STUDIES IN MEDIEVAL HISTORY AND CULTURE

Edited by

Francis G. Gentry

Professor of German
Pennsylvania State University

A ROUTLEDGE SERIES

Studies in Medieval History and Culture

Francis G. Gentry, *General Editor*

The Contested Theological Authority of Thomas Aquinas
The Controversies between Hervaeus Natalis and Durandis of St. Pourçain
Elizabeth Lowe

Body and Sacred Place in Medieval Europe, 1100–1389
Dawn Marie Hayes

Women of the Humiliati
A Lay Religious Order in Medieval Civic Life
Sally Mayall Brasher

Consuming Passions
The Uses of Cannibalism in Late Medieval and Early Modern Europe
Merrall Llewelyn Price

Literary Hybrids
Crossdressing, Shapeshifting, and Indeterminacy in Medieval and Modern French Narrative
Erika E. Hess

The King's Two Maps
Cartography and Culture in Thirteenth-Century England
Daniel Birkholz

Pestilence in Medieval and Early Modern English Literature
Bryon Lee Grigsby

Race and Ethnicity in Anglo-Saxon Literature
Stephen J. Harris

Aspects of Love in John Gower's Confessio Amantis
Ellen Shaw Bakalian

The Medieval Tradition of Thebes
History and Narrative in the OF Roman de Thèbes, Boccaccio, Chaucer, and Lydgate
Dominique Battles

Worlds Made Flesh
Reading Medieval Manuscript Culture
Lauryn S. Mayer

Empowering Collaborations
Writing Partnerships between Religious Women and Scribes in the Middle Ages
Kimberly M. Benedict

The Water Supply System of Siena, Italy
The Medieval Roots of the Modern Networked City
Michael P. Kucher

The Epistemology of the Monstrous in the Middle Ages
Lisa Verner

Desiring Truth
The Process of Judgment in Fourteenth-Century Art and Literature
Jeremy Lowe

The Preaching Fox
Festive Subversion in the Plays of the Wakefield Master
Warren Edminster

Non-Native Sources for the Scandinavian Kings' Sagas
Paul A. White

Kingship, Conquest, and *Patria*
Literary and Cultural Identities in Medieval French and Welsh Arthurian Romance
Kristen Lee Over

Saracens and the Making of English Identity
The Auchinleck Manuscript
Siobhain Bly Calkin

SARACENS AND THE MAKING OF ENGLISH IDENTITY
The Auchinleck Manuscript

Siobhain Bly Calkin

Routledge
New York & London

Published in 2005 by
Routledge
Taylor & Francis Group
270 Madison Avenue
New York, NY 10016

Published in Great Britain by
Routledge
Taylor & Francis Group
2 Park Square
Milton Park, Abingdon
Oxon OX14 4RN

Transferred to Digital Printing 2009

Part of Chapter Five was previously published as "Violence, Saracens, and English Identity in *Of Arthour and of Merlin,*" *Arthuriana* 14, no. 2 (2004): 17–36. Reprinted with permission.

International Standard Book Number-10: 0-415-97241-8 (Hardcover)
International Standard Book Number-13: 978-0-415-97241-3 (Hardcover)
Library of Congress Card Number 2005013420

Library of Congress Cataloging-In-Publication Data

Calkin, Siobhain Bly, 1973–
    Saracens and the making of English identity : the Auchinleck manuscript / by Siobhain Bly Calkin.
        p. cm. -- (Studies in medieval history and culture)
    Includes bibliographical references and index.
    ISBN 0-415-97241-8 (alk. paper)
    1. English literature--Islamic influences. 2. Islam and literature--England--History--To 1500. 3. Islamic Empire--Foreign public opinion, English. 4. National characteristics, English, in literature. 5. Romances, English--History and criticism. 6. Romances, English--Manuscripts. 7. Manuscripts, Medieval--England. 8. Islamic Empire--In literature. 9. Manuscripts, English (Middle) 10. Saracens in literature. 11. Crusades in literature. 12. Auchinleck manuscript. I. Auchinleck manuscript. II. Title. III. Series.

PR129.I75C35 2005
820.9'38297--dc22   2005013420

ISBN10: 0-415-97241-8 (hbk)
ISBN10: 0-415-80309-8 (pbk)

ISBN13: 978-0-415-97241-3 (hbk)
ISBN13: 978-0-415-80309-0 (pbk)

Publisher's Note
The publisher has gone to great lengths to ensure the quality of this reprint but points out that some imperfections in the original may be apparent.

Taylor & Francis Group
is the Academic Division of T&F Informa plc.

Visit the Taylor & Francis Web site at
http://www.taylorandfrancis.com

and the Routledge Web site at
http://www.routledge-ny.com

For My Parents and for James

Contents

Series Editor's Foreword

Far from providing just a musty whiff of yesteryear, research in Medieval Studies enters the new century as fresh and vigorous as never before. Scholars representing all disciplines and generations are consistently producing works of research of the highest caliber, utilizing new approaches and methodologies. Volumes in the Medieval History and Culture series include studies on individual works and authors of Latin and vernacular literatures, historical personalities and events, theological and philosophical issues, and new critical approaches to medieval literature and culture.

Momentous changes have occurred in Medieval Studies in the past thirty years, in teaching as well as in scholarship. The Medieval History and Culture series enhances research in the field by providing an outlet for monographs by scholars in the early stages of their careers on all topics related to the broad scope of Medieval Studies, while at the same time pointing to and highlighting new directions that will shape and define scholarly discourse in the future.

Francis G. Gentry

Acknowledgments

Many people have shaped *Saracens and the Making of English Identity* over the course of its development, and it gives me great pleasure to acknowledge their influences here. This book began as a dissertation written at the University of Notre Dame, and I would like to thank my supervisor, Jill Mann, for her incisive comments and helpful suggestions, and for her generosity in reading later revisions of my dissertation material. Special thanks are also due to Maura Nolan for her cheerful willingness to comment on portions of this book in the final stages of its composition, and for her insightful suggestions for revision. I would also like to thank Dolores Frese, Graham Hammill, and Katherine O'Brien O'Keeffe for their interest in my work.

I am also deeply appreciative of the friendly support of my colleagues in the English Department at Carleton University over the past three years. I am particularly grateful for their kind tolerance of my obsession with Saracens and for the lively interest they have taken in my project, even when it is far removed from their immediate research areas. Leanne Groeneveld and Paul Keen have read and commented on portions of this book, while Percy Walton, Brian Greenspan, and Sukeshi Kamra have all discussed knotty aspects of my research with me. Their enthusiasm and insights are much appreciated. I would also like to thank Carleton University for various research grants that enabled me to complete this book.

Colleagues working elsewhere have also been very generous with their time and energy. I would like to thank Lisa Lampert and Suzanne Conklin Akbari for their helpful suggestions on Chapter Three, and Jacqueline Stodnick for her unfailing common sense advice about multiple aspects of the book-writing process. Earlier versions of this material were presented at various Kalamazoo congresses and at the New Medievalisms Conference in 2004, and I very much appreciate the questions and comments I received at these gatherings. Portions of Chapters One, Three, and Five appeared first in articles in *Florilegium, The Journal of English and Germanic Philology,* and *Arthuriana,* and I am grateful to these periodicals for permission to republish that material here.

Finally, I would like to thank my husband James, my parents, and my brother and his family for their support and encouragement throughout my work on this book. They understand better than anyone the sacrifices, effort, and time that have gone into this text, and James in particular will rejoice with me to see its appearance in print.

Introduction

MUSLIMS, SARACENS AND MEDIEVALISTS

The purportedly Muslim figures who appear in medieval western literature usually bear little or no resemblance to historical Muslims of the period. Edward Said states, "we need not look for correspondence between the language used to depict the Orient and the Orient itself, not so much because the language is inaccurate but because it is not even trying to be accurate."[1] Similarly, Norman Daniel and Dorothee Metlitzki identify repeated stereotypical misrepresentations of Islam in medieval literary texts, noting such inaccuracies as the representation of Islam as a polytheistic religion or the portrayal of alcohol-drinking Muslims.[2] The Muslims depicted in medieval western texts, then, constitute no act of mimesis but are rather wholly fictional figures. They are Orientalist constructs, representations of the East produced in the West for western consumption that enshrine western ideas of easternness rather than any empirical reality of the East. As Said clearly demonstrates in *Orientalism,* however, such inaccurate depictions of the East often reveal a great deal about the western situation of their production and circulation. *Saracens and the Making of English Identity* explores how representations of Muslims in a fourteenth-century English manuscript engaged the particular historical and cultural landscape in which they appeared. The book emerges out of a confluence of interests in postcolonial theory, depictions of alterity, and medieval manuscript culture, and reflects a historicist belief that the significance of cultural artifacts like the Auchinleck manuscript and its texts lies in the situation of their compilation and dissemination. The book argues, in brief, that although the depictions of Muslims in the Auchinleck manuscript may be mimetically inaccurate, they engage in multi-facetted ways some of the central concerns of the manuscript and the culture that produced and consumed its texts.

To acknowledge the distance between what Said terms "depict[ions of] the Orient and the Orient itself," I use the word "Saracen" to refer to representations of Muslims in medieval writings, and the word "Muslim" to refer to the lived realities of medieval Muslims.[3] The term "Saracen" derives from Classical Greek and Latin words that meant "Arab."[4] According to Diane Speed, the word "Saracene" was available in Old English as a Latin borrowing from the ninth century onwards, and meant Arab or Muslim.[5] The word first appears in Middle English in the mid-thirteenth century as "Sarasin" or variant spellings thereof[6] and, according to the *Middle English Dictionary*, usually means "Turk, Arab, or Muslim," although it can be used generically to mean "pagan."[7] The *Middle English Dictionary* actually cites the generic meaning "pagan" as that associated with earlier occurrences of the word, and suggests that the meaning "Turk, Arab, or Muslim" was available only from c. 1300 onwards. This seems rather odd given the word's original meanings in Latin and Old English as well as the fact that, as Norman Daniel notes, writers "throughout the Middle Ages" used the term to "mean 'Arab' or 'Muslim,' or both."[8] Indeed, Diane Speed has challenged the *Middle English Dictionary*'s assertion that "Sarasin" did not connote Muslims until 1300.[9] Nevertheless, even the *Middle English Dictionary* agrees that by the time the Auchinleck manuscript was compiled in the 1330s, the Middle English term "Sarasin" meant Turk, Arab, or Muslim. This book, then, examines the Saracens of the Auchinleck manuscript as western, Orientalist representations designed to connote, albeit inaccurately, historical Middle Eastern Muslims.

Representations of Islam have attracted medievalists' interest throughout the latter half of the twentieth century. In the 1940s, William Wistar Comfort and C. Meredith Jones identified common, stereotypical traits of Saracen characters in Old French literature.[10] In the 1960s, Richard Southern and Norman Daniel discussed the challenges posed to medieval European Christianity by Islam, and studied various thinkers' responses to these challenges,[11] while in the 1970s Dorothee Metlitzki explored the role of Arabic science and philosophy in medieval England and traced the common, stereotypical traits of Saracen characters in English literature,[12] a task Norman Daniel performed for Old French *chansons de geste* in the next decade.[13] Much of this early work concentrated on identifying stereotyped representations of medieval Muslims and signaling the historical misrepresentations involved, concerns which also animate the first two chapters of Edward Said's *Orientalism*.[14] This body of foundational work has been complemented by more recent work by medievalists. For example, John Tolan has surveyed European responses to Islam in theological and historical texts dating up to 1300, while Sharon Kinoshita and Lynn Ramey have studied the depictions of Saracens in Old French romances and *chansons de geste*.[15] Carol Heffernan and Geraldine Heng have also discussed the Saracens of romance, but devote their attention to Middle English romances.[16] Heffernan examines Chaucerian depictions of the East as well as those found in *Floris and Blauncheflur* and *Le Bone Florence of Rome,* while Heng analyzes romance portrayals of Muslims as part of her larger study of how the genre engages history and participates in cultural explorations of race, nation, and place. Much of this recent work has focussed on how medieval representations of the East relate to actual Muslims of the time, and what such representations reveal about perceptions of racial and religious difference in the Middle Ages. In other words, much of this work looks East in its focus.

Although Saracen characters reveal much about western ideas of the East, and suggest much about cross-cultural contact between East and West, they also engage the specific western contexts of their moments of appearance in complex ways. This book studies one manuscript in order to analyze how Saracens engage issues at play around the time of that manuscript's compilation and initial reading in the country where it was produced. *Saracens and the Making of English Identity* is thus a book as much (perhaps even more) about western understandings of domestic issues in the West as it is a book about western ideas of the East. Rather than viewing Saracen characters solely as depictions of the East, this book considers them western representations of a continuum of otherness that includes foreigners close to home as well as Middle Easterners. It argues that Saracens can represent both proximate alterities within western Europe, and a historical Muslim presence of which Christians were aware and with which they interacted many times. Mimetic inaccuracy enables Saracens to oscillate between West and East. Sometimes the Auchinleck manuscript confronts readers with Saracens who seem to be western knights and ladies, while at other times, Auchinleck's Saracens evoke an extremely powerful, technologically advanced, and sophisticated Muslim civilization which both impressed medieval Christians with its scientific knowledge and immense wealth, and menaced them militarily with its many victories over crusaders and its capacity for territorial expansion.[17] Saracens in Auchinleck thus represent a range of alterity and oscillate in such a way that they address both local western issues as well as ideas stemming from East-West cultural contact and the very real anxieties Muslim civilizations occasioned for European Christians.[18]

This book's concentration on one manuscript also contributes in other ways to the study of western depictions of Islam. Many analyses of Saracens attend primarily to either romance or religious writings,[19] and have therefore not been able to address the fact that texts about Saracens appear in manuscript contexts in which romance and religious materials are found side by side. My focus on the Auchinleck manuscript requires consideration of the portrayal of Saracens in saints' legends and texts designed to facilitate lay piety as well as in romances belonging to the Matters of Britain, England, France, and Araby. Such a focus also takes account of the fact that, as Andrew Taylor notes, "medieval reading was often 'intensive' rather than 'extensive,' with people reading the same books over and over again."[20] Studying the Saracens portrayed in one manuscript thus facilitates an appreciation of the ways in which various depictions of Saracens may have fleshed each other out intertextually, as texts in that manuscript were re-read or re-heard by people. Although scholars today cannot re-create a medieval audience, the conjunction of texts within one manuscript forms an identifiable literary horizon of expectations and experiences within which Saracen characters would have been situated by medieval audiences.[21] The medieval book thus constitutes the locus *par excellence* for exploring the various cultural functions Saracens served for the western communities that so avidly compiled and disseminated tales about them in the later Middle Ages.

THE AUCHINLECK MANUSCRIPT

Edinburgh, National Library of Scotland, Advocates 19.2.1 is known more informally as the Auchinleck manuscript, and has long been recognized as one of the most important vernacular English manuscripts pre-dating Chaucer. It is a large book composed entirely of texts written in English,[22] and has been identified on paleographic and textual grounds as an English product assembled during the 1330s.[23] In its present form,[24] the manuscript consists of forty-four items, of which all but nine represent the earliest extant Middle English versions of these texts.[25] In addition, only four of the surviving manuscripts that pre-date Auchinleck include English romances, and none contains more than two romances while Auchinleck contains eighteen including its Breton lays.[26] Auchinleck also includes hagiographic legends and other types of religious narrative, works of religious instruction, poems of satire and complaint, humorous tales, debates, monitory pieces, a chronicle, and a list of Norman Barons.[27] The manuscript is thus remarkable both for its size and for the range of genres it encompasses.

   Given these characteristics, it is no surprise that the Auchinleck manuscript has long been a subject of scholarly inquiry. In the late nineteenth century it was studied, and many of its texts edited, by a number of German philologists including Carl Horstmann, Eugen Kölbing and Julius Zupitza.[28] In the 1940s, Laura Hibbard Loomis devoted many articles to discussion of

the manuscript's contents and production.[29] In response to Loomis's work on
book-production before Chaucer, many scholars have studied Auchinleck as
a cultural artifact testifying to early methods of book assembly, and have frequently sought to refine or refute Loomis's claim that the manuscript was the
product of a commercial, lay bookshop in London.[30] Other scholars have
edited or analyzed individual texts in Auchinleck, focusing mainly on lais or
romances found therein and referencing the larger manuscript context as a
guide to dating.[31] Interestingly, a point made by Loomis in the 1940s is still
largely true today of scholarship involving Auchinleck's texts. She wrote:
"Despite an enormous amount of meticulous study of individual texts, literary criticism has but rarely concerned itself with medieval English books as
wholes rather than parts."[32] This general trend has recently begun to be
reversed. Seth Lerer's *Chaucer and His Readers,* for example, examines a number of Chaucer's works as they appear in fifteenth-century manuscripts,
while collections of essays devoted, respectively, to the Vernon and Harley
manuscripts[33] and the texts therein appeared in 1990 and 2000.[34] Andrew
Taylor's *Textual Situations* also focuses on manuscripts as whole entities and
as essential contexts for well-known texts.[35] Loomis' point, however, still
characterizes most scholarly work on the Auchinleck manuscript. Only
Thorlac Turville-Petre's chapter on Auchinleck in *England the Nation* and
Jean Harpham Burrows's dissertation analyze multiple texts and genres from
Auchinleck.[36] *Saracens and the Making of English Identity* provides another
wide-ranging analysis of the manuscript, and examines hagiographic legends
and texts that elaborate medieval chronicle entries, as well as romances
drawn from the Matters of France, England, Britain, and Araby. This book's
breadth thus represents a way of reading that engages the varied contents of
Auchinleck, and respects the inter-textual play of the medieval book.

 Saracens and the Making of English Identity also draws attention to
aspects of Auchinleck that have been overlooked. One of the most startling
omissions in scholarship on Auchinleck, which emerges upon consideration
of the manuscript as a whole, is the topic of the manuscript's many representations of otherness, particularly of eastern otherness or of Saracens. Saracen
characters, or references to Saracens and the East, appear in fifteen of the
forty-four extant items, and many of the texts containing such references and
characters run to thousands of lines of verse in their original state. The fifteen
texts that include Saracens are: *Þe King of Tars* (1228 lines),[37] *Seynt Mergrete*
(824 lines), *Seynt Katerine* (660 lines), *[On þe seven dedly sinnes]* (308 lines),
(Floris and Blauncheflur) (861 lines), *(Guy of Warwick)* (6848 lines), *(Guy of
Warwick, stanzaic continuation)* (3588 lines), *Reinbrun gij sone of warwike*
(1522 lines), *Sir beues of hamtoun* (4444 lines), *Of arthour & of merlin* (9772

lines), *(Roland and Vernagu)* (880 lines), *Otuel a kniȝt* (1738 lines), *(Kyng Alisaunder)* (c. 963 lines),[38] *Liber Regum Anglie* (2369 lines)[39], and *King Richard* (c. 1046 lines).[40] These numerous and often extensive depictions of Saracens may well have passed unnoticed because the Auchinleck manuscript also contains a number of texts that evince a lively sense of English group identity. Nineteen of the forty-four extant items explicitly refer to their existence in "Inglisch" as opposed to any other language, the heroes of most Auchinleck romances are geographically linked to specific places in England, and the political and historical texts discuss situations and events in England. While this English focus is often identified as a key characteristic of Auchinleck, the manuscript's many depictions of non-English peoples and places are not often noted. A number of Auchinleck texts, however, do not refer to England, contain English characters, or explicitly draw attention to their presentation in English. *Saracens and the Making of English Identity* examines Saracens in both these and more explicitly English-focused texts, and shows how the Saracen characters throughout the manuscript relate to what has been identified as one of Auchinleck's central projects: the articulation of a sense of English national identity. *Saracens and the Making of English Identity* thus not only provides a fuller understanding of the cultural functions of Orientalist constructs in the West, but also explores the complexity of Auchinleck's invocation of "Inglisch" identity.[41]

While scholars frequently cite Auchinleck or its texts as evidence of a vernacular English self-consciousness in the early fourteenth century, they often confine their analyses to passing observations of the manuscript's references to English locales or language, [42] or to efforts to link texts found in Auchinleck to specific great families of England.[43] Only Thorlac Turville-Petre investigates with comprehensiveness the manuscript's repeated appeals to an English readership and English communal identity, and even his study spans a brief thirty pages. He devotes one chapter of *England the Nation* to the Auchinleck manuscript, and, after mentioning the manuscript's impressive assembly of English-language texts, he concentrates on identifying the places in the manuscript where England is mentioned. As a result, *England the Nation* does not explore how texts not explicitly linked to England may contribute to Auchinleck's construction of an English community. Furthermore, while Turville-Petre does briefly mention the Saracens of Auchinleck, he considers these characters straightforward manifestations of late medieval English crusading fervor and offers no further analysis of how they might contribute to the assertion of national identity that he discerns in Auchinleck.[44] Depictions of otherness, however, can play a crucial role in a group's definition, formation, and assertion of its identity, and *Saracens and the Making of English*

Identity argues that Saracens in Auchinleck do much more than testify to an English interest in crusade. The otherness of these characters demands medieval English readers' consideration of what counts as cultural, ethnic, and religious difference, what is to be done about such difference, and how differences and borders between groups are to be negotiated. Saracen characters also promote awareness of the role of violence in the formation of a group's cultural, ethnic, and political identity, and they reveal the ways in which sex and gender play into constructions of group identity. Texts involving Saracens thus allow Auchinleck to do much more than merely assert an English vernacular identity; they offer the manuscript and its audience an imaginative way of exploring the processes and problems of making such an assertion in the early fourteenth century.

IMAGINING ENGLISHNESS IN THE EARLY
FOURTEENTH CENTURY

Two problems emerge when one attempts to discuss English identity in the early fourteenth century. The first is that of terminology: is one speaking of an English nation or sense of national identity at this point in time? This is a problem posed most frequently by modern theorists of nationhood, many of whom construct the Middle Ages as an "Other" in contradistinction to which they trace the emergence of nations in the early modern era. One need only think of Benedict Anderson's influential assertions that nations are an ideological phenomenon linked to print culture, and that trans-national dynastic and religious allegiances precluded nation formation in the Middle Ages, to perceive the inscription of the medieval period as an originary "Other."[45] Ironically, however, recent work by medievalists clearly shows that Anderson's definition of a nation as an "imagined political community"[46] works very well for medieval realms and communities. As Geraldine Heng puts it,

> Though the arguments [among medievalists] are multifarious, occasionally contradictory, and undeniably *en procès*, a consensus has emerged that discourses of the nation in the medieval period, like nationalist discourses of the eighteenth and nineteenth centuries, hinge critically on Ben Anderson's famous formulation of the nation as an 'imagined (political) community,' while departing in local, period-specific details—political, economic, governmental—from nationalist formations in postmedieval centuries.[47]

Recent work by Heng, John Gillingham, Lesley Johnson, Thorlac Turville-Petre, Felicity Riddy, and Diane Speed has done much to affirm the existence of a discourse of national identity in England in the later Middle Ages, and to indicate the ways in which this discourse is linked to notions of kingship, religion, language, literature, and geography.[48] Moreover, the Middle English language itself includes in its lexicon the word "nacioun" as a designation for peoples and political states.[49] It thus seems clear that some sense of nation did exist in England in the fourteenth century, albeit one constructed very differently then than now.

This book, while greatly indebted to work focussed on defining "nation" and affirming its presence in late medieval contexts, does not participate directly in such efforts at definition and affirmation. Instead, I accept that some sense of national identity existed in England in the fourteenth century, and explore why and how assertions of English identity might take place in and around portraits of religious others. I trace the complex and shifting nature of English identity at this time, and examine the situations that both promoted and worked against claims of a cohesive English identity. I further accept as a premise the idea that Auchinleck's assertions of English identity might best be read as interpellations, a term coined by Louis Althusser. Althusser argues that a subject's group and ideological affiliations are constructed by the act of hailing, that is to say the act of identifying a subject in some sort of communication and having the subject acknowledge his or her status of having been hailed (i.e. by responding in some way). The act of hailing, and the recognition of oneself in the hail, construct an identity.[50] Auchinleck's numerous appeals to "Inglisch" readers work in precisely this way: they hail a specific readership and audience, and in the act of hailing that readership as already extant, they bring it into existence. The term "interpellation" thus denotes a process of identity formation rather than an invocation *tout court* of an already-established identity, and reminds readers today that Auchinleck's many appeals to a specific readership may well represent efforts to craft a sense of cohesive English identity at a time when such an identification was neither self-evident nor stable. *Saracens and the Making of English Identity*, then, accepts that some sense of England as a cohesive political, linguistic, and geographic community circulated among the English in the early fourteenth century, but recognizes that definitions of this community and its larger role in Britain and the world were very much up for grabs at the time.

The complex and shifting nature of English identity and identifications in the early fourteenth century is the second problem to be confronted when conceptualizing "Englishness" at this time. By the later Middle Ages, the English community had repeatedly been confronted with the problem of determining who or what was "Inglisch" given the numerous influxes of

Angles, Saxons, Jutes, Danes, and Frenchmen[51] into an island once inhabited largely by Celts. Is a bilingual, Norman-descended aristocrat English by the 1330s, or is he or she ethnically and culturally different? The complexity of this historical situation is further compounded by new developments in the early fourteenth century. Culturally, this period marks the post-Conquest re-emergence of English as a prestigious language of literature and historical record. French had, since the mid-thirteenth century, increasingly become an acquired second language rather than a mother tongue, even for the aristocratic, French-descended inhabitants of England.[52] Not until the early fourteenth century, however, does one find chronicles and romances being written and disseminated in English on a fairly wide scale. Indeed, Auchinleck itself contains the earliest extant English versions of a number of Anglo-Norman romances. Accordingly, one can see at the time of Auchinleck's compilation (and indeed in the compilation itself) a new and widespread use of the English language for literary purposes. This indicates that by the 1330s English was once again a language considered appropriate for high-status cultural functions, and that it had risen measurably within the hierarchy of linguistic prestige in England.[53] Politically, too, a number of recent developments were complicating questions of ethnic identification in fourteenth-century Britain.[54] As Edward I and his descendants made concerted efforts to subject Wales and Scotland to English rule, their actions raised the question of whether the Welsh and Scots could, in some way, be made "Inglisch" by their subjugation to an English king. Likewise, Edward III's claim to the French throne combined with increasing military and political friction involving the French to raise questions about how these two peoples were politically, militarily, and culturally both similar and distinct. Thus, linguistic, political, ethnic, and geographic definitions of Englishness in the early fourteenth century were both fluid and complex as well as subject to renegotiation. Accordingly, any assertions of English identity like those found in Auchinleck demand consideration of what vision of England and the English is being advanced, and how it engages the issues at play in the early 1300s.

To effect such consideration, *Saracens and the Making of English Identity* pursues questions such as: How does Auchinleck direct itself to fourteenth-century English readers and their concerns? Why and when does anyone want to be identified as "Inglisch" at this time? How does one go about achieving such identification? What pressures, according to the manuscript's texts, underlie and/or compromise assertions of English identity in the early fourteenth century? What is the role of religion in defining or establishing Englishness? These questions may not be fully answered by the

Saracen characters of Auchinleck, but the manuscript's figures of religious alterity certainly offer an extremely helpful lens through which to consider them. Indeed, it should come as no surprise that depictions of religious others can prove so helpful when assessing medieval articulations of English identity. As Geraldine Heng notes, "nationalism . . . in the Middle Ages is always and fundamentally traversed, determined, and articulated by religious investments: a specificity of medieval nationalism."[55] Although the centrality of religion in the Middle Ages has often been identified by theorists of nation as impeding or precluding nation formation during the period, medieval texts themselves clearly indicate that religion can be a crucial element in crafting a sense of identity that imaginatively binds together the members of a political community. Indeed, the pertinence of Auchinleck's Saracens to questions about how people construct and articulate a sense of national identity has only become clearer to me over the course of my work on this study. Developments since the events of September 11, 2001 have made more broadly apparent the fact that depictions of religious others, be they Muslim or Christian, play fundamental roles in articulations of nation throughout the world today. As a result, contemporary theorists of nation formation and articulation may well derive valuable insights into the present from consideration of the medieval past and its religiously inflected articulations of group identities like Englishness. What this book contributes to such studies is an awareness that the connections between depictions of religion and articulations of nation are not always simple or superficial. While religious others can serve as simple binary opposites against which to define a group identity, they can also represent alterities within a community or closely linked to it and, as such, explore issues very close to home. Religion and nation intersect in many different ways, to many different ends, as the Saracens of the Auchinleck manuscript make abundantly clear.

SARACENS AND THE MAKING OF ENGLISH IDENTITY

Saracens and the Making of English Identity opens with an examination of the figure of the noble Saracen warrior, a character frequently identified by scholars as a mimetically inaccurate replica of a western knight. This figure is found in many romances and appears in Auchinleck in *Otuel a Kniȝt, Roland and Vernagu, Sir Beves of Hamtoun,* and the three *Guy of Warwick* tales.[56] Upon consideration of these texts, it becomes clear that while noble Saracen knights may be stereotypical replicas of their western counterparts, they work extremely effectively to explore the interplay of sameness, differentiation, and difference in the articulation of communities' identities. Saracen knights thus serve in Auchinleck to illuminate issues involved in early fourteenth-century efforts to define English identity in relation to France.

The second chapter focuses on the only female Saracen who appears in the texts studied here, the princess Josiane in *Sir Beves of Hamtoun* who converts to Christianity and then marries the text's eponymous English knight. Josiane engages questions about how individuals may assume, alter, and affirm group identities. Because she is female, Josiane offers a specifically gender-inflected vision of this process and, because she is Saracen, she explores the ways in which foreign women might craft a place for themselves in English society. Indeed, her position and experiences so closely resemble those of England's foreign queens in the thirteenth and fourteenth centuries that Josiane illustrates intersections of group and gender identity extremely pertinent at the time of Auchinleck's compilation.

One of the issues at play in Britain in the 1330s was the relationship of England to Scotland, and disagreement over the nature of this relationship prompted various efforts to define and redefine what was English and, specifically, what was subject to the English king. Chapter Three argues that Saracens in two Auchinleck texts engage material pertinent to these fourteenth-century debates. Specifically, the chapter claims that Saracens in *Þe King of Tars* and *Floris and Blauncheflur* explore how the cultural borders defining communities are established, the extent to which borders may be rewritten so as to integrate disparate peoples, and the ways in which efforts to promote such integration may provoke vehement assertions of differentiation. Interestingly, the Auchinleck texts whose Saracens most directly engage these issues of importance in England are romances that do not explicitly mention England, and are often classified as belonging to the Matter of Araby or Matter of the East. *Þe King of Tars,* a text set in the Middle East which recounts the marriage of a Saracen Sultan to a Christian princess and the monstrous offspring their union produces, forms the keystone of this chapter, while *Floris and Blauncheflur,* a romance which depicts a rather different vision of cross-cultural union, serves as a helpful foil to *Þe King of Tars* and offers an alternative perspective on the issues explored.

Chapter Four introduces another genre into this study of Auchinleck's Saracens, and examines the appearance of Saracen persecutors in two of the manuscript's hagiographic legends: *Seynt Mergrete* and *Seynt Katerine.* The characterization of these Saracen persecutors raises the specter of historical Muslim wealth and power for a western audience, and indicates both fourteenth-century English identification with pan-Christian concerns and projects, and the extent to which such identification defined Englishness at this time.

Finally, a discussion of the hybrid Middle Eastern and Northern European Saracens of *Of Arthour and of Merlin* concludes *Saracens and the Making of English Identity*. Chapter Five examines how these hybrid Saracens engage the larger history of England as well as the fourteenth-century moment of the manuscript's compilation. The chapter argues that, in this Arthurian text, Saracen characters work to define Englishness historically, and powerfully illustrate the role of invasion and war in the formation of English political, cultural, and linguistic identity.

The Saracens in the Auchinleck manuscript range from noble knights and princesses to monstrous giants, and from religious persecutors of Christians to reminders of pre-Christian paganism in England. Together, these various Saracens offer the manuscript and its audience an imaginative way of coming to terms with ideas about group formation, the maintenance of communal borders, the roles of sameness and difference in assertions of group identity, the place of gender norms and religious affiliations in communities' self-definitions, and the role of violence in assertions of cultural or political identity. As Saracens in Auchinleck raise these issues, they allow the manuscript to complement its assertions of English vernacular identity with consideration of some of the complications involved in making such assertions in the early fourteenth century. In short, Saracens in Auchinleck indicate for their audiences the challenges of imagining and articulating a united English identity at a period when the English language was just beginning to regain its prestigious status, when the English people, on the eve of the Hundred Years War, found themselves increasingly at odds with their French cousins, and when matters of English, Welsh, and Scottish sovereignty began to acquire new and pressing significance.

Chapter One

The Perils of Proximity: Saracen Knights, Sameness, and Differentiation

INTRODUCTION

The first Saracens to be studied in detail in this book are the Saracen warriors depicted in *Roland and Vernagu, Otuel a Kniʒt, Sir Beves of Hamtoun,* and the three Guy of Warwick tales (*Guy of Warwick, Guy of Warwick (stanzaic continuation)*, and *Reinbrun gij sone of warwike*).[1] *Roland and Vernagu* and *Otuel a Kniʒt* represent the earliest extant English translations of French Matter of Charlemagne material recounted in *chansons de geste* and chronicles. *Roland and Vernagu* narrates Charlemagne's campaign against Saracens in Spain and a duel between the French hero, Roland, and a Saracen giant named Vernagu. *Otuel a Kniʒt* relates the arrival of a Saracen knight named Otuel at Charlemagne's court, a battle between Otuel and Roland, Otuel's conversion during the course of this battle, and the convert's subsequent participation in Charlemagne's campaigns against Saracens. *Sir Beves of Hamtoun* and *Guy of Warwick,* on the other hand, belong to the category of Matter of England romances. *Sir Beves* recounts the life and deeds of an English knight raised by Saracens who marries a converted Saracen princess, while the three Guy of Warwick tales narrate, respectively, the eponymous hero's martial deeds before marriage, his martial deeds and penance after marriage, and the martial deeds of his son Reinbrun. While the six texts differ in subject matter, they all involve extensive depictions of battles and single combats between Christians and Saracens. As a result, these tales allow me to examine a number of representations of noble Saracen knights.

The oddest aspect of this stereotypical figure of otherness, who appears in many tales of Saracen-Christian interaction, is his extremely close resemblance to the Christian knights he fights.[2] Indistinguishable in appearance, dress, and behavior from his Christian counterparts, the Saracen knight seems to exist simply to provide an arena for Christian knightly endeavor. Given his similarities to Christian characters, the Saracen knight cannot really engage questions of lived racial and religious difference in the Middle Ages, and various scholars have dismissed the figure as a meaningless clone of his Christian counterparts.[3] Nonetheless, this mimetically inaccurate Saracen does raise the question of what it means to assert differences in situations where the samenesses between groups are many and the differences few and malleable. In a fourteenth-century context, such situations evoke England's interactions with fellow Europeans more than they do English involvement in crusades to the Middle East. Indeed, Saracen knights in the texts discussed here acquire cultural importance not in relation to issues involving the Middle East, but in relation to issues involving France. The Saracen knights in Auchinleck serve as reflexive comments on England's efforts in the early fourteenth century to rewrite the longstanding cultural and political ties between England and France, and thereby define an English identity in contradistinction to that of France. Saracen knights investigate how such assertions of difference are made in contexts of shared similarities. In particular, Saracen knights show how the class[4] affiliations shared by members of different groups can both frustrate efforts to assert the cultural or political identities distinctive of each group and, paradoxically, provoke a more vociferous assertion of the same cultural or political identities. These figures also reveal what constitutes the differentiation of communities and demonstrate the role of individual will in effecting this differentiation as well as the social factors limiting the individual's exercise of free will in such endeavors. Finally, Saracen knights hint at the dangers of too much similarity between communities in conflict with each other. All these issues were central to fourteenth-century articulations of Englishness given the paradox of the country's French-influenced past and present tense relationships with continental France.

ENGLISH AND FRENCH POLITICAL PROXIMITY

To understand the stakes involved in Auchinleck's representation of Saracen knights, it might first be useful to grasp how central were issues of group identity, sameness, and differentiation in England during the period of Auchinleck's compilation and circulation (c. 1330–40). Two historical events illustrate this point and situate the work done by Auchinleck's Saracens in the immediate context of French-English identity and conflict. The first example is that of the 1340 Parliament in England, and it demonstrates how English and French identities in England were so intermingled by this time that the two insular cultures could not be disentangled despite increasing

English antagonism towards the continental French. When Edward III summoned his parliament in 1340, one of the Statutes passed was that to end the "obsolete procedure of 'presentment of Englishry'" whereby the local hundred could be fined whenever "a Norman was found slain within its boundaries by an unknown hand."[5] The procedure was abolished because it was no longer possible to distinguish an Englishman from a Norman.[6] By 1340, then, England was populated by people embodying an indistinguishable mix of French and English heritages. At the same Parliament, however, Edward and the country's representatives were primarily preoccupied with his efforts to raise money for a campaign against the French to forward his claim to the French throne.[7] This campaign itself, ironically, derived from England's close connections with continental France and its people: Edward could assert his right to the French throne because, through his mother, he had as strong a claim to the position left vacant by his uncle's death as the other continental aspirants. Once again, the tangled interweaving of French and English identities is made clear. The campaign, however, constituted a direct assault on the French, and thereby promoted a strong sense of division between English and French identities and polities. Nevertheless, as the Presentment of Englishry and Edward's genealogy show, the English identity that was to be asserted in the coming Hundred Years War had some of its foundations in the country's French past. A background of sameness with the French thus underlay a military situation in which the two sides had to be differentiated in order to do battle against each other.

The second historical incident to be noted from this period of Auchinleck's compilation is Philip of France's decision in 1335 to move the fleet assembled for a renewed crusade against Muslims from Marseilles to Normandy.[8] Edward III read this action as evidence of Philip's intention to support the Scots in their conflict with the English over Scottish sovereignty, and "accused Philip of seeking every occasion to aid and maintain the Scots and of trying to keep him [Edward] at war in Scotland so that he might not pursue his rights elsewhere."[9] At this point, the hostility between English and French is made clear, and with it, the distinct differentiation of English and French in the European political arena of the 1330s despite their shared history. However, the action narrated also exemplifies the ways in which European monarchs frequently could, and did, deploy efforts directed against Muslims to their own ends. Here, a fleet collected and financed with the understanding that it would be used to return the Holy Land to Christian control is summarily redirected to more immediate European goals by the French king. Representations of Muslims and the need to make war on them thus serve ends much closer to home. Just as the Saracens of Auchinleck relate more to specifically English issues than to Muslims of the fourteenth century, so actual Muslims of the period played roles in the Anglo-French-Scottish conflict that so preoccupied England during the late thirteenth and early fourteenth centuries.

These two examples demonstrate the complexities involved in early fourteenth-century efforts to define and assert an English identity. United by political history, the ties of frequent French-English marriages, and the English possession of patrimonial lands located in continental France, the English and French of this period shared certain concerns and characteristics. On the other hand, divisions between the two peoples could not but appear as the rulers of the two countries clashed over acts of homage, lands in France held by the English king, political prestige in Europe, and the place of the Scots in Britain.[10] Meanwhile, Muslims not immediately involved in this process were nevertheless implicated in it as forces gathered to attack them were redirected to other ends. Depictions of the East and its peoples clearly served immediate political functions in late medieval Europe.

ENGLISH AND FRENCH CULTURAL PROXIMITY

Problems of sameness and differentiation in relation to France were also played out in the cultural life of England during this period. Various aspects of the Auchinleck manuscript exemplify this point. The romance *King Richard,* for example, mentions early on the fact that "Romaunce make folk of Fraunce" (10), and identifies "þis romaunce [as] of Freyns wrouʒt" (19).[11] Despite clear acknowledgement of the French cultural inheritance underlying the romance, the narrator proceeds to add that many "lewed no can Freyns non" (22) but that they like to hear "Of douʒti kniʒtes of Inglond" (28). Having thus distanced the English from their French past and claimed "Inglisch" interest in his subject matter, the narrator tells a tale that contains, even in its current fragmentary state, multiple examples of French-English conflict (lines 95–6, 163–4, 208–14, 261–64, 287–89, 307–8, 320–21), most of which is caused by French perfidy and the fact that "þe king of Fraunce nold [Richard] no gode" (164). *King Richard* thus acknowledges a shared cultural heritage uniting the French and English, but simultaneously depicts a deep and abiding enmity between the two groups.

The Auchinleck texts that contain extensive portraits of noble Saracen knights do not comment as explicitly as *King Richard* on the French-English relationship of the later Middle Ages, but their literary history makes the same point. The narratives on which this chapter concentrates represent the earliest extant English translations of French texts that enjoyed widespread popularity among both the continental French and the Anglo-Normans in England. *Roland and Vernagu* and *Otuel a Kniȝt* are English versions of Matter of France tales, while *Sir Beves of Hamtoun* and *Guy of Warwick* translate earlier Anglo-Norman texts. All draw heavily upon French literary sources, yet each also circulates in English, a choice of language which testifies to efforts to end the cultural prominence of French literature in post-Conquest England.

Roland and Vernagu derives from an Old French prose text, the *Estoire de Charlemagne* or the *Redacted Johannis Turpin* which dates from 1206 and survives in eighteen manuscripts.[12] This text, in turn, draws on the popular twelfth-century Latin prose *Chronicle of the Pseudo-Turpin* while adding some other material.[13] The Auchinleck *Roland and Vernagu* is the only extant Middle English text that narrates Charlemagne's conquest of Spain and the battle between Roland and the Saracen giant Vernagu on this campaign. It thus combines French-focused material with a language of presentation that reflects English self-consciousness. In addition, lest the redactor should be accused of distracting people's attention from England, the tale states at its opening that Charlemagne rules all of "fraunce . . . & Inglond."[14] This textual evocation of Charlemagne as a king of England unites French and English, and reflects England's complex relationships with Charlemagne, France and the realm's French-influenced past. William of Malmesbury, for example, claimed that at the Battle of Hastings William of Normandy's men sang a version of *The Song of Roland*. The veracity of this assertion is debated by scholars,[15] but, whether true or not, the chronicler's anecdote certainly indicates a perception of Charlemagne as a French interpolation into insular culture. The legacy of the Conquest meant that Charlemagne was an interpolation destined to remain part of English heroic tradition. Despite Charlemagne's Frenchness, the English for many years saw him as part of an ideological tradition of martial valor and excellence in which they participated. For example, Ambroise (a jongleur who recorded Richard I's crusade from a distinctly pro-Richard, pro-English/Anglo-Norman stance) lamented the passing of the good old days of Charlemagne's era when there was no dissent among different branches of the Frankish peoples, and contrasted this with his own era when French-English divisions were continually a problem for crusaders.[16] Ambroise's pithy and derogatory remarks about the Continental French on the third Crusade embody a distinct insular position and consciousness, but they are still articulated in the French language. *Roland and Vernagu* continues the French-based tradition of Charlemagne, but takes the sense of insular identity voiced by Ambroise into new arenas through the use of the English language to relate the deeds of Charlemagne. The appearance of the French king and his nobles in Auchin-leck thus testifies to the complicated French heritage underpinning English identity. It is entirely appropriate, therefore, that the Saracen knights in this Matter of France tradition explore problems of sameness and differentiation.

The Auchinleck *Roland and Vernagu* ends with news of Vernagu's death reaching the Saracen Otuel, a character not mentioned in the *Pseudo-Turpin*.[17] The story of this character emerges in *Otuel a Kni3t*, which imme-diately follows *Roland and Vernagu* in Auchinleck and narrates the conversion of a Saracen warrior at Charlemagne's court. *Otuel a Kni3t* is the earliest extant English translation of material contained in the French *chan-son de geste Otinel. Otinel* exists as a self-contained tale in three contexts today: an Old French version from a fourteenth-century manuscript[18] in the Vatican (Vatican City, Biblioteca Apostolica Vaticana, Regin. Lat. 1616); and two Anglo-Norman texts, one a fragment of 292 lines dating from the mid-dle of the thirteenth century (Paris, Bibliothèque nationale, nouvelles acqui-sitions françaises 5094),[19] and the other a complete version dating from c. 1300 (Cologny-Geneva, Bodmeriana Library, 168).[20] André de Mandach believes that the *Otinel* tale may actually have originated in an Anglo-Nor-man linguistic and cultural context.[21] While De Mandach's claim is still a hypothesis rather than a proven fact, there is certainly no denying the popu-larity of the tale in England. In addition to the Anglo-Norman versions and the one in Auchinleck, two more English versions exist in fifteenth-century manuscripts: *Otuel and Roland* in the Fillingham manuscript (London, British Library, Additional 37492) and *Duke Rowland and Sir Otuell of Spayne* in London, British Library, Additional 31042.[22] Tales of Otuel thus represent a large proportion of Middle English Charlemagne material, since only thirteen texts of this material exist today.[23] Auchinleck contains the ear-liest extant English versions of this Charlemagne material, and thereby testi-fies to the complicated mixture of French and English heritages in fourteenth-century England.[24]

Sir Beves of Hamtoun, too, translates into Middle English an earlier Anglo-Norman original. *Boeve de Haumtone* survived to modern times in three manuscripts, although one of these (Leuven, University Library, G.170)[25] was burned in 1940. The remaining two manuscripts of the Anglo-Norman tale survive, and date, respectively, to the second half of the thir-teenth century (London, Lambeth Palace, 1237, Nos. 1, 2)[26] and to c.1300 (Paris, Bibliothèque nationale, nouvelles acquisitions françaises 4532). Once more, Auchinleck represents the earliest extant translation of this material into English, and *Sir Beves,* like *Otuel,* was very popular in England. It exists in seven later medieval English versions: Cambridge, University Library, Ff.

2. 38 (mid to late fifteenth century)[27]; Cambridge, Gonville and Caius College, 175 (fifteenth century)[28]; Naples, National Library, XII. B. 29 (fifteenth century); London, British Library, Egerton 2862 (formerly the Duke of Sutherland manuscript) from the end of the fourteenth century; Manchester, Chetham Library, 8009 (also known as Mun. A. 6. 31)[29]; Oxford, Bodleian Library, Douce 19 (fragmentary printed edition); and an early printed text.[30] All the Middle English versions differ significantly from one another and from the Anglo-Norman original, and testify to a practice of free-spirited translation and interpolation.[31] Scholars posit the existence of a now lost Middle English version pre-dating that of Auchinleck and serving as the base text for both it and the other variants,[32] but no definitive evidence has yet come to light to support this assertion. While not as French-focused as the Charlemagne texts discussed in this chapter, *Sir Beves* does derive from England's French literary heritage. Given this heritage, it is not surprising that *Sir Beves* also explores, through its Saracens, problems of sameness and differentiation in articulations of a group identity.

Guy of Warwick shares a similar history. The three tales in Auchinleck together translate into English an Anglo-Norman romance that circulated in the thirteenth and fourteenth centuries. *Gui de Warewic* appears to have been quite popular as sixteen manuscripts of it exist today, ten of which are fairly complete and six of which are fragmentary.[33] Auchinleck is the earliest extant complete English translation of the narrative, and is the only English version to divide the story of Guy's life into three sections. *Guy of Warwick (stanzaic continuation)* and *Reinbrun gij sone of warwike* are unique metrical constructions, while *Guy of Warwick (couplet version)* is one of the earliest renditions of the narrative in couplets. Another early fourteenth-century couplet version did exist, but is in fragments today (London, British Library, Additional 14408 and Aberystwyth, National Library of Wales, Binding Fragments 578[34]). Fifteenth-century versions of *Guy* are found in Cambridge, Gonville and Caius College, 107 and Cambridge, University Library, Ff. 2.38.[35] Another fragmentary version exists in London, British Library, Sloane 1044.[36] Given the number of extant *Guy of Warwick* texts, it is clear that this romance, like *Sir Beves,* represents a popular Englishing of French cultural inheritances, and stands at the forefront of fourteenth-century efforts to provide readers with "Inglisch" subject material in the English language and thereby craft a wholly English literary tradition.

To lay out the literary history underlying the appearance of these texts in Auchinleck is to indicate the scope of Auchinleck's achievement in providing for its audience one of the earliest collections of secular texts in the Middle English language. Indeed, Auchinleck is often venerated for this achievement by scholars of English identity[37] and by scholars of Middle English romance.[38] The manuscript, too, expresses a sense of pride in its use of the English language by drawing readers' attention to the language of presentation in texts such as that entitled *Þe pater noster undo on englissch*. As several scholars have noted, such evocations of the vernacular testify to an emergent sense of English identity that draws heavily upon language for its self-definition. What few people have pointed out, however, is the concomitant act of homage Auchinleck pays to the strong tradition of French language and culture in England. By drawing upon the Matter of France as well as Anglo-Norman texts for its material, the manuscript reflects the inescapable influence of post-Conquest French patrons, politics, and art on early fourteenth-century English literature and the emergent group identity it embodies. This French inheritance functions both as a catalyst for the articulation of a new "Inglisch" identity through use of the English language, and as an unavoidable historical component of the same Englishness. Auchinleck itself thus embodies the country's challenge of negotiating its sameness and difference in relation to France.

The tales of Saracen and Christian knights studied in this chapter bear witness to the "Englishing" of French literary inheritances in another way, too. While the French sources of these texts are usually classified as *chansons de geste* by scholars,[39] their English descendants are most often identified as romances. Susan Crane's *Insular Romance* discusses *Sir Beves* and *Guy of Warwick* in detail,[40] while the *Manual of the Writings in Middle English* provides entries for all the texts discussed here in its first volume, entitled *Romances*.[41] The generic categorization of medieval literature is problematic at the best of times since it is difficult to bridge the gap between medieval methods of classification and modern scholarly ones. Nevertheless, as Paul Strohm has shown, the term "romauns" did have an early genesis in English, and was most often used to refer to texts originally written in French that possessed an element of the fabulous.[42] The term *chanson de geste,* however, has no history in Middle English, while the term "geste," which does appear in Middle English, identifies any "poem or song about heroic deeds," and thus constitutes an extremely fluid generic identification that encompasses "romauns" rather than excludes it.[43] Scholars of medieval French literature, however, use the term *chanson de geste* very specifically to designate tales that recount the battles and conflicts of French knights both among themselves and against external enemies such as Saracens.[44] The same Old French scholars have used the term "romance" to indicate tales that focus more on the quests of individual knights and their courtly relationships with women.[45] As Sarah Kay has pointed out, however, the dividing line between the two genres in Old

French is not absolute and the two types of texts complement each other by emphasizing shared issues of interest in different contexts. *Chansons de geste* often address the question of marriage and dynastic relationships with women, albeit usually with Saracen princesses rather than Christian European ladies, and romances such as those about Arthur and his knights do explore male-male relationships in the knightly world and the conflicts they involve, albeit more often in relation to strange knights than in relation to brothers-in-arms and the different generations of men in a family.[46] Even with Kay's careful refinements of genre definition, however, it is still possible to distinguish between texts like Chrétien de Troyes's *Chevalier de la charette,* which concentrates on Lancelot and Guinevere's relationship and on an individual knight, and those of the Guillaume d'Orange cycle which concern themselves more with Saracen-Christian conflict and marriage, inept kings, and various knights' valiant deeds in large-scale battles. While not denying that the two types of literature are related, one can classify them by emphasis fairly readily. When one comes to English texts, however, even this somewhat clear defining line fades. Scholars often characterize insular romances as tales purportedly about individual knights that are more concerned with social, familial and dynastic issues and with battle, and less concerned with the nuances of love relationships, than their French counterparts.[47] In other words, scholars identify English romances as more likely to demonstrate the qualities of both French romance and *chanson de geste.* The Auchinleck texts discussed here manifest such characteristics, and, although they are usually categorized as romances, clearly incorporate elements traditionally associated with *chansons de geste. Roland and Vernagu* adds lines about Otuel that ultimately stress Vernagu's familial alliance with him and thereby alert readers to the implications of Roland's deeds in a Saracen dynastic context. *Otuel a Kniȝt* excises the details of the love affair between Otuel and Belecent so lavishly narrated in the French source.[48] *Sir Beves of Hamtoun,* meanwhile, interweaves the narration of a love relationship with more lengthy descriptions of Saracen-Christian conflict and dynastic vengeance. *Guy of Warwick* minimizes the love relationship between Guy and Felice, and devotes many more lines to Guy's battles against Saracens and other opponents. The texts studied in this chapter thus seem to embody an insular melding of French romance concerns about individual knights and their loves and deeds with French *chanson de geste* concerns about Saracen-Christian conflict, familial alliances, and dynastic duties. Moreover, all these texts could be designated by the Middle English term "romauns," because of their language of origin. Given these issues, then, perhaps it is problematic to discuss French and English "romance" as if they are comparable categories. Instead, it might be more helpful to consider English romance as a descendent of both French romance and *chanson de geste* in which the characteristics of both are intertwined more fully than in their French manifestations.

SAMENESS AND SARACENS

The various Englishings of French literary inheritances described above reveal both English cultural dependency on the French and English independence. They thus indicate the complicated task of articulating a distinct fourteenth-century "Inglisch" identity given the country's shared heritage with France. Indeed, the literary and political situations detailed above point to problems of sameness and desired differentiation in assertions of a community's unique identity. It is just this problem of defining group identity in a context of shared similarities and minute differences that the Saracen characters in *Roland and Vernagu, Otuel, Sir Beves,* and *Guy of Warwick* address. I do not mean to say that these texts intentionally or explicitly define English and French identities. Rather, they offer to their readers a representation of Saracen-Christian interaction that raises questions about what constitutes sameness, what it implies for various group identities, and how groups are to be distinguished given a context of similarity and shared values. These issues constitute the challenge of articulating English identity in relation to France and England's French heritage; thus, the Saracen characters relate to Auchinleck's project of articulating English identity, but in a reflexive rather than mimetic manner. In other words, they do not assert an English identity as much as explore how such an assertion is made and what it means or involves. In this way, the Saracen knights discussed here serve an important cultural function in Auchinleck despite their oft-cited stereotypical and clone-like nature.

The main type of Saracen in *Otuel a Kniʒt, Roland and Vernagu, Sir Beves of Hamtoun,* and *Guy of Warwick* is the Saracen warrior, a literary figure with a long history that both precedes his appearance in Auchinleck and shapes the functions he serves therein. The Saracen warrior is a common fixture of French *chansons de geste* and their Middle English translations. Unmimetic as he is, this figure appears most commonly in one of two forms; he is either a beast-like source of power to be feared and fought, or a ferocious knightly opponent whom the Christians would like to convert to their side. The following quotations from the *Chanson de Roland* describe the two types of Saracen warriors. Members of a Saracen emir's forces appear " . . . as chefs gros: / Sur les eschines qu'il unt en mi les dos / Cil sunt seiet ensemble cume porc."[49] An emir himself, however, is depicted thus:

Cors ad mult gent e le vis fier e cler.
Puis que il est sur sun cheval muntet,
Mult se fait fiers de ses armes porter.
De vasselage est il ben alosez,
Fust chrestïens, asez oüst barnet. (895–899)

[He has a well-proportioned body and his face is fierce and open,
When he is mounted on his horse,
He bears his arms very fiercely.
He is renowned for his bravery,
If he were a Christian, he would be a very worthy knight.]

The same two types of Saracens are found in *Beves of Hamtoun* and *Guy of Warwick*. Beves fights two Saracen giants of "loþeliche semlaunt"[50] who are fearsome in demeanor and thirty feet tall (lines 1853–920 and 2505–43). These Saracens, however, are ultimately defeated by Beves and do not serve as battle opponents as frequently as do more knightly Saracens who are admirable fighters and masters of European techniques of battle. *Guy of Warwick* presents readers with one particularly monstrous Saracen named Amoraunt in the *Stanzaic Continuation*. Amoraunt is "so michel of bodi y-piȝt, / [that] Oȝains him tvelue men haue no miȝt" (63. 1–2).[51] He also stands four feet taller than any other man, and is "As blac . . . as brodes brend" (62.10). Apart from Amoraunt, most Saracens in *Guy of Warwick* are noble, knightly warriors who resemble their Christian opponents. *Guy of Warwick (couplet version)*, for example, presents to readers the Saracen Costdram:

So strong he is, & of so gret miȝt,
In world y wene no better kniȝt;
For þer nis man no kniȝt non
Þat wiþ wretþe dar loken him on. (2907–10)

The Saracen figures who appear in *Otuel a Kniȝt* all fall into this category of noble warrior and are explicitly described as "bold kniȝt" and "douȝti kniȝt."[52] Likewise, *Roland and Vernagu* depicts Vernagu, the French hero's opponent, as a valiant warrior who is able to appreciate Roland's act of courtliness in laying a stone beneath the Saracen's head as he sleeps. Vernagu, however, is still a giant with magical powers, and thus blurs somewhat the division between monstrous and knightly Saracens. Ultimately, though, his duel with Roland, his esteem for courtly behavior, and Roland's efforts to convert him by theological exposition cast Vernagu more as noble warrior than as animalistic monster. All the texts studied here, then, present readers with depictions of Saracen warriors as noble Saracen knights.

As scholar after scholar makes clear, the stereotypical nature of these Saracens lies in their bizarre similarity to the literary figure of the European Christian knight. The character supposed to represent alterity is essentially no different from his Christian counterpart, as becomes evident when one examines how Saracen and Christian opponents evaluate each other, how they fight each other, how the two groups reward their members, and how the supposedly different religious communities worship their gods. As will be seen, the samenesses that emerge from analysis of these characteristics assert and validate one specific group identity, that of western knightliness, while downplaying other group identities rooted in religion and culture. Thus, Saracen knights comment both on the problems class affiliations can pose to the assertion of cultural or political identities, and, indirectly, on the process of defining English identity in relation to France.

The first similarity between Christian and Saracen that one notices in these texts is their shared attitudes towards the role of the body in evaluating someone's worth. Saracens participate in the bodily economy of the Christian knights they fight. In other words, like their Christian fellows, Saracen warriors use bodily appearances, genealogies, and physical acts to ascertain value and to constitute knightly honor. Similarly, their Saracen bodies and acts reinforce Christian notions about how a knight's body should look and comport itself. For example, in *Otuel*, Charlemagne's squire discerns the then unconverted Otuel's noble martial identity on sight: "Þe skwier þou3te wel by si3t, / Þat Otuwel was a dou3ti kni3t" (87–88). Otuel, even though he is Saracen, can be identified correctly as a noble fighting man. This diagnosis is borne out by his martial stance and acts in Charlemagne's hall (he kills a knight who attacks him from behind—lines 163–72), and by his eventual disclosure of noble genealogy. When Charlemagne asks Otuel,

> "Of what linage þou art come."
> Otuwel answerde þis;
> "A kinges sone ich am, iwis,
> Soþ to segge & nou3t to lye,
> Ich am þe kinges cosin garsie." (336–40)

Otuel's body thus fits the knightly economy in both its appearance and its origins. Because he, a Saracen, fits so neatly into knightly categories, he proves the applicability of these categories across cultural boundaries. In *Sir Beves*, Saracen warriors reinforce Western standards in a slightly different way—by using those same standards when they are judging Christian foreigners. Beves, having been sold to Saracen traders, is presented to the Saracen King Ermin, and Ermin swears,

> "Be Mahoun, þat sit an hi3,
> A fairer child neuer i ne si3,
> Neiþer a lingþe ne on brade,
> Ne non, so faire limes hade!
> Child," a seide, "whar wer þe bore?
> What is þe name? telle me fore!" (535–40)

Beves' genealogy and appearance are evidently valued not only by his own culture, but also by Saracen culture. As a result, knightly values, and differentiation from other types of people, are reinforced and made to seem universal by Saracen participation in the same bodily economy.

Depictions of Saracen battle behavior also suggest that Saracens use their bodies militarily the same way that Christian knights do. As Norman Daniel points out, in the *chansons de geste* "there is no pretense that the horrors of war were not evenly distributed between them, or that Christians and Saracens conducted war in any way differently."[53] Because he fights back, and does so in the same manner as his Christian opponent, the Saracen validates his opponent's training in violence. This sameness of fighting techniques is most noticeable in the descriptions of single combat. For example, the battle between Roland and the yet-unconverted Otuel begins thus:

> Þei riden to-gedire wiþ speres kene,
> Þat were steue & nou3t longe;
> & þe kni3tes were boþ stronge,
> & smyten eiþer in oþeres sscheld
> Þat boþe hors fellen in þe feld,
> & risen a3ein op fram þe grounde,
> & boþe kni3tes were hole & sounde.
> Þo þe stedes were risen boþe,
> Þe kni3tes woxen boþ fol wroþe,
> & drowen swerdes ate laste,
> & eiþer hu3 on oþer faste. (446–56)

Both warriors begin the attack on horseback, reinforcing the increasingly anachronistic idea that individual mounted combat is a universal modus operandi for fighting others.[54] Spears, borne by "stronge" knights, bear down on shields, and each knight smites so hard that he fells the other's steed to ground. Finally, both knights are seized by rage as their efforts are thwarted, and each resorts to his sword as hand-to-hand combat replaces mounted charge. The parallelism of weapons, armor, and methods of battle means that the Saracen shares and reinforces the Christian knight's ideas about how to train and how to comport himself in battle.

Saracen-Christian parallelism is also seen in the rituals structuring knightly encounters on the battlefield. For example, when Beves and Yuor fight each other in formal single combat in *Sir Beves*, the two opponents begin by praying for success:

> To hire godes þai bede i*n* eiþ*er* side;
> Beves bad help to Marie sone
> And king Yuor to sein Mahoune;
> Ase Beves bad helpe to Marie,
> To Teruagaunt Yuor gan crie. (4144–48)

Guy of Warwick, too, suggests that Saracens and Christians share battle rituals. After Guy has slain the noble Saracen Costdram in battle, he sends the Saracen's head to the Emperor of Constantinople. Later, when Guy encounters the Saracen Esclandar on the battlefield, Esclandar tells him " . . . neu*er* schal y bliþe be, / Til ich [your] heued binim þe; / Bihoten ich it haue a maide*n* of pr*i*s" (*Guy of Warwick (couplet version)* 3049–51). Saracens and Christians alike feel that sending an enemy's head to a person one serves constitutes the proof *par excellence* of success in battle and earns esteem for the victorious warrior. Both cultures also share the more formal ritual of trial by battle to determine legal redress in tricky situations. The first part of *Guy of Warwick (stanzaic continuation)*, for example, depicts Guy serving as a champion in two trials by battle, the first to settle a dispute between a Saracen sultan and one of his subordinate Saracen kings, and the second to settle a dispute between a Christian European emperor and one of his earls. Rituals of chivalry, too, traverse the Saracen-Christian divide. For example, in both *Roland and Vernagu* and *Guy of Warwick* Saracens engaged in single combats with Christian champions appeal to the Christian's sense of chivalric fair play to call for a temporary halt in battle (*Roland and Vernagu* 611–52 and *Guy of Warwick (stanzaic continuation)* stanzas 113–114). Saracens clearly know the traditions of noble Christian knights well. And even when they do not, they recognize the inherent values of such traditions. In *Otuel a Kni3t*, for example, the Saracen Otuel learns from, and imitates, one of Roland's chivalrous actions:

> Otuwel þoute on errore deede,
> Þo he [Roland] hadde slawe his stede,

Hou roulond houede stille as ston,
Til he [Otuel] was risen & gon;
& he [Otuel] stod al stille,
& leet roulond risen at wille. (489–94)

Here, the Saracen is shown not only to practice battle in the same manner as
his Christian counterpart, but even to recognize and admire the one act in
which he has not been trained by his Saracen background. The code of battle
is so similar between the two types of knight that Otuel is able to perceive,
and approve of, the desire for honorable victory that underlies Roland's
actions. Of course, this parallelism of fighting methods was not a reflection
of reality, as is made clear by the crusader Ambroise's comments about the
differences in armor and weapons that made historical Muslims quicker at
raiding and escaping pursuit than their more heavily-armed Christian counterparts.[55] In the fictional world of Auchinleck, however, Christian knights
need not fear that they will encounter Saracens who raise questions about the
efficacy of traditional western methods of battle.

It is not only in battle, however, that Saracens resemble their opponents and thereby suggest a sense of cross-cultural knightliness. Like their
Christian counterparts, Saracen characters in *Otuel* and *Sir Beves* exhibit a
decided acquisitiveness, and a sense that war, profit, and knightly honor are
inherently compatible.[56] In *Otuel*, the narrator points out that the Saracen
Garsie "was lord of londes ynowe, / & ʒit he þouʒte wit maistrie, / Habben
al cristendom to gye" (38–40). The universal language of profit also underlies the duel between Beves of Hamtoun and Yuor of Mombraunt. Yuor
offers single combat with an incentive:

"ʒif þow slest me in bataile,
Al min onour, wiþ outen faile,
Ich þe graunte þourʒ & þourʒ,
Boþe in cite and in bourʒ!" (4133–36)

Beves happily accepts this, and claims Yuor's realm after he has defeated the
Saracen. In these cases, both Saracens and Christians demonstrate a
healthy interest in wealth acquisition. The same base values operate in both
cultures.

The texts studied here also suggest that, whatever the religious affiliation of knights, military prowess will be recognized and rewarded in the
same way—with financial and political power. For example, in *Guy of Warwick (couplet version)*, the narrator praises the Emperor of Constantinople
for offering Guy and his companions "riche tresour . . . / Gold and siluer

gret plente" (4463–64) in recompense for their martial achievements. Similarly, when Otuel kills Clarel, a Saracen who has insulted Charlemagne, Charlemagne

> . . . ӡaf otuwel, þat douӡti kniӡt,
> A god Erldam þat selue niӡt.
> Al þat in þe ost was,
> Maden murþe & solas,
> Þat otuwel hadde so bigunne,
> & hadde so þe maistri wonne. (1339–44)

Here, both land and public acclaim are awarded to the now-Christian noble knight who has displayed martial might. However, even Saracens can be given such treasures by Christian rulers, if they demonstrate enough military proficiency. Otuel, before he converts, is offered marriage with Charlemagne's daughter (and the position of power and wealth such marriage entails) after he has demonstrated his martial valor. Once Roland has "feled þat otuwel smot ariӡt, / & þat myӡt was in his arm" (510–11), he promises Otuel Belecent for his wife should he become Christian (see lines 512–18). Likewise, the Saracen king, Ermin, rewards Beves's martial appearance and bearing by offering him marriage to Josiane and "al me lond after me liue!" (560). If Saracen rulers, despite their membership in a different culture, also recognize knightliness with financial and political power, then knights of both groups are assured of wealth and status, and yet another characteristic unites Saracen and Christian warriors.

By this point, it should be clear that the identities being affirmed by Saracens and Christians in these texts are not those of different religious faiths, but rather a shared membership in one communal body, namely a brotherhood of knights that cuts across cultural borders. If there is any doubt about this, the representation of the two groups' religious practices dispels it. To begin with, warriors from both groups venerate their gods by fighting, and regard the field of battle as the proving ground *par excellence* of their respective gods' strengths. For example, Saracens in *Guy of Warwick* read their defeat at Guy's hands as evidence that "Our godes ous hateþ," and that "Mahoun ne Apolin / Be nouӡt worþ þe brestel of a swin" (*Couplet Version* 3678–80). Similarly, when a Saracen knight tells Beves that he should "Anoure þe god, so i schel myn, / Boþe Mahoun and Apolyn!" (605–6), Beves responds by challenging the knight to fight, saying

> "Ich wolde for me lordes loue,
> Þat sit hiӡ in heuene aboue,

Fiȝte wiþ ȝow euerichon,
Er þan ich wolde hennes gon!" (615–18)

The Saracen accepts this as a worthy cause for battle, and the melee begins.
Beves honors his God as the Saracens do theirs—by attacking the unbeliever.
His body and theirs become the sites of divine manifestation, and the relative
status of the Christian God is asserted by Beves's victory. The determination
of holy hierarchy by conflict also appears in *Otuel a Kniȝt*. Clarel tells the
recently converted Otuel that

"Bi mahoun, þat ich onne bileue,
Oppon þi bodi ich wolde preue,
Þat mahoun may mo miracles make,
Þan he þat þou art to itake." (1173–76)

Otuel is only too willing to take this challenge up, and proves, by killing
Clarel, the relative superiority of his new God. Both Christians and Saracens,
then, suggest that the best way to worship God is to fight as knights do on a
battlefield. [57] Not for either group are the more traditional Christian practices of church attendance or donations to religious orders. Even Guy, the
most penitent and religiously self-aware knight presented in these texts,
atones for his sins not by joining a monastery or going to confession but by
fighting Saracens. Moreover, Guy's life-changing recognition that he has
never done a good deed for God is effected not by a priest or hermit, but by
his solitary contemplation of the nighttime sky (*Stanzaic Continuation* stanzas 20–21).[58] In these texts, knights sort out religious problems in their own
way, without any interference by clerics.

    Other events, too, assert the religious self-sufficiency of noble warriors.
Moments of Saracen conversion to Christianity emphasize the knightly ability to transcend faith differences single-handedly. In these tales clerics simply
are not needed to regulate inter-faith relationships since knights obtain
numerous converts with little or no clerical assistance. For example, Beves
Christianizes the Saracen princess Josiane simply by being around her. She
falls in love with him, and changes her religious affiliation in order to marry
him. As she says to Beves, "þow me to wiue tok, / Whan ich me false godes
for-sok" (2185–86). Beves, for his part, has no false modesty about his role in
Josiane's conversion; he tells the priest who will perform the baptism that
"ȝhe wile, for me sake, / Cristendome at þe take" (2583–84). As Beves makes
clear, the knight's role in conversion is originary and formative, and is the
foundation upon which any subsequent clerical involvement rests. Otuel's
change of faith also asserts the knightly order's self-sufficiency in religious

matters. No priest is involved in his conversion. Instead, the prayers of Charlemagne and his "Lordinges" (566) result in God sending a dove to alight directly on Otuel's head and effect a change in his will. Worthy knights are converted by direct contact with the divine, and clerics appear merely to perform the baptism ceremony that affirms a change wrought by God (see lines 635–38). Even the unsuccessful conversion depicted in *Roland and Vernagu* endows Roland with the ability to explain mysteries of the Christian faith to Vernagu, and when this effort fails, an angel comes directly from God to tell Roland that no cleric could do any better and that he may now proceed to kill Vernagu.[59] Literary knights thus prove themselves adequate to every religious situation they encounter, and clerics find themselves relegated to the position of a rubber stamp.

As one examines the details of what constitutes the similarity between noble Saracen warriors and their Christian counterparts, it becomes apparent that the two supposedly different groups have one common identity—that of knightliness. Warriors may be Saracen or Christian in these texts, but they share criteria for the evaluation of people's social standing, methods of battle, ideas about the suitable recompense for martial endeavor, and concepts of how divinity is manifested in their worlds. Similarities between fictional Saracens and Christians indicate that knightliness occurs throughout the world, among different peoples. This has the effect of portraying knighthood as a natural phenomenon rather than as an artificial construct peculiar to western society. The Saracen warrior thus suggests the existence of a universal brotherhood of knights. What we have, in essence, is the assertion of a class identity that transcends cultural or religious affiliations.

Saracen knights thus comment reflexively on a key problem involved in defining a group identity: any group affiliation is only one of a subject's multiple communal identities, and can be overwritten at any time by another type of group identity. Moreover, the particular overwriting depicted here suggests the dominance of socio-economic characteristics over cultural ones. What a person values, and how a person earns a living and comports him- or herself, matter more in these texts than what a person worships or where he or she comes from. Consider the implications of such a representation in a manuscript like Auchinleck, which strives so valiantly to assert a national identity premised on a people's shared linguistic and geographic characteristics. Given the point of class universality made by Saracen and Christian knights in the texts discussed here, any assertion of a group identity founded on principles other than class appears a rather fragile and tenuous, perhaps even futile, effort. Indeed, the challenges posed by class affiliations to articulations of English identity were particularly noticeable in the early fourteenth century. Even as cultural products like Auchinleck and the conflicts of the Hundred Years War helped to differentiate the English from the French, ties of blood and socio-economic status still bound nobles from the two countries together, sometimes to the detriment of attempts to distinguish the warring nations. For example, in his chronicle of the Hundred Years War Froissart describes an incident at the sack of Caen in 1346 in which "Sir Thomas Holland [an English knight] rescued the comte d'Eu and the comte de Tancarville who were in fear of their lives from some English archers."[60] The three had been travelling companions earlier in their lives on knightly voyages, and Holland is described as being "tous joians" when he is able to save his fellow French nobles. Here, class identity operates across French-English boundaries even when the two nations are at war with each other, and when the situation from which Holland's fellow nobles had to be rescued was one created by Holland's countrymen. This is not to say that the historical class identity of knights and nobles in England was simple or uniform. There were rich and poor, weak and strong, powerful and powerless mounted and landed warriors in England in the fourteenth century,[61] and not all of them would have felt Holland's desire to intervene on behalf of the French nobles (although many might have been motivated to do so, as Holland was in part, by the lure of hefty ransoms for such high-ranking prisoners of war!). Still, there is no denying that historical situations did exist in which people's affiliations with one socio-economic group could, and did, override efforts to assert English unity. [62] (One might consider clerics and their links to Rome as another example of such a group). The similarities between Saracen and Christian warriors in certain Auchinleck texts thus point to one of the largest impediments to creating a heightened sense of Englishness during the early fourteenth century: the English people's participation in multiple group identities, and the ways in which some of these identities, such as class, could undermine assertions of communal English identity and of differentiation from the French.

SAMENESS AND INTERPELLATIONS OF ALTERNATE IDENTITIES

When the similarities connecting groups are emphasized, as in the texts discussed here, one becomes aware of the constructed and contingent nature of assertions of difference. In other words, when the samenesses between groups seem to predominate, one is particularly struck by moments when differences between the groups are vehemently asserted. Such moments provoke questions about why and in what circumstances differences are emphasized.

The contingency and strategy underlying choices of when to assert a specific identity are also shown in these texts, most particularly in *Otuel a Kniʒt.* This narrative indicates that similarities between knights, even as they undermine Saracen-Christian differentiation, can also, at times, paradoxically promote vehement assertions of cultural and political difference. Christian and Saracen warriors in these texts may be bound together by knightly concerns and values, but such class unity can be undermined by individuals' desires for recognition within the sameness of the community to which they belong. Such desires can lead knights to downplay their class affiliations with their opponents, and assert their differences from these characters. Ironically, however, such assertions of difference seem to be expressly provoked by knightly sameness.

Because these characters are all knights, their very class identity promotes martial competitiveness and individual quests for prestige. Knights are valued for their performances in battle and receive rewards for outstanding performances. Each knight thus wants to be like his fellows, but better than them too, and such desires mean seeking out opportunities for displays of martial prowess. Otuel outlines this situation explicitly when, after he has converted, he comments that Roland, Oliver, and Ogier have stolen away to attack Garsie's forces in order to prove their greater prowess in relation to him:

> "Roulond, oliuer, an ogger þe stronge,
> Oue[r] þe water alle þre,
> Beþ went for envie of me,
> To loke wher þei miʒten spede,
> To don any douʒti deede,
> Among þe sarazins bolde." (1018–23)

The erstwhile Saracen here lays bare the rivalry underlying certain knightly actions. Other events promote similar competitiveness and efforts to find forums for martial display. For example, once Ogier has been captured, the way is opened for a heretofore unmentioned "ʒong kniʒt, þat sprong furst [b]erd" (1445) to enter the field of battle and have his actions described in as much textual detail as those of the high-ranking warriors Roland, Oliver, and Otuel. The "ʒong kniʒt" displays his martial prowess and achieves narrative recognition for it. His story demonstrates the benefits that accrue from opportunities for individual display, and thus promotes knightly competitiveness and efforts to create such opportunities.

The drive to achieve differentiation within the brotherhood of knights, however, is not without its drawbacks. Quests for knightly honor can undermine the solidarity of the brotherhood, and pose problems for the rulers who rely on knights to advance their political ends. The raid by Ogier, Roland, and Oliver, provoked by their desire to win honor in combat, results in Ogier's aforementioned capture by Saracens and his separation from his comrades. This event, while it offers the "ȝong kniȝt" an opportunity for recognition, compromises Charlemagne's efficacy on the battlefield. While the "ȝong kniȝt" may replace Ogier, imagine how much better Charlemagne's military position at this point would be had he the services of Ogier at his disposal in addition to those of the "ȝong kniȝt." Ogier's desire for differentiation from his fellow knights thus creates problems for the larger group to which he belongs.[63] Too much sameness can be a community's curse.[64]

As shared ideals of knighthood promote competitiveness and disunity, they also foster knights' links to group identities other than knighthood. Class sameness at times promotes assertions of cultural and political difference. Saracen warriors are marked by religious difference and thus participate in a group identity foreign to their Christian opponents even as they share a class identity. What the Saracens reveal, however, is that Christian characters are troubled by, and react to, the otherness of Saracens only when those "foreigners" are performing better at knightly functions. In other words, the Saracen irritates his Christian counterparts most when he is doing a better job at the same tasks that Christian knights are supposed to perform. The problem, essentially, is that of envy and competitiveness, of similarity in a separate entity provoking aggression.[65] The above-mentioned actions of Roland, Oliver, and Ogier illustrate the manifestation of this type of situation among members of a particular body of knights. When knights are linked by class but differentiated culturally and politically, however, shared knightly competitiveness can provoke strategic assertions of these alternate identities.

Such provocation and assertion are seen most clearly when the as yet unconverted Otuel boldly declares his martial prowess by recounting the capture of Rome by Saracens:

> "King garsie þe weie nam,
> To þe Cite of rome he cam,
> Twenti þousende was þe sawe,
> Þat were þare of sarazin lawe:
> Corsouse m[i swerde ful] harde fel,
> & bot þere Freinche flechs fol wel." (127–32)

Upon hearing these words,

> Estu3t of leggers, a freinshe kni3t,
> He sterte op anon ri3t,
> & kypte anon in his hond
> A gret muche fir brond,
> & to otuwel a strok hadde ment. (133–37)

Although Otuel has already cursed Charlemagne and bandied challenges with Roland, it is when he describes his martial prowess that he provokes his hearers into physical action. It is almost as if, having heard of Otuel's violent deeds, Estu3t must perform one himself to prove his knightly value. Because Otuel has deliberately cast his deeds as an attack on "Freinche flechs," he affords the French knight an excuse to attack him. The narrator explicitly introduces Estu3t's violent response with reference to his "freinshe" identity, and this casts the knight's response as an action provoked by Otuel's description of knightly prowess being exercised on, rather than by, "Freinche flechs." Estu3t's French group affiliation allows him to act according to the code of knightly honor that he shares with Otuel, and to display to others his own martial prowess after Otuel has described his. Knightly sameness here, in the form of love of battle and of competitive display, encourages the assertion of cultural and political difference as a reason for combat.

Otuel next provokes knightly aggression and promotes political differentiation when he invokes his martial prowess (rather than Charlemagne's decree) as defense against further attacks by the French. After Estu3t's attack, Charlemagne orders his knights to refrain from harming Otuel, but the Saracen refuses to give up his sword to a Frenchman and insists that the weapon is his best protection. Otuel here flaunts the battle prowess he shares with his Christian counterparts, but differentiates himself from them by disdaining the efficacy of Charlemagne's regal decree as a safeguard. It is at this moment that the French knight fated to die attacks Otuel from behind. Otuel thus incites the most deadly enmity when he behaves most like a Christian knight (by invoking his physical abilities as the guarantee of his safety), and yet maintains his political differentiation from the French knights. The Saracen is most irritating, and threatening, when he enacts military prowess more freely and successfully than the Christian knights themselves, yet remains distinct from them.

Thus, while a class affiliation might sometimes undermine borders between communities, as in the case of Thomas Holland, at other times the desire for differentiation within one class group might provoke members' vociferous assertions of their alternate communal identities. In *Otuel,* too much shared knightliness results in the cultural and political divisions between warriors being emphasized and claimed. It is not differences that provoke a strategic, forcible erection of boundaries between groups, but samenesses. Similarly, it was not Edward III's differences from the French that initiated the Hundred Years War, but rather his closeness to the French throne and his similarities to other French claimants of that throne. Even within England, the shared knightliness that prompted warriors of different political stripes to participate in the same tournaments also led to pointed and deadly assertions of political difference. In the time of Edward II when the magnates were trying to convince king and Parliament that Piers Gaveston was a drain on England financially, socially, and politically, and ought to be exiled, their political antagonism towards Gaveston was heightened by his knightly triumphs over them in tournaments.[66] Juliet Vale notes that in 1341, a tournament at Roxburgh turned into a serious rather than a mock battle when English and Scots nobles met on the tourney-field.[67] Divided into teams based on allegiances, the knightly brotherhood could not help but express in a purportedly social venue the very real political antagonisms occasioned by the English-Scottish wars of the fourteenth century.[68] As a result, the tournament became noteworthy for the severity and number of wounds suffered by the participating knights.[69] Likewise in *Otuel,* knightly competitiveness exists throughout, but plays itself out most forcibly when other group affiliations come into play. The problem, however, is not simply that differences provoke aggression, but that samenesses do so. The Saracen is most upsetting when he is participating in knightly endeavors and performing them better than the Christians, and it is these shared class situations that prompt vehement assertions of the cultural differences separating Saracen and Christian knights.

WILLED DIFFERENTIATION

Although Saracen and Christian knights may choose when to emphasize their political and cultural differences over their class samenesses, there is no denying that some difference ultimately separates the two groups. Because the Saracen warrior so closely resembles his Christian counterpart, however, he demands an analysis of what constitutes the minute difference between these two figures. The obvious answer is religious affiliation, but what this is is harder to define. As scholars repeatedly point out (and as shown earlier), the Saracen knight of romance does not lead a religious life so very different from that of his Christian colleague.[70] The event of a Saracen warrior's conversion, however, requires some articulation of what differentiates him from a Christian knight, and of how such differences are constructed and re-constructed by individuals.

In *Otuel,* Otuel's conversion to Christianity is effected by the direct intervention of God, who sends the Holy Spirit to alight on the Saracen's head during his duel with Roland:

> A whit coluere þer cam fle,
> Þat al þe peple miȝten se,
> On otuweles heued he liȝte
> Þoru þe uertu of godes miȝte.
> & otuwel, þat douȝti kniȝt,
> Wiþ-drouȝ him anoon riȝt
> Fram roulond, & stod al stille,
> To fiȝte more he ne hadde wille. (577–84)

As the passage shows, this divine visitation does not immediately convert Otuel; instead, the dove alters Otuel's will to fight. The eventual Christianization thus rests on Otuel's individual will. Indeed, the rhetoric surrounding this conversion is peppered with references to will. At the start of the duel, Charlemagne asks the lords attending the duel to pray God to "ȝive otuwel wille to day, / For to reneien his lay" (571–72).[71] Otuel, too, expresses his Christianization as an effect of will. He says to Roland: "ȝef þou wolt holden þat þou me het, / . . . / For soþe, þan is mi wille went" (587–90). In Otuel's conversion, God effects a change of will, but not a change of group affiliation. God simply gives the Saracen the desire to alter his group identity, but does not magically accomplish this for him. Conversion and group identity thus become states dependent on individual agency. The text suggests that assertions of group identity are acts of will rather than reflections of hard-and-fast boundaries between groups.

Perhaps the clearest evidence that Saracen-Christian differentiation is a product of will is offered by the Saracen knight Clarel in *Otuel.* Clarel is one of four Saracen kings encountered by Roland, Ogier, and Oliver when they sneak across the river to prove their martial prowess. After the French heroes have killed three of the four kings, Clarel refuses to flee the battle, but instead fights fiercely, unhorses Roland (792–94), and is overcome and taken captive only when Ogier and Oliver join the fight (813–18). Clearly an equal to the Christian knights in war, Clarel also proves to be their equal in honorable behavior when, later, fortune's wheel turns and Clarel shows clemency to the captured Ogier in return for earlier clemency he received from the three French knights. Clarel tells Ogier, "Þou holpe to saue mi lif a day, / Ich wole sauen þin, ȝef I may" (979–80). Clarel is thus essentially indistinguishable from Charlemagne's knights in all respects save one: his adherence to Saracenness. Indeed, later in the text, it is Clarel who rebukes

Otuel for his conversion and challenges him to single combat to prove "Þat mahoun may mo miracles make, / Þan he þat þou art to itake" (1175–76). This combat, like so many others, is described in terms of parallel acts on the parts of the two knights (see lines 1281–336). Otuel, however, emerges triumphant, and with that his differentiation from the equally doughty Clarel is trumpeted. The death, at the convert's hands, of his erstwhile Saracen comrade constitutes proof that Otuel definitively abandoned his Saracen ties when he decided to become Christian. So similar to the Otuel who appeared at the start of this tale, Clarel ultimately must die to affirm Otuel's change of group identity. His similarity to his eventual killer, however, clearly suggests that it is only an act of will that separates the two knights of Saracen origin, and determines their eventual ends in the text.

This emphasis on will as the basis of conversion and group identity is not unique to *Otuel*. In *Roland and Vernagu*, Vernagu's will emerges as an insurmountable obstacle to his conversion. Despite Roland's lengthy exposition of such key tenets of Christianity as the unity of the Trinity (701–18), the Incarnation (721–45), and the Resurrection (749–84), Vernagu shows no interest in conversion, and concludes the theological discursus by saying "Now we wil fiȝt. / Wheþer lawe better be, / Sone we schul y-se" (787–89). God then sends Roland an angel who advises him to

> " . . . sched þe schrewes blod,
> For he nas neuer gode,
> Bi lond no bi se:
> Þei alle prechours aliue,
> To cristen wald hi*m* schriue,
> Gode nold [h]e neuer be." (809–14)

The angel's words demonstrate Vernagu's intractability in the face of multiple efforts to alter his religious status. No matter who might try to make Vernagu a Christian, the angel insists that the Saracen will remain unchanged, a claim borne out by the complete inefficacy of Roland's attempts at theological persuasion. Here, there is no will on either side for Vernagu to alter his religious affiliation. Vernagu would rather fight to determine the strength of the respective deities, and the Christian side as represented by the angel asserts that Vernagu is essentially immovable and therefore should be killed. Vernagu's Saracenness is not as great a problem as his unwillingness to change.

Sir Beves of Hamtoun, too, represents religious identity and its concomitant group affiliation as something determined by will. While delivering a letter for the Saracen King Ermin in whose household he has lived since childhood, Beves happens upon his cousin Terri who has been sent from

England to seek Beves. Terri, unaware of Beves's identity, asks Beves for news about himself, and

> Beves be-held Terri & lou3,
> & seide, a knew þat child wel inou3:
> "Hit is nou3t," a seide, "gon longe,
> I se3 þe Sarsins þat child an-ho*n*ge!" (1305–8)

Even when Beves sees Terri's distressed reaction to this news he does not enlighten his cousin, but maintains his claim that he is dead. Moreover, when Terri asks about the message Beves carries, Beves claims that the Saracen king who entrusted it to him "'wolde *loue* me non oþer, / Þan ich were is owene broþer'" (1331–32). With the lie about his death, Beves willfully severs his connections to his Christian identity, and with his assertion of Ermin's brotherliness, he writes himself into a more Saracen identity.[72] Acts of will thus shape his apparent group affiliations. These identifications, however, can be rewritten and realigned, as Beves shows. After this experience, Beves decides to perform a more Christian identity. When he encounters Saracens emerging from their worship, he alights from his horse to kill their "prest," and throw their gods in a ditch (1348–56). Here, his choice to descend from his horse and wreak havoc on a scene that, given his upbringing in Ermin's household, cannot have been unfamiliar to him aligns Beves once more with the Christian heritage he has just denied. In *Sir Beves* then, as in *Otuel* and *Roland and Vernagu,* the group identities of "Saracen" and "Christian" rest on a foundation of choice and action.

Making the distinction between Christian and Saracen rest on changeable will represents religious identity as a constructed differentiation between peoples. The idea that people could will themselves to have a certain religious identity in life was a central tenet of Christianity. The gift, or problem, of free will from God meant that every person had the power to choose good or evil as his or her way of life. This notion informs Augustine's representation of the ethical life as one of struggle against one's baser desires.[73] Augustine's concerns about free will and the power to choose awry also explain his assertion that sometimes force may be used to convert people to Christianity for their own good.[74] Karl Morrison, in his study of clerical thinking about conversion in the twelfth century, also shows that religious men and women articulate in their writings a sense of life with God as a continual effort to improve one's will and deflect it from sinful desires. The Latin term used to describe this process was "conversio," the same as that used to describe a Saracen's decision to become Christian.[75] To find the conversion of Saracens depicted as an act of will, therefore, accords well with certain religious ideas from the Middle Ages.

Such a representation of Saracen conversion demands the attention of today's reader because it reveals a fascinating medieval idea about the relative permanence of cultural group identity. While medieval people often asserted the indissolubility of boundaries dividing different cultural groups from each other, they also at times articulated notions of boundary permeability, of the possibility of inclusion and integration.[76] One avenue of inclusion is conversion or movement to a Christian relationship with God that, in literature at least, is credited with the power to efface all sorts of boundaries and identity markers. In the *Chronicle of Lanercost,* for example, an English scholar described as "less careful of his comfort" than his fellows is found speechless and black-skinned. This situation, however, is reversed when his fellows recite the Gospel and thereby force the evil spirit causing the man's problems to depart his body.[77] Skin color becomes an impermanent and shifting indication of one's relationship to God. The same idea underlies the change of the Soudan's color in *Þe King of Tars.* After he converts to Christianity, this Saracen character's skin changes from black to white.[78] In the Middle Ages, then, conversion had the power to change in deep ways one's group affiliations and the appearances that designated these. However, as explained above, conversion was a process often understood and represented as dependent on the will of the individual. Hence, in an individual's agency rested the ability to change one's group identity, and in literature at least, this power of change even extended over the biological markers of one's cultural affiliations. Religious difference, and all the struggles and deaths it provoked in the later Middle Ages, become an effect of agency and a product of individual desire. Heretics, Saracens, and Christians can thus all be said to have willed their group affiliations and the conflicts derived from such affiliations.

I should point out, however, that such notions of conversion and its relation to will appear in literary contexts where the Saracens and Christians are represented as knights who share similar motivations, methods of combat, and behaviors. When Saracens closely resemble their Christian opponents, conversion becomes both possible and desirable. When the Saracen enemy is a monstrous creature like Amoraunt in *Guy of Warwick (stanzaic continuation),* or when he is defined solely by bestiality and color, as in the *Itinerarium peregrinorum,* the idea of conversion is not usually pursued. Rather, these Saracens are characterized so as to highlight all the borders separating them from their Christian enemies. In *Guy of Warwick,* for example, Guy's first words upon seeing the black giant Amoraunt are "It is . . . no mannes sone: / It is a deuel fram helle is come" (95.10–11). Similarly, the

Itinerarium Peregrinorum describes one group of Saracens as "a fiendish race, forceful and relentless, deformed by nature and unlike other living beings, black in colour, of enormous stature and inhuman savageness," and another as "a devilish race, very black in colour."[79] In these texts, black skin color is coupled with unhuman attributes, and the two together work to mark out an indissoluble boundary between Saracens and Christians. With such descriptions, Saracens like Amoraunt are distanced from their Christian opponents, and their very humanity and concomitant possession of free will are called into question. The powerful possibilities of conversion, agency and inclusion outlined above are thus confined to Saracens who closely resemble Christians, and were clearly ignored by writers who wished to facilitate Christian military action rather than conversion. Such writers' ends were best served by representing Saracens as devilish fiends, and thereby justifying attacks on them. This is clearly an aim of the *Itinerarium,* a record of European crusade. It is also an aim of the *Stanzaic Continuation* of *Guy of Warwick,* the text that recounts Guy's religious awakening and penance. Putting his martial abilities to godly ends is Guy's aim in this tale, not winning converts, thus it is unsurprising that battle is the focus of Saracen-Christian interaction and that a particularly monstrous Saracen appears here rather than in the other *Guy of Warwick* tales in Auchinleck.

In *Otuel,* however, all the Saracens are noble knights and conversion is therefore an option to be pursued. Here, the difference defining Saracen-Christian conflict is shown to rest on an act of will and not on a difference in nature. *Otuel* thus raises the question of why the fighting continues if the conflict is merely a product of will. Only if Christian and Saracen warriors share certain desires for, and investments in, battle can it continue. In *Otuel,* knights from both sides display interest in honor, vengeance, and booty. Honor, for example, provokes the duel between Roland and Otuel. Otuel claims that Saracen warriors will kill all the French knights who dare to fight, and this prompts Roland to challenge him to battle so that the Saracen shall never afterwards "Despice freinchs man" (290). Neither will permit the other to denigrate the prowess of the body of knights to which he belongs, and Otuel even tells Roland that "ʒef þou hauest wille to fiʒte, / Whan euere þou wolt let þe diʒte, / & þou sschalt finde me redi diʒt" (295–97). Vengeance emerges as a motive for continuing war when Clarel and Otuel both want to fight Roland because he has killed a relative of theirs (341–54; 727–32). Similarly, Roland challenges Otuel to battle to reprove him for insulting Charlemagne (265–90), who is a relative of Roland's (517). Finally, Christians and Saracens share a lust for the booty of battle that precludes settlement of their conflict. Garsie hungers for land (38–40), while Otuel expresses interest in Roland's offer of an advantageous marriage and the benefits it entails upon his conversion to Christianity (587–94). All these shared interests mean that neither Saracens nor Christians desire an end to different religious identities and the conflicts they entail. The two types of warriors constitute a brotherhood of those who benefit from war and so the will to convert simply is not there on either side. And while Charlemagne evinces a desire for Otuel to change his will and convert (see lines 570–72), he evinces no such desire when, later, Clarel and Otuel embark upon single combat. Conversion ultimately serves not to end conflict but merely to recast the sides involved. In its depiction of Otuel's conversion, then, *Otuel a Kniʒt* articulates a role for will in defining difference and thereby calls into question the absolute separation of the identities of Christian and Saracen. Charlemagne's later lack of interest in converting Saracens and ending conflict speaks all the more powerfully because of this, since the audience can now read this lack of interest as not a natural but a willed state of affairs. In the end, when *Otuel* attributes a role to will in conversion, it ultimately emphasizes the investment of groups in maintaining conflict between themselves, and the self-interest that can underpin assertions of differences between groups. Such self-interest, as John Barnie demonstrates, was very much part of English involvement in the Hundred Years War, particularly in its early years when battles went well, and booty and profits poured into English coffers and were transported home. According to Barnie, "The disputed inheritance [of Edward III] might be used as a rallying point for patriotic sentiment and as a justification in royal propaganda, but the reasons for the widespread support of Edward's cause in the 1340s and 50s should be sought . . . above all in the opportunities which the war offered for personal advancement and enrichment."[80] Once again, similar Saracens raise issues at stake in the English-French relationship of the early 1300s.

WILLED IDENTITIES AND THE AUCHINLECK MANUSCRIPT

When religious difference becomes a matter of will and an identity motivated by socio-economic investments, one is forced to recognize that tales purportedly about Muslims are less accurately characterized as tales of historical alterity, and more accurately identified as commentaries on the social contexts surrounding the production of western manuscripts. In Auchinleck, the figure of the convertible Saracen knight embodies a vision of group identity and its construction that is central to the manuscript's engagement with English cultural identity. As mentioned earlier, two of the knightly tales that posit a role for will in the definition of a character's religious identity are

English translations of Matter of France material popular both in continental France and among the Anglo-Normans in England. Interestingly, when English regains its popularity as a language for the transmission of culture in the fourteenth century, relatively few Matter of France texts make their appearance in this language. One logical reason for this is the increasing tension between the English and French at this time. Given the simmering conflicts between the two nations, it is unsurprising that the Matter of France with its veneration of French rulers and nobles was less popular among the English than tales of the insular hero King Arthur.[81] What is intriguing, however, is that the extant English versions of the Matter of France suggest a penchant for stories recounting the conversions of noble Saracen knights to Christianity. Tales of converted Saracens make up seventy per cent of the surviving metrical Matter of Charlemagne in English.[82] English translations of the French material thus seem to testify to a particular insular interest in tales in which group affiliations are redefined through acts of will.

This emphasis on will in tales of Saracen knights is key to understanding how the converted Saracen warrior clarifies Auchinleck's larger project of articulating a sense of Englishness. As shown, the figure of the similar Saracen lays bare the role of will in defining a group identity. In *Otuel,* Auchinleck ensures that this fact is not missed by including repeated references to Otuel's will that do not appear in the older Old French and Anglo-Norman versions of the text.[83] As a result, Auchinleck highlights the ability to will new identities for oneself. In so doing, the manuscript draws attention to its own efforts to articulate an "Inglisch" cultural identity. Auchinleck, too, successfully wills a change of identity. The manuscript deliberately chooses not to reproduce for its audience material in certain languages. Instead, Auchinleck contains the earliest extant English translations of the Matter of France, and is composed almost entirely of unilingual English texts that are often presented with prologues or epilogues explaining how the English version serves as an alternative to texts written in French or Latin. For example, the narrator of *Of Arthour and of Merlin* begins his tale by saying

> Of Freynsch no Latin nil y tel more
> Ac on I[n]glisch ichil tel þerfore:
> Ri3t is þat I[n]glische vnderstond
> Þat was born in Inglond.
> Freynsche vse þis gentil man
> Ac euerich Inglische Inglische can,
> Mani noble ich haue ysei3e
> Þat no Freynsche couþe seye,
> Biginne ichil for her loue

Bi Ihesus leue þat sitt aboue
On Inglische tel mi tale—. (19–29)[84]

With such explicit articulations of a choice to narrate in English rather than
French or Latin, Auchinleck testifies to an "Inglisch" will to know and possess texts in the insular vernacular. This will represents a change of identity
and group affiliation. By turning their backs on French and Latin as media
of communication, Auchinleck, its compilers, and its readers enact Englishness as something separate from these other language traditions, and different from the insular literary culture of the past, such as that patronized by
the French-speaking and French-focused courts of Henry II and Eleanor of
Aquitaine. The tale of Otuel's conversion, as it emphasizes choice and
agency, lays bare the role of will in shaping group identity at a time when,
and in a place where, a material product of English culture was willfully
crafting a vernacular, insular identity distinct from France and the French
concerns of preceding periods of English literary history.

The complications involved in rewriting group identities by acts of will
are made clear when one considers Auchinleck's inability to completely sever
cultural ties with France. Even as Auchinleck deliberately rewrites the French
language, it cannot erase the historical bonds England shares with France,
and these remain evident in the explicitly acknowledged French aspects and
origins of its texts. In this way, Auchinleck exposes the complicated historical
intertwinings shaping groups, and coloring any assertion of a distinct fresh
identity. Willed assertions of difference are effective but they cannot rewrite
history altogether. The limitations of will are not just evident in Auchinleck
as a whole, however. They also appear in the text from that manuscript that
most clearly assigns a role to will in defining group identity.

THE LIMITATIONS OF WILL: ALLEGIANCES, HIERARCHIES, AND WILLING AWRY

Although the convertible Saracen Otuel makes clear the role of will in effecting cultural differentiation, there is no denying that such acts of will cannot
achieve a completely clean break from the past. In *Otuel,* the eponymous
knight's post-conversion adventures suggest that social factors make the
assumption of a new group identity, and the abandonment of an old one, a
process that involves more than an individual's willed action. The groups,
too, must have their say in the process, and while a willed change of community may initially appear quite simple, subsequent events usually suggest that
this is not quite the case.

Inasmuch as Otuel willfully changes his religious community, he also rewrites his military allegiance. Since the Saracens and Christians in this text resemble each other so closely in their martial comportment and values, Otuel's change of religion amounts to a change of sides in a war. As Norman Daniel puts it, because Saracens and Christians in *chansons de geste* are so undifferentiated in their religious practices, religious identification should be regarded very much as an allegiance.[85] Conversion thus does not only mark a change of faith but also a change of political identity. Otuel's willed Christianization is as much a willed shift of loyalties from his Saracen overlord Garsie to Charlemagne as it is a willed change of religion. The details of the text support this perspective, and in so doing reveal the difficulties involved in willfully altering one's communal identity and situate them in a context much more familiar to the English audience of this tale than that of religious conversion.[86]

At first, Otuel's conversion projects a myth of wholeness, and of the smooth integration of strangers into a new community. When Otuel is touched by God's dove, his will to fight dissipates, and he decides to accept Roland's earlier offer of marriage with Charlemagne's daughter Belecent. Otuel says to Roland,

> "ȝef i sschal wedden þat faire may,
> Ich wille bileuen oppon þi lay,
> & alle myne godes forsake,
> & to ȝoure god ich wille take." (591–94)

With these words, Otuel links himself to his new Christian community by demonstrating both a willingness to enter sexually and religiously into the group and an esteem for powerful alliances that his Christian counterpart Roland (given his offer) evidently shares. Otuel's use of the words "forsake" and "take" also casts his decision as a change of allegiance, albeit not temporal but divine. Charlemagne's response to this news, however, suggests that conversion is a change of loyalties in the temporal sphere. He says

> "I *gra*nte wel þat it so be,
> For whi þat he [Otuel] wille dwelle wiþ me.
> Þanne hadde ich þe [Roland] and oliuer,
> Otuwel, & gode ogger,
> In all þe world in lenkþe & brede,
> Þer nis king þat nolde me drede." (623–28)

Charlemagne agrees to Roland's plan because it ensures that Otuel will remain with Charlemagne and that the king will be able to call on the military services of Roland, Oliver, Otuel, and Ogier combined. To Charlemagne's mind, this conversion represents a shift in Otuel's military loyalties, and is a political windfall for him. In addition, by listing Otuel as an integrated member of his key group of knights, Charlemagne projects an image of knightly cohesiveness and force to be deployed in accordance with one ruler's (his) set of desires and needs. In its first moments of existence, then, Otuel's willed change of identity seems to promote unity in Charlemagne's realm and entourage, and even benefit the Christian community as a whole. It seems quite clear to the partisan audience that a change of Otuel's temporal allegiance has occurred, and that this change is a correct, logical, and divinely sanctioned move. The intervention of God, and the Christian-Saracen context, mean that no hint of disloyalty accrues to Otuel, and that no reproach can be made regarding his conduct in switching overlords. Moreover, it appears from Charlemagne's words that Otuel will at once become an integral member of the French king's retinue. At this point, Otuel makes changing group identity through acts of will look easy.

Nevertheless, despite the suggestions of an easily achieved change in communal identity, Otuel's conversion does not work quite so cleanly as it seems to at first. He does not really become the fourth member of a quartet involving Roland, Oliver, and Ogier. Instead, as mentioned above, these three sneak off without Otuel to ford a river and fight Saracens (lines 701–6). Otuel, once he discovers what has happened, reports to Charlemagne that the three have crossed the river

> " . . . for envie of me,
> To loke wher þei miȝten spede,
> To don any douȝti deede,
> Among þe sarazins bolde:
> . . . . .
> To sechen hem ich wole ride.
> Þauȝ þei habben envie to me,
> Ich wille for þe loue of þe,
> Fonden whoþer i miȝte comen,
> T[o] helpen hem ar þei weren inomen." (1020–30)

Otuel clearly views this act as an instance of competitive disunity, and his words point up the division that still exists among the four knights even when on the same side. No quartet is working here. Admittedly, his words do reflect his new status in their expression of an unswerving loyalty to Charlemagne. The truth is, however, that this loyalty is in doubt and must be repeatedly attested by Otuel after his conversion. His past still haunts him, as is made clear when, after baptism, he vows not to wed Belecent until "þi [Charlemagne's] werre to þe ende be brou3t ,/. . . . . / Whan king garsie is slawe or take, / Þanne is time mariage to make" (647–50). Otuel apparently feels the need to prove his altered identity by fighting for his new lord against his former one. Charlemagne, too, seems to require Otuel's willed change of sides to be manifested in battle, since he responds to Otuel's vow by saying "Nou i se þou louest me wel" (652). More than one battle is required to affirm Otuel's new allegiance, however. In addition to engaging the Saracen Clarel in single combat, Otuel must also pursue other Saracen kings and even Garsie himself to demonstrate his new identity as Charlemagne's knight. As the repeated battles show, Otuel's willed change of allegiance is neither as straightforward nor as easy as it first appears in the duel with Roland. Not only does Otuel not become one of Roland's inner circle, but Otuel is required repeatedly to assert his loyalty by deeds. Jonathan Elukin notes of Jews in the Middle Ages that those "who converted to Christianity found it difficult to convince Christians that they had abandoned their Jewish identities."[87] Otuel seems to be in the same position. However straightforward his abandonment of Saracenness appeared, events subsequent to his conversion clearly indicate that it is no simple matter for Otuel to become part of Charlemagne's retinue, and that integration is not achieved simply because an individual chooses to redefine his communal identity. Residues of past identities remain, whether one wills them to or not. Admittedly Otuel does achieve some integration towards the end of the text. After Ogier rejoins the battle, the narrator states

> Þo alle foure weren ifere,
> Þar nere none strokes dere,
> Þo dou3ti kni3tes smiten so sore,
> As þau3 þei ne hadden nou3t fou3ten 3ore,
> Þat wiþ inne a litel stounde,
> Sarazins 3eden alle to grounde. (1679–84)

These lines imply that, after enough battles, Otuel has proved his right to belong to Charlemagne's forces, and to be included in the inner quartet of fighters. Moreover, it is at this point that Garsie flees and is captured by Otuel. Sure allegiance and comradely cohesion thus constitute the ending note of Otuel's tale. The full inclusion of Otuel in his new community just takes much longer to effect than one might have expected from the initial events surrounding his willed conversion.

Otuel a Kniȝt, however, does not content itself with depicting only the difficulties posed by the new group one desires to enter; it also gives full voice to the vituperation and resentment one must endure from one's former community. The Auchinleck text attributes to its Saracen characters a fully developed and justified sense of betrayal at Otuel's change of loyalties. His former comrades frequently utter reproaches about his conversion, sometimes explicitly couching these in terms of temporal allegiance and treason. Clarel, for example, greets the revelation of Otuel's changed identity by saying

> "Allas!" [. . .] "whi destou so?
> So wrecheliche hauestou do.
> ȝit i re[d]e þou turne þi mood,
> & leef on mahoun, ore þou art wod,
> & ich wole pese, ȝef þou wilt,
> Þat þou hauest garsie a-gult." (1157–62)

While recognizing Otuel's act as a rejection of Mahoun, Clarel immediately proceeds to categorize the purportedly religious event as a political deed tantamount to treason against Garsie. The sense of political betrayal is further emphasized by Auchinleck's representation of Garsie's goals during the final general engagement. In the Old French and Anglo-Norman texts, Garsie's main aim is to defeat Charlemagne and conquer France, and his main obstacle is Roland.[88] In Auchinleck, however, Garsie is focused on Otuel and the convert becomes both the main hindrance to the Saracen king's possession of France and the target of that Saracen's military action. The Auchinleck Garsie states first that "Aȝenes otuwel myn herte stant" (1514), and then says to his advisors,

> " . . . what is þi reed
> Þat þe þef traitour nere ded?
> Certes fraunce hadde be wonnen,
> Ne hadde his tresoun be bigunnen" (1517–20).

In these speeches Garsie clearly articulates both his desire for Otuel's death and his sense that Otuel is the main impediment to his conquest of France. Moreover, Garsie's final orders in this scene are that Baldoff of Aquilent repel the Christians while Garsie himself "wole after come, / & helpe þat otuwel were nome" (1537–38). Otuel is clearly the main object of Garsie's enmity here, and Garsie's use of terms such as "þef traitour" (1518) and "tresoun" (1520) represent Otuel's infraction as political rather than religious. Such characterizations bring to the fore Otuel's former loyalties and the problems created by his broken allegiance. After the initial seeming ease of conversion and integration, the complicated underpinnings of changing allegiances are made clear, and the difficulties for all involved in the process are laid bare.

The conversion of Otuel, then, addresses the problem of knights changing their allegiances. Benjamin Kedar writes that "conversion of the Muslim enemy was an important component of the fantasy world of the western knight" during the era of crusade. He also notes that fantasies of this type seemed to proliferate, or be especially comforting, at times when the crusades were not going well for the westerners.[89] I would suggest that Otuel's miraculous conversion by God's dove articulates a similar knightly fantasy—that changing allegiances is a straightforward, clean-cut and easy process. In other words, where there's a will, the way is simple. As events unfold after Otuel's conversion, though, this fantasy is exposed for the imaginary escape from reality that it is. The latter part of the poem clearly demonstrates the messiness, difficulty, reproaches, and deadly challenges experienced by knights when they desired to change their group affiliations. Furthermore, Auchinleck 's representation of Garsie emphasizes the political treason involved in Otuel's conversion, and thus explicitly makes changing one's religious identity an act of changing allegiances. In this way, *Otuel a Kniȝt* analyzes the difficulty of redefining one's group identity through acts of will in a context more closely related to the lived experience of the manuscript's English audience than that of religious conversion.

Issues of political allegiance were repeatedly at stake in England in the late thirteenth and early fourteenth centuries. The Lanercost chronicler, for example, frequently cites incidents of what he considers treason and oath-breaking by the Welsh and Scottish during the respective wars between these peoples and the English.[90] The question of homage and fealty, of course, was at the very heart of these conflicts since Edward I represented them as rebellions by the Welsh and Scots against their liege lord, which is to say himself. Allegiances and loyalties were also repeatedly renegotiated in the years immediately preceding Auchinleck's circulation. During the reign of Edward II, the murder of Piers Gaveston at the command of the Duke of Lancaster so troubled the Duke's erstwhile allies, the earls of Pembroke and Warenne, that they returned their loyalties to Edward, and seceded from the magnates' camp and efforts to limit Edward's powers.[91] The end of Edward II's reign must also have involved a number of shifts in loyalty as first Mortimer and Isabella attracted allies for their deposition of Edward II, and then Edward III asserted his authority by imprisoning and executing Mortimer.

English tensions with France during this period also revolved around questions of allegiance and fealty. In the thirteenth century, Henry III of

England signed a peace treaty with the King of France which made Henry a vassal of the King of France and a peer of the French realm.[92] From then on, the French king had sovereign rights in the duchy of Aquitaine and could require the English king, as Duke of Aquitaine, to render homage and to answer for military activity deemed hostile to the French king's sovereign interests.[93] This led to efforts to characterize actions taken by the same man as actions taken either by the Duke of Aquitaine (subject to the King of France) or the King of England (sovereign in his own right). The political and military interests of the French and English kings determined, respectively, whether the English king's actions were those of a disloyal subject, or those of a sovereign protecting his realm's interests. The clash between the political roles of vassal and sovereign, as well as disagreement over what were the "precise boundaries of the[] respective possessions" of the King of France and the Duke of Aquitaine, created much tension between England and France and led to repeated conflicts and treaty negotiations until the death of the French king Charles IV in 1328.[94] Shortly after this, Edward III decided to advance his claim to the French throne and thereby provoked more questions about allegiances. Given the historical complexities of claiming, following, and changing allegiances in this period, it is clear that Saracens in *Otuel* address problems facing English kings, nobles, and knights in the early fourteenth century.

The complications involved in altering allegiances and group identities are further revealed by Auchinleck's Saracens when one examines the role hierarchy plays in Otuel's conversion, and in the conversion of the Soudan of Damascus in *Þe King of Tars*.[95] Otuel is converted by the change in his will wrought by a divine visitation. Although the emphasis on will attributes some agency to the convert, the appearance of the white dove sent by God asserts the power of the divine to shape the human. While in this tale divinity focuses its power on human will, and thereby allots a leading role to human will in changes of identity, the fact remains that this will can be influenced and re-directed from above. As the text articulates a space for agency in the definition of group affiliation, it minimizes the rebellious potential of this space by reaffirming the subject's capacity to be guided by hierarchies of power. Such minimization is even more noticeable in *Þe King of Tars*. Here the Saracen Soudan, a powerful ruler, is enticed to convert by the miraculous re-shaping of his formless child, and by the religious instruction administered by his Christian wife and her priest. He is also himself the object of a divine miracle upon his conversion, when (as mentioned before) his skin color changes from black to white. Through these miracles the Soudan becomes, like Otuel, a subordinate object of divine power, but the assertion of hierarchy does not end there. In this text, the Soudan's divinely influenced choice to become Christian means a willed change of identity for his people. This alteration, however, is not one they desire but a change willed for them by their ruler. Having become Christian, the Soudan informs his barons that

> . . ."Houso it bifalle,
> ȝe mot ycristned be.
> Miseluen, ich haue Mahoun forsake
> & Cristendom ich haue ytake,
> & certes, so mot ȝe." (1037–41)

The alternative, should they not wish to become Christian, is beheading (1054–56). Indeed, this alternative is common in tales of Saracens, and also shows up in Auchinleck's *Sir Beves of Hamtoun* where Beves and his son Gii make Gii's newly-won "londe of Ermony / . . . cristen wiþ dent of sword" (4018–19). As these texts both demonstrate, one's group identity can be coerced by those who rule over one and possess the military might to effect their desires. Hierarchical superiors can dictate one's group affiliation by altering one's will (as God does with Otuel), or by offering a choice in which to live is to will a change in one's group identity (as in *Þe King of Tars* and *Sir Beves*).

Such assertions of hierarchy limit individual agency in the assumption of a new communal identity. They foreclose any possibility of willing the wrong choice, and suggest that refusing to change one's group affiliations is impossible in some situations. For example, the Soudan's forced conversion of his Saracen subjects indicates the impossibility of him allowing them to choose an identity separate from his. If he decides to convert to Christianity and they refuse, their choice suggests that his decision is flawed, and this undermines his authority. Moreover, his change in position represents a weakness, a moment when traditional Saracen beliefs and customs are successfully challenged and replaced, and it is important that other cultural practices, such as subjugation to the Soudan, not be allowed to change. If they did, the Soudan would lose his entire base of identity since he exists textually only as a "soudan" and is given no named identity separate from that word, which defines him as a ruler of Saracens. Thus, to ensure that group-dependent aspects of his identity still exist even after he has abandoned Saracenness, the Soudan must forcibly re-align his people's religious identity to be recognized as a legitimate Christian ruler. Re-defining his identity involves asserting his right to rule, which existed when he was a Saracen sultan, but doing so in a manner that simultaneously asserts and proves his new

Christian identity. The ideal mechanism for asserting this dual role is to attack Saracens, as the Soudan does. Forcing his people to do something, violently coercing their acquiescence to his will, re-establishes the Soudan's position as ruler. Moreover, it does so in a manner that is fully accepted and used by Christian rulers in their turn, as seen in *Sir Beves*. In addition, making Saracens the objects of the Soudan's violence casts the Soudan in the light of the ideal Christian knight, and thereby affirms his recent conversion.[96] Interestingly, while the physical enforcement of political hierarchy constrains the Saracen subjects' exercise of will in relation to their group identity, it simultaneously re-asserts the power of individual will to redefine group identity: the wholesale conversion of these characters comes about because the Soudan desires it. Hierarchy grants him agency even as it limits that of his subjects. Hierarchy thus both minimizes the role of some people's will in defining group identity while reasserting that role for the wills of other types of people. Ultimately, however, *Þe King of Tars* still shuts down the possibility of willing awry, which is to say that it forecloses the possibility of characters choosing a group identity other than that of Christianity.

Other texts in Auchinleck, however, do raise the possibility of characters willing awry only to shut it down in other ways. As discussed below, Beves has moments when he appears to affirm a Saracen identity for himself only subsequently to reject such a possibility. The only other characters in the texts discussed here who desire a Saracen identity despite having the option to convert are Saracen giants.[97] In *Sir Beves*, the giant Ascopard is on the verge of receiving baptism at Beves' command when he rebels at the thought of being immersed in a specially built font:

> Whan þe beschop him scholde in schoue,
> A lep anon vpon þe benche
> And seide "Prest, wiltow me drenche?
> Þe deuel 3eue þe helle pine,
> Icham to meche te be cristine!" (2592–96)

Ascopard thus refuses Christian identity with an act of agency. Ultimately, however, this is shown to be the wrong choice because Ascopard betrays Beves to his Saracen enemies and thereby wins the narrator's opprobrium, a situation that would not have arisen had Ascopard converted and truly switched his allegiance to Beves and his Christian activities. In addition, the comedy of the scene recounting Ascopard's refusal of the "right choice" minimizes the danger posed by the moment when a character on the side of the hero desires a non-Christian identity. In *Roland and Vernagu,* the giant

Vernagu also proves intractable in his adherence to his Saracen identity. As described above, he does not heed Roland's theological exposition, and according to the angel, he will never heed any Christian's efforts to "save" him. Once again, though, the error of his ways is demonstrated for the reader. God empowers Roland to kill Vernagu, and the Saracen himself is not presented as an admirable or even scary character. Instead, he falls asleep during a duel with Roland and starts to snore. Humor is again used around the figure of the Saracen giant to diminish the attractiveness of his erroneous use of free will, and to situate such uses of agency in the realm of the comical and the monstrous rather than in the realm of the admirable hero knight. The possibility of using one's will to assume the wrong group identity is thus shut down and refused by texts that, in other contexts, assert a role for will in the definition of group identity. The anxiety surrounding the possibility of willing awry, however, cannot disappear altogether, and the use of humor when relating such actions may constitute rather nervous laughter about a possibility which did exist historically at the time of Auchinleck's production, and which provoked a great deal of anxiety among writers who paid attention to Christian behavior in the Latin Crusader kingdom of Outremer. Such nervous laughter may also reflect an awareness of the easily-made mistake of choosing awry in the political arena closer to home where allegiances and loyalties often changed or had to change, some-times with disastrous consequences.

FRATERNIZING WITH THE ENEMY[98]

The anxiety of choosing awry is essentially an anxiety created by too little differentiation between Saracen and Christian in these texts. A wrong choice (of Saracenness) is possible in these narratives simply because the differences separating Saracen and Christian knights are so negligible and rest on an act of will. The anxiety posed by too little differentiation has two dimensions. The first emerges when one thinks of the Saracen knights in these tales as Orientalist constructs who resemble western European Christians more closely than actual Muslims. The Saracen knights fight like their Christian counterparts, share the same values of acquisitiveness and competitiveness, and usually resemble their opponents physically (i.e. they are not depicted as bestial or of different color). As a result they resemble the French and English knights of the later Middle Ages, and are able to explore English concerns about sameness, differentiation, and allegiance extremely effectively. When considered in this light, the anxiety provoked by too little differentiation between Saracen and Christian is a general anxiety about the political and military dangers of too much similarity and fraternization between communities in conflict with each other. When the samenesses between warring groups are many and the differences few, the lines demarcating sides in a conflict necessarily appear rather artificial, and raise the possibility of people changing allegiances, or of not battling the enemy viciously enough. The idea of the enemy's absolute otherness and concomitant deserved destruction is also harder to promote in such contexts. This anxiety is not unrelated to French-English relations of the fourteenth century. As is shown by Froissart's tale of the English knight Thomas Holland rescuing his fellow French nobles, samenesses could occasionally undermine the oppositions of the Hundred Years War. Too much fraternization, and too little differentiation, must necessarily be matters of anxiety for warring parties.

There is a second dimension to the anxiety occasioned by too little differentiation of Christian from Saracen in these tales. In *Otuel, Roland and Vernagu, Sir Beves,* and *Guy of Warwick* the Saracen knights who resemble western European Christians participate intimately in an exploration of issues involved in late medieval assertions of English identity. These characters, however, unlike England's opponents in the Hundred Years War, are not western European Christians but rather fictional depictions of historical Muslims. This is not a cause for consternation when the Saracens are depicted solely so as to evoke familiar, western European others. However, the similarity between Saracen and Christian knights does induce anxiety when medieval writers and readers are confronted with literary traces, in the Saracens, of actual Muslim civilizations. Such traces raise the question of what it means to undertake investigations of a European Christian identity like Englishness in relation to figures of historical, geographic and religious Otherness. When explorations of European identity are rooted in the representation of Saracen and Christian sameness, but also take place in a context that evokes historical Muslims, such explorations provoke cultural anxiety about maintaining distinct divisions between Christians and non-Christians. In these cases, although the Saracen knight's sameness enables consideration of the issues discussed in this chapter, it also provokes fear that a Christian knight can be too similar to his Saracen counterparts.

Of the texts discussed in this chapter, only *Sir Beves* and *Guy of Warwick* can be said to contain literary traces of actual Muslim civilizations, and only *Sir Beves* manifests significant anxiety about the perilous proximity of Christian knights to characters reminiscent of historical Muslims. The Matter of England texts differ from *Otuel* and *Roland and Vernagu,* which are situated in Europe and narrate military campaigns carried out by Christians and Saracens in efforts to expand their land-holdings. While it is true that in these Charlemagne tales one might find traces of the historical Muslim presence in Spain, the events primarily take place on battlefields and consist of wars that reassuringly draw definitive lines between Christians and Saracens. *Guy of Warwick,* too, uses battle to maintain a clear division between Saracen and Christian knights. No Saracen is converted in any of the Guy texts in Auchinleck; instead, they are killed or defeated. *Guy of Warwick* does, however, present a portrait of Saracen-held lands in Africa and the Middle East, of Saracen political power, and of inter-Saracen conflicts. In the *Stanzaic Continuation,* Guy fights the Saracen Amoraunt as part of a trial by battle to resolve a conflict between two Saracen rulers in the East, while in *Reinbrun gij sone of warwike,* the Christians Herhaud and Reinbrun end up on opposite sides of a battle between a Saracen "emeraile" and a Saracen king in Africa. In depicting such a complex Saracen political scene, *Guy* evokes a sense of a self-contained non-Christian world and thereby reminds its audience of historical Muslim civilizations in the Middle East in the Middle Ages. Because Saracen-Christian interactions in this text never move beyond war, however, the slight evocations of historical Islam in *Guy* promote no anxiety about proximity. *Sir Beves,* on the other hand, narrates the life story of an English Christian boy who is sold to Saracens at a young age, grows up in a Saracen court, serves a Saracen ruler in various inter-Saracen conflicts, and eventually marries a converted Saracen princess. In this context of multiple and extended interactions on and off the battlefield, the Saracen characters slide disconcertingly from rather familiar, almost western European, foes into evocations of the historical Muslim world with its courts, rulers, and complex politics. Accordingly, there is a troubling aspect to *Sir Beves's* representation of Saracen-Christian similarity and to the text's emphasis on the role of will in altering one's group identities. Here, the possibility of willing awry raises the specter of a Christian knight being assimilated into a culture that evokes, in some way, historical Muslims. It is therefore unsurprising that *Sir Beves* explores how such assimilation might happen, and then shuts down this possibility in ways that, through the sense of excess associated with them, communicate a clear anxiety about Christian characters too closely resembling Saracen characters who evoke aspects of medieval Muslim society.

Historically, one of the concerns prompted by crusade and settlement in the East was the fear that western Christians involved in these activities might lose their sense of proper mores and become too similar to their Muslim opponents. As Geraldine Heng notes, crusaders were "enjoined to rescue from infidel pollution the sacred places of the Holy Land, not to visit the contagion of heathen pollution upon themselves."[99] Thus, inhabitants of the crusader kingdoms were adjured not to intermingle sexually with Sara-cens,[100] and were roundly condemned by their western counterparts for becoming too eastern, too non-Christian. According to the author of the *Itinerarium peregrinorum,* the fall of Jerusalem in 1187 occurred because res-idents of the crusader kingdoms forgot their (western) Christian origins:

> Then the Lord's hand was aroused against His people—if we can prop-erly call them "His," as their immoral behaviour, disgraceful lifestyle, and foul vices had made them strangers to Him. For shameful practices had broken out in the East, so that everywhere everyone threw off the veil of decency and openly turned aside to filthy things.[101]

Getting too close to Saracens was also a charge leveled against later crusading forces. In Roger of Wendover's chronicle entry for 1229, crusaders from the Holy Roman Empire, including the Emperor himself, are accused of eating and drinking with Saracens, and of preferring Saracens and their customs to Christians.[102] Even writers advocating renewal of crusade in the early four-teenth century, after the fall of Acre in 1291 and the effective end of the western Christian presence in the Holy Land, raised concerns about future crusader inhabitants of the East "going Saracen." Pierre Dubois, for example, proposes a plan for the renewed conquest and western settlement of the Holy Land in his tract *De recuperatione terre sancte,* written about 1306. He wor-ries that future settlers of the Holy Land may lose touch with their Christian roots: "Suppose that those who dwell in that land live wickedly . . . that men congregated there from practically every part of the world begin to lead wicked lives and accustom themselves to such a manner of living? And instead of changing it, fix it as a habit, which is another nature, since it alters nature?"[103] Dubois also fears that his plan to marry beautiful, well-educated Christian women to Saracen rulers (and thereby convert these rulers to Christianity) might give rise to the women's participation "in their husbands' idolatry [eorum ydolatria]."[104] Evidently, fourteenth-century writers share their predecessors' concerns about maintaining a distinctive western Christ-ian identity in the East. Sarah Lambert summarizes the anxieties thus: "Operating on the borders of Christendom, it was vitally important for [Christian crusaders in the East] to recognize and stick to the rules, to iden-tify fully with 'us' and to know and recognize 'them.'"[105] How to recognize and affirm this distinction is precisely the problem facing the Saracen-raised Beves in *Sir Beves of Hamtoun* as he finds himself being assimilated into Sara-cen behaviors and group affiliations Other than those to which he was born in England.

Beves finds himself becoming Other to his heritage as an English Christian knight at a number of points in his tale. For example, during his teenage years at the Saracen Ermin's court, Beves learns that he does not know the date or meaning of Christmas. To add insult to injury, however, his ignorance and the information that effaces it are both communicated to him not by a fellow Christian, but by a Saracen:

> A Sarasin be-gan to say
> And askede him [Beves], what het þat day.
> Beves seide: "For soþ y-wis,
> I not neuer, what dai it is,
> For i nas boute seue winter old,
> Fro Cristendome ich was i-sold;
> Þar fore i ne can telle nouȝt þe,
> What dai þat hit miȝte be."
> Þe Sarasin be-held and louȝ:
> "Þis dai," a seide, "i knowe wel inouȝ:
> Þis is þe ferste dai of ȝoul,
> Þe God was boren wiþ outen doul;
> For þi men maken þer mor blisse
> Þan men do her in heþenesse." (591–604)

Here, it becomes evident that the Saracen-raised Beves has no access to his cultural heritage, or to knowledge about it, except as mediated by Saracens.[106] Essentially, people Other to him control knowledge about his culture, and this power of theirs makes him an object of ridicule. The situation of having another group mediate ideas about one's group identity is precisely the process enacted by the figure of the Saracen knight in the texts discussed here. Repeatedly in Auchinleck, Saracens communicate ideas about, and comment on, what it means to assert an English identity. *Sir Beves,* however, points to problems of shame and cultural dispossession when Saracens are the repositories of too much information about a Christian identity, and know more about being Christian than Christians themselves do, especially in contexts where these omniscient Saracens rather disconcertingly resemble historical Muslims in their political and military power.

The danger that Beves is losing his English, Christian cultural identity is also powerfully figured in the scene discussed earlier in this chapter when Beves tells his cousin Terri that the cousin Terri seeks (i.e. Beves) is dead, and later asserts that the Saracen King Ermin loves him (Beves) as a brother. In this episode, Beves disavows his Christian family and attempts to construct for himself a Saracen one. He cuts himself out of a Christian web of affiliations, and assumes Saracen familial connections. In this way, he enacts most forcefully his own estrangement from the identity to which he was born, and communicates a desire to replace his Christian identity with a Saracen one.

Given the similarities between the Saracen world in which Beves grows up and the historical Muslim one, suggestions that Beves might "go Saracen" and literally make himself the brother of Christianity's enemies provoke considerable narrative anxiety. This anxiety can be detected in the excess that accompanies Beves's textual efforts to recollect himself and assert his Christianity. It is almost as if, having come perilously close to abandoning his English Christian heritage, Beves must then prove beyond the shadow of a doubt his refusal to abandon his origins. One way in which Beves affirms his Christian identity after such moments of potential assimilation is through recourse to violence. As in *Otuel,* when an individual character's links to Saracens loom too large, violence emerges as that which is needed to demarcate and construct boundaries between Saracen and Christian after such boundaries have been compromised. For example, after the Saracen knight teaches Beves about Christmas Day, Beves affirms his Christian identity by claiming that he does remember one thing about Christmas Day: that Christian knights tourney and fight on this day (609–18). He then challenges the Saracens to a bloody battle in which he kills fifty of them. Through violence that opposes him to Saracens, Beves forcibly draws boundaries between him and them, and thereby reasserts his Christianness. The sheer number of Saracens he kills, however, indicates an excessive, almost paranoid desire to differentiate himself from them. Beves's behavior after his encounter with Terri again asserts Christian identity through violence. As mentioned earlier, after he has left Terri Beves attacks Saracens worshipping their gods by killing the Saracen "prest," throwing the Saracen idols in a fen, and laughing "hem alle þer to scorn" (1349–57). Although he has lived in Saracen lands for many years by this point, Beves has never yet performed so significant a Christian knightly feat as the destruction of Saracen idols. The new violence of this act, and Beves's scornful laughter upon completion of the deed, re-draw the boundaries differentiating him from his Saracen environs. Having brushed up very close against an act of changing his allegiances, an act of conversion (if, indeed, he has not committed one), Beves must now once more remind himself of who he really is, and of the boundary that should separate him from his Saracen overlord. Again, however, his reminder seems rather excessive. His act is unprovoked by Saracen taunts, and his laughter seems rather harsh—perhaps nervous? This act also seems a rather meaningless Christian drop in the very large ocean of

Saracen worship that has constituted Beves's surroundings in Ermin's realm. The only reason for Beves's sudden change in comportment seems to be a somewhat unfocussed need to affirm to himself as violently as possible that he is different from the world in which he finds himself.

The sense of excess, or of hyper-correction, accompanying Beves' efforts to assert his Christian heritage can also be seen in narratorial efforts to construct Beves as a second St George and thereby decisively dissociate the hero from his lapses into Saracen behaviors and affiliations. St George was important to crusaders and was said to have inspired them in a vision at the Battle of Antioch in 1098, and to have appeared during the march to Jerusalem in 1099.[107] He thus represents an explicitly anti-Muslim corrective to Beves's moments of assimilation into Saracen culture. St George was also a particularly important saint in England. His arms were used by Edward I to identify English troops campaigning in Wales in 1277, and the saint's banner was raised when Edward captured the Castle of Carlaverock in 1300.[108] St George also served as the central patron of the Order of the Garter, and letters patent issued in 1351 referred to him as "the most invincible athlete of Christ, whose name and protection the English race invoke as that of their peculiar patron, especially in war."[109] Narratorial efforts to depict Beves as a second St George thus strongly affirm not only Beves's Christian, but also his English, heritage. Through his resemblance to St George, Beves becomes not just any English Christian knight, but the epitome of English Christian knighthood in a Saracen-Muslim context. Beves's battles against Saracens, an action associated with St. George, have already been detailed at various points in this chapter. His identification with St. George extends beyond these, though: Beves also fights a fearsome dragon that spews venom, is twenty-four feet long, and has sides as hard as brass and a breast as hard as stone (2660–78, 2711). In case Beves's similarity to the dragon-fighting St George should pass unnoticed, the narrator explicitly states that the hero "nemenede sein Gorge, our leuedi kniȝt" (2817) at a moment of need in his battle against the dragon. Beves's Christian identity is further affirmed by the fact that he finally defeats the dragon only after he repeatedly prays to God for aid (2839–40, 2860–68). Thus Beves, once so perilously close to becoming Saracen, firmly establishes himself as a model English, Christian knight. Interestingly, this St George-like battle is an addition to the tale made by its English translator, and the invocation of St George is unique to Auchinleck.[110] These alterations suggest a keen editorial interest in depicting Beves as the epitome of English Christian knighthood,[111] an interest which makes perfect sense given Auchinleck's larger fascination with places, people, and issues "Inglisch." The same editorial interest, however, ensures that the dangerous potential of Beves's acculturation to the Saracen world is decisively contained and rejected, although, again, the sense of excess and of hyper-correction does communicate an anxiety about Christian proximity to Saracenness in this text.

In *Sir Beves,* then, the problem of too close a relationship to Saracenness, too little differentiation, is outlined and anxiously resolved. Too much similarity is especially dangerous for Beves, who lives in a Saracen world that evokes, in its geography, power, and politics, historical Muslim civilizations. *Sir Beves* thus anxiously explores the possibility of Christians in the East "going Saracen," and suggests a reliance on violence and on hyper-exemplary Christian behavior as methods for combating acculturation to the Saracen-Muslim world and way of life. As it does so, the poem identifies potential hazards both when communities in conflict are very closely linked and when figures of geographical and cultural otherness are depicted as similar to western Christians and as intimately involved in explorations of western Christian identities like Englishness.

DA CAPO AL FINE

The Saracens of *Roland and Vernagu, Otuel a Kniȝt, Sir Beves of Hamtoun,* and *Guy of Warwick* largely fall into the category of noble Saracen warrior. This figure is fascinating not because he radically differs from his Christian opponents, but because he radically resembles them. This character's close resemblance to Christian knights provokes consideration of how groups may be differentiated when the samenesses connecting them are many and the differences few. In particular, Saracen knights in these texts point out how class affiliations can both frustrate and facilitate attempts to assert a cultural or political identity. They also explore what constitutes the differentiation of groups, how and when cultural differences are asserted, and what role individuals and their free will can play in both the differentiation of groups and the changing of one's affiliations or allegiances. Finally, the Saracen knights in *Sir Beves* participate in a textual exploration of the dangers posed to Christians by too little differentiation from cultural others, particularly when such others connote in some way the historical Others of medieval Christians. As Saracen knights investigate the various issues listed above, they and their literary origins indicate some of the complex challenges involved in asserting a fourteenth-century English identity in contradistinction to that of France. Unlike the language of the texts in which they appear, however, Saracen knights in these texts do not directly assert an "Inglisch" identity but rather explore how such an assertion is made given a relationship of extensive sameness and minimal difference similar to that between England and France in the early fourteenth century. In this way, the Saracen knights of *Roland and Vernagu, Otuel, Sir Beves,* and *Guy of Warwick* serve an important cultural function in Auchinleck's efforts to imagine Englishness.

Chapter Two

Saracens and She-Wolves: Foreign Consorts and Group Identity

INTRODUCTION

While the rest of this book analyzes male Saracen characters in Auchinleck, Chapter Two focuses on a female Saracen character, the princess Josiane in *Sir Beves of Hamtoun*. As a princess of "Ermonie" who converts to Christianity and marries an English baron, Josiane is a Saracen who becomes explicitly linked to England, and who is charged with the task of finding and asserting her identity as Beves's "Inglisch," Christian countess. It is therefore unsurprising that this Saracen provides a close examination of the processes through which individuals assume and alter their communal identities. Because she is a woman who traverses the borders between two cultural groups, Josiane offers a unique, gender-specific view of this process of changing one's group identity. Her position in many ways resembles that of the historical foreign queen, and medieval cultural constructions of the foreign queen help us to appreciate the ways in which Josiane engages questions about asserting group identities and thereby explores issues pertinent to Auchinleck's interpellations of "Inglisch" identity. Admittedly, many of the challenges Josiane faces in asserting her new group identity relate to her religious difference from Beves and his people, and thus she does not exactly resemble historical foreign queens in late medieval England who were all Christian from birth. Nevertheless, Josiane's experiences do reflect some of the challenges faced by England's foreign consorts in the early fourteenth century. Upon consideration of some of the acts of English foreign queens during this period, it becomes clear that as Josiane crafts a place for herself in English society, she reveals the processes through which foreign consorts of the period could shape public perceptions of themselves, of their English kings, and of England's place on the world stage. In particular, as Josiane goes about becoming a Christian, English countess, she demonstrates more clearly than other Saracen characters in

Auchinleck the performative nature of identity, and the ways in which religious affiliations, gender stereotypes, and culturally-specific ideals of womanhood can be enacted by women to achieve their own ends and to obtain entry into specific communities.[1] In so doing, Josiane raises more stridently than her male Saracen counterparts anxieties about how permanent, stable, and accurate people's identities are if the mere deployment of verbal or physical tropes effects an individual's entrance into, and acceptance by, a new community. Because Josiane is a wife who becomes a mother, she also draws attention to the sexual and familial integration of foreigners, especially religious others, into a group different from that of their origins, and explores the level of acceptance accorded such foreigners. Finally, Josiane demonstrates ways in which people's anxieties about the accuracy of a claimed identity can be allayed. Her experiences suggest that while an individual's own assertion of a specific group affiliation must be regarded with some suspicion, the behavior of others can testify to the veracity of the assumed identity. She thus offers an intriguing insight into a group's desire and need for external affirmation and legitimization. All told, Josiane provides for readers a unique meditation, from a female perspective, on the processes involved in asserting, defining, and assuming a group identity like Englishness.

THE SARACEN PRINCESS AND THE FOREIGN QUEEN

Josiane's ability to comment on the assumption of group identities is due in large part to the fact that she is a Saracen princess who converts to Christianity. This figure is surprisingly popular in western medieval literature.[2] Found frequently in French *chansons de geste* and their translations, she also turns up in chronicles such as Orderic Vitalis's *Ecclesiastical History* and Matthew Paris's *Chronica majora*.[3] There is even a tale of Thomas Becket's life and passion which identifies the English saint as the offspring of a Christian man and the converted daughter of a Saracen emir.[4] In most texts, the princess embodies a Christian's ideal of female Saracen behavior: she falls madly in love with a western knight, may betray her family or Saracen allies for his sake, and eagerly undergoes baptism to become both Christian and eligible for marriage to the hero.[5] In some Old French texts, admittedly, Saracen princesses are ferocious opponents of Christians and would rather die than convert,[6] but the majority of western texts recount a Saracen princess's willing conversion to Christianity even though there are few, if any, attested historical cases of Saracen women abandoning their heritage and menfolk for Christianity and its adherents.[7] While the popularity of princess conversion tales probably reflects a medieval Christian taste for texts in which Saracens lose out to more attractive and superior Christians on domestic as well as military fronts, another possible reason for the popularity of Saracen princesses is their resemblance to the historical figure of the foreign queen. Like the Saracen princess, the foreign queen is a woman of high estate who mediates between two distinct cultural groups. For this reason, tales about Saracen princesses who traverse the borders between communities may have seemed particularly relevant to western audiences. The Saracen princess considered in this chapter certainly resembles representations of foreign queens in England, and offering some details about these resemblances and about the foreign queen's socio-cultural position clarifies how Josiane works so effectively to explore issues involved in the assertion of group identities.

First, it is important to note the physical resemblances between Saracen princesses and foreign queens. Jacqueline de Weever's book, *Sheba's Daughters,* argues that while unconvertible Saracen women are primarily depicted as dark-skinned or as giantesses, and hence as physically different from western Europeans, those Saracen women who fall in love with Christians and convert epitomize medieval European ideals of beauty. Their skin is as white as snow, their figures are slight, and their complexions are described as a mixture of white and red.[8] This phenomenon appears in *Sir Beves:* Josiane the Saracen is described as " . . . faire . . . & briȝt of mod, / Ase snow vpon þe rede blod,"[9] while Beves' mother, a Scot, is likewise "faire and briȝt" (27). The effect of such similarities between Saracen and Christian is to create a situation in which Josiane represents a level of biological and cultural differentiation more frequently encountered by Auchinleck's English audience than that of actual Middle Eastern peoples. A Saracen who looks like a western European and eventually converts is, essentially, a Christian European. The character of Josiane, considered this way, clearly resembles the western royal consort who comes from abroad to enter intimately into a ruling family and to provide a distinct people with their next ruler. Although foreign to the realm she adopts, the foreign queen is not physically dissimilar to people there even though she probably represents a different culture. Physically and racially, then, Josiane fits the western model of the foreign queen. There are, however, other more important aspects of the foreign queen figure that help to illuminate Josiane's relevance to an English audience of the fourteenth century.

Historically, the foreign queen was a constant presence in the English political scene during the reigns of Henry III, Edward I, Edward II, Edward III, and Richard II. In Edward II's reign (and therefore during the decades immediately preceding Auchinleck's compilation), the foreign origins of royal consorts became particularly important. During the 1320s, the French connections of Edward II's queen, Isabella, allowed her to negotiate a compromise between him and her brother, the French king, over the French king's insistence that Edward pay homage to him for Edward's French lands. Edward refused so to humble himself, and Isabella resolved the impasse by arranging for Edward II's son and heir, the future Edward III, to pledge fealty to his uncle in his father's stead. Isabella also, however, arranged a marriage between her son and Princess Philippa of Hainault that ultimately provided her with the forces necessary to overthrow Edward II and depose him.[10] For this achievement, Edward II's foreign queen became known to later centuries as the "she-wolf of France."[11] Her actions were so significant that the idea of the foreign queen could not help but be a part of English people's political horizons during the 1330s when Auchinleck was compiled.

While foreign queens were a historical fact of life for the English in the thirteenth and fourteenth centuries, my interest in them lies in the complex symbolic role such figures played for the peoples around them by serving as sites where gender, sex, and multiple group identities met. In this aspect of her existence the foreign queen resembles most closely the literary Saracen princess and sheds light on how this character who converts to Christianity and changes her group identity functions in a text like *Sir Beves*. In particular, the foreign queen and the Saracen princess share an ability to model interactions between peoples and rulers, and to indicate the complex intersections of group identity, power relations, sexual roles, and individual acts. The case of Isabella of France exemplifies some of these intersections. Because Isabella was French and connected to the French king, she was able to influence her brother's course of action. Because, however, she was also married to the English king and the mother of an English heir apparent, her acts advanced English interests in maintaining peaceful relations with France. As an individual with familial connections to two different peoples, Isabella was uniquely situated to intervene in this English-French dispute, a fact recognized by papal envoys who urged her involvement.[12]

The cultural position of being on the borders between communities and their respective rulers is a defining component of the foreign queen's identity and a central reason for her power and prestige. She represents a realm and way of life outside the king's jurisdiction, and this endows her with a certain political status in relation to the king. Her status, however, is complicated by her gender and sexuality. Because she is the king's wife, the foreign queen is subject to him and circumscribed by his power, given medieval Christian clerical and legal models of marriage and husbandly governance.[13] Her position therefore lies on the threshold between subject and sovereign. The queen's sexual relations with the king also emphasize the liminality of her position. As the king's sexual partner, the foreign queen has intimate access to him and his body. This is essential for the begetting of an heir and the continuance of the king's dynastic sovereignty. Sexual relations, however, and the carnality they imply, foreground the king's human limitations—his fleshliness and his subjection to temporality and death. Thus, the queen's sexuality and reproductivity ground the king in human embodiment and subjection to time and succession even as they ensure his dynasty's continuance. In the sexual context, the queen's foreign connections also complicate her symbolic relation to the king. In sex with her, the king's body is inescapably interwoven with, and exposed to, the foreign. Intimacy with a foreign queen thus suggests the king's vulnerability to outside influences. All told, the foreign queen occupies a liminal position in relation to the king, and represents both his power and his weakness. Her prestige reinforces his position at home by manifesting publicly his connections to royalty in the world at large. Her links to other powers allow her to serve as a mediator between him and foreign powers, and thus facilitate his geopolitical interests. The foreign queen also represents a realm where her husband is not king, and where no one is subject to him. Her gendered social subjection to him as wife, however, mitigates the threats posed by this foreignness. Ironically, though, her sexual duties as wife again place the king on a border between immortality and mortality, and between familiarity and foreignness.

Complex intersections between individual acts, sexual roles, gender norms, and group relations define the foreign queen and position her on various thresholds of intimacy and exteriority, subjection and sovereignty. This positioning has implications for her role in relation to her husband's realm and subjects. Foreign to them, she represents all the dangers of another mode of governance or of cultural behavior. As the wife of their monarch and mother of their future ruler, however, the foreign queen occupies a position at the center of the realm's self-conception. Thus, in relation to her adopted subjects and land, the foreign queen again plays a liminal role, both central to these people's polity and estranged from it because of her origins. Louise Fradenburg discusses the foreign queen's liminality in *City, Marriage, Tournament*. Here Fradenburg defines the queen as liminal because she is both foreign to her new people and exists outside the lines of their direct political governance—by the late Middle Ages the queen can only effect change or political action through her influence on her husband, not in her own right.[14] In this respect, she is liminal, and Fradenburg points out that "the very outsidedness of the liminal to particularized hierarchical interests can make the liminal seem 'above' or 'beyond' such interests."[15] In other words, as both outsider and disenfranchised royalty (relatively speaking), the foreign queen appears removed from particular power struggles, and thus can serve as a symbolic space for all her husband's realm and subjects. Because she is an outsider and without direct power, she transcends political rivalries and in-fighting, but because she is a queen and has special access to the monarch, she possesses a prestige and status that make her a very powerful symbol for people and the realm. According to Fradenburg, the foreign queen could be "a potential threat, . . . protection, [and] a banner under which to ride against the enemy" for her people.[16] As a link to powers abroad, the queen might offer a portal through which foreigners could gain influence in a polity. On the other hand, as the vessel of dynastic continuity and a symbol of her husband's status, the queen could be used as a unifying force within her adopted realm. Ultimately, by representing both the realm and foreign threats to it, the queen suggests the continuity of the realm in the face of all events, even as her very origins are a constant reminder of the realm's vulner-ability as an entity. She embodies both the group's identity and threats to that identity simultaneously. The foreign queen thus finds herself at the meeting point of various components of a polity's self-conception.

The foreign queen's position as a specifically gendered border between cultures is complex and multi-facetted. Indeed, I have only sketched out some aspects of her liminal situation here. In many ways, however, her position and that of Josiane in *Sir Beves* are similar. Like the foreign queen, Josiane is the daughter of a foreign ruler, the Saracen King Ermin. She also abandons her homeland and native culture (including her Saracen religion) to become Beves's Christian wife. Admittedly, by marrying Beves she does not become a queen in England; there she is Beves's countess. Eventually, though, Beves wins a kingdom for himself and Josiane becomes a queen.[17] Both as this Christian knight's countess and as his queen, however, Josiane occupies a position that mediates between two cultures and peoples. As she does so, this female Saracen reflects and precipitates concerns about communities' identi-ties, just as foreign queens do. In this way Josiane complements other Saracen explorations of identity formation and group affiliations in Auchinleck. Her contribution is particularly important because, as Josiane raises issues about the performance, permanence and affirmation of identities, she draws atten-tion to the ways in which gender and gender expectations play into identity formation in a way that no male Saracen in Auchinleck does.[18]

PERFORMING IDENTITY

Perhaps because she possesses so many different affiliations and symbolic roles, the foreign queen is often represented in situations where she seems to perform and affirm certain aspects of her identity. One such situation is that of intercession with the king in an effort to introduce clemency into his political decisions. Frequently identified with either the [b]iblical Esther (who intervened with her husband to preserve the Jewish people) or, in the later Middle Ages, with the Virgin Mary and her mediation with Christ on behalf of Christians, Christian queens often found themselves petitioned to act on behalf of various subjects.[19] Lois Huneycutt has demonstrated the ways in which Queen Matilda, Henry I's Anglo-Saxon queen, manifested in her private letters and acts of literary patronage an awareness of her intercessionary duties as queen as well as conscious efforts to model her behavior on that of Esther. John Carmi Parsons, meanwhile, has pointed out the prevalence of moments and motifs of intercession in both the acts and the cultural constructions of English queens in the later Middle Ages.[20] Intriguingly, various records of intercession suggest a calculated performativity in such acts. For example, Froissart recounts how Edward III's Queen Philippa petitioned the king to reverse his decision to execute six burghers of Calais in 1347.[21] As Paul Strohm points out, Froissart's account is "Sorely lacking in factual authority," but provides "an archive of the major presuppositions of intercessory queenship."[22] In sum, a heavily pregnant ("durement enchainte") Queen Philippa casts herself on her knees before Edward, points out that she has not made many demands on him since her arrival, and beseeches him for the son of Mary and for love of her (Philippa) that he "show a merciful disposition to these six men."[23] The queen, moreover, has not been directly involved in discussions ere this, but rather "comes late to the gathering of Edward's retinue, and . . . follows a step behind when they step out to view the hostages."[24] In this way, she occupies what Fradenburg identifies as the queen's traditionally liminal position in relation to the king's political power, and it is this liminality that makes her act so dramatically powerful.[25] The queen literally erupts out of the borders of the men's discussion. This incident demonstrates a certain performativity on her part through careful deployment of both rhetoric and the body. Speaking as intercessor, the queen explicitly invokes the Marian precedent for her actions and mentions the infrequency of her demands on the king. In this way, she constructs herself both as the agent of a religious power beyond politics and as a political bystander. She verbally emphasizes her liminality in relation to the king's political role and depicts her act as that of a person removed from power; she thereby protects herself from charges of interference in the king's governmental prerogative. The queen's deployment of her body, too, performs her feminine subjection to the king and minimizes the temerity of her interruption. Her subservient, kneeling position enacts her subordination to his rule.[26] As a foreign queen with external connections, this act of self-humbling is particularly powerful because the queen also embodies, as she subordinates herself to Edward, a people who are not his subjects. Because of her own bloodlines, Philippa possesses a political prestige that commands the king's respect, but she willingly humbles this prestige before him, thereby further aggrandizing him. Also, while her physical position humbles Philippa, her visible pregnancy serves to remind the king of her centrality to his dynastic continuance and thus to his power.[27] In these ways, she encourages his clemency through a type of flattery or, more accurately, through a verbal and bodily enactment of his kingly status and prestige. Because the queen is also his wife, however, the king may accede to her request without diminishing his royal prerogative or losing face before his advisors. His concessions instead appear as the magnanimous gifts of a loving husband. In her role as intercessor, then, the queen's efficacy derives from her liminal position as foreign yet subordinate, and as frail with pregnancy yet powerful because this same bodily fragility is central to the king's dynastic ambitions. Such efficacy, however, is only achieved through the queen's careful performance of various aspects of her identity of subordination and power.[28]

The centrality of performance in acts of intercession like this highlights the ways in which the foreign queen, because she embodies so many different individual and group affiliations, can choose to invoke her associations in a careful construction of her personal and social identity. This is one aspect of the foreign queen figure that Josiane incarnates in her role as Saracen princess. Her actions in *Sir Beves* reveal the ways in which feminine deployments of rhetoric and the body serve to construct identity and mediate between the individual, her lover, and her community or a community to which she wishes to belong.[29]

Josiane, in many ways, performs herself into a Christian identity as Beves's consort. Her actions suggest that Christian identity is something that can be verbally deployed and constructed. For example, after Beves has been a member of the Saracen King Ermin's court for a few years, he finds himself on Christmas Day provoked into battle against a party of his erstwhile Saracen comrades. This battle is precipitated by one Saracen's mockery of Beves's ignorance about what it means to be Christian. The sting of this charge apparently lingers, for when Josiane sends messengers to summon Beves to her so that she may tend his wounds and amend his relations with Ermin, Beves furiously declares

> "I nele rise o fot fro þe grounde,
> For speke wiþ an heþene hounde:

ȝhe is an honde, also be ȝe,
Out of me chauℳber swiþe ȝe fle!" (691–94)

Beves's words indicate an anger rooted in religious identity and the difference
between Christians and Saracens. Josiane appears to recognize this because,
after hearing the words of his rebuff from her messengers, she approaches
Beves saying "Lemman, . . . gent and fre, / For godes loue, spek wiþ me!"
(707–8). Her invocation of the Christian God rather than of a deity associated with Saracens[30] suggests that Josiane shares a set of beliefs and thus an
identity with Beves. This is not at all the case, however, because at this point
Josiane is still an unconverted Saracen with no plans or promises to convert.
Indeed, before this she has mentioned no desire at all to be Christian, and, in
her only preceding speech, swore by the Saracen gods "Mahoun" and "Tervagaunt" (659). Interestingly, this Saracen oath appears when Josiane is
requesting a favor from her Saracen father, namely that he listen to Beves's
side of the story before punishing him for killing Saracens. The two speeches
juxtaposed suggest that Josiane is intensely aware of her various audiences
and of how speech defines a religious group identity for her and thereby
enables her to achieve specific goals. In the conversation with her father,
Josiane's appeal to Saracen deities constructs her as an ally of her father and
shields her against charges of identifying too closely with the Christian man
she wishes to protect. In the interaction with Beves, on the other hand,
Josiane clearly realizes the need to construct herself as Christian, or Christian-like, in order to come near him at this moment.[31] Moreover, Josiane's
rhetorical gestures towards both religious identities succeed—her father
grants the favor she requests while her invocation of the Christian God
appeases Beves and prompts him to cast aside his anger, speak to her, and
allow her to kiss him and heal his wounds (lines 709–17). Josiane essentially
performs her way into a religious identity acceptable to her Christian lover,
much as Philippa performed a wifely and queenly identity acceptable to her
husband and effected his mercy in the above story of intercession. Josiane's
speeches, and Beves's acceptance of her oral performance of Christianity,
however, work a little differently: they challenge assumptions that particular
group identities are stable or secure. Indeed, these characters suggest that
religious group identities are a matter of enactment: to be Christian is to act
like one—here, by invoking the Christian deity.

To understand the full significance of Josiane's words here, it is helpful
to situate this incident within the literary history of *Sir Beves*. The Christmas
Day battle does not exist in either of the extant Anglo-Norman versions of
the tale, and is considered a later English translator-poet's interpolation into

the tale.[32] As Auchinleck contains the earliest extant Middle English version of *Sir Beves*, the incident may have originated with this manuscript's compilers (although it could reflect a now-lost earlier tradition of the *Sir Beves* tale). The origin of this episode, however, does not interest me as much as the effect of its inclusion. Incorporating this event into *Sir Beves* foregrounds the issue of religious difference within the tale. In the Anglo-Norman version reconstructed by Stimming[33] there is no Christmas Day battle, and the religious divisions between Josiane and Beves do not surface until a much later scene (also found in the Middle English versions) where Josiane promises to convert for Beves's love. Instead, Beves's first battle in the Anglo-Norman version revolves around a boar hunt and Beves's need to defend his trophy (the boar's head) from envious Saracen knights who wish to steal it from him. In Auchinleck and other Middle English versions, however, Beves's first battle occurs because of Saracen-Christian enmity. In addition, his angry words likening Josiane to a "heþen honde" (completely absent from the Anglo-Norman) establish early in their relationship the problems posed by their different religious identities. In this way, the English versions emphasize the complications religious affiliations create in inter-personal relationships, and indicate almost from the tale's beginning the need for Josiane and Beves to mediate between two cultures.

While the various English versions of *Sir Beves* use the Christmas Day battle to highlight issues surrounding religious difference, not all of them recount the incident in a manner that demonstrates the potential role of rhetorical performance in changing one's identity.[34] The Auchinleck version studied above clearly suggests that Josiane can rhetorically perform a Christian identity. The Chetham manuscript, however, recounts events thus:

> Forth they [the messengers] went wyth that may
> To Beves chamber, there he lay;
> Beves lokyd up stoutly thoo
> And Iosyan in her armes two
> Toke hym vp and kyssud hym swete,
> His malincoly there to abate:
> She said: "Beves, leman, thyn ore!
> Thou arte wounded fferly sore." (577–84)

Here, Josiane has no speech in which she can be seen to perform a Christian identity. Similarly, the Gonville and Caius College manuscript reads:

> Forþ þey wente in þat stounde
> And Beffs in hys chaumbyr þey ffounde

> Iosyan caste here armys abouten his swere,
> On here he made a loþly chere
> ʒhe keste him on moþ & on chin (705–9)

while the Cambridge University Library manuscript reads:

> Forþ sche wente in þat stounde
> And Beffs in hys chaumbyr ffounde
> Sche caste here arme abouten his swere,
> And he made on hur loþly chere
> ʒhe keste him moþ & chin. (705–9)

In all three cases, Josiane's invocation of a Christian God does not appear. She merely performs a lover's relationship to Beves rather than the religious and love identities she performs in Auchinleck and the other manuscripts (Egerton and Naples) that include her Christian-like speech. The representation of Josiane in Auchinleck thus emphasizes the potential of performance as a method of changing one's group identity.[35] As noted elsewhere in this book, the Auchinleck manuscript includes material some other manuscripts omit, and in so doing draws attention to the processes involved in defining a group identity

In Auchinleck, the interaction between Beves and Josiane suggests that conscious and appropriate deportment can engineer one's entry into a specific group identity. Josiane's words apparently overcome cultural difference while also suggesting the instability of group identities. Josiane's verbal performances, however, also demonstrate that rhetorics of identity can be deployed to serve individuals' particular ends. Josiane repeatedly draws attention to this issue in *Sir Beves* by verbally and physically invoking gender stereotypes, and then using these to further her own interests and achieve individual and group affiliations she desires.[36] In a number of episodes, Josiane uses proverbial portraits of feminine identity to construct her self-identity and her membership in various groups. In this gender-specific manner she offers some provocative commentary on identity definition on both personal and communal levels, and enacts the same sort of behaviors as the interceding foreign queens described above. She thus, like the foreign queen, draws attention to the ways in which gendered group identities (such as womanhood or motherhood) can be manipulated by individuals, and perhaps have to be when that individual is female.

In the trope described above, the queen interceding with her husband uses traditional medieval stereotypes of feminine subordination to men to achieve specific ends.[37] Josiane's conscious and explicit deployment of gender norms resembles very closely this aspect of queenly intercession. Twice, in references absent from the Anglo-Norman versions of *Sir Beves,* Josiane verbally invokes what she presents as proverbial platitudes about women to help her achieve individual identities she desires. The first such invocation occurs when she is apologizing to Beves for telling him that his behavior towards her made him better suited to dig ditches than to be a knight and interact with ladies (see lines 1118–24). Josiane approaches Beves to make amends and behaves thus:

> 3he fel adoun & wep wel sore:
> "Men saiþ," 3he seide, "in olde riote,
> Þat wimmannes bolt is sone schote.
> For-3em [sic] me, þat ichaue misede,
> And ich wile ri3t now to mede
> Min false godes al for-sake
> And cristendom for þe loue take!"
> "In þat maner," queþ þe kni3t,
> "I graunte þe, me swete wi3t!" (1190–98)

In this incident Josiane performs a subordination of herself to Beves, a subordination, moreover, that is both gendered and religious. Like the interceding queen's genuflection, Josiane's prostrate position immediately constructs her as Beves's inferior. Her words explicitly cast this position of inferiority as a gendered one. Josiane begins her apology with a proverbial reference to men's assertions about women: "Men saiþ . . . Þat wimmannes bolt is sone schote" (1191–92). She then adds "For-3em me, þat ichaue misede" (1193), and this constitutes an admission that "Men" are right about women. With this admission, Josiane places men in the superior position of the knower to the known. Men become the knowing subjects while women become the objects of masculine observation, study and knowledge. In this way, Josiane (like the interceding queen) uses words and gender norms to represent the male with whom she is involved as her superior. Her appeal to proverbs, however, highlights the cultural field within which she is operating, and in so doing makes her act here rather performative. Josiane has taken a gender cliché and used her body and words to enact and validate that cliché before the man with whom she wishes to be reconciled. In addition, she again demonstrates an awareness of the importance of religious identity to Beves, and offers her conversion to Christianity as an incentive for Beves to forgive her. In this way, Josiane represents herself as occupying an erroneous religious affiliation, a construction that further builds up Beves's image as the sole adherent to the "true" faith in a Saracen world. Josiane's words and body

thus enact a relationship between her and Beves that places Beves in a superior position to Josiane. This reverses earlier interactions where Josiane
seemed to have the upper hand, directing Beves's actions, nursing him, and
condemning certain of his speech acts and behaviors. Interestingly, Beves says
"In þat maner . . . I graunte þe, me swete wiȝt" (1197–98). His words "In þat
maner" seem to suggest that when Josiane behaves thus, and deploys herself
so as to affirm Beves's gender and religious superiority, he will grant her
desires. In this way, Josiane's performance of proverbial gender and religious
subordination ultimately advances her own ends, just as queenly intercession,
while appearing to advance the interests of others, really advanced the queen's
own interests by affirming her position of political power and access to the
king. Such behaviors suggest that broad generalizations about gender and
religious identities can be performed by individuals in ways that enable them
to achieve some sort of agency even when these individuals are operating
from the liminal and apparently disempowered position of supplicant.

Josiane again displays the ways in which proverbial gender norms can
be turned to an individual woman's benefit later in the text. When Beves is
away reclaiming his English heritage, the now-Christianized Josiane finds
herself importuned by the Earl Miles to become his wife. Josiane refuses, but
after Miles has disposed of her giant guardian Ascopard, she is unable to protect herself and is forcibly married to the earl. Josiane, however, defends herself from Miles's sexual advances through the performance of a stereotypical
gender norm. When she and Miles are brought to bed on their wedding
night, she says to Miles

> "Ich bidde, þow grau*n*te me a bone,
> . . . .
> Ich bidde þe at þe ferste frome,
> Þat man ne wi*m*man her i*n* come;
> Be-lok hem þar oute for loue o me,
> Þat noman se our priuite!
> Wi*m*men beþ schamfast i*n* dede
> And namliche maidenes" . . . (3194–202)

With these words, Josiane casts her individual request as the manifestation of
a maidenly modesty that is the norm for women. Whether it is may be
debated, but Josiane certainly represents maidenly modesty as a gender norm
and uses it to justify her individual actions. The fascinating part of this
episode is the use to which Josiane puts this invocation of maidenly modesty.
Once Miles has dismissed his attendants, he locks the door and tells Josiane
that because he acceded to her request he must now draw off his own boots,

something he has never done before. As he sits down to do this, Josiane makes a noose out of a towel, throws it around Miles's neck, and hangs him from the bed-curtain rail (see lines 3214–24). By deploying a rhetoric of maidenly modesty, Josiane engineers a situation in which she is able to defend her body from a would-be rapist. She shows how women can use a supposed aspect of their group identity as women to advance their individual interests.[38] Here, Josiane's obvious personal interest is to remain unviolated. This physical state, however, is important not only for her personal well-being but also for her desired future position as Beves's consort: Beves has been strictly enjoined by the hierarchy of the Christian Church to marry a virgin. Thus, Josiane deploys gender norms that ultimately maintain for her the identity prescribed for Beves's wife. While this may not be the most empowering motivation from a modern feminist perspective, Josiane's desire to maintain her status as Beves's consort does reflect the historical desires of medieval Englishwomen. Maintaining their status as king's consort was important to late medieval English queens who, as mentioned before, actively performed the feminine gender role of intercessor in order to affirm publicly their queenly position, and the power that accompanied this. What may, perhaps, speak more appealingly to modern feminists and identity theorists is the way in which Josiane inhabits a cultural system from within and deconstructs it by using stereotypical ideas about women to prevent the forced bodily subordination of rape. Interestingly, Josiane's invocation of proverbs is conspicuously absent from these episodes in the extant Anglo-Norman versions of the tale. Once again, the Auchinleck version highlights intriguing ideas about group identity and the ways in which it can be manipulated and deployed.

Josiane's performances of specific gender identities, while they may not ultimately subvert patriarchy, do deploy certain patriarchal models to an individual woman's ends. The situation is not unrelated to ideas put forward by certain postcolonial identity theorists like Bhabha about how indigenous colonized peoples at times take over the rhetoric of their colonial masters and deploy it to their own ends, thereby subverting the colonial intentions within that rhetoric to the desires and resistance of the colonized.[39] There is another point of correspondence between ideas outlined by modern theorists and the depiction of the Saracen princess in *Sir Beves of Hamtoun*: namely, the fact that in contacts between different peoples, representations of womanhood are often deployed to particular political or cultural ends.[40] These representations of womanhood are usually ideological constructs particular to a given culture, and not mimetic representations of women actually living in that culture. The point, though, is that political and ethnic groups do seem able to agree, at times, that certain modes of feminine comportment define their members.[41] This notion of culturally specific gender behavior, while not fully explored in *Sir Beves* or in other tales of Saracen princesses, is at least raised in the tale studied here. I do not mean to suggest that Josiane serves as a model of historical "Inglisch" or Muslim womanhood for Auchinleck readers. Her nature as a stereotypical Saracen means that she really bears no resemblance to actual Muslim women of the fourteenth century, and the reality is that women, whether Muslim or "Inglisch," medieval or modern, are too implicated in racial, class and ethnic identities for one model ever to apply to all of them, even within one country. Later fourteenth-century "Inglisch" womanhood was no exception to this, and while Josiane does embody certain cultural and historical characteristics of the foreign queen figure in England, she cannot be said to incarnate every "Inglisch woman." That said, there is no denying that ideological constructions of culturally-specific gender behavior do exist, however unrepresentative of historical reality. In *Sir Beves,* the character of Josiane indicates the existence of such culturally specific gender expectations, and shows how a foreign woman can facilitate her incorporation into Beves's English Christian society by choosing to behave in a manner specific to Beves's culture.

Josiane's performance of womanly modesty in Miles's bedroom allows her, through murder, to ensure the acceptability of her body to Beves's culture and her fulfillment of his culture's requirement that her body be virgin if she is to be Beves's consort. This, of course, can be linked to Christian veneration of virginity and to more pragmatic patriarchal concerns about dynastic succession (which were part of English medieval society, but certainly not unique to it). While this requirement is mentioned in the Anglo-Norman version of *Beves,* there it is only articulated once—when Beves tells Josiane that his confessor requires him to marry a virgin. In the Anglo-Norman version the confessor does not explicitly articulate this at all, but in Auchinleck and the other English versions this injunction is represented both in the confessor's direct speech and in Beves's later reference to it. Josiane's encounter with a lion and lioness is another place where the English versions of the tale emphasize Josiane's requisite virginity. While the Anglo-Norman version states only that lions are not permitted to harm the children of kings, a number of English versions state that the lions cannot harm Josiane "For þe kind of Lyouns" means that "A kynges douȝter, þat maide is, / Kinges douȝter, quene and maide both, / Þe lyouns myȝt do hur noo wroth" (2391–94). In these ways, English versions of *Sir Beves* emphasize the need for Josiane's Saracen body to conform to Christian-required norms, and make virginity a cultural and religious prerequisite for Josiane's incorporation into Beves's society.

Other incidents in *Sir Beves* also show how culturally-specific gender behaviors are a problem to be resolved before the foreign princess can acquire a new, "Inglisch" identity. Once Beves returns to fight the lions surrounding Josiane, she attempts to use her special status as virgin princess to assist Beves in his battle: "She seide, she wolde þat oon [lion] hoolde, / While þat he þat other quelde. / A-boute þe nekke she hent þat oon" (2409–11). Beves, however, vehemently opposes this action. He says

> . . ."Dame, forsoth, y-wys,
> I my3t 3elp of lytel prys,
> There y had a lyon quelde,
> Þe while a woman a nother helde!
> Thow shalt neu*er* vmbraide me,
> When þ*ou* comest hoom to my contre:
> But þ*ou* let hem goo both twoo,
> Haue good day, fro þe y goo!" (2413–20)

In the Anglo-Norman version, Beves even uses this moment to paint a verbal picture of his future life "en Engletere," when he will be boasting to his barons that he killed two lions only to have Josiane jump into the conversation and say that she held one for him.[42] As these various versions show, Beves links a notion of appropriate gender behavior for men and women to his native land and culture. The sense of boasting (note the use of the word "3elp" in Middle English) connotes a masculine world of deeds and tales of knightly prowess into which Josiane's body must not intrude if Beves is to preserve face in his homeland. To Beves's mind, Josiane may only become his bride and enter his English community if she disciplines her body to perform non-aggressive roles in battle. These roles, however, are foreign to Josiane. When the fight seems to be going badly for Beves, she again intervenes:

> Þo Iosian gan vnder-stonde,
> Þat hire lord scholde be*n* slawe;
> Helpe him 3he wolde fawe.
> Anon 3he hente þat lioun:
> Beves bad hire go sitte adoun,
> And swor be god in trinite
> Boute 3he lete þat lioun be,
> A wolde hire sle in þ*at* destresse
> Ase fain ase þe liounesse. (2470–78)

By entering the fray once more, Josiane reveals her difficulty in conforming to the roles Beves indicates she should play to fit into his life in his country.

She forcibly disciplines her body in response to his last threat, though, and abandons the martial activity of holding a ferocious, rampaging beast for the more ancillary activity of returning Beves's shield to him:

> Þo ȝhe ne moste him nouȝt helpe fiȝte,
> His scheld ȝhe brouȝte him anon riȝte
> & ȝede hire sitte adoun, saun faile,
> And let him worþe in þat bataile. (2479–82)

As the last lines of this quotation show, Josiane has understood, and accepted, that in Beves's culture his role is to fight while hers is to spectate[43] and to equip the warrior. In this episode she learns, with difficulty, how to comport her body so that it will conform to the gender roles Beves indicates are hers. She thus shapes her body into a culturally-specific and approved mode of feminine behavior. By so doing, however, she lays bare for the audience the ways in which culturally-specific gender behaviors are a challenge to be overcome in efforts to change one's group identity, and again indicates the role of performance, or conscious deployment of one's body and words, in individual efforts to reshape community affiliations.

Josiane's initial tendency to martial activity is a trait shared by many Saracen princesses in literature.[44] In the tale of *Fierebras,* for example, the eponymous hero's sister Floripas embroils herself in the escape attempts of her father's Christian captives, and even murders her own nurse by throwing her out of a window when this woman attempts to interfere in Floripas's plan. As Sarah Lambert, notes, however, "Once [women] have crossed the boundaries into Christendom, they have to move into the background" in narratives about Christians and Saracens.[45] While it is important to qualify this assertion by pointing out that in tales like *King Horn* Christian heroines do play very assertive and aggressive roles, there is no denying that female literary Saracens frequently take the initiative in events only to cede this assertiveness after their conversion. What is unique about the depiction of Josiane in *Sir Beves of Hamtoun* is that the circumscription of the Saracen woman's activity is explicitly performed for the reader. Moreover, Beves links this circumscription to his notion of the gender norms in his native English society, and thus emphasizes how specific cultural norms can problematize an individual's efforts to claim a new group identity.

Although *Sir Beves* clearly displays an awareness of how culturally-specific gender norms influence individuals' efforts to alter their group identities,[46] it should be noted that the second example I offer of this situation (the interaction between Beves and Josiane in the lions incident) is only partially extant in Auchinleck. The manuscript does not omit this episode, but a freak of history has resulted in the disappearance of the folio recording the start of the battle and Beves's fascinating reference to the traditions of his home country. Editors usually use the Egerton manuscript (London, British Library, Egerton 2862) to supply the matter narrated on the missing folio. That version of *Beves,* the Anglo-Norman tale, and the Naples manuscript contain the reference to Beves's home country and therefore to an "Inglisch" set of gender expectations for knights' ladies. Two of the later Middle English versions, however, (the Chetham and Cambridge University Library manuscripts) do not contain this reference to Beves's home country. These manuscripts also omit Josiane's later attempt to re-enter the fray and her subsequent behavior modifications. Lines recounting these events in detail do appear in Auchinleck, however (lines 2465–82). They open the folio immediately following the lacuna, and are the ones quoted and analyzed above as the moment of Josiane's bodily self-discipline. Because these details about Josiane's interactions with the lions and with Beves appear in Auchinleck, it seems justifiable to include the entire incident in my discussion, and to use the Egerton manuscript, like editors of the Auchinleck *Sir Beves* before me, to supply the missing lines. I cannot help but believe that should the missing folio ever turn up, it would probably contain a reference to Beves's home country similar to those found in the Anglo-Norman, Egerton, and Naples (Naples, National Library, XII. B. 29) versions. The Anglo-Norman and Egerton manuscripts are chronologically closest to Auchinleck, while the Egerton and Naples manuscript versions resemble Auchinleck most closely in content.[47]

In sum, the Saracen princess Josiane reveals the ways in which group identities can be performed, and how such performances can assist an individual to alter his or her group affiliations. Repeatedly, Josiane can be seen consciously fitting herself into a model of group identity, be that identity Christian, feminine, or a notion of womanhood particular to Beves's English culture. She demonstrates most fully the various identities that can be performed, and the many different ways in which performance redefines group identities and advances personal interests. Josiane thus promotes an awareness of how the individual and the group interact in the process of identity formation and assertion. She also indicates the possible variety of such interactions given individuals' involvements in multiple group identities. As she does so, Josiane draws attention to how gender and biology play into ways of performing identity and influence the types of identities one is expected to perform in order to change one's group affiliations.

PERMANENCE AND PASSING

As Josiane foregrounds the role of performativity in the assertion of individ-ual and communal identities, she raises the possibility of discrepancies between performed and actual group affiliations. Sometimes her actions clearly work to present her as someone she technically is not, as when she swears by a Christian God before she has been baptized or has even expressed a desire to convert. She thereby passes for a permanent and established mem-ber of the Christian community even though she is not Christian. One might be tempted to overlook the disquieting possibilities of this discrepancy by attributing it to a medieval poet's readiness to put Christian words in the mouth of a Saracen, or by pointing out that Josiane does actually convert later in the poem. The Auchinleck *Sir Beves,* however, does not permit the disquieting aspects of performativity to be shelved so easily. It includes a later example of identity performance that cannot be dismissed along either of these lines, and that works in tandem with Josiane's performative display to provoke consideration about the relative permanence and veracity of an asserted identity.

After having been imprisoned for seven years in the Saracen King Brademond's dungeon, Beves enlists divine assistance and manages to kill one of his two jailers. The problem he then faces is how to entice his other jailer to enter the dungeon so that that Saracen, too, may be killed and prevented from interfering in Beves's escape. To accomplish this, Beves slyly poses as the living jailer's now dead companion, and does so rhetorically—through his speech. Beves calls out to the living jailer, "For þe loue of sein Mahoun, / Be þe rop glid bliue adoun / And help, þat þis þef wer ded!" (1625–27). Inter-estingly, it is not through use of a Saracen language that Beves convinces his jailers that he is Saracen. Unlike some French *chansons de geste* which express repeated concern about the linguistic differences between Saracens and Christians,[48] *Beves of Hamtoun* does not even suggest that there could be lin-guistic incomprehensibility between Saracens and Christians. The whole world, apparently, communicates in the "Inglisch" language so valued in Auchinleck. Accordingly, it is Beves's choice of words, his invocation of a Saracen deity, that implies Beves's membership in a Saracen community. Moreover this rhetorical suggestion proves efficacious. The living jailer enters Beves's cell, and thereby indicates that Beves's speech has successfully cast Beves as a Saracen. The jailer is mistaken, and Beves is not really Saracen at this point, but acceptance into a group is again effected by a deployment of rhetoric; the notion of performing one's way into a religious identity surfaces once more. Beves's ability to construct himself as Saracen solely through the use of religious references constitutes another point of difference between Middle English and Anglo-Norman versions of the tale. In the Anglo-Norman, Beves merely calls to the jailer to come and help him with a heavy stone, and the jailer does so. Once more, Auchinleck and some other English versions of the tale foreground the question of religious difference and place it in a performative context.[49] They endow rhetoric with the power to shift easily a person's apparently stable and permanent group affiliations, and thereby point out the malleability of these affiliations and the ease with which false ones may be assumed.

This incident, because it involves Beves's assumption of an identity he never intends to hold, clearly suggests that false religious identities are easily assumed, and that they pass muster with individuals who actually do belong to the religion enacted. Josiane's acceptance by Beves when she performs Christianity conveys the same message. Repeatedly, the Auchinleck *Sir Beves* confronts its audience with the phenomenon of religious passing. It therefore provokes thought about how permanent and stable a group identity is, and how the permanence and veracity of an identity can be accurately discerned. Historically, this was very much an issue in the later Middle Ages. There are repeated examples of Christians, even as they express a desire for converts to their faith, ultimately finding themselves unable to trust such converts or accept them as true Christians. For example, concerns about the permanence and comprehensiveness of conversion turned up in England in the late thirteenth and early fourteenth centuries. A dossier assembled in the fourteenth century in support of Thomas Cantilupe's canonization records Cantilupe's outrage over the suggestion that

> a certain knight who was a Jew and called Henry of Winchester, the Convert, should have *testimonium et recordum* [sic] over Christians who clipped or forged the king's money—that is to say, that he should have authority and power such that at his command and testimony, or by his written record, other men could lose life and limb.[50]

Cantilupe, the future candidate for canonization, apparently told King Edward I "that it was not proper that this convert and Jew should have such power over Christians; he [Cantilupe] would not consent to it and with tears sought permission from the lord king to resign from his council."[51] Thus, as Stacey explains, "By the middle of the thirteenth century in England, there was clearly an irreducible element to Jewish identity in the eyes of many Christians, which no amount of baptismal water could entirely eradicate."[52] Indeed, these anxieties about the permanence or definitiveness of a convert's Christianness were sometimes justified, as "rabbinic tradition had long allowed Jews to accept baptism if the only alternative was death, while exercising a mental reservation which allowed them to remain as secret Jews in good standing."[53] Whether Jewish converts truly did become Christian or not, there is no denying that anxiety about the sincerity of their conversion, and fear that a performance of Christianity could pass for Christianness itself, did exist in England in the 1280s. Cases of supposed Jewish apostasy were brought to Edward I's attention in this decade, and Stacey even suggests that Edward's expulsion of the Jews from England in 1290 may have reflected, in part, a general English frustration that more Jews had not converted to Christianity in response to the efforts of Edward and his father. Historically, then, the performances of religious identity enacted by both Josiane and Beves in Auchinleck engage what had been a widespread English concern about the permanence and veracity of changes in religious identities less than a generation before the manuscript's compilation.

Medieval Christian anxieties about the efficacy of conversion and about the crossing of communal boundaries involved therein tended to manifest themselves frequently as concerns about the body of the convert and that body's sexual interactions with Christians. This is completely understandable since sexual relations with non-Christians were a charged topic in the Middle Ages. The Council of Nablus, held in 1120, condemned sexual intercourse and marriage between Muslims and Christians, while in the 1140s, Gratian's *Decretum* reinforced and disseminated a condemnation of inter-faith sex more widely.[54] In 1215, the Fourth Lateran Council decreed that Jews or Muslims living in Christian realms should differentiate their bodies from Christians' by wearing identifying clothing so that Christians would not unwittingly copulate with members of these other faiths. [55] Given this Christian anxiety about sex with religious others, it is not surprising that sex should prove a charged issue for converts to Christianity. As Steven Kruger argues, "the condemnation of interfaith sexual contacts translated into uncertainty about the licitness of sexual and family relations with new converts to Christianity," and "uncertainty about whether religious conversion truly transformed [Muslim and Jewish] bodies, cleansing them of their impurities, repairing their imperfections, and removing the tinges of animality that clung to them in Christian fantasies."[56] These uncertainties can be seen in the fact that, as both Kruger and Stacey point out, the surest route by which a convert could achieve integration into Christian society was by entering holy orders and practicing the celibacy enjoined thereby. When sexual activity and procreation between converts and Christians entered the picture, in contrast, the convert's previous religious existence was often raked up, even many generations after conversion. The children conceived between

Christians and converts found it difficult to escape their mixed origins and to function socially in the same manner as the offspring of long-time Christians. For example, in his attacks on Pope Anacletus II in the early twelfth century, Bernard of Clairvaux repeatedly brought up the fact that Anacletus's great-grandfather was a Jewish convert.[57] Such behavior clearly shows how incomplete was the integration of converts into the structures of Christian society, since Anacletus's long-distant Jewish heritage could still be deployed against him many years after his progenitor's conversion. Similarly, Kruger notes that "Pope Clement IV in 1268 rebuked Alfonso III of Portugal for allowing marriages of Christian men to women of Saracen and Jewish *origin*," an act that clearly differentiates between converts and Christians in a sexual and procreative context.[58] Kruger also points out that

> in late-fourteenth-century Aragon, 'the death penalty for all sex relations between Jews and Christians' was reiterated in such a way as to 'include new converts.' And in 1459, Pope Pius II granted the annulment of the unconsummated marriage between a Christian man and a woman of Jewish heritage who was accused of 'Judaizing' and heretical' behavior; the Pope's treatment of the connection between the woman's unorthodox behavior, her ancestry, and the possible Jewishness of her future progeny expresses a strong suspicion of the insincerity and incompleteness of Jewish conversion and some sense of a hereditary aspect of Judaism that might not easily be overcome—perhaps especially when female converts are involved.[59]

The sexual and familial integration of foreigners into medieval Christian communities was thus a moment when the origins of these foreigners came back to haunt them, when the efficacy of any convert's performance of Christianity was questioned, and when the permanence and veracity of a convert's change of religious and cultural affiliation could be challenged.

This anxiety about the sexual and familial assimilation of foreigners understandably shows up in the representation of Josiane in *Sir Beves of Hamtoun*, since she is both a convert and a foreign consort when she conceives children with her Christian husband. Moreover, her actions throughout the text have repeatedly displayed the ease with which identities, be they true or false, can be performed so as to ensure one's acceptance into a group. She therefore cannot escape a suspicion that maybe her baptism and conversion are, in fact, merely another performance that has masked her Saracenness rather than eradicated it. For these reasons, it is not surprising that Josiane's integration into the familial and social structures of Beves's society appears less than complete in the latter part of the tale. Once Beves has regained his patrimony, married Josiane, and sired a child on her, Josiane plays no role in his English adventures. Beves travels on his own to the king's palace, and his main activity here is a horse race that ultimately leads to his exile from England. It is at this moment of exile from his native heritage that Josiane re-enters Beves's story in any memorable way. After she and Beves have left England, Josiane gives birth to twin boys in a forest. Immediately after labor, she is kidnapped by the treacherous Saracen Ascopard and returned to her erstwhile Saracen husband King Yuor. At the very moment that the converted Josiane bodily ensures Beves's dynastic succession, her Saracen past returns to haunt her. The physical proof of her and Beves's sexual union precipitates an invocation of her Saracenness, and Josiane, despite her conversion, is once again classified as Saracen. As was often the case historically, a convert finds the definitiveness and permanence of her conversion called into question precisely when she manifests a physical, bodily incorporation into Christian society. Auchinleck once again raises the question of how integration into a new community is achieved, and indicates the anxiety surrounding the sexual manifestation of such integration. The female Saracen's body thus facilitates consideration of how sexual relations play into the assumption of a new group identity,

This incident, however, is even more fraught with inter-group tensions and concerns about how women's bodies mediate between groups than the above discussion indicates. The fact that Ascopard engineers Josiane's reclamation by the Saracen world of her origins is particularly significant. Ascopard is the monstrous Saracen giant who pursued Beves and Josiane when they were first reunited and fled from the realm of Josiane's first husband, King Yuor of Mombraunt.[60] After defeating Ascopard in battle, Beves wished to kill him, but Josiane interceded for the Saracen's life. Moreover, as part of her intercessionary speech Josiane again invoked a Christian identity before she had actually converted. She beseeched Beves, "Sire, . . . so god þe saue, / Let him [Ascopard] liuen & ben our knaue!" (2545–46). Because this incident, like the one linked to the Christmas Day Battle, occurred before Josiane had actually converted to Christianity, the preservation of Ascopard's life is inextricably linked with another example of Josiane rhetorically performing an identity that is not yet hers. In addition, in this act Josiane mediates between Christian and Saracen societies rather than definitively renouncing one in favor of the other; she assumes a position on the borders of two communities that is precisely that of historical foreign queens, those other renowned intercessors. Ascopard's salvation, then, is a moment when Josiane stands on the border between the Saracen associations of her past and the Christian associations of her future as Beves's wife. This borderline and performative moment, however, returns to haunt Josiane when Ascopard kidnaps her and forcibly re-implicates her in her former Saracen associations at precisely the moment when she has manifested physically her acceptance by Beves and integration into his Christian familial structure. Her inescapable links to her Saracen heritage re-emerge to impede her wholesale inclusion into Beves's society as venerated dynastic matriarch, and to demonstrate that Josiane's Christian identity, like that of most converts, must ever be accepted with some reservations.

Although other Middle English versions of *Sir Beves* recount this kidnapping in brief detail, the Auchinleck manuscript devotes a significant number of lines to it, and thereby ensures consideration of the incident's implications for Josiane's efforts to assert a Christian identity. Moreover, while other manuscripts do not explicitly remind readers that this event is linked to Josiane's mediation between two groups earlier in the text, Auchinleck includes a speech in which Josiane recounts her past intercession:

> ʒhe seide: "Ascopard, freli frende,
> For bounte, ich dede þe while
> And sauede þe fro perile,
> Þo Beves þe wolde han slawe
> And i-brouʒt of þe lif dawe,
> Ich was þe bourʒ, þe schost be trewe" (3652–57).

In Auchinleck, then, the eruption of Josiane's Saracen past in her kidnapping is combined with explicit reference to earlier acts of hers in which she straddled the borders between peoples and negotiated a compromise between Saracen and Christian. Right after the labor and childbirth that should have marked Josiane's final incorporation into English, Christian society as valued mother, Auchinleck's readers are confronted with explicit reminders that she is not fully Christian—that she possesses a Saracen past and that she has, through her intercessionary acts earlier in the text, worked to forge relationships between Christian and Saracen communities rather than preserve the separateness of these two groups. The definitiveness of her converted identity is thus called brilliantly into question, as is the possibility of ever successfully severing one's ties to a former group identity.

The Auchinleck *Sir Beves* continues its evocation of Josiane's Saracen past by including in its narrative events following her kidnapping that do not appear in other Middle English manuscripts.[61] In Auchinleck, Josiane responds to her kidnapping by redoubling her efforts to reject her Saracen connections and prove her worthiness for full inclusion in Christian society. Ironically, however, even these efforts require that Josiane rely on her Saracen heritage. As Ascopard leads her to Yuor, the Auchinleck Josiane uses herbs and a knowledge of "fysik and sirgirie" gleaned "in Ermonie" (3671–72) to make herself "in semlaunt & *in* ble / A foule mesel on to se" (3687–88). By doing so, she repulses Yuor and decisively terminates his interest in reclaiming her as his queen (3695–98). Paradoxically, Josiane uses her Saracen upbringing to sever ties to one aspect of her Saracenness. The same type of effort occurs later in the text. When Sabor (Beves's uncle) falls ill and needs money for medicine, Josiane proves that she is a loyal member of Beves's family group (and worthy of reclamation from her Saracen links) by using her minstrelsy skills to obtain the necessary money and medicine. These minstrelsy skills, however, are another product of Josiane's Saracen upbringing according to Auchinleck: "While Iosian was in Ermonie, / ʒhe hadde lerned of minstralcie, / Vpon a fiþele for to play" (3905–7). Thus, even Josiane's care for Beves's extended family reaffirms her Saracenness. Josiane does, however, achieve partial inclusion into Beves's world from these efforts, and is reunited with Beves after working so hard to distance herself from her Saracenness. Intriguingly, however, after Josiane's kidnapping and subsequent efforts to prove the veracity of her conversion, Beves never returns to England to reclaim his patrimony and install Josiane as his "Inglisch" wife and countess. He visits England once more to rectify kingly abuses, but then resigns his baronage into the hands of his cousin and assumes the kingship of the Saracen kingdom of Mombraunt. In this way, the convert-Christian couple suggests that the place for them socially is not a Christian England, but rather a kingdom close to Saracen lands and interests. Despite Josiane's efforts to fit in to Christian English society, her Saracenness cannot be completely obliterated, and her union with Beves ultimately results in Beves settling in a kingdom close to that of Josiane's Saracen father in which both she and her English husband are accepted.

Given Beves and Josiane's exile from Beves's native land, a reader tends to perceive these characters' inter-faith marriage as an act involving rather negative consequences. There is, however, a silver lining to their intermingling. Beves's relocation to a Saracen kingdom and his assumption of this land's throne may exclude him from his English lands and political status, but they do result in English acquisition of a foreign land—indeed, of two foreign lands, since one of Beves's sons inherits the Saracen kingdom of Josiane's father. The other son, interestingly, ends up inheriting England itself. In this way, the incomplete incorporation of the converted Josiane into Beves's society ultimately aggrandizes English geo-political influence by placing English nobles in positions of power in two foreign lands as well as in their native land. Attempts to include Josiane in Christian society physically and sexually may provoke differentiation and a certain level of exclusion, but this does not end her links to Christianity, and the partial integration achieved by her and Beves advances Christian ends and develops English Christian influence abroad. Geo-political benefits accrue from an inter-faith union that differentiates Saracen from Christian but does not uncouple the two. Josiane's inability to achieve definitive inclusion in English, Christian society is thus not entirely negative. Indeed, the geo-political implications of Josiane's union with Beves may explain why, as Jennifer Goodman has argued, individuals engaged in the early conquest and colonization of the Americas found medieval tales like *Sir Beves* so appealing and pertinent to their experiences, and bought printed versions of them so frequently.[62]

The geo-political benefits of Josiane's union with Beves clearly resemble those achieved historically by monarchs' marriages to foreign queens. These women often brought dowry lands with them, and even if they did not, were expected to facilitate friendly relations between polities. The nature of the anxiety that surrounds a female convert's sexual assimilation into a group and provokes a reassertion of her difference, may also be clarified by consideration of the foreign queen. For this figure, moments of sexuality and reproduction were contexts in which her foreign origins arose to haunt both her and the group to which she now belonged. The intimate, sexual insertion of the newcomer into her adopted community could not be decisively distanced, on the group's part, from the threat of foreign invasion and all the fears surrounding the idea of such an invasion. Because the queen was a foreigner, her sexual interactions with the king inevitably entwined him with foreignness and represented his vulnerability to attack or influence from without his realm. Her sexual and reproductive acts could also pose a much more literal threat of invasion. For example, the remarriage of Henry III's mother to the Count of Poitiers meant that Henry found himself in later life with a number of Poitevin half-brothers to support. His efforts to provide for his foreign family aroused great resentment among the English.[63] In this way, Henry's mother's reproductive relationships created a problem for Henry, and were perceived in England as the root of a mini-invasion by Poitevin nobles in the thirteenth century. Edward II's French queen, too, demonstrated how justified people were in associating the sexuality of foreign queens with threats of invasion. While Edward's relationship with Isabella enacted an intimate exposure of the English to the foreign, the really menacing combination of queenly sexuality and invasion from abroad was manifested later in their relationship. In 1326, fed up with Edward's refusal to remove Hugh Despenser the Younger from court, Isabella refused to return home from France.[64] Her actions occasioned widespread fears of foreign invasion in England,[65] and these fears proved to be justified when later in the year Isabella and her lover, Roger Mortimer, returned to England with an army of foreigners to overthrow Edward. The queen's sexual partner played a leading role in the defeat, deposition, and death (or so many believe) of Isabella's kingly husband in 1327.[66] In this way, a foreign queen's sexuality was directly involved in an invasion of England, and validated a general tendency to associate the sexual integration of foreigners into a community with danger to that same community. While the re-emergence of Josiane's Saracen affiliations at the moment of her genealogical inclusion in Beves's society probably does not represent a literal fear of Saracen invasion in the text, it does clearly represent fears about a foreigner penetrating too deeply into an English Christian community and thereby, perhaps, contaminating it. The character of Josiane thus facilitates consideration of the ways in which foreign consorts' sexual acts impact upon polities, an issue of immense pertinence in England during the transition between the reigns of Edward II and III in the years immediately preceding Auchinleck's compilation. Once again, as a female Saracen, Josiane allows for an exploration of inter-group relations and anxieties in situations manifestly not part of a Saracen warrior's or persecutor's masculine experience.

AFFIRMATION

While foreign consorts could menace the ruler they married and his realm, they could also work to affirm his status, and this process of identity affirmation is explored by Josiane in *Sir Beves*. As the preceding sections of this chapter show, the performativity of identity can provoke anxieties about the veracity and stability of the identities claimed by people. Combating such anxieties means finding a way to demonstrate repeatedly the validity of one's claims to specific identities. The most convincing affirmation of an identity, however, is not a person's own performance of an identity he or she claims, but other people's enactments of that person's claimed identity. In other words, people read the veracity of an identity not through an individual's own performance of that identity, but through the behaviors and performances of others around that individual. This way of creating a sense of identity was particularly important for kings, as Louise Fradenburg points out in *City, Marriage, Tournament*. She suggests that many late medieval Scottish kings consciously staged tournaments in ways that would reinforce in spectators' eyes the superior position and power of the king.[67] The king's queen, too, testified to his public position. I have already discussed the ways in which queenly intercession affirms a king's claim to be the natural font of political action. I have also indicated the similar ways in which Josiane's humbling of herself before Beves as she begs his pardon affirms his identity as a Christian man without his having to assert anything himself. There are other ways, too, in which Josiane's status as Beves's foreign consort enacts his claimed identities and demonstrates how claimed identities may be publicly affirmed by the behavior of others.

Like a foreign queen, Josiane repeatedly represents to readers both the vulnerability and invulnerability of Beves's position as an English, Christian noble. Peggy McCracken identifies this ability to display a ruler's political status as a phenomenon peculiar to consorts.[68] She claims that the consort's body is what allows her to play the role of identity barometer in relation to her partner and his polity. In particular, McCracken argues that female consorts participate in a socio-symbolic "system that locates political integrity and legitimacy in the body of the queen," that equates the state of the queen's body with the state of the king's rule, and that uses accusations about the purity of the queen's physical body to menace the king's sovereignty.[69] Josiane's body works very much in this way in *Sir Beves of Hamtoun*.

First, Josiane's body figures forth the vulnerability of Beves's identity as a Christian, English knight. Whenever Beves is involved in sensitive redefinitions of his identity, Josiane is either forcibly married off to a suitor she dislikes, or kidnapped. For example, King Yuor marries Josiane against her will at a moment when Beves, imprisoned in Brademond's dungeon, finds himself striving to maintain his claim to Christian knightliness. Beves is in prison because he mistakenly believed, as mentioned earlier, that the Saracen King Ermin loved him as "is owene brother" (1332). For this reason, Beves trustingly delivered a letter from Ermin to King Brademond in which Ermin ordered Brademond to kill Beves. Brademond instead imprisoned Beves, and in the dungeon our Christian knight degenerates into a being who fights monsters with clubs rather than swords, and whose hair grows to his feet. Moreover, a battle with a flying adder scars Beves's face so horrendously that Josiane cannot recognize him upon their eventual reunion (1572–74). During this episode, then, Beves finds himself distanced from his identities as both knight and Christian. He is less than knightly because he fights the monstrous snake with a club rather than a sword, and because his appearance is not that of most literary knights given his scar and hair length. He is less than Christian at this moment, and is in prison, because he mistakenly believed himself to be a Saracen's brother. Beves's identity as Christian knight, therefore, is in doubt at this point. His vulnerability is proclaimed publicly by the subjection of Josiane to marriage with a man she does not desire. Just as the queen's body signifies the health of her husband's kingship and realm, so Josiane's body here enacts for readers the ill health of Beves's knightly and religious identities, and his inability to define who he is or protect what is important for his dynastic succession (namely his intended bride) from foreigners like the Saracen Yuor. Josiane's marriage, against her will, to Yuor announces Beves's declined state to the world.

The same sort of enactment of Beves's status by Josiane occurs later in the text. When Beves returns to England to reclaim his patrimony, Josiane finds herself forcibly married to Earl Miles and menaced with a very public rape of her body (see lines 3162–94). The vulnerability of her body to this attack mirrors Beves's vulnerability as he seeks to re-establish himself as an English noble by confronting his mother and her lover, and by avenging his father's murder and his own subsequent disinheritance. Should Beves fail in this endeavor, he will call into question his very appellation as Sir Beves of Hamtoun as well as his right to membership in the English polity. His "Inglisch" identity is thus very much at risk at the moment when Josiane finds herself fending off violation by Miles. Beves's Englishness is also in question later in the tale when he is exiled from England and forced to resign his barony into the hands of another. When Beves is deprived of both his geographical claim to Englishness and his status as land-owning noble, Josiane's own Saracen identity returns to haunt her and she is kidnapped by Ascopard. Like more recent invocations of the female body's vulnerability in assertions of national identity (consider the appearance of a book entitled *The Rape of Kuwait* after Iraq's invasion of the country),[70] *Sir Beves* uses Josiane's body to figure forth the fragility of Beves's Christian and English knightly identity at moments when he is redefining his social role and group affiliations. The female body of Beves's consort reflects the state of his rule as Earl of Southampton, and the security of his religious and class identities.

While Josiane's body at times enacts the instability of Beves's identities, it also suggests the ultimate stability of these identities. She shares what Fradenburg identifies as the foreign queen's paradoxical power to represent both the vulnerability and invulnerability of her husband's kingship and his realm. Even as Josiane's body is subjected to moments of threatened rape, the character repeatedly engineers a defense of her physical integrity. When Beves languishes in prison and she is wed to Yuor, Josiane refuses to accept her father's claim that Beves has abandoned her and married another. Instead of resigning her body to Yuor's sexual advances, she puts on a magical ring that prevents men from having intercourse with her (1469–74). In this way, Josiane maintains the pure integrity of her body just as Beves's wife must, according to his confessor (1965–70). Similarly, as we have seen, when forcibly married to Earl Miles and escorted to his bed, Josiane deploys a rhetoric of female modesty to protect herself from rape and arrange events so that she can murder Miles. Admittedly, moments of physical and sexual vulnerability on Josiane's part reflect challenges to Beves's claims to certain identities, and menace the purity and continuity of Beves's lineage. Nevertheless, her ability to overcome her attackers and rewrite these moments of vulnerability as ones of triumphant self-defense symbolizes the ultimate invulnerability of Beves and his identity. No one is going to deprive him of his chosen wife, nor of a suitable lineage. Moreover, no violation of Josiane's body will occur even when Beves is faced with the challenge of renegotiating his identity. All will work out fine in the end for Beves, just as it does for his partner when his problems repeatedly complicate her life. Josiane thus performs and affirms Beves's identities as land-owning, Christian, English knight, and proclaims the durability of these identities.

Josiane also testifies to Beves's social prestige more directly than by mirroring in her body the vulnerability and invulnerability of his identities. At times she interacts with Beves so as to make his knightly status apparent to others. For example, after Beves's escape from Brademond's dungeon Josiane's actions towards Beves identify him as a knight more than his own behavior does. When Beves, fleeing Brademond's dungeon, arrives at Josiane's palace he is dressed in the lowly garb of a palmer and petitions Josiane for alms. Nothing about him proclaims his knightly status. Josiane, however arranges his reunion with various public symbols of his status. Before she even recognizes Beves, she tells him

> "Þe semest . . . man of anour,
> Þow schelt þis dai be priour
> And be-ginne oure deis:
> Þe semest hende and corteis." (2121–24)

With the words "anour," "hende," and "corteis," Josiane ascribes a noble identity to Beves. In addition, she sets him to preside over her table of palmers, thereby proclaiming to all his superior status. Josiane's affirmation of Beves's identity does not stop there, however. She also arranges for his reunion with his noble steed Arundel, and this clearly re-establishes Beves in his knightly identity. Historically, horses were the defining symbol of the knight, who was initially nothing more than a mounted warrior.[71] In the later Middle Ages, good horses were prized and venerated as symbols of knightly, noble status, and, since they cost a great deal (especially when they had to be armed for battle), they were prominent evidence of their master's elevated social status.[72] Josiane's actions towards the fugitive, scarred, and disguised Beves thus proclaim that he is a noble knight. Josiane affirms his true status and identity even when appearances belie them.

Josiane's own status, too, serves to reinforce and proclaim Beves's status to the world. She is, as Beves points out to the bishop who baptizes her, " . . . of heþenesse a quene, / And ȝhe wile, for me sake, / Cristendome at þe take" (2582–84). Josiane's queenly status makes her willingness to convert for Beves's sake a powerful assertion of his value. She also announces his prestige publicly to Christians and Saracens alike; her repeated choice of Beves for her consort, and her rejection of other Saracen and Christian suitors in his favor, represent him as superior to all other nobles. In these ways, Josiane's acts testify to Beves's status in the world outside England. This situation resembles closely the way in which a foreign queen's foreignness announces her king's status in the world outside his realm, and constructs him as a figure of international repute and respect. The foreign queen's own identity serves to affirm her husband's claim that he is worthy to be his people's ruler. She is both a status symbol for him, and an external validation of his right to rule.

Josiane's ability to represent the solidity of Beves's political, religious and social identities exposes his dependence on factors and people outside of himself. One needs external symbols and foreigners for an asserted identity to be recognized both at home and abroad. The same type of recognition is needed when one is striving to assert a group identity like that of Englishness. Consider, for example, how nascent nations produced by the break-up of other countries work tirelessly to be recognized in forums like the United Nations, or to establish diplomatic relations with other sovereign nations since such relations construct them, in turn, as sovereign nations. In other words, a group cannot unilaterally assert a political and national identity; such an act has international implications and relies, in part, upon foreign recognition for its efficacy. Thus, to find in Auchinleck a portrait of a Saracen woman which reveals the many ways in which a foreigner can affirm an English noble's identity is to find in a manuscript busily engaged in asserting an "Inglisch" identity an awareness of the role of external recognition in successful assertions and redefinitions of group identities

Although England had been accepted internationally as a political entity long before Auchinleck's compilation, the nature of its international role and status was certainly being redefined in the late thirteenth and early fourteenth centuries. English monarchs of this period repeatedly display a hunger for foreign recognition of England as a power to be reckoned with in western Europe. Simon Lloyd, for example, notes how a sense of competition with France and the Capetian monarchs entered into King Henry III of

England's interest in crusading in the mid-thirteenth century.[73] Lloyd argues that reports of the French king Saint Louis's crusading victories and collection of holy relics provoked efforts on Henry's part to represent himself publicly as an equally religious ruler, and to foreground in various rituals English saintly relics. Lloyd also suggests that Henry was rather jealous of the French king's papally-bestowed title of Defender of the Faith,[74] and that he repeatedly tried to find ways of obtaining similar accolades for himself. Henry III was not the only English monarch to desire, and strive for, a role of importance on the European stage. His son, Edward I, appears to have been equally interested in asserting English prestige internationally. Not only was Edward a renowned and avid tourneyer abroad in his youth,[75] but he also took crusading vows and served in the Holy Land with such distinction that for years afterward messengers from foreign powers interested in fighting Muslims sought alliances with him. The Mongols, for example, repeatedly sent envoys to Edward I to discuss the possibility of combining forces against Muslims in the Middle East, and English chroniclers dutifully detail this evidence of the English monarch's prestige in the wider world.[76] Even French writers such as Pierre Dubois dedicated and addressed treatises on crusade to this English king.[77] Edward I also strove ceaselessly to compel Welsh and Scottish acceptance of English sovereignty. His acts of colonization and conquest contributed to making his kingship and realm more grandiose and politically important in the larger world. Edward III, too, sought to distinguish himself and England on the field of battle and in the practice of chivalry. His wars against France, tournament activities, and creation of the Order of the Garter all served this end and garnered international prestige for him and his kingship.[78] Auchinleck's representation of Josiane as an enabler and promoter of Beves's public status thus draws attention to the ways in which recognition by others plays a crucial role in assertions of an identity. Desires for international recognition and a prominent role on the world stage were very much part of assertions of "Inglisch" identity in the thirteenth and early fourteenth centuries.

In sum, individuals' abilities to perform identities can occasion anxieties about the permanence and veracity of asserted group affiliations. These anxieties, however, can be allayed when the identities claimed by an individual are verified by the acts of others. Josiane's multiple enactments of Beves's Christian, knightly status function in this way and repeatedly affirm Beves's prestige both abroad and at home. She thus draws attention to the fact that an identity cannot be asserted unilaterally but instead must be recognized by others and performed by them to take effect. Josiane highlights this aspect of identity in a way that other Saracen characters in Auchinleck do not, and as a result this female Saracen indicates how central external recognition is to any project of asserting an "Inglisch" identity.

CODA: GOOD QUEEN/BAD QUEEN

Josiane's acts in *Sir Beves* evoke in various ways the functions of foreign queen figures. It should be noted, however, that Josiane is not the only foreign queen in the text. Beves's own mother is a foreign consort as well, and the juxtaposition of her behavior with Josiane's indicates the dangers posed when such a figure does not wish to fit in to her husband's culture or further his interests.

Like Josiane, Beves's mother invokes models of male-female interaction, but her aim is not to preserve herself from harm or to reconcile herself and her husband. Instead, she appeals to models of husbandly devotion and wifely dependence to engineer her husband's murder, the dispossession of her son, and the fulfillment of her sexual desire for another man. Beves's mother begins by expressing dissatisfaction with her elderly husband:

> Hadde ich itaken a ȝong kniȝt,
> Þat ner nouȝt brused in werre & fiȝt,
> Also he is,
> A wolde me louen dai and niȝt,
> Cleppen and kissen wiþ al is miȝt
> And make me blis. (61–66)[79]

To remedy this, she plans an ambush of her husband by her lover. On the appointed day, the lady lingers in bed as if she is sick ("Ase hit wer nede" the text says (177)). When her husband sympathetically asks whether he can get anything to comfort her, she demands the body of a wild boar and tells him where he may find such a beast (181–92). Sir Gii dutifully proceeds according to her instructions, and is ambushed and killed by the lady's lover, the Emperor of Almeyne. Beves's mother thus performs feminine frailty and plays on husbandly concern in order to obtain her own desires. Once these are obtained and she is reunited with her lover, she orders her son put to death, and, when this fails, sells him to Saracens. Unlike Josiane, who played on tropes of maidenly modesty to preserve herself and the virginity needed for Beves's dynastic legacy, Beves's mother uses her performative abilities to ends contrary to Beves's dynastic, land-holding interests.

In another episode, Beves's mother demonstrates her refusal to fit into the gender norms of Beves's society as he defines them elsewhere in the text. In the lions incident, Josiane masters her desire to participate in martial masculine endeavor and, instead, learns to play the role of spectator dictated for her by Beves, which Beves suggests is a normal female role in his society. Beves's mother, however, repeatedly refuses to be a spectator. Instead, she engineers and directs masculine martial endeavors, as when she arranges the murder of her husband. Likewise, when the adult Beves returns to reclaim his patrimony from his mother and the Emperor, this lady actively dictates her new husband's martial activities, telling him where he may obtain the knights necessary for battle against Beves, and who will come to his aid as an ally (see lines 3313–32). Indeed, one of the allies she suggests is her own father, the King of Scotland, and his forces. In this case, the queen's foreign affiliations become a threat to the realm of her first husband. The incursion of outside powers that a foreign queen can represent for her adopted people becomes a reality and, as Scots soldiers battle Englishmen, we see in *Sir Beves* the realization of worst case scenarios involving foreign queens.

Thus, Beves's mother in many ways serves as a foil to Josiane and her behavior as a foreign consort. While Josiane and Beves's mother do incarnate some of the same aspects of the foreign queen, their different behaviors demonstrate, respectively, the benefits and the dangers a foreign consort can bring to a ruler and his polity. The Saracen princess advances a vision of her English husband as internationally desirable, ensures the continuity of his dynasty, and accepts her subordination to him. Beves's mother, on the other hand, impugns her English husband's sexual performance, overthrows him and disinherits his dynasty, and avoids behavior that would aggrandize him in any way. What is most interesting about this foreign consort, however, is the fact that she is explicitly identified as "þe kinges douȝter of Scotlonde" (26). In *Sir Beves,* then, a comparison of Scottish and Saracen foreign queens is implied. While the Scots queen proves to be perfidious and murderous, the Saracen embodies ideal foreign consort behavior. Admittedly, Josiane's Saracenness does raise some concerns in the text, but compared to Beves's mother Josiane is a model foreign queen. Her Saracen origins may taint Beves a little and require that he ultimately rule in countries other than England, but this move beneficially expands English geo-political power. Moreover, the offspring Josiane and Beves produce are worthy to reign in England, as is shown by one son's marriage to the English king's daughter and succession to his father-in-law's throne. Dynastically, Josiane is a winning choice for bride. Beves's mother, a Scot, is not. She betrays her English husband and organizes military endeavors such that she introduces into an English barony German and Scottish fighting forces. She thus represents all the harm a foreign consort can effect in her adopted realm. As a result, the Scots appear worse than Saracens in this English romance.

Such a depiction was not unknown in the English-Scottish conflict over Scottish sovereignty in the late thirteenth and early fourteenth centuries. Indeed, rhetoric on both sides during this period repeatedly cast the conflict in terms reminiscent of crusade, and likened the opposing side to Saracens. For example, "Edward II described the Scots as if they were pagans, whose purpose was to destroy the English Church both materially and spiritually. He declared that the Scots burned churches, shed Christian blood, and intended to 'impose tribute on our people and Holy Church.'"[80] Around the same time, a pro-English chronicler indignantly recorded that Scottish prelates "corrupted the ears and minds of nobles and commons, by advice and exhortation, both publicly and secretly, stirring them to enmity against the king and nation who had so effectually delivered them [i.e. the English king and nation]; declaring falsely that it was far more justifiable to attack them than the Saracens."[81] In this way, rhetoric about a distant Other was used to condemn the more proximate Other of the English-Scottish conflict. The same type of move can be discerned in *Sir Beves* when the Scottish foreign queen behaves worse than the Saracen one, and the Scottish character is represented as posing a much greater threat to English baronial and dynastic interests than the religious convert. Beves's mother manifestly refuses to act in a manner that affirms her English husband's power, and instead does everything she can to undermine his and his heir's position as earls of Southampton. Beves's mother thus enacts a Scottish refusal to acknowledge or accept English sovereignty. The distant Other, the Saracen queen, serves to condemn this proximate Other's intransigence by playing a more affirming role in relation to English Christian identities and claims to sovereignty. The representations of Saracen and Scottish consorts thus contrast with each other so as to suggest Scottish rebellion against assertions of English geopolitical prominence, and to condemn the Scots for such rebellion by showing that even non-Christians acknowledge and work to affirm English sovereignty. Once again, a Saracen character in Auchinleck serves as a provocative commentary on challenges facing assertions of "Inglisch" identity in the early fourteenth century.

Chapter Three

Monstrous Intermingling and Miraculous Conversion: Negotiating Cultural Borders in Þe King of Tars[1]

INTRODUCTION

The striking conjunction of Saracen and Scottish consorts in *Sir Beves of Hamtoun,* although a small part of that lengthy romance, begs consideration of the ways in which other Saracen characters in Auchinleck might engage the complex insular politics of the early fourteenth century. This is not to say that Saracens in Auchinleck should be expected to comment explicitly upon these politics. Indeed, a fundamental premise of this book is that Saracens *implicitly* address issues of local western interest by exploring the larger questions that underlie these issues. One such underlying question is the extent to which the integration of different peoples is either desirable or possible. In the late thirteenth and early fourteenth centuries, the incorporation of foreign peoples into English society was very much at issue. Not only did chroniclers repeatedly articulate concerns about the appointment of "aliens" to positions of clerical and political power in England, but multiple efforts were underway to redefine the English king's sovereignty as extending over the Welsh, Scots and French as well as the "Inglisch." One ramification of these efforts was the potential integration of English, Scottish, Welsh, and French subjects. If the English king were successful, one man and his administration would reign over four peoples; political unity would exist where before there had been some diversity. Thus, both domestic and international affairs around the time of Auchinleck's compilation posed questions about the desirability and possibility of integrating different peoples. This chapter contends that Saracen characters in Auchinleck, although they do not comment explicitly on this domestic context, do explore situations in which two different peoples intermingle, and test the possible extent of such cultural integration as well as the forms it can take.

Western texts about Saracens constitute an ideal venue for the consideration of cultural intermingling since a number of these texts depict the conversion of Saracens and the incorporation of these erstwhile others into a Christian community. Chapters One and Two of this book examine, among other things, the respective integrations of Otuel and Josiane, two new converts, into Christian communities. The fact that such integration is inherently part of many tales about Saracens may help to explain these characters' popularity and frequent appearance in Auchinleck; if fourteenth-century English audiences were not interested in stories about the intermingling of peoples, such stories simply would not appear as often as they do. Neither *Otuel a Kni3t* nor *Sir Beves of Hamtoun,* however, foregrounds the issue of cultural integration to the extent that *Þe King of Tars,* the central tale studied in Chapter Three, does. While the texts discussed heretofore depict converts working their way into their new societies, *Þe King of Tars* describes the monstrous progeny of a truly inter-faith marriage between an unconverted Saracen king and a Christian princess, and represents conversion as a comforting alternative to the radical intermingling of two peoples. *Otuel* and *Sir Beves* thus brush up against a question about cultural borders and the integration of peoples that *Þe King of Tars* complicates and engages in full. The question's importance is made clear by the number of texts that address it in some way, but the depth of thinking on the issue is discerned most readily through analysis of *Þe King of Tars.*

From its very beginning, *Þe King of Tars* establishes the differences separating Christian and Saracen, but also simultaneously challenges these distinctions and explores the extent to which the cultural borders dividing these disparate communities can be rewritten. As characters in this tale examine the possibility of rewriting the borders that define and divide two cultural groups, they postulate the possibility of integrating the two groups. Saracen characters and their interactions with Christians offer two models for re-writing these borders and integrating the two communities. The first model is that of the monstrous, inter-faith child, and is the most radical since it posits a wholesale intermingling of Christian and Saracen. The second model is a much more traditional medieval re-writing of cultural borders, and takes the form of conversion from Saracenness to Christianity. This re-writing of cultural borders is much less radical in that it merely rewrites an individual's religious affiliations and not the defining borders of a religious identity. Ultimately, however, in both cases *Þe King of Tars* articulates anxieties about cultural integration and suggests that any move towards the integration of different groups will provoke or involve differentiation, albeit in a variety of ways. Saracen characters in *Þe King of Tars* thus highlight for readers of Auchinleck the ways in which drives toward the integration of disparate peoples are often intertwined with assertions of cultural difference, and show how these two processes are connected.

To argue that *Þe King of Tars* addresses questions pertinent to articulations of English identity in the fourteenth century may seem rather surprising. This Auchinleck text belongs, along with its fellow *Floris and Blauncheflur,* to what has often been called the Matter of Araby or Matter of the East, and both texts have generally been ignored in discussions of the manuscript's investment in English identity.[2] Set in the Middle East, these texts contain neither English characters nor settings, and do not call attention to the fact that their language of presentation is English. Both narratives, however, depict cultural intermingling and thus explore a phenomenon very much involved in articulations of "Inglisch" identity around the time of Auchinleck's compilation. *Þe King of Tars* offers the more explicit and thorough consideration of this issue and forms the centerpiece of this chapter. *Floris and Blauncheflur,* even though much of its opening in Auchinleck has been lost, provides a fascinating alternative vision of cultural intermingling and is discussed at the end of this chapter as an interesting foil to *Þe King of Tars.* Both tales clearly demonstrate that a tale does not need to be about England in order to lay bare issues that underpin interpellations of "Inglisch" identity.

INTEGRATING FOREIGNERS AND APPEALING TO "INGLISCH" IDENTITY

Assertions of a sense of English community in the thirteenth and fourteenth centuries frequently accompany acknowledgement of foreign presences within the political and religious institutions of the realm. Indeed, chronicles from the period abound in references to problems caused by "aliens" for Englishmen. Often, these aliens are foreigners from the Continent who are represented as depriving the English of their rightful patrimonies and prestige. Roger of Wendover, in his *Flores historiarum,* refers to a Flemish plot concocted between King John and his allies in 1215 for the Flemish to "come to England with their wives and children, with the intention of expelling and totally exterminating all the natives, and of possessing the land themselves by perpetual right."[3] Matthew Paris, in his *Chronica majora* entry for 1247, records complaints about papal exactions and recounts the forced insertion of the Pope's family and countrymen into English benefices as well as King Henry III's unpopular advancement of his "uterine brothers" and their entourages from Poitiers and Savoy.[4] According to Matthew, the many marriages arranged between royal wards and foreigners favored by the king made "native nobles and indigenous Englishmen" feel that they were being despised, and resulted in "the nobility of England devolv[ing] in a large measure to unknown foreigners."[5] He adds that "the pride and insults of these foreigners had provoked the determined hatred of the English."[6] The *Chronicle of Bury St. Edmunds* describes the acts of barons in 1263 who "seized the property, wherever it was to be found, of the Roman clergy . . . , and conferred or gave their churches to whomsoever they chose. They treated aliens in the same way."[7] Fourteenth-century chronicles contain similarly resentful references to the integration of foreigners into English society. One northern chronicler, for example, explicitly highlights the foreign origins of Edward II's unpopular protégé, Piers Gaveston, in his condemnation of Gaveston's treatment of English nobles. The chronicler writes in his 1311 entry: "[Piers], confident that he had been confirmed for life in his earldom, albeit he was an alien and had been preferred to so great dignity solely by the king's favor, had now grown so insolent as to despise all the nobles of the land."[8] Here, the incorporation of a foreigner into the high ranks of the nobility promotes the denigration of the English nobility. Including foreigners in English institutions could even prove fatal to Englishmen according to some chronicles. The *Anonimalle Chronicle,* written in the second half of the fourteenth century, records that in 1327 Edward III's Hainault forces "killed many of the English at night" in York, and adds that the marauding Scots escaped from King Edward at Stanhope Park in England partly "because of the jealousy that the [English] lords felt towards the Hainaulters."[9] In this case, foreign elements within the king's retinue are blamed for the deaths of Englishmen and for military failures against the Scots. Each of the chroniclers cited here, then, articulates grave concerns about the insertion of foreign elements into English dynastic, political, religious and military structures. The intermingling of peoples may be a fact of life, but it is dangerous and decidedly undesirable. Moreover, in these examples accounts of the integration of foreigners into English society are interwoven with concomitant assertions of a distinct native population. The presence of identifiable foreign elements within domestic structures fosters the articulation of a cohesive sense of Englishness; integration provokes differentiation. Already the historical pertinence to an English audience of the questions explored in *Þe King of Tars* is becoming clear.

Integration was also an issue among the different cultures of Britain during this period, as English kings worked to number Wales and Scotland among the holdings of the English Crown. Edward I campaigned against the Welsh in 1276–77 and 1282–83, and Welsh uprisings were put down by English forces in 1287, 1294–5, and 1316.[10] Similarly, English relations with Scotland consisted of protracted wars from 1296–1328, and from 1333–57.[11] Repeatedly, English people were asked to finance and serve in conflicts designed to integrate the Welsh and Scots into the English political system by forcing them to submit to English sovereignty. Indeed, rhetoric surrounding these conflicts often expressed a sense that these people were already part of the English polity. The pro-English *Chronicle of Lanercost,* for example, describes the Scots as "deceitful and ungrateful for the benefits they had received from King Edward [I]," and condemns them for "declaring . . . most preposterously that their own oath to King Edward [I] had been made under compulsion, and therefore might be broken under compulsion."[12] Here, the Scottish-English conflict is couched as a matter of disloyal behavior by subjects of the English king who are already integral members of his polity. Ironically, however, appeals for military and financial assistance against the Scots depicted the Scots as a decidedly unintegrated people, as a people so culturally different from the "Inglisch" that, as mentioned in Chapter Two, they intended "to destroy the English Church both materially and spiritually."[13] Military service against the Scots, recruiting propaganda for these wars, and administrative re-organization of military service all fostered similar assertions.[14] Descriptions of the Scots in the early 1300s, then, slipped rhetorically between claims that they were recalcitrant members of the English polity and appeals to make war on them because they were so culturally different from the English. Regal efforts to integrate the Scots and English politically, and thereby collapse the categories of "enemy" and "loyal subject," led to strident assertions of the differences between these two peoples. Interpellations of a cohesive "Inglisch" identity in the early fourteenth century thus emerged as part of efforts to integrate non-English people into the English polity.

One last point of intersection between the historical context of Auchinleck's circulation and *Þe King of Tars* should be noted. As this tale of the East explores the phenomenon of cultural integration, it postulates the existence of a child who incarnates the intermingling of two different peoples. Such a child might also be found in early fourteenth-century England. Edward III was the son of a French princess (Isabella, Charles IV's sister) and an English king (Edward II). Because of this French-English inter-marriage, Edward III was both the King of England and the nephew of a French king who died without a direct heir. As a result, this King of England could claim to be King of France as well, a claim which he began to pursue in the 1330s. Inter-marriage between different groups thus produced a child who collapsed the borders between them. The pursuit of this child's claims of dual inheritance prompted some concerns. Would the subjects of the King of England become subjects of the King of France if Edward succeeded in advancing his claim? How would the French and English peoples be kept distinct? Edward III's own intermingling of cultural affiliations thus prompted consideration of the ways in which the cultural borders dividing peoples and polities could be renegotiated. Although *Þe King of Tars* does not directly mention French-English interactions of the fourteenth century, its tale of the collapse of distinct identities effected by inter-marriage and sexual reproduction engages issues of crucial importance to England around the start of the Hundred Years War

The above discussion of England in the late thirteenth and early fourteenth centuries is not intended to be exhaustive, but rather to sketch out the proximate historical horizon of experiences within which tales about the intermingling of peoples might have been read in early fourteenth-century England. This national historical horizon is explicitly brought to readers' attention in other Auchinleck texts. The manuscript's only chronicle, the *Liber Regum Anglie*, repeatedly lists Wales, Scotland and (sometimes) parts of France among the holdings of English kings from Brut to Edward I, and narrates the forced annexation of these lands by Edward I and others.[15] Thus, the manuscript as a whole evokes for readers the local western contexts within which *Þe King of Tars's* narrative of cultural integration in the East acquires additional importance. Admittedly, however, *Þe King of Tars* does not mention England, the English, or the particular situations outlined above. Its consideration of cultural intermingling takes place within a literary context of Saracen-Christian interaction in which groups are separated by religious faith and race. *Þe King of Tars* thus explores questions of integration and the differentiation it provokes along borders more clearly defined, and rigidly patrolled, in the Middle Ages than those separating the English from the Welsh, French, or Scottish. The text clearly focuses on questions about religious difference and the desirability (or lack thereof) of Saracen-Christian interaction, as will my discussion of it. Nevertheless, given limited English experience of Muslim-Christian intermarriage, the lived relevance of the story's depiction of cultural integration may well have been found in contexts much closer to home for "Inglisch" readers. Those contexts are laid out here as one sounding board against which *Þe King of Tars* resonates. This is not to say that *Þe King of Tars* does not also address western ideas about religious difference and Saracen-Christian intermingling. Rather, the "Inglisch" history sketched out above shows that even as *Þe King of Tars* explicitly draws our attention to the East and questions of religious interaction there, it considers a larger issue of cultural integration at play in more immediate local contexts in the West as well.

THE LITERARY HISTORY OF *ÞE KING OF TARS*

Before I trace my way through *Þe King of Tars's* rich and provocative consideration of cultural integration, it might be helpful to offer a full summary of the narrative and its literary origins as these explain some of the most intriguing aspects of the text's depiction of cultural intermingling. In *Þe King of Tars,* a Saracen Sultan of Damascus proposes marriage to the Christian Princess of Tars. When his suit is refused, he decides to win her by force, and wages a bloody battle against her father, the King of Tars, in which thirty thousand Christians are killed. The Soudan[16] thus wins his lady as she agrees to wed him rather than have any more Christians die fighting for her. After moving to his court, the lady pretends to convert to Islam, but secretly continues to believe in Christ. Upon her apparent conversion to Saracenness, the Soudan marries her and they beget a child born as a "rond of flesche yschore" lacking eyes, nose, feet, hands, limbs, and any other defining features.[17] Each parent reads this monstrous offspring as a sign of the other's false belief, and the Soudan appeals to his gods to heal the lump. When he is unsuccessful, the Lady arranges for the lump's Christian baptism after which it becomes a handsome little boy. The Soudan, suitably impressed, converts to Christianity and in so doing changes his skin color from black to white. He then proceeds, with the aid of his father-in-law, to convert his subjects to Christianity or kill them.

The history of this narrative has been thoroughly laid out by Lillian Herlands Hornstein, Robert Geist, and Judith Perryman.[18] All three agree that *Þe King of Tars* represents an extensive literary elaboration of events recorded in medieval chronicles. The historical events upon which this narrative is built are a series of Tartar military successes in the Middle East.[19] In 1279 a Mongol ruler named Abaga triumphed over Egyptian Muslim forces in Syria.[20] Unlike the *King of Tars* story, however, Abaga's forces did not convert Damascus to Christianity, nor did they have any Christian allies. In 1281, Abaga's brother, united with Christian Armenians and Georgians, battled unsuccessfully against the Muslim Sultan near Damascus.[21] Finally, in 1299, a battle occurred between Muslim Egyptians, and Ghazzan (Abaga's grandson) and his Christian allies from Armenia and Georgia after which, eventually, Damascus was taken. This event is described thus in the 1300 entry in the *Chronicle of Bury St. Edmunds:*

> New joy, new felicity had recently broken upon us from the east. For the great king Ghazan, khan (that is emperor) of the Tartars, made the king of Armenia the chief and leader of his army. Thereupon on the last day of December the first battle was fought against the sultan of Cairo at a place between the two great cities of Gamela and Damascus. There the Saracens were defeated and slain and the sultan fled into the city of Gamela. The leader of the Tartars with the whole of his army pursued him and besieged and captured the said city. The sultan, therefore, fled to Damascus, where at first thousands of Saracens on both sides fell, but at length all the sultan's forces were routed. The sultan himself with only five companions, fled through the wilderness of Cairo to Algar. After this the sultan sent thirty horses laden with gold to the Emperor Ghazan and announced that he wished to hold all his territories from him. Ghazan kept the gold but gave the ambassadors no reply at all, asserting that the treasure he had received was his own and not another's. And lo! when the enemies of the Christians had thus been brought to naught and destroyed, the great khan restored to the Christians all the lands which in former times they possessed.[22]

Perryman summarizes events thus: "On balance, it is probable that the victory of 1279 began the tradition of the Tartar king fighting on behalf of the Christian faith, but that the victory of Ghazzan in 1299 [recited above] gave it its popularity."[23]

A number of European chroniclers reported these historical events shortly after they had occurred. Almost immediately, the events became intertwined with motifs of miraculous conversion and monstrous birth.[24] An originary source from which the various chronicle entries and the Auchinleck text derive their narrative of military conquest, monstrous birth, and miraculous conversion has not been found. Geist, however, argues that the combination may result from an initial chance association of these incidents within a chronicle entry. He points out that the *Annales Polonorum* entry for 1274 records a "story of the conversion of 'rex Thartarorum,' and, juxtaposed to it, without logical relationship[,] the story of an abnormal birth that was transformed by baptism."[25] He suggests that this juxtaposition may have been misread as one event or that a chronicler may have decided to add a causal relationship to the events, and that such an act gave rise to the chronicle narrative underlying *Þe King of Tars*.[26] As Perryman and the *Annales'* editors point out, however, the annals to which Geist refers were written no earlier than 1340–41.[27] They therefore cannot be a direct source for either the Auchinleck text or any of the chronicle analogues that pre-date it. Some similar chronicle entry may underlie these texts, but no such entry has been found or is known to exist.[28] Moreover, none of the analogues has been linked to any other in a direct, causal textual relationship, so the exact origins of the story, and of the Auchinleck tale, are unclear.

The chronicle analogues to *Þe King of Tars* that do exist resemble the Auchinleck text in that they include a Christian wife's conversion of a non-Christian king, their monstrous child's "miraculous transformation," and a military defeat of Saracens "near either Damascus, . . . , or Jerusalem."[29] Six texts that pre-date Auchinleck[30] contain this narrative: the Anglo-Latin *Flores historiarum* (written 1300–1307),[31] Villani's Italian *Istorie Fiorentine* (probably written 1307–30),[32] Rishanger's Anglo-Latin *Chronica* (written 1307–27),[33] a Hispano-Latin letter to Jayme II of Aragon (written 1300–1307),[34] the Germano-Latin *Annales Sancti Rudberti Salisburgenses* (written 1280–1300),[35] and Ottokar's German *Österreichische Reimchronik* (written 1306–8).[36] The first three record the events under the year 1299, the letter to Jayme II of Aragon does not date the events, and the two German chronicles record the events under the year 1280. None of these chronicles is precisely duplicated in *Þe King of Tars*. The Auchinleck tale is unique in its identifications of the Princess as the daughter of the Christian King of Tars rather than the Christian King of Armenia, and of the converted ruler as a Saracen sultan of Damascus rather than a king of Tartars who attacks Saracens.[37] The Saracenness of the Soudan, so central to *Þe King of Tars,* thus represents an Auchinleck diversion from its chronicle analogues, and may testify to a particular manuscript interest in Saracens. The precise nature of the child born of inter-faith marriage also varies in these texts, with only the *Istorie Fiorentine* identifying it, like Auchinleck, as a lump. In addition, the sultan's conversion does not appear in all the analogues, nor, when it does appear, is it ever accompanied by the miraculous change of skin color recounted in Auchinleck.[38] Finally, the conversion of the sultan's people is not always mentioned, but when it is there is no suggestion of the forced, violent conversion that concludes *Þe King of Tars.*[39]

One other Anglo-Latin chronicle that pre-dates Auchinleck should be noted among these analogues even though it does not follow the general story outline. The fourteenth-century *Chronicon de Lanercost* contains an entry for 1280 which describes a lump-child born to the King and Queen of Norway who is made human by the intervention of St Francis.[40] This analogue lacks the emphasis on Christian interactions with non-Christians, does not involve conversion, and is not even set in the Middle East. It is, however, an English narrative that recounts the birth of a monstrous lump and this lump's subsequent healing through divine intervention. The *Chronicon* is particularly interesting because it links its lump story to formative political events in England and Scotland during the late thirteenth and early fourteenth centuries. The *Chronicon* relates its tale of lumpish birth as part of its record of the marriage between the King of Norway who had initially been born as this lump and a Scottish princess. The *Chronicon* also narrates the birth of their daughter. This marital connection between Norway and Scotland did indeed exist historically, and became crucially important for English-Scottish relations when the daughter born of this marriage died at sea en route to Scotland to claim the throne in 1290.[41] Her death led to a contest over the Scottish kingship, which Edward I was invited to resolve. This appeal to Edward enabled the English king to construct himself as overlord of Scotland, and was invoked by him both as evidence of his claim to Scotland and as a justification for his protracted wars against the Scots. In the *Chronicon de Lanercost,* then, a tale of monstrous, lumpish birth and miraculous healing similar to Auchinleck's *King of Tars* is situated at the start of the convoluted chain of events that ultimately evolves into the English-Scottish war that provoked so many questions about integration and differentiation in early fourteenth-century Britain. Moreover, the *Chronicon* lump is connected to depictions of the integration of disparate cultures. It opens a narrative that culminates, within the 1280 entry, in a description of the Scottish princess's arrival in Norway and her formative influence on her new people. In other words, the tale of lumpish birth also introduces a description of the Scottish princess's incorporation into her new community, and her introduction into that community of elements of her own culture. The *Chronicon* states "She comported herself so graciously towards the king and his people that she altered their manners for the better, taught them the French and English languages, and set the fashion of more seemly dress and food."[42] Once again, lumpish births and cultural integration are narratively connected. Thus, although no direct links between the Auchinleck *King of Tars* and the *Chronicon de Lanercost* can be demonstrated, the two texts intriguingly resemble each other in that they both interweave depictions of undefined, lumpish children with narratives about the integration of disparate peoples and cultures.

Apart from the various chronicle entries discussed above, the Middle English poem contained in Auchinleck does not appear to have any literary analogues or potential sources.[43] The Middle English poem can, however, be found in two manuscripts other than Auchinleck: the Vernon manuscript (Oxford, Bodleian Library, English Poetry a. 1), and the Simeon manuscript (London, British Library, Additional 22283). The earliest version is that found in Auchinleck as the other two manuscripts date to the late fourteenth century.[44] Perryman suggests that both the early fourteenth-century Auchinleck text and the later texts of Vernon and Simeon may derive separately from a single composition, now lost.[45] Ultimately, however, Auchinleck represents the earliest extant verse elaboration of chronicle entries like those detailed above, and shares only with its later English versions the identification of the non-Christian ruler as a Saracen, the depiction of the same ruler's change in skin color upon conversion, and the violent confrontation between the Soudan and his own people.

DEFINING, CONSTRUCTING, AND PROBLEMATIZING CULTURAL BORDERS IN *ÞE KING OF TARS*

As *Þe King of Tars* narrates its version of this chronicle tale of inter-faith marriage in the Middle East, it explores issues of integration and differentiation that, as shown above, were also involved in articulations of "Inglisch" identity in the thirteenth and early fourteenth centuries. These issues include: how cultural difference and otherness are defined and constructed, the possibility of unifying different cultural groups, the forms such integration may take, and the ways in which integration provokes differentiation. To explore such matters, the text must first indicate what constitute the differences between Saracens and Christians, and the extent to which such differences preclude integration. Thus, from its very beginning the text defines the borders separating Christian and Saracen. It also, however, challenges the accuracy of such differentiation, and thereby hints at the constructed, contingent nature of cultural borders and at the possibility of integrating disparate peoples.

The early sections of *Þe King of Tars* detail events leading up to the marriage between the Soudan and the Princess, and the birth of their offspring. From its opening, the text works to identify the differences that constitute cultural borders. For example, the early part of the text links Saracens with beasts, an idea underlying many medieval representations of Saracens[46] and found elsewhere in Auchinleck. The Christian King of Tars, according to the Soudan's messenger, calls the Soudan "Heþen hounde" (93) and the narrator describes the inter-faith battle over the Princess as "Þer hewe houndes on Cristen men" (169). Similarly, the Princess, once given to the Soudan, dreams of her situation as comparable to being chased by a hundred black hounds (421–30) and almost caught by one in particular (440–41). References like these, as Perryman notes, "show[ ] the heathen state as beast-like . . . and the Christian state as human."[47] As a result, the differentiation of Saracen and Christian is emphasized.

Þe King of Tars also draws on the typical medieval literary stereotype of the raging Saracen to differentiate Christians and Saracens.[48] When the Soudan hears that his suit has been rejected by the King of Tars,

> Also a wilde bore he ferd;
> His robe he rent adoun;
> His here he rent of heued & berd.
> He schuld venge him wiþ his swerd,
> He swore bi seyn Mahoun.
> Þe table so heteliche he smot
> It fel into þe flore fot-hot,
> & loked as a lyoun.
> Al þat he rau3t, he smot doun ri3t;
> . . . . .
> Al þus þe soudan ferd ypli3t,
> Al þat day & alle þat ni3t. (98–110)

Wildness and bestiality are once again associated with the Saracen, and so is fierce anger. As Perryman notes, the Soudan's tantrum stands in marked contrast to the Christian princess's reasoned discussion with her parents.[49] The Princess speaks "wiþ wordes stille" (274) and "Wiþ resoun ri3t & euen" (276). The differences between Christian and Saracen are thus further emphasized.

The differences are also highlighted by the Christian response to the Soudan's offer of marriage. While the Saracen ruler is prepared to overcome, or at least blur, the Christian-Saracen divide through marriage, his proposal prompts the King of Tars to declare that he "wald arst spille min hert blode / In bateyl to ben yslawe" (41–42) rather than give his daughter to a Saracen. Similarly, the Princess herself says

> "Ihesu, mi Lord in trinite,
> Lat me neuer þat day yse
> A tirant forto take.
> . . . .
> 3if him arst tene & wrake." (61–66)

The Princess eventually withdraws her opposition to prevent any more bloodshed (223–37), but her mother's initial reaction to this is to refuse her assent to the match since such a wedding means her daughter's destruction: "Y no schal neuer þerto conseyle / Our douhter forto schende" (263–64). This Christian opposition is, historically, quite accurate. For example, the

Council of Nablus decreed in 1120 that "male Saracens who married Latin women should be castrated," and the Church's prohibition of inter-faith marriage was in effect at the time of *Þe King of Tars's* composition.[50] Historically, Muslims also often opposed such inter-faith unions, licit or illicit,[51] but this is not a point of similar tenet identified in *Þe King of Tars*. The Christians' reactions instead further delineate a distinction between Christian and Saracen. Thus, *Þe King of Tars* opens with events and statements that reinforce the division of Saracen from Christian.

At other places, however, the poem challenges the accuracy of this division, thereby hinting at the constructed and contingent nature of difference even as it invokes it. To begin with, while it is certainly true that connotations of bestiality fall squarely on the Saracen side of the divide, at other points *Þe King of Tars* undercuts the division such references work to create. For example, although the King of Tars does not behave "Also a wilde bore" or a "lyoun" (98, 105) when he is angry, his fury at the Soudan's marriage proposal does push him to the brink of madness. According to the narrator, "Almost for wretþe he [the king] wex ner wode" (38). Perryman considers this a contrast with the Soudan's behavior, and to some extent it is, but madness is not that far removed from a bestial temper tantrum in medieval literature.

Other aspects of the early part of *Þe King of Tars* also complicate the task of identifying the supposedly clear difference between Christian and Saracen. For example, the action begins when the Soudan is presented as having succumbed to "amor de lonh," a love born out of hearsay,[52] for the King's daughter:

> Þe los of hir [the Princess of Tars] gan spring wide
> In oþer londes bi ich a side;
> So þe soudan herd it say.
> Him þou3t his hert it brast ofiue
> Bot 3if he mi3t haue hir to wiue
> Þat was so feir a may. (19–24)

This type of physical desire for an unseen woman is explicitly associated with Saracen lands in some medieval lyrics,[53] but it is usually western Christian men who experience it upon hearing about women in the East.[54] Thus, *Þe King of Tars* uses a literary trope usually associated with the desires of western, Christian men to describe a Saracen man,[55] and this portrait of desire complicates the definitive division the text seems to draw between the two identities.

In addition, the poem explicitly points out other attitudes shared by Christian and Saracen men. It explains that, having won the lady by battle, the Soudan will not marry her until she converts to his law:

> Noiþer for fo no fre[n]de
> For noþing wold he neyʒe þat may
> Til þat sche leued opon his lay,
> Þat was of Cristen kende.
> Wel loþe war a Cristen man
> To wedde an heþen woman
> Þat leued on fals lawe;
> Als loþ was þat soudan
> To wed a Cristen woman,
> As y finde in mi sawe. (405–14)

Here, the poet deliberately highlights a Saracen desire for married people to share one religious belief, and points out how such a desire traverses Saracen-Christian borders. The text thereby again attributes to the Soudan some resemblance to Christian men, and complicates the definitive division the text initially seemed to draw between people of two faiths. Interestingly, this evocation of Saracen-Christian similarity seems particularly troubling within the text. The narrator's "As y finde in mi sawe" indicates a desire to validate his observation in some way, and perhaps to acknowledge that his point might be a problematic claim for some. His words may point to a discomfort created by the way in which similarities between Christian and Saracen men open up the possibility of rewriting the cultural groups' borders.

The Princess, too, blurs Saracen-Christian differentiation. The day after her arrival at the Soudan's court, she is brought before his Saracen idols[56] and acquiesces in apparent apostasy of the Christian faith after the Soudan threatens to kill her father if she will not become Saracen (470–80). At this point, the last significant action before the climactic birth of the "flesche," the tale's undercutting of differentiation becomes most apparent. The Princess says, "To Mahoun ichil me take, / & Ihesu Crist, mi Lord, forsake / Þat made Adam & Eve" (487–89). The narrator elaborates on this scene, describing the Soudan's joy and instructions in the Saracen way of worship, and then describes how the Princess

> . . . kist Mahoun & Apolin,
> Astirot, & sir Iouin,
> For drede of wordes awe.
> & while sche was in þe temple [þer]

Of Teruagant & Iubiter
Sche lerd þe heþen lawe. (499–504)

At this moment, the Princess is, for all intents and purposes, a Saracen. Since lines 383–84, she has been "cladde, / As [heþen][57] wiman were," and now she has performed the religious acts of a Saracen. Her appearance and behaviors are those of a Saracen woman. The Princess, however, is still Christian, or so the text assures its readers by depicting the Princess, the night before her apostasy, as experiencing a dream in which Jesus promises to help her in her time of need (421–56). The text also tries to contain the implications of her actions by stating, after twenty-five lines describing her physical acts of Saracen worship, that " . . . þei sche al þe lawes couþe, / & seyd hem openliche wiþ hir mouþe, / Ihesu for3at sche nou3t" (505–7).

As various medieval texts and scholars make clear, however, it is no small matter that the Princess takes on the appearance of a Saracen. One crusade chronicle, for example, claims that "appearance is governed by character. Whatever sort of character the ruler has, it is naturally reflected in outer appearance."[58] For this medieval writer, internal "character" and external "appearance" are not as separable as *Þe King of Tars* might have us believe. The medieval romance *Silence,* which depicts a woman who dresses and successfully passes as a male squire and knight, contains a similar suggestion. As Susan Crane points out, passages in *Silence* indicate that the adoption of specific clothes and the performance of duties attached to those clothes effect a deep and substantial alteration of the individual that verges on the biological: "Although Nature keeps insisting that only Silence's clothes are masculine, she [Nature] spends three days at the end of the romance 'a repolir / Par tolt le cors et a tolir / Tolt quanque ot sor le cors de malle' [refinishing Silence's entire body, removing every trace of anything that being a man had left there]."[59] Here, the effects of masculine garments and behaviors cannot be erased merely by removing the garments and ceasing the behaviors.

Given such assertions about the permeability of the boundaries between the body, its clothing, and its cultural identities, the Princess of Tars's Saracen attire, visible acts (kissing the idols), and words (she says all the Saracen laws "openliche wiþ hir mouþe" (506)), cannot be taken lightly. They suggest rather strongly that the Princess should be categorized as Saracen at this moment. The text still, however, doggedly insists that she is Christian and that "No minstral wiþ harp no crouþe / No mi3t chaunge hir þou3t" (509–10). The Princess thus represents a serious case of category confusion, and exemplifies the challenges of determining who is Christian and who is Saracen. At this point, the tale's undercutting of differentiation is most apparent.[60] The heroine conveys the appearance of one identity (Saracenness), and yet supposedly retains another diametrically opposed identity (Christianity). One is squarely confronted by the question of whether the Princess has successfully maintained that division between Saracens and Christians that was so emphasized by her family, and yet so problematized by other parts of *Þe King of Tars*. Her situation suggests that it is very difficult to maintain the borders between Christianity and Saracenness when the distinctions between the two are somewhat fuzzy and when one is completely immersed in a Saracen world. Once more, the definitiveness of the boundaries between Christian and Saracen is challenged in *Þe King of Tars*.

Ultimately, however, the poem requires the reader to accept that the Princess is still Christian. The text assures us, after twenty-five lines of strong suggestion otherwise, that

> Þe soudan wende niȝt & day
> Þat sche hadde leued opon his lay,
> Bot al he was bicouȝt .
> For when sche was bi hirselue on
> To Ihesu sche made hir mon,
> Þat alle þis world haþ wrouȝt. (511–16)

Unless we wish to misread events as the Soudan does, we must accept that the Princess is still essentially, in some way, Christian. There is no doubt, however, that her behavior seriously raises the question of how difference is different, how sameness is same, and of how these categories of different and same get constructed in the establishment of cultural borders. As a result, the possibility of rewriting these borders, and integrating Saracens and Christians, is opened up.

MONSTROUS INTERMINGLING

Given the text's rather anxious assurances that the Princess is still really Christian, one must accept that events following her seeming apostasy represent an integration of Saracen and Christian cultures, an integration for which preceding events have prepared the audience by challenging ideas about the insurmountability of the borders between the two groups. Those borders are decisively surmounted when, after the Princess's apparent conversion, the Soudan weds her, and they conceive a child (565–67). Since the newlyweds are still different, still Saracen and Christian despite the Princess's performance of Saracenness, the text's narration of this event constitutes a radical exploration of integration because it depicts what were for medieval Christians the ultimate union of separate entities: marriage and sex. To begin with, marriage theologically made man and woman one unit.[61] In addition, medieval western Christians understood that "sexual relations, whether licit or illicit, meant that the partners became one flesh,"[62] or, as David Nirenberg summarizes the canonical position, "'unity of flesh' was achieved whenever there was 'mixing of blood.'"[63] Inter-faith sexual relations were thus a charged issue in the Middle Ages since they undermined the separation of religions. As a result, prohibitions of inter-faith sex and marriage abounded.[64] While most literary texts, like *Sir Beves of Hamtoun,* avoid contravening this cultural taboo by having the non-Christian convert before marriage, *Þe King of Tars* depicts intercourse that falls squarely into the prohibited area. [65] As a result, *Þe King of Tars* does not present a minimal integration of Saracen and Christian, or a negotiation of differences in which some distinctiveness may be maintained, but rather a culturally charged unification of peoples. Two separate peoples become the one flesh that medieval Christians believed resulted from the mingling of bloods in sexual intercourse. *Þe King of Tars* thus presents in its narrative the most intimate integration of peoples possible for western Christians in the Middle Ages.

This integration, moreover, produces offspring and thereby incarnates the breakdown of the borders separating Christians from Saracens. Such incarnation extends *Þe King of Tars's* depiction of the integration of different peoples. It also represents the radical possibility of escaping cultural categorization and division altogether. The child of the unconverted Princess and her Saracen husband constitutes a being which unites Christian and Saracen identities, and therefore defies religious identification. Theoretically, the child offers the possibility of no longer needing to concern oneself with cultural differences since it conflates such differences. As *Þe King of Tars* examines the question of Saracen-Christian integration, it thus explores the possibility of an existence which eludes religious differentiation and thereby tears down cultural borders.

The physical form such existence takes, however, is troubling:

& when þe child was ybore
Wel sori wimen were þerfore,
For lim no hadde it non.
Bot as a rond of flesche yschore
In chaumber it lay hem bifore
Wiþouten blod & bon.
For sorwe þe leuedi wald dye

For it hadde noiþer nose no eye,
Bot lay ded as þe ston. (577–85)

The intermingling of Saracen and Christian, and the collapse of the borders separating two peoples, produce a fascinating, disconcerting lump of flesh. Such a representation of Saracen-Christian integration raises many questions.

First, one must consider why a lump of flesh should appear as the progeny of Saracen-Christian union. Other medieval portraits of such unions do not depict the children produced as lumps. For example, Wolfram von Eschenbach's *Parzival* narrates a situation in which a black Saracen Queen (Belacane) and a white Angevin knight (Gahmuret) give birth to a black-and-white spotted boy (Feirefiz).[66] Lived situations of Christian-Saracen sex, such as those in Spain or Outremer, certainly did not give rise to any fantastical ideas about lumpish children. As David Nirenberg points out: "No Iberian writer fantasized, as the German Wolfram von Eschenbach did, that the offspring of a Christian-Muslim couple would be mottled white and black: they knew better."[67] One might posit that the Auchinleck "flesche" is thus a product of ignorance on the part of an English redactor. But this answer, in addition to presuming information for which we have no concrete evidence, does not explain why a lump should appear, as opposed to Wolfram's vision of mottled humanity, or as opposed to any other form. To understand the situation presented in Auchinleck, one must examine the literary history underlying the text and its lump of "flesche," the careful textual construction of the relationship between the "flesche"'s mother and father, and the reproductive theory that might be at play in this situation.

Chronicle analogues helpfully illuminate *Þe King of Tars* by showing avenues of development that it either does not follow in its representation of a mixed heritage child as a lump of "flesche," or that it embroiders in interesting ways. In the analogues that pre-date Auchinleck, the union of two faiths produces a child that is somewhat monstrous. In Ottokar's *Österreichische Reimchronik,* the child is half-beautiful and half-ugly. Here the half-and-half divide signals the incompatibility of the two religious identities. The use of half-and-halfness to express irreconcilable division between two different cultural groups also turns up in the *Annales Sancti Rudberti Salisburgenses,* where the child is half-smooth and half-hairy, and in the letter written to Jayme II of Aragon in which the child is half-animal, half-human. In the Anglo-Latin *Flores historiarum* and Rishanger's *Chronica* the child is presented as entirely hairy. Only in the Italian *Istorie Fiorentine* and the Anglo-Latin *Chronicon de Lanercost* does the offspring appear as the undifferentiated lump also found in Auchinleck. Lillian Herlands Hornstein suggests that the cases where the child is either lumpish, hairy or otherwise bestial may result from a version of events similar to that in the Lanercost *Chronicon,* which states that the child "resembled more the offspring of a bear than a man, as it were a formless lump of flesh."[68] Hornstein points out that medieval bestiaries often portrayed the bear's offspring born as a shapeless lump which had to be licked into shape by its mother's tongue.[69] She writes, "To one transcriber or translator the bear's-cub simile might mean the shapeless lump of the bear in the bestiary, to another the rough hairy qualities of the animal."[70] She also suggests that there may have been a misreading of "ursus" ("bear") for "hirsutus" ("hairy"). It should be noted, however, that no conclusive evidence supports Hornstein's hypothesis since she posits an as yet unfound originary reference common to many parts of Europe which concretely exists only in the Lanercost *Chronicon.* Even if she is correct, however, it is important to note that some chroniclers decide to maintain the half-and-half divide so expressive of the parents' religious difference, while others embrace the unformed lumpishness, and use baptism as a type of mother bear's tongue to lick the mixed heritage child into Christian shape. Creative choice may certainly have played a role in the varying interpretations of a reference to bear-like offspring.

The literary-historical answer to the question of why a lump appears in Auchinleck's *King of Tars,* then, seems to be that the "rond of flesche yschore" (580) represents a tradition also found elsewhere (e.g. the Italian *Istorie Fiorentine*) which may have been chosen to convey a reference to bear-like offspring. This is not to say, however, that no significance should be attached to the representation of integrated peoples as a lump in Auchinleck. On the contrary, the lump engages issues that a half-and-half child does not. While a half-and-half child suggests that sex does not intermingle cultures to the extent that they become indistinguishable, a lump insists that cross-cultural intercourse means the end of any ability to differentiate cultural groups and inheritances. For example, Wolfram von Eschenbach uses his character Feirefiz, the black-and-white spotted boy, to signal visually the separateness of Saracen maternal inheritances (black skin spots) from Christian paternal ones (white skin spots). For Wolfram, it is important that what is Christian be separated from what is Saracen, a fact seen in the repeated motif of Christian men severing relations with Saracen women in *Parzival.*[71] The Middle English *King of Tars,* however, frustrates any such desire to distinguish Christian from Saracen and preserve the separateness of the two groups. The lump's uniform physical form decisively refuses a biological division of Christian and Saracen, and instead confronts readers with a situation in which cultural inheritances cannot be disentangled. The Middle English tale thus radicalizes its portrait of the integration of differences effected by inter-faith sexual union.

Interestingly, English versions of the chronicle story seem particularly invested in the mixed-heritage offspring's unity of being. In all the English versions (Anglo-Latin and vernacular), the child is either uniformly hairy or uniformly lumpish, both situations that insist on a thorough integration of the parents' differences. The lump version of the story also seems to have cir-culated particularly widely in England. Only one non-English source uses the lump motif, and only in England does the story (in its lump motif ver-sion) take on an extensively developed literary form. Of the three Middle English versions of *Þe King of Tars,* the Auchinleck text appears most heavily invested in the offspring's formlessness. The Auchinleck poem consistently uses the term "flesche" to describe the lump of flesh between birth and bap-tism,[72] while the Vernon and Simeon manuscripts merely use the term "flesche" at the offspring's birth to describe its formlessness. The two later manuscripts then exclusively label the lump as "child," "hit," or "wrecche." Auchinleck thus continually returns its readers' attention to the formlessness of the mixed faith offspring while the other manuscripts downplay this mon-strosity. The wholeness of the lump, and the fact that no aspect of it can be differentiated from another, explain why this monstrous image is so repeat-edly emphasized in Auchinleck. The image drives home to readers the extent of the cultural intermingling that has occurred; nothing of either Saracen or Christian can be definitively identified in this mixed heritage offspring and, consequently, one is forced to confront the fact of pervasive cultural integra-tion that it represents. Emphasizing the lump's monstrous appearance both communicates this fact, and keeps attention riveted on it.

Other aspects of the Auchinleck text also work to focus audience atten-tion on the fact that the lump inextricably conflates two peoples. Unlike some analogues of the tale (namely the *Istorie Fiorentine*), the Auchinleck text contains no accusation that the queen has committed adultery or bes-tiality. The Auchinleck Soudan also does not deny involvement in the pro-duction of the "flesche." In the *Flores historiarum,* the father disowns the child and orders it burned, while in the *Istorie Fiorentine,* the letter to Jayme II of Aragon, and Ottokar's *Österreichische Reimchronik,* the mother and child are condemned to death as the father attempts to sever any links to them. These narrative incidents in the analogues temporarily distract read-erly attention from the sexual intermingling of cultures that has occurred, and postulate other possible explanations for the monstrous birth. *Þe King of Tars,* however, insists from the moment of the lump's appearance that both father and mother shaped it. Indeed, the Princess explicitly states that "Þe child was ȝeten bitven ous to" (604). The Auchinleck text thus immediately focuses the reader's attention on the fact that the "flesche" constitutes a monstrous intermingling of both his parents' group identities.

This notion of equal parental responsibility for the appearance of the "flesche" is borne out by medieval theories of reproduction that may also underlie Auchinleck's rather bizarre portrait of a lump. First, the Soudan can be seen to carry some biological responsibility for his offspring's monstrosity. After the dissemination of Aristotelian thought, it was generally agreed that male sperm played the formative role in human reproduction. As Joan Cadden explains it, "woman supplie[d] the matter for reproduction, and sperm [wa]s the agent."[73] Other thinkers asserted that sperm "ma[d]e the foetus human or animal," or that weak sperm failed to transmit the father's characteristics to the child.[74] A child is thus a mixture of its mother's matter and its father's shaping form. Given this model, the Soudan in *Þe King of Tars* seems to have failed to perform adequately in the conception of the "flesche." The Soudan's defining characteristic in this text, however (as shown by his lack of any other appellation than the Saracen-linked title "Soudan"), is his Saracenness, thus his religious identity can be seen to have been inadequate to the task of shaping a Christian woman's matter. The Princess, however, is also a potential problem. Medieval writers often asserted that images presented to the woman's spirit during conception influenced the form of the embryo; thus, an adulterous woman might give birth to a child "resembling the deceived husband and not the natural father" since her shame brought her husband's image to mind during the act of conception.[75] Gerald of Wales further clarifies the mother's role in shaping the appearance of her child when he recounts the story of a queen who meditated upon the image of a black person in a painting so much that her child was born black.[76] Accordingly, the "flesche"'s form, or lack thereof, could reflect its mother's failure to envision a proper child emerging from her union with the Soudan. At the time of the lump's conception, the Princess is the only character, besides the narrator, who knows that her marital relationship with the Soudan sits squarely within the prohibited space of Saracen-Christian sex and thereby undermines that divide between Christian and Saracen that the early part of the text, and particularly her Christian family, established. Her awareness of compromised cultural borders may thus have played a role in the formation of the lump. All told, medieval reproductive theories assert that both parents have the potential to cause deformity in a child. Such theories thus offer no decisive answer to the question of which parent is responsible for the "flesche" in Auchinleck, but instead leave the question of responsibility open while suggesting the existence of some problem in the sexual intermingling of the two parents.

According to the Auchinleck *King of Tars,* the main problem in the sexual intermingling of the Soudan and the Princess is religious difference. Whatever the literary history or the scientific ideas that may underlie the lump's appearance in Auchinleck, both parents read this appearance in religious terms. Each actively blames the other's belief system for the deformation. The Soudan says to his wife, "Þe childe þat is here of þe born / Boþe lim & liþ it is forlorn / Alle þurth þi fals bileue" (592–94). The lady immediately ripostes, however: "Leue sir, lat be þat þou3t. / Þe child was 3eten bitven ous to; / For þi bileue it farþ so" (603–5). The Soudan and the Princess thus explicitly indicate that the "flesche" is a product of both its parents and an entity that intermingles Saracenness and Christianity. Why the parents both immediately blame religious difference for the "flesche"'s appearance is unclear, but the fact that they do so emphasizes that the "flesche" is to be read as a physical commingling of two disparate religious identities.

The problem for the "flesche," then, is not simply that it is of the wrong faith; rather, it is too intermingled to have one faith. It represents a wholesale integration of Christian and Saracen, and occupies an undefined space between the two religions even as it unites them and incarnates that unification. Lacking limbs, blood, bones, and features, the "flesche" lies beyond the realm of human definition and identification. From a Christian perspective (which is that of the poem), the "flesche" exists outside the law. It is the product of a union considered illegal in Canon Law, and it defies all customary laws about human appearance. It exists outside of language because it has no power of speech and no name. It also exists outside of religious identification; one cannot call it Christian because it is not baptized, but one cannot call it Saracen since it is so indeterminate. The lump thus escapes identification, and embodies a monstrous indeterminacy created by the loss of defining cultural borders.

David Williams argues that in medieval Europe border-problematizing monsters like the "flesche" served as a way of getting outside traditional epistemologies or ways of conceptualizing, analyzing, and categorizing phenomena.[77] According to Williams, medieval monsters reminded people of "the fragility and incompleteness of ontological and cognitive orders," and served as "the third term, the copula, the mediation between all those entities doomed, by logic and language, never to be joined."[78] In the light of such ideas, the monstrous "flesche" can be read as a mediator of binary division and an integration of disparate entities. Because the "flesche" is produced by both its parents, it conflates the categories of Saracen and Christian, and problematizes the differentiation of these groups by its very existence. The "flesche" therefore provokes a questioning of how cultural

borders get constructed, and opens a space for the re-writing of these borders somewhere in between them, in the space in which it exists.

As it lies outside, and challenges, religious and social categories while
being linked to them through its parentage, the "flesche" can be read both
positively and negatively. To lay out these readings, I wish to draw not only on
Williams's work, but also on that of Julia Kristeva. While Kristeva's notion of
abjection may seem quite removed from *Þe King of Tars,* it is a modern analysis of the social position of being outside the Law, a set of prohibitions that
she identifies as involving language, religion, and morality as well as societies'
legal systems and decrees. She works out what it means to occupy this position in a thorough manner that helps one to think about various aspects of
the "flesche." Admittedly, the time period to which her model mainly refers is
far distant from the one I am dealing with, but she does link her ideas back to
Christian notions that are very much at stake in the situation I am discussing.[79] Thus, both Williams and Kristeva help one to think through the
cultural function of the "flesche" within its medieval text.

This cultural function is very much linked to the lump's position of
exteriority in relation to religious and social constructs. To occupy a position
that contravenes such constructs is to occupy a position beyond traditional
cultural borders. Williams and Kristeva both identify positive aspects to the
position of existing outside traditional cultural borders. Williams identifies
this position both as that of monstrosity in the Middle Ages, and as akin to
the mystical "via negativa," which produces new knowledge of God by tran-
scending affirmative, rational, logic- and language-bound statements that
never really get at God's true nature because God is beyond categories.[80]
Monsters thus offer a more comprehensive way of thinking about, and understanding, the divine. Kristeva also recognizes a positive aspect to existing outside traditional cultural borders. She considers this position one from which a
true re-ordering of social elements can take place, a re-ordering that would
elide the harshness of the subject's lived relationship to language and social
dictates.[81] As she explains it, this position is "edged with the sublime," and
constitutes "the moment when revelation bursts forth."[82] Another way in
which she expresses this is to state that the more the subject strays away from
the epistemological categories constraining social existence, "the more he is
saved."[83] Reading the "flesche" in this aspect of its position is quite interesting. Because it lies outside, or in between, the binary opposition between
Saracen and Christian, the "flesche" offers a mode of existence unstructured
by religious borders. In other words, the "flesche" represents a space in which
two peoples can be interwoven into a new, undifferentiated entity. The lump
posits an alternative mode of interaction between differentiated peoples, and a

re-definition of their identities and cultural borders. In this way, the "flesche" offers a vision of Saracen-Christian integration and an alternative to war and hostility between the two groups.

Such an integration, however, is depicted as completely undesirable in *Þe King of Tars*. The women who assist at the birth are described as being "Wel sori" at the sight of the "flesche" (578), while the lump's mother "For sorwe . . . wald dye" (583), and lies "in care & wo" (602). The Soudan, too, is grieved by his offspring's shapelessness: "In hert he was agreued sore / To sen þat selcouþe si3t" (686–87). Whatever potential for integration is represented by the "flesche," it is not one that any character in the poem desires. The intermingling of peoples produces a biological indeterminacy that horrifies and troubles the community to which the child belongs. Kristeva best explains the nature of such horror. She argues that a position beyond the borders of society, while it offers an opportunity for new modes of existence, menaces the societies to which it is related with collapse and chaos because the prohibitions that define social identity and contain aggression are perverted or ignored. Kristeva describes the situation as "the *fading away* of all meaning and all humanity," and as a "moment of . . . suicide."[84] She links this type of borderline position with repugnance and horror, calling it "death infecting life" among other things.[85] This situation seems analogous to the effects the "flesche" has on its viewers, and suggests the problems posed by a fusion of Christian and Saracen. What would Christianity look like without differentiation from other groups? How would it define itself without an "other" to fight, conquer, or convert? No such Christianity was widespread at the time of *Þe King of Tars*'s composition and circulation when the Papacy actively constructed others opposed to it for investigation, examination, and punishment,[86] and when, as Lisa Lampert has shown, Christianity continued to define itself, as it had for centuries, "by claiming its difference from Judaism and from Jews."[87] Saracens, too, were serviceable "others" in relation to whom Christian uniqueness could be asserted, but in *Þe King of Tars* the lump enacts an integration of Christian and Saracen that threatens such religious self-definition with chaotic overthrow. Ending differentiation, as the lump does, would deprive Christianity of its defining foes, and reproduce socially the horror of the lump's own indeterminacy. A mode of existence like that of the "flesche" would get rid of faith's defining differentiating components, those boundaries that ideally structure social behavior, and offer nothing except integration in their place. The "flesche" and the horror it provokes in *Þe King of Tars* thus testify to a need for those divisions problematized earlier in the poem, and ultimately elided by sexual intercourse between the lump's parents. The text produces, in the "flesche," an exceptional situation, outside nature, of non-differentiation. As the reactions of the characters show, there is nothing desirable about unification in these terms, and so it is no surprise that after the appearance of the "flesche" *Þe King of Tars* forcibly re-inscribes the divisions between Saracen and Christian, and vehemently asserts the differences between the two groups. Cultural differentiation emerges as the necessary counterweight to the hideousness of cultural integration.

Cultural differentiation reappears when the Soudan and Princess decide that their respective gods should be invoked to heal the lump. When prayers to the Saracen gods prove futile (see lines 625–72), the "flesche" is given Christian baptism, upon which

> It hadde liif & lim & fas,
> & crid wiþ gret deray.
> & hadde hide & flesche & fel,
> & alle þat euer þerto bifel. (776–79)

With baptism, adherence to one law, the Christian, is firmly imposed on the "flesche," and this ends its hideous indefinition and integration of Christian and Saracen identities.

Christening here is presumably accompanied by the lump's acquisition of a Christian soul, and this shapes the formless body since, in the later Middle Ages, the soul was believed to provide form to the matter of human flesh.[88] With the firm choice of one cultural identity, a clear form emerges from the "flesche." The benefits of differentiation, and the superiority of Christianity, are asserted simultaneously, and the borders separating Saracen from Christian are resurrected.

In sum, the "flesche" in *Þe King of Tars* offers readers one monstrous model for the integration of Saracen and Christian communities. The "flesche"'s existence posits a space in which the borders separating and defining Christianity and Saracenness may be completely torn down, and in which a new, intermingled cultural entity unstructured by borders may emerge. Precisely this "unstructuredness," however, demands that the "flesche"'s space of integration be shut down. No borders and no structure mean no social, cultural, or biological intelligibility, and thus no humanity for the "flesche." So the text, having blurred the borders separating Saracen and Christian, and pushed lack of differentiation to its collapsing point, displays that collapse as a horror, and decisively resurrects the cultural borders of religion. Re-writing cultural borders in a way that tears them down and intermingles separate entities is thus represented as a monstrous, disturbing possibility. Whatever model of cultural integration is to be practiced between disparate groups, it must involve differentiation. Henceforth the text advocates conversion, and its concomitant affirmation of difference, as the preferred, less radical method of integrating peoples.

MIRACULOUS CONVERSION

As the second model of integration discussed in this chapter is conversion, I would like to outline briefly some general characteristics of this process. First, even though conversion incorporates non-Christians into a Christian community, it is rooted in differentiation, and is therefore a much less radical model of integration than that offered by the lump and its intermingling of Saracen and Christian. The changing of an individual's religious beliefs, and his or her subsequent inclusion into a new group, is not an integration of two different groups in the sense of an equivalent interpenetration of various elements of each group's identity as they unite to form a new entity. Rather, conversion rewrites individual differences in a way that simultaneously asserts the borders between, and the differences defining, religious groups. To advocate conversion as the preferred method of dealing with cultural difference is therefore not to advocate an intermingling of Christian and Saracen but instead to suggest that Saracens should abandon their defining differences in favor of becoming Christian. Conversion means conformity to the cultural borders separating Saracen from Christian rather than compromise of them. A Saracen convert is defined precisely by his or her adherence to the norms distinguishing a Christian community from a Saracen one. Conversion thus forcibly pulls individuals over that space of indeterminacy and cultural intermingling where the "flesche" exists, not to break down the borders between peoples, but rather to re-draw the lines marking those borders around ever larger numbers of Christians. To examine the issue of integration within a context of conversion, then, is to examine it within a context that already involves a certain amount of differentiation.

The second point to be made about conversion is that widespread medieval models of the process underlie its depiction in *Þe King of Tars.* Two of the best-known conversions in the Middle Ages were those of St. Paul,[89] and St. Augustine of Hippo. The biblical account of Saul's metamorphosis from vehement persecutor of the Christian Church into one of its foremost apostles emphasizes the role of miraculous, divine intervention in conversion. As Saul travels to Damascus in pursuit of Christians, a light from heaven descends on him, and the voice of God rebukes him, thereby changing Saul's beliefs and turning him into one of Christ's most important proselytizers. The same type of divine intervention can be seen in Augustine's narrative of the experience that finally enabled him to abandon the pleasures of the flesh for those of the spirit. Shamed by the account of another man's conversion to Christianity, Augustine laments his own inability to make a full commitment to the Christian way of life. He then hears a message from God directing him to read a part of the Bible which advises him to pay no heed to the lusts of the flesh.[90] This incident enables Augustine to renounce his past and take the final steps toward baptism. As both these narratives make clear, model conversions in the Middle Ages involved divine intervention and, with it, a definitive turn away from sin to Christ.

Another notion of conversion is also conveyed in these two narratives, as has been discussed by Karl Morrison in reference to twelfth-century monastic life. This notion is that of conversion as an ongoing struggle.[91] Augustine's *Confessions* articulate this most clearly. Not only must Augustine wrestle against lust and other sins before his definitive acceptance of Christianity, but even afterwards, he recounts daily struggles to remain in a right relationship with God.[92] Paul, too, finds himself struggling to do the work of God, although he must battle not only against sin, but also against the suspicion his sudden conversion engenders among his fellow apostles. They refuse to accept him as one of their own until the apostle Barnabas, a witness to events on the Road to Damascus, vouches for the sincerity of Paul's conversion.[93] The two narratives, even as they affirm a role for the divine in conversion, indicate a decidedly human aspect of the process which is well exemplified in tales of Saracens: namely, that conversion does not guarantee instantaneous or easy assimilation into the way of Christ. One must continually prove the veracity of one's conversion and, in Paul's narrative at least, there is a recognition that the human capacity for dissimulation might make it difficult for converts to convince their new communities of their changed identity.[94]

The Saracen sultan's conversion in *Þe King of Tars* manifests three characteristics of conversion listed above: conversion's links to differentiation, its susceptibility to divine intervention, and its need to be repeatedly attested. The Sultan's experience also suggests that conversion is an incredibly powerful way of re-writing cultural borders, albeit according to a model of assimilation rather than one of lumpish intermingling.

After the "flesche" has been shaped by Christian baptism, the Princess informs the Soudan, who is rejoicing in what the text now terms "þis child" (807), that he has no further claim to the child or her unless he converts:

> "3a, sir, bi seyn Martin,
> 3if þe haluendel wer þin

Wel glad miȝt þou be."
"O dame," he seyd, " hou is þat?
Is it nouȝt min þat y biȝat?"
"No sir," þan seyd sche,
"Bot þou were cristned so it is
Þou no hast no part þeron, ywis,
Noiþer of þe child ne of me." (808–16)

At this point, the child can be definitively ascribed to one parent. With the clear inscription of one religion, the lines of possession in the child are firmly drawn. Not even half will belong to the Sultan unless he converts. We have moved from a space of indeterminacy to one of strict divisions like those figured in the half-and-half products of inter-faith unions in some analogues to *Þe King of Tars.* With her claim of ownership, however, the Princess attempts to erase completely the role of the Saracen in the child's creation. She renounces the sexual begetting of the child invoked by the Soudan so as to revoke the sexual union of differences that created the "flesche." The only parental influence is now Christian and, if the Soudan will not convert and become Christian, he cannot exist as a parent. The text thus moves towards a firm construction of difference, and the Princess's words effectively re-draw the borders separating Christian from Saracen.

The text itself also re-draws these borders rather startlingly. After the lump's formation, the reader is suddenly told, for the first time, that the child's father is black. When the Soudan approaches his son after the child's shaping, the text states "Þan cam þe soudan, þat was blac" (799). No explicit reference is made to this fact before this point.[95] The Soudan's blackness thus emerges after the horror of indeterminacy has been raised and rejected, and serves to mark the divisions between Saracens and Christians more emphatically since we know from the first stanza of the tale that the Princess is "As white as feþer of swan" (12). Biological distinctions appear after the horror of inter-faith procreation to establish a physical border between Christian and Saracen. No longer will it be possible to mimic religious affiliation the way the Princess did earlier; henceforth visual cues signal one's group identity and difference from others.

This color border, however, does not just divide Saracen from Christian, but also articulates Christian ideas about the respective rightness of the two religions. In the later Middle Ages, blackness was frequently used in the West to indicate a state of sinfulness. In one of his sermons on the Song of Songs, Bernard of Clairvaux, discussing black skin, states

> I recognize here the image of our sin-*blackened* nature; I recognize the
> garments of skin that clothed our sinning first parents. He [Christ] even

brought this blackness on himself by assuming the condition of slave, and becoming as men are, he was seen as a man.[96]

As Bruce Holsinger notes in his discussion of this sermon, "black skin [in this sermon] . . . represents a necessary but temporary aberration [caused by the earthly, sinful life] that endures only to be redeemed by the cleansing whiteness of salvation."[97] The *Chronicle of Lanercost* too, as mentioned in Chapter One, describes how an Oxford scholar is found "speechless, behaving as if on the point of death; but, which is very wonderful, his whole body presented such a horrible appearance that you would have believed him to be a filthy Ethiopian rather than a Christian."[98] The scholar's friends then recite the Gospel (even though they can only remember bits of it), and this forces the evil spirit to leave the man who "shortly afterwards returned from the sooty appearance to his natural looks."[99] Here, possession by an evil spirit results in blackness, and the color is reversed by an appeal to the divine. In all these cases, skin color reflects the state of one's relationship with God. Differentiation by color in *Þe King of Tars* thus can be read as defining the religious borders separating Saracen from Christian, conveying a judgement of the two faiths, and asserting the superiority of Christianity. The subsequent narration of the Soudan's actual conversion further develops this clear differentiation of the two groups even as it offers a model of how one Saracen might be incorporated into a Christian community.

The Soudan, suitably impressed by his son's formation, agrees to his wife's request that he convert. After three days of instruction, the Soudan is baptized and his black skin is bleached white: "His hide, þat blac & loþely was, / Al white bicom, þurth Godes gras, / & clere wiþouten blame" (928–30). What we have here, then, is a moment in the Middle Ages when skin color serves as the sign of "ultimate, irreducible difference between cultures, linguistic groups, or adherents of specific belief systems."[100] The Soudan's conversion and change of color constitute, as various scholars have recently noted, a moment when certain modern understandings of race intersect with a medieval text.[101] What is rather different about this medieval text, however, is that skin color characterizes a group rather than an individual, and can be changed when an individual changes his or her group affiliations. Skin color becomes an impermanent and shifting marker of the differences between cultures. It can be altered by baptism and by an individual's renegotiation of his or her relationship to the Christian God. This event evidently relates to notions of divine intervention in conversion. As in the cases of Saints Paul and Augustine, God emerges to facilitate his worshipper's entry into a Christian community. Here, however, God does not effect the convert's change of identity as He does in the cases of Paul and Augustine. Instead, God's grace emerges after baptism to remove a physical barrier to the Soudan's acceptance by his new community, and to testify to the sincerity of his conversion. The Soudan's wife, for example, knows that he has converted not from his words but from his changed appearance: "Þan wist sche wele in hir þou3t / Þat on Mahoun leued he nou3t / For chaunged was his hewe" (943–45). A divine act thus allows Christians to perceive physically the authenticity of the Soudan's Christian identity. The miracle constitutes proof of conversion, not any human action, which is quite understandable given the Princess's earlier false conversion in the tale. Moreover, because God's grace and the miracle it effects are presented as consequences of conversion, conversion is depicted as a process able to eradicate any differences that might impede a convert's integration into his new community. In this text, unlike in *Sir Beves of Hamtoun*, conversion can decisively re-write even the most marked of cultural borders.

Conversion, however, still reinforces differentiation. No trace of the Soudan's Saracen origins remains when he is Christian. Instead his appearance is changed to conform to the borders dividing Saracen from Christian in the text. Unlike his son's lumpishness, then, the Sultan's conversion does not challenge cultural differentiation, but reasserts the division of Saracen from Christian. The individual identification of Saracen or Christian can be rewritten here, but union of the two groups as separate and different entities cannot ever be accomplished. In this model of integration, then, the incorporation of a Saracen into a Christian community is successful, but only because it affirms ideas about how the groups are different. Integration here renews differentiation.

The same renewal of differentiation can be seen in another aspect of the text's ending. After the Princess perceives the Soudan's conversion through his "chaunged . . . hewe" (945), she insists that he

"Do cristen þi lond, alle & some,
Boþe eld & 3ing.
& he þat wil be cristned nou3t,
Loke to þe deþ þat he be brou3t,
Wiþouten ani duelleing." (956–60)

The Princess urges her husband to prove his integration into the Christian community in the most concrete way possible: by turning his back on his former communal links with Saracens and forcibly severing those links with death unless his erstwhile people join him on the Christian side of the Saracen-Christian divide. Unlike the situation in some analogues to *Þe King of*

Tars where the non-Christian's household converts upon seeing the miracle of the child's formation at baptism, the Princess's words demand that the Soudan's conversion, and that of his Saracen people, be interwoven with force and violence. Here, as in Otuel's duel with Clarel in *Otuel a Kni3t,* physical violence must be deployed to patrol the borders between Saracen and Christian, and decisively differentiate the two after one individual has changed his group affiliations. The Princess's attitude suggests that violence is necessary to combat the possibility of recidivism or deceit on the Soudan's part, even though his change of religion has been marked by divine miracle.[102] The Soudan, moreover, agrees, and forcibly converts or kills all of his Saracens. Incorporating the Soudan into Christianity thus provokes a renewed, definitive, and bloody re-establishment of difference in *Þe King of Tars.* Integration once again prompts revitalized, and more forceful, assertions of the borders separating two religious groups. Yet again, the possibility of intermingling two different peoples is denied. The Soudan's conversion means conformity to the cultural borders separating Saracen from Christian rather than compromise of them, and the erstwhile Saracen participates in Christian efforts to eradicate Saracenness. The tale of his conversion thus shuts down any possibility of cultural integration as the intermingling or coexistence of two equivalent and equally valued identities.

In sum, *Þe King of Tars* offers two models for cultural integration and the rewriting of borders defining disparate communities. The most radical model is that presented by the lump-child. This figure posits a mode of integration in which Saracen and Christian are so intermingled that the cultural borders dividing and defining the two no longer exist. Cultural borders appear completely re-writable here, but this re-writing produces such monstrous indefinition that it cannot be accepted. The need for differentiation is firmly invoked, and adherence to one set of cultural practices is imposed on the lump. The text then offers a more traditional medieval model for re-writing cultural borders: conversion. In *Þe King of Tars,* conversion is a divinely inflected process that has the power to erase and re-write an individual's identity markers so as to fit him into the parameters of his new, Christian community. While this process can re-write an individual's ability to conform to cultural borders, it does not challenge or re-write the borders themselves. Instead, it affirms their existence and the centrality of differentiation. Integration here involves differentiation both on a personal and a cultural level. *Þe King of Tars* thus leaves the reader with no real hope for a just and fair integration of different peoples. The text suggests that the only way to resolve difference is to obliterate it through definitive re-alignment (often through violence) of one's identity, or else face the monstrous indeterminacy of the "flesche" as a mode of existence in which differences are intermingled rather than obliterated. The text as a whole thus explores the opposition of the categories of Saracen and Christian, troubles this opposition, pushes the collapse of division to its utmost point, and, having shown that collapse as a horror, forcibly re-inscribes the original differences without any of the earlier undercutting of these divisions. Saracen characters in *Þe King of Tars* thus complement the Auchinleck manuscript's assertion of "Inglisch" identity by offering a thought-provoking exploration of issues and processes of cultural integration and differentiation very much at stake both in any assertion of group identity, and in England's specific fourteenth-century grapplings with the incorporation into its polity of both Continental foreigners and foreign peoples closer to home such as the Welsh and Scots.

CODA: AN ALTERNATE AUCHINLECK VISION OF CULTURAL INTEGRATION

While *Þe King of Tars* offers a rather dark vision of integration, and leaves the reader contemplating two fantastic choices, monstrous intermingling or miraculous conversion, the Auchinleck manuscript includes another text which provides a much more positive vision of Saracen-Christian intermingling. *Floris and Blauncheflur,* too, depicts an inter-faith relationship and locates most of its events in the East. It, however, suggests the possibility of a harmonious integration of Saracen and Christian, and even if it, too, in the end, insists on conversion to seal the union, this tale of the East represents that conversion as a much less violent process.

To suggest that *Floris and Blauncheflur* provides a harmonious vision of East-West interaction might seem to align this reading with the traditional scholarly reading of the romance as "an idyllic love story set in the exotic East."[103] Such a reading has recently been challenged by writers such as Kathleen Coyne Kelly and Carol Heffernan who offer a "darker reading" of the poem either by emphasizing Blauncheflur's slavery or by tracing suggestions of possible incest in the tale.[104] While Kelly and Heffernan have made clear the poem's darker aspects, there is no denying that in the context of the Auchinleck manuscript, and especially in relation to *Þe King of Tars, Floris and Blauncheflur* offers a rather positive vision of Saracen-Christian interaction. This is perhaps first discerned in the poem's origins itself. The Middle English tale, most scholars agree, represents a translation of the Old French *Floire et Blancheflor,* a text which, as E. Jane Burns notes, "results from a complex literary mixing of elements found in Graeco-Roman or Byzantine romances, more indigenous French materials, biblical antecedents, traditional

Arabo-Persian tales, and passages from the *Pilgrim's Guide to Compostela*."[105] The proportionate role of these various elements in the story of Floris and Blauncheflur is still debated, but most scholars agree on the heterogeneity of the list. In its origins, then, this Auchinleck tale reflects a harmonious inter-mingling of influences from East and West.[106] Unlike *Þe King of Tars* which derives, ultimately, from Christian records of Christian-Muslim conflict, *Floris and Blauncheflur* emerges from a more peaceful conflation of literary inheritances from both Christian and Muslim cultures.

The narrative itself also offers, in contrast to *Þe King of Tars,* a less stark division of Saracen and Christian. To begin with, manuscript lacunae mean that the opening of *Floris and Blauncheflur* is lost in all four manuscripts con-taining the Middle English tale. As a result, the identification of the lovers as Christian and Saracen, and the story of how Christian Blauncheflur and her mother end up enslaved at a Saracen court in Spain, are lost to modern readers. Two of the manuscripts do include references to Blauncheflur's mother as "þe Cristen woman" (London, British Library, Egerton 2862, lines 3, 247, and London, British Library, Cotton Vitellius D. iii, line 46),[107] but all other open-ing references to the religious differences of Floris and Blauncheflur are lost. Assuming that the lovers' religious affiliations were originally made clear in all manuscripts before the books were damaged, it is still striking to find that reli-gious identifications are not emphasized and reiterated in the extant portions of the tale. According to De Vries's comprehensive glossary, the words "hethen" and "paien" do not appear in any manuscript of the tale, the adjective "Cristen" appears only in the three instances noted above, and the term "sarazin" appears only once, in Auchinleck. In Auchinleck, however, "sarazin" describes two of the Amerail of Babiloine's men (694), not Floris. Indeed, in the 861 lines of the Auchinleck text that we have, neither lover's religious identification is ever specified. The adjective "Cristen" does not appear at all, much less in conjunc-tion with Blauncheflur's name, and Floris's Saracenness is never mentioned. Compare this to *Þe King of Tars*. Leaving aside the text's opening 100 lines in which characters' religious affiliations are made clear by uses of the terms "heþen," "Cristen," and "Sarazin" as well as various invocations of deities, one finds in the remaining 1128 lines forty-one occurrences of the word "Cristen" and twelve occurrences of the word "Sarrazin." In addition, references to Christ, Mahoun, and "heþens" appear frequently, as does the Saracen title "Soudan," which is the male protagonist's only appellation. Thus, even if the opening of *Þe King of Tars* had been lost, there would still be plenty of refer-ences to clarify the main characters' religious affiliations. In *Floris and Blauncheflur,* however, no such references appear, a fact which minimizes the reader's awareness of the religious divisions between the two lovers. Admittedly, the ending of the Auchinleck text, which is complete, does narrate a conversion and thereby remind readers of the lovers' religious difference. Even this reference blurs identification, however. The text states,

> & þai [Floris and Blauncheflur] com hom [to Spain] whan þai miȝt,
> & let croune him to King,
> & hire to Quene, þat swete þing,
> & vnderfeng Cristendom of prestes honde,
> & þonkede God of alle his sonde. (849–53)

In this passage, the subject of the single preterite verb "vnderfeng" in "vnderfeng Cristendom" is unclear. One must assume, based on the French tale, that Floris is meant, and this is how De Vries glosses the difficult line, but there is no denying that the text's reference is rather murky and seems to imply that Blauncheflur "vnderfeng Cristendom." Rather than repeatedly confronting readers with the fact of the lovers' religious differences, then, the Auchinleck *Floris and Blauncheflur* downplays the faith affiliations of the two lovers, a situation very different from *Þe King of Tars* where the two lovers' religious identifications prove central to everything that happens. As a result, *Floris and Blauncheflur* emphasizes the love uniting Floris and Blauncheflur rather than the religions dividing them.

Readerly awareness of Floris and Blauncheflur as lovers separated by religious difference is further minimized by the fact that these inter-faith lovers are represented as a cohesive unit working against the desires of a Saracen ruler. When Floris succeeds in finding Blauncheflur and gaining admission to her chamber, the two become the objects of the Saracen Amerail's anger. Narratively, the line of opposition is drawn between the Saracen ruler and the Saracen-Christian couple rather than between the two lovers themselves, which is the case in *Þe King of Tars*. As a result, the tension in *Floris and Blauncheflur* seems to lie between East and West rather than between Christian and Saracen. The western lovers become the targets of an eastern ruler's enmity. Floris, identified at various points as "of Spaine a Kynges sone" (404, 804), shares a geographical origin with Blauncheflur and, like her, travels a long way by sea to "Babiloyne." He may be Saracen and she may be Christian, but in "Babiloyne" they are both foreigners. Geography unites them, and separates them from the eastern Amerail and his Saracen retainers. Even that opposition between East and West is troubled, however, as the narrative continues.

When Floris and Blauncheflur are caught in the tower of maidens by the Amerail, they plead for mercy and are granted a respite from execution until the Amerail has consulted his "baronage" (650). When brought in front of the baronage for judgement, each lover attempts to pull the other's neck back from the sword and volunteer his or her own neck instead. As a result, "Al þat ise3en þis / Þerfore sori weren iwis" (770–71). The Amerail himself "chaungede mod and chere, / For aiþer for oþer wolde die" (775–76). Eastern, Saracen pity for the western lovers means that the lovers are spared. The lines of opposition drawn earlier in the narrative are thus overcome by a shared respect for self-sacrificing love. The cultural borders between East and West that seemed to be in play fall down, and Floris and Blauncheflur are happily married and feted in the Saracen East. East and West harmoniously intermingle, as do Saracen and Christian lovers. *Floris and Blauncheflur* thus offers a rather positive vision of westerners finding a home in the East, and of Saracen-Christian integration in theologically unifying marriage.

This is not to say, however, that this situation endures. As in *Þe King of Tars,* borders between cultures, regions and religions are re-erected after a situation in which they were collapsed. Shortly after the wedding, Floris is summoned home by the death of his father and Spain's concomitant need for its new king. He adamantly refuses the Amerail's pleas that he stay in "Babiloyne," saying "I nel bileue for no winne; / To bidde me hit were sinne" (846–47). East-West intermingling ceases once Floris is called westward. The summons home also means the end of Saracen-Christian intermingling as it is after the lovers return to Spain that conversion to Christianity occurs in the Auchinleck text. The westerners cannot stay in the East, and in the West there is no space for their Saracen-Christian union, a fact which provoked the lovers' journey East to begin with, since Blauncheflur was originally sold to merchants in order to remove her from Floris's loving attention. Floris and Blauncheflur can be a happily married inter-faith couple in the East, but once they return home, their inter-faith union must be regularized and homogenized. Conversion, and differentiation of Christian from Saracen, once again replace integration.

That conversion, however, and all the interactions along the way, offer a much more positive vision of Saracen-Christian interaction than *Þe King of Tars.* Unlike *Þe King of Tars* where Saracen-Christian battle is the starting and end point of the narrative, and the foundation of all conversions depicted, *Floris and Blauncheflur* contains no depiction of Saracen-Christian, or even East-West, battle. Some violence and hostility certainly underlie Blauncheflur's sale to merchants, but ingenuity and compassion, rather than battle, characterize the interactions between peoples in *Floris and Blauncheflur.* Rather than fighting to win his love, Floris poses as a merchant and gains entry to the Amerail's tower of maidens through conversation and "ginne" (419). Similarly, rather than being converted by miracle or violence, Floris seems to be converted by love for Blauncheflur, and there is no evidence that he then forcibly converts his realm. Perhaps, as a Spaniard, Floris can mediate between East and West and between Saracens and Christians without violence because he understands the different cultures involved. Whatever the reason, *Floris and Blauncheflur* suggests that Saracen-Christian intermingling may ultimately prove untenable, but that constructive, non-violent Saracen-Christian interaction is possible without divine intervention.

Saracens and English Christian Identity in *Seynt Katerine* and *Seynt Mergrete*

INTRODUCTION

In Chapter Four, we move from depictions of Saracens engaged in war or marriage to depictions of Saracens engaged in the religious persecution of Christians. This shift reflects the fact that the two texts studied in this chapter generically diverge from the texts discussed so far. Rather than being Middle English romances, translations of French *chansons de geste*, or elaborations of chronicle entries, these narratives are saints' legends. Studying saints' legends like the Auchinleck *Seynt Katerine* and *Seynt Mergrete* can be rather daunting. How does one presume to analyze and contextualize texts that are defined generically by their adherence to tropes of martyrdom attached to many different saints' legends? As Hippolyte Delehaye points out, "Every martyr, as a rule, is animated by the same sentiments, expresses the same opinions and is subject to the same trials, while the holy confessor who has earned his reward by an edifying life must needs have possessed all the virtues of his profession, which the hagiographer . . . delights to enumerate."[1] The saint is characterized precisely by his or her repetition of certain saintly acts, and his or her similarity to other saints. Given this aspect of saints' legends, they seem to invite study that focuses on their hagiographic generality and samenesses. As Patrick Geary notes, however, such study is not necessarily the best way to arrive at a full understanding of the cultural functions of saints' legends in the Middle Ages. He states: "If we want to understand values reflected in the hagiography of a period, texts must be seen in relation to the other texts with which they were associated, read, or gathered, not in relation either to timeless views of Christian perfection or simply to other contemporary hagiographic texts."[2] In other words, assertions of the common exemplarity of saints, or of their similar glorification of God, indicate some of the cultural significance of saints' legends in the Middle Ages, but preclude

reflection on ways in which the same texts also interact with the specific circumstances of their historical appearances in various places and
manuscripts.[3] To do justice to a saint's legend and its import at a given historical moment of circulation, Geary advocates scholarly attention both to the
textual tradition within which the legend emerges and to the material context in which it circulated. Antecedent texts are thus inescapable components
of individual manifestations of saints' legends like those in Auchinleck, but
not the sum of a text's cultural relevance at the moment of its circulation.
Geary appears to call for both a contextualization of saints' legends within a
framework of antecedent texts, and a contextualization and analysis of saints'
legends as they appear within their manuscripts. Such a program of study
seems to me the best way to indicate the indebtedness of *Seynt Katerine* and
Seynt Mergrete to a long tradition of legends while simultaneously recognizing that such tradition-shaped texts still participate in, and illuminate in
unique ways, the cultural project of the Auchinleck manuscript in which
they appear. To this end, I begin by mapping out the general hagiographic
traditions underlying the Auchinleck *Seynt Katerine* and *Seynt Mergrete* and
the Saracens therein. I then proceed to demonstrate how these tradition-
shaped texts and their depictions of Saracens illuminate Auchinleck's interpellations of English group identity.

　　While, as shall be seen, the Saracens in *Seynt Katerine* and *Seynt Mergrete* are neither unique nor originary, they do complement other Auchinleck
Saracens. Because these Saracens, unlike their manuscript fellows, appear in
saints' lives, [4] they are part of texts designed to promote lay piety as much or
more than to entertain. As a result, the cultural functions served by Saracens
in *Seynt Mergrete* and *Seynt Katerine* differ somewhat from the cultural functions served by Saracens in other Auchinleck texts. Rather than exploring
issues of group identity that relate primarily to English people as inhabitants
of England in the early fourteenth century, Saracens in these saints' lives
directly engage questions of identity that relate to English people as members
of a wider, pan-Christian medieval community, and reveal that "Inglisch"
identity at this time is by no means separable from Christian group identity.
In other words, these texts indicate that English identity as conceived in
Auchinleck is religious as well as political, linguistic, cultural, and historical.

　　In *Seynt Mergrete* and *Seynt Katerine*, this religious Englishness takes
two forms. The first is that of religious education and practice—these saints'
lives and their Saracens offer guidance to a lay English, Christian audience
about ideal Christian attitudes and behaviors. In particular, Saracens in these
texts serve to clarify Christian ideas about female sexuality, about people's
proper relationship to physical luxuries, and about the objects that should be

worshipped by a religious community. The second form religious English-ness takes is somewhat more complicated. Western Christianity in the Middle Ages was not just a particular way of life; it was also a geo-political identification that brought with it international involvement in Christian politico-religious endeavors in foreign lands. The principal arena of such endeavor in the later Middle Ages was the Holy Land, and English people were extensively involved in Middle Eastern crusades.[5] Saracens in *Seynt Mergrete* and *Seynt Katerine* reflect this aspect of "Inglisch" identity. Their characterization, geographic affiliations, technological expertise, and power communicate a sense of the historical existence of Muslims and Byzantine Greeks, and of western interactions with these peoples in the Middle East. In various ways the Saracens in these saints' lives slide disconcertingly from being the familiar domestic others of medieval literature to being slightly menacing evocations of actual Middle Eastern Otherness and its power. Saracens here thus complement their Auchinleck fellows by evoking more fully the historical presence of Middle Eastern Otherness. By so doing, the Saracens in *Seynt Mergrete* and *Seynt Katerine* introduce contemporary historical resonances of eastern power, of western defeats at eastern hands, and of western political expulsion from the Holy Land into the usually ahistorical genre of the saint's life. As a result, the actions of the saints in these saints' lives take on a new aspect. The evocation of historical eastern power enables in *Seynt Mergrete* and *Seynt Katerine* an imaginative revision of late thirteenth-century crusading setbacks, and the enunciation of a vision of Christian triumph somewhat similar to that espoused by authors of crusading treatises in the early fourteenth century.

CONTEXTUALIZING *SEYNT KATERINE, SEYNT MERGRETE,* AND THE SARACENS THEREIN

Saint Katherine of Alexandria was reputedly martyred at the beginning of the fourth century, but no clear proof of her historical existence has been found. [6] Indeed, in 1969 the Vatican removed her feast day from its calendar of saints, indicating as it did so that her existence was questionable.[7] The earliest extant reference to St Katherine consists of "a few lines of her lost acts in a fragmentary Greek martyrology dating from the first half of the eighth century."[8] Around 800 A.D. some relics believed to be hers were found at Mount Sinai and a convent there was subsequently dedicated to her.[9] The *Menologium Basilianum*, compiled around 886, contained a fragmentary martyrology of Saint Katherine, and this version was recast by Symon Metaphrastes around 960.[10] All Greek texts post-dating the Metaphrastes version are drawn from a tenth-century narrative of St Katherine known as the Pseudo-Athanasian text.[11]

The cult of St Katherine appears to have been introduced to the West in the eleventh century. According to a monk of Saint-Trinité-du-Mont in Rouen who wrote between 1054 and 1090, "Symeon, a monk of Mount Sinai, brought bone particles and oil from St Catherine's shrine to Rouen in about 1030, the year in which the abbey of Saint-Trinité was founded."[12] This abbey soon became the abbey both of the Holy Trinity and of St Katherine,[13] and a monk named Ainard wrote a now-lost lengthy Latin account of the saint. Nevanlinna and Taavaitsainen assert that this Latin life by Ainard is the Vulgate version of the legend.[14] Wogan-Browne and Burgess, in contrast, claim that Ainard's life is now lost and that an anonymous author wrote the Vulgate tale.[15] Whatever its origins, the Vulgate version of the tale derives from the Pseudo-Athanasian Greek text, enjoyed wide popularity in the West, and is found today in more than a hundred extant manuscripts, many of which date from the late eleventh and the twelfth centuries.[16] An abridged version of the Vulgate *St Katherine*, known as the Shorter Vulgate, also enjoyed considerable circulation in the West, and was the basis for the tale of St Katherine included in Boninus Mombritius's collection of saints' legends published in1480.[17] Although this printed *Sanctuarium* post-dates Auchinleck and the other English texts of Saints Katherine and Margaret discussed here, it is considered by scholars to represent a collection of Latin saints' legends that circulated widely in the West centuries before the print publication by Mombritius. Accordingly, various vernacular saints' legends that pre-date Mombritius's *Sanctuarium* are often identified as being based upon a Mombritius-type source, despite the apparent anachronism of such a reference.[18] Mombritius-type legends of both St Katherine and St Margaret exist, and were used frequently as sources for vernacular legends of these women in the Middle Ages. The other Latin version of St Katherine's legend that enjoyed considerable popularity in the West is that found in Jacobus de Voragine's *Legenda aurea*. This Latin collection of biblical stories and saints' legends is usually dated to c. 1255–1270.[19] Some 1,000 manuscripts of this text survive, as well as many print editions in Latin and in various western vernaculars,[20] and these all testify to the work's tremendous popularity in the later Middle Ages.

The earliest known record of Katherine in Britain is found in a late tenth-century psalter from Shaftesbury, but St Katherine is not included in any calendars or martyrologies of the Old English period.[21] Thus, the cult of Katherine appears to have begun "its full development in Britain with the Norman Conquest."[22] "William the Conqueror granted the abbey of Saint-Catherine-de-Mont a sub-priory at Harmondsworth,"[23] while a hospital dedicated to St Katherine was founded in Rochester, Kent, in 1108.[24] Records of a Latin miracle play about St Katherine exist from the late eleventh or early twelfth century,[25] and manuscripts of both the Latin Vulgate legend of Katherine and of the *Legenda aurea* version seem to have been available to English hagiographers.[26] In addition, extant manuscripts from the thirteenth century onwards contain prayers and hymns to the saint in both Anglo-Norman and English.[27] In the late 1100s, a Benedictine nun of Barking called Clemence composed an Anglo-Norman poem recounting Katherine's martyrdom[28] and this exists in four manuscripts.[29] Anne Savage and Nicholas Watson also note that sixty-two English churches were dedicated to St Katherine.[30] Evidently, St Katherine of Alexandria was very popular among the English, a fact further evinced by the recent publication of an entire book examining her cult in late medieval England.[31]

Given such popularity, it is no surprise that many Middle English versions of St Katherine's story exist.[32] The earliest English-language legend of St Katherine is an alliterative prose version found in three early thirteenth-century manuscripts which contain the collection of saints' lives and writings on virginity known as the Katherine Group.[33] St Katherine also appears in seventeen manuscripts of the *South English Legendary*, a collection of saints' lives that circulated from the late thirteenth century onwards.[34] According to the dates of extant manuscripts, the next appearance of the legend of St Katherine in England is that which concerns us here, namely the *Seynt Katerine* found in the Auchinleck manuscript of the early fourteenth century.[35] Katherine's tale is also found in many later collections of saints' lives including two fifteenth-century manuscripts of the *Northern Homily Collection*, the fifteenth-century manuscript of the *Scottish Legendary*, Osbern Bokenham's *Lyvys of Seyntys*, the 1438 English translation of the *Legenda aurea*, and Caxton's 1483 *Golden Legend*.[36] She also appears in Mirk's *Festial* (c. 1400) and in a variety of fifteenth-century miscellanies.[37]

St Margaret of Antioch also enjoyed great popularity in England, and Bella Millett identifies her and Katherine as "by far the most popular subjects for vernacular saints' lives" in medieval England.[38] Like the other saint discussed in this chapter, however, Margaret boasts a complicated history before her appearance in England. Her martyrdom is traditionally associated with the persecution of Christians under the Roman emperors Diocletian and Maximian (305–313 A.D.), but there is no record of her in accounts of Christian persecutions around this time in Antioch, nor is there any evidence of an early cult focussed on her.[39] For these reasons, Margaret's saintly status has been challenged and, like St Katherine, she was withdrawn from the Vatican's official calendar of saints in 1969.[40]

The earliest extant records of St Margaret's legend and veneration date from the end of the eighth century.[41] She was known to the Byzantine Church as Marina,[42] and her life is included in the ninth century menology of Emperor Basil.[43] Another Greek version, "said to have been taken from an account written by Methodius, Patriarch of Constantinople (842–846 A.D.) is still extant," and Symon Metaphrastes includes a version of St Margaret's legend in his tenth-century martyrology.[44] Magennis and Clayton argue that the Methodius-linked narrative, which they call the Greek *Passio a Theotimo*, served as a major source for Latin hagiographers of Margaret in the West, especially the recension known as BHG no. 1165.[45]

The earliest extant Latin versions of Margaret's legend date from the late eighth century.[46] Margaret appears in the martyrologies of Hrabanus Maurus (d. 856), of Wandelbert (a ninth-century Benedictine monk of Prüm), and of Notkerus Balbulus (d. 912).[47] Magennis and Clayton discuss in detail six Latin versions of St Margaret's legend circulating in the medieval West: the Mombritius version, the Turin version, the Casinensis version, the Paris version, the Caligula version, and the Rebdorf version.[48] Many of these are found in multiple manuscripts, and the legend of St Margaret evidently enjoyed significant readership. In addition, her tale is found in Vincent of Beauvais's *Speculum historiale*, and in the widely read *Legenda aurea*, a version that combines elements of Vincent's version and the Mombritius version.[49] Latin legends of St Margaret were clearly available to both Anglo-Saxon and post-Norman Conquest inhabitants of England.[50] In addition, St Margaret appears "in almost all of the surviving calendars of the Anglo-Saxon Church," and in a number of its litanies.[51] Relics of St Margaret are also "attested in all three of the manuscripts containing lists of relics in Anglo-Saxon monastic houses."[52] After the Norman Conquest, one also finds a number of churches dedicated to St Margaret,[53] as well as six Anglo-Norman poetic versions of her legend written before the end of the thirteenth century,[54] and a verse version by Wace.[55]

Many English language versions of St Margaret's legend exist, the earliest of which are in Old English. Her tale is found in the *Old English Martyrology*, in the late eleventh-century London, British Library, Cotton Tiberius A. iii manuscript, and in the early twelfth-century Cambridge, Corpus Christi College 303 manuscript.[56] The earliest extant Middle English legend of St Margaret is the early thirteenth-century alliterative prose version that forms part of the Katherine Group of texts.[57] The legend is also found in seventeen manuscripts of the *South English Legendary*, which circulated in England from the thirteenth century onwards.[58] A version composed in quatrains and frequently identified as *Meidan Maregrete* is found in the thirteenth-century manuscript Cambridge, Trinity College 323 (also referred to in older texts as Trinity College B 14. 39) as well as in later fifteenth-century recensions.[59] The Auchinleck *Seynt Mergrete* is sometimes identified as a fourteenth-century variant of this thirteenth-century Trinity College version,[60] although D'Evelyn lists the Auchinleck text separately as a unique version.[61] St Margaret's legend is also found in a number of fifteenth-century manuscripts and in hagiographic collections such as the *Scottish Legendary*, Bokenham's *Lyvys of Seyntys*, the 1438 English translation of the *Legenda aurea*, and Caxton's 1483 print *Golden Legend*.[62] The saint also appears in Lydgate's legends of saints and in Mirk's *Festial*.[63]

The sheer number of legends involving Katherine and Margaret makes the attribution of one particular vernacular version to a specific Latin or vernacular antecedent extremely difficult. However, scholars who specialize in source studies have used elements of these saints' legends to trace a general trajectory of inheritance for English manifestations of these tales. These scholars suggest that the Auchinleck *Seynt Katerine* has as its ultimate source the "*Legenda aurea* with additions from the Vulgate version."[64] The Auchinleck *Seynt Mergrete*, and the thirteenth-century *Meidan Maregrete* that predates it, are believed to share a common source that ultimately derives from a Mombritius-type version of the legend.[65] Other English-language texts mentioned above also pre-date the Auchinleck legends, and thus are chronologically capable of having influenced the authors and scribes of Auchinleck. While a whole book could be written about the respective similarities and differences of *Seynt Katerine* and *Seynt Mergrete* to these various versions, I will merely situate the Saracens of *Seynt Katerine* and *Seynt Mergrete* in relation to these antecedent texts.[66] Of course, the number of manuscripts and texts is such that this cannot be anything more than a general positioning, especially in relation to the Latin sources of these legends since most of these exist in multiple manuscripts with all the variation that that entails. A general outline, however, suffices to contextualize the Saracens of the Auchinleck legends as I am interested in the Auchinleck tales not as originary or original representations of Saracens but as part of a particular manuscript context.

In *Seynt Katerine*, the saint's persecutor, Emperor Maxens of Greece,[67] is described thus:

Mahoun he held for his god:
He trowed in þat fals lay;
. . . . . .
Sarraȝin he was ful strong,
Wiþ cristendom he seyd nay,

For alle þat leued on Jh*e*su Crist
He stroyd hem boþe ni3t & day. (17–24)⁶⁸

A Saracen presence is further established by the fact that Katerine proclaims
her Christianity "Among þe sarra3ins so blake" (426). Another "Sarra3in"
(450) invents a device of spiked wheels to torture Katerine and sets it up for
use before a crowd of "wicked sarra3ins" (491), while the retainers who
remain loyal to Maxens are described as "Þe sarra3ins þat wiþ him held"
(627). Throughout the Auchinleck text, then, Katerine's suffering and martyrdom are depicted as the effects of explicitly Saracen persecution, and
Christians and Saracens are set up as diametrically opposed religious groups.
While the sense of diametrically opposed religious communities is found in
all antecedent versions of Katherine's legend, the identification of the non-
Christian community as Saracen is not. Neither the *Legenda aurea* nor the
Latin Vulgate version describes Katherine's persecutors as Saracen, and neither text identifies any of the pagan gods to whom Christians must make
sacrifice as "Mahoun."⁶⁹ No Saracens appear in the early thirteenth-century
Katherine Group *Seinte Katerine* either. There, Katherine's persecutors are
described as "heaþene folc,"⁷⁰ and the ingenious engineer of the torturous
wheels is a "burh-reve" (100) The persecutors' idols, however, are identified
as "maumez" (16), a term which means pagan idols, but which also evokes
specifically Saracen idols for late medieval Christians.⁷¹ The *South English
Legendary* also avoids the term "Saracen" and calls Katherine's persecutors,
among other things, "þis liþere men" (231).⁷² It states explicitly, however,
that these persecutors worship "maumet3" (30) and pray to "Mahoun"
(261). Thus, a strong Saracen coloring is attached to Katherine's persecutors
in the *South English Legendary* even though they are not actually called Saracens as in Auchinleck. In sum, Saracen persecutors do not appear to be a fea-
ture of the Latin sources of the Auchinleck *Seynt Katerine*, nor do they
appear explicitly in English versions of the legend that pre-date Auchinleck.
The English texts, though, do use words such as "Mahoun" and "maumet3"
that suggest a Saracen element in Katherine's persecutors. The depiction of
Katherine's persecutors in the Auchinleck *Seynt Katerine* thus develops in
more detail suggestions of Saracenness found in preceding English versions
of the legend. Some English texts that post-date Auchinleck also identify
Katherine's persecutors as Saracens, including those in Cambridge, Caius
College 175 (fifteenth-century) and in Cambridge, University Library, Ff. 2.
38 (also fifteenth-century).⁷³ Other fifteenth-century English versions of the
legend, however, omit all references to Saracenness altogether, including one
manuscript of the *Northern Homily Collection*⁷⁴ and Southwell, Minster

Library, Southwell Minster 7.[75] Thus, while the appearance of Saracens in *Seynt Katerine* is not without precedent, it does represent a textual trajectory that is by no means universal.

In a similar evocation of Saracenness in the Auchinleck *Seynt Mergrete*, the Christian heroine prays to be saved "Fram þis foule Saraȝins" (72),[76] and her persecutor Olibrious is called "þat sarraȝin" (105). Mergrete is also ordered to worship Mahoun (298), and Saracen converts are said to "forsake Mahoun" (326). The Latin Mombritius version that has been identified as the ultimate source of this tale differs from the Auchinleck text significantly. In the Latin, Margaret's persecutors are called "impii" and "viri sanguinum" (197).[77] There is no reference to Saracens or to Mahoun. What is found in the Mombritius text, however, and in many other Latin versions of Margaret's legend, is a description of the second devil Margaret fights in her prison as appearing in the form of a black-skinned man. The particular Mombritius text printed in *The Old English Lives of St Margaret* reads thus: "[Margaret] vidit alium diabolum sedentem ut homo niger habens manus suas ad genua conligatus."[78] In the Auchinleck *Mergrete*, however, Mergrete "seiȝe a wele fouler þing | sitten in a wro: / He hadde honden on his knes | and eiȝe on euerich to—" (214–15). In the Auchinleck text, then, the blackness of the devil who resembles a black man has disappeared to be replaced by eye-filled toes. However, a persecutor who resembles the former devil has been added. Although *Seynt Mergrete* itself does not explicitly state that Saracens are black, black skin is an attribute of Saracens in texts surrounding the saint's legend,[79] thus a readerly context of black Saracens has been established by the manuscript. Imaginary devils and racial characteristics are thus separated out from each other in Auchinleck, and skin color marks human rather than supernatural enmity to Christianity.

The same distinction can be seen when the Auchinleck legend is compared to the two Old English legends edited by Clayton and Magennis. These texts follow Mombritius, and differ from Auchinleck, in their description of the second devil as "swilcne anne sweartne man, and his honda to his cneowum gebundenne,"[80] and as "sweart and unfæger, swa him gecynde wæs."[81] They also identify Margaret's persecutors as "hæþen[ ]"[82] and "hæþan folc"[83] rather than as explicit Saracens who worship Mahoun. The early thirteenth-century alliterative *Seinte Marherete*, too, identifies Margaret's persecutors as "heþene folc" (46),[84] and represents the second devil as "muche deale blackre þen eauer eani blamon" (61).[85] Unlike the Latin and Old English versions, however, *Seinte Marherete* uses the term "maumeȝ" (75) to describe the idols worshipped by Margaret's persecutors, and this evokes associations with Saracens even though no Saracens are explicitly present in the text. The *South English Legendary* does not identify Margaret's persecutors as Saracen, but describes them merely as "heþene" (5)[86] worshippers of "false godes" (91). This legendary also minimizes its description of the second devil, and merely states that he appeared in the likeness of a man without specifying any skin color. In the thirteenth-century *Meidan Maregrete*, however, the second devil has eyes on his toes and knees (183)[87] while Margaret's persecutors are described repeatedly as "saresin3" (64). This text not only pre-dates Auchinleck, but has been suggested by some scholars as a direct source of the Auchinleck tale, although there is no consensus on this claim and D'Evelyn categorizes the two as different versions in her bibliography.[88] Whatever the actual relationship between the two tales, however, there is no denying that an English tradition of Saracen persecutors of St Margaret existed before Auchinleck. Saracen persecutors also turn up in the fifteenth-century text in Oxford, Bodleian Library, Bodley 6922 where the second devil dwindles to a mere "foulere best" (329).[89] The Auchinleck *Seynt Mergrete* is thus by no means unique among English texts in its depiction of Saracen persecutors and in its rewriting of the Mombritius version's second devil. The Auchinleck text is also not the first English text to introduce Saracens into Margaret's persecution. The Auchinleck legend does, however, belong to a rarer tradition; many English texts do not explicitly identify Margaret's persecutors as Saracens, and a number of fifteenth-century versions, like Lydgate's, make no reference to Saracens, Mahoun, or a black man-like devil (in Lydgate's tale the devil merely appears in the likeness of a man for his second visit).[90]

From the above, it should be clear that the Auchinleck saints' lives discussed in this chapter are not the only versions of these lives to represent Katherine's and Margaret's persecutors as Saracen. However, the Auchinleck versions do seem to emphasize the Saracen element of their narratives more than do the few antecedent versions that contain what are often muted or indirect suggestions of Saracen persecution. Moreover, it is evident from the above comparisons that the Auchinleck versions' explicit inclusion of Saracen characters represents a rather uncommon textual trajectory in tales of Katherine and Margaret. An extensive tradition of non-Saracen persecutors, or of not-explicitly-Saracen persecutors, also existed and was in wide circulation at the time of Auchinleck's compilation in the 1330s. Thus, a certain amount of choice, or at least of endorsement of a now-lost source's choice, may very well underlie these Auchinleck saints' lives. Ultimately, it is impossible to determine whether the Saracen presence in these tales occurs as a result of happenstance or choice. What is important in the context of this discussion, however, is not whether the Saracens in these Auchinleck tales are originary and unique, or quite common, but rather how the Saracen persecutors of *Seynt Katerine* and *Seynt Mergrete* function both within the larger manuscript context of Auchinleck and within the tales themselves.

SARACEN PERSECUTORS, THE AUCHINLECK CONTEXT, AND CHRISTIAN ENGLISH IDENTITY

The Saracen persecutors in *Seynt Katerine* and *Seynt Mergrete* represent a different type of Saracen from the Saracen princess of *Sir Beves*, or the warring and/or invading Saracens of *Roland and Vernagu, Otuel a Kniȝt, Guy of Warwick, Reinbrun gij sone of warwike, Sir Beves, Þe King of Tars*, and *Of Arthour and of Merlin*. In the two saints' lives, Auchinleck readers are presented with a portrait of Saracen political power and a Saracen-run state. Unlike *Sir Beves, Þe King of Tars*, and *Guy of Warwick* however, where one also sees life in a Saracen state, in the saints' lives Saracen political power is devoted exclusively to the persecution of Christians; Saracen characters either actively torture Christians, order them tortured, or observe them being tortured. The interactions between Saracen and Christian are thus not those of war, invasion, love, forced marriage or conquest, but rather interactions between Mahoun-worshippers and Christ-worshippers within a polity controlled by Mahoun-worshippers who value religious homogeneity. This situation evidently bears some resemblance to the Soudan's realm in *Þe King of Tars*, but that text is different in that it depicts inter-faith interactions between separate polities, and addresses the issue of religious integration. The two saints' legends, by contrast, depict inter-faith interactions within a polity, and are not about integration at all, but about the enunciation of religious difference. Martyrdom and conversion, not compromise, are the saints' goals; thus, the strict borders between Christendom and Saracenness are never challenged as they are in *Þe King of Tars*. Instead, because of the saints' lives' genre, religious practices become the focus of attention and much of the action involves the explicit articulation and enactment of the differences between Christian and Saracen religious positions. As is normal in medieval depictions of Saracens, Saracen religious practices do not resemble historical Muslim ones at all. In the saints' lives, however, because of the genre's religious focus, Saracen religious practices do have greater theological implications than in other genres studied in this book. In a saint's legend, Saracen religious practices serve as a foil which clarifies the centerpiece of the text, namely the saint's exposition of doctrinal Christian ideas and practices.

By serving as foils in theologically-focussed texts, Saracens in the two saints' lives participate in an aspect of Auchinleck not frequently discussed:

the manuscript's involvement with issues of lay piety. Because Auchinleck contains so many of the earliest extant English versions of French romances and *chansons de geste*, and thus so many foundational English tales of knightly adventure, its less original texts about Christian living have not received much critical analysis. These texts, however, account for eighteen of the manuscript's forty-four extant items. In addition to the two saints' lives discussed in this chapter, Auchinleck includes seven items that depict models of Christian living and of divine involvement in daily life (*St. Patrick's Purgatory and the Knight Sir Owen, Þe desputisoun bitven þe bodi & þe soule, The Clerk Who Would See the Virgin, Speculum Gy de Warewyke, Hou our leuedi saute was ferst founde, The Sayings of St Bernard, The Four Foes of Mankind*), six items that provide readers with information about central Christian figures and events (*The Legend of Pope Gregory, The Life of Adam and Eve, The Harrowing of Hell, Life of St Mary Magdalene, Anna our leuedis moder, The Assumption of the Blessed Virgin*), and three items that offer English readers access to basic Christian tenets and prayers in their own language (*On þe seven dedly sinnes, Þe pater noster vndo on englissch, Dauid þe king*).[91] While these texts are often rather short and do not occupy as many folios as the lengthy romances, they do constitute a significant portion of Auchinleck. Through these religiously focussed texts, the manuscript develops readers' awareness of Christian prayers, tenets, history, and identity, and thereby fosters lay piety. Saracen characters' ability to serve as a foil to Christian practices enables them to play a role in this project of fostering lay piety. As I will argue later in this chapter, their representation of an inverse, unideal mode of religious behavior clarifies for readers what are ideal Christian tenets and behaviors.

Even as they function thus, however, Saracens in *Seynt Katerine* and *Seynt Mergrete* also participate in their Auchinleck fellows' explorations of ideas about English identity. Efforts to foster lay piety by no means work at cross-purposes to efforts to construct a sense of communal, "Inglisch," vernacular identity. While the eighteen texts mentioned above develop knowledge of Christian worship and identity, they use the vernacular as their mode of communication. Some of the texts explicitly interweave their project of instruction with the language of their enunciation, and assert that they have been written in English precisely so that English lay people may better know what they are doing and saying when they worship. For example, the narrator of *Þe pater noster vndo on englissch* states that the text has been translated into English for the benefit of "Lewede men, þat ne beȝ no clerkes" (3),[92] while *On þe seven dedly sinnes* identifies itself as a text written in English specifically to communicate central articles of belief to "children and wimmen and men / Of twelue winter elde and more" (12–13).[93] Texts that actively foster lay piety thus also actively participate in that other project so central to Auchinleck: the interpellation of an English community interested in reading texts in its own language.

Auchinleck's interest in lay piety essentially defines the English community as a community engaged in learning about, and practicing, Christianity. In Auchinleck, then, Englishness is a religious identification as well as a political, linguistic, cultural, and historical one. This religious Englishness manifests itself in two ways in the saints' lives discussed here. First, these texts and their Saracens instruct a lay English, audience about ideal Christian attitudes towards sexuality and luxury, and about the appropriate objects of worship for Christians. The Saracens of *Seynt Mergrete* and *Seynt Katerine* thus serve as a guide to moral living for an English Christian community, and represent that community as one concerned about its spiritual health. In addition to being guides to model Christian life, however, these Saracens also remind readers of England's role as a Christian nation on the international stage and thereby manifest another facet of religious Englishness.

To be a western Christian nation in the later Middle Ages was to participate in pan-Christian politico-religious endeavors in foreign lands. The principal target of these endeavors in the later Middle Ages was the Holy Land, held by Muslims and Byzantine Christians until the surprise success of the First Crusade in 1098 established a western Christian presence in the area. English leaders and forces participated in this crusade and in most thereafter, and such crusading endeavors were a great source of English pride as well as a focus of national attention. For example, every English king from Henry III to Edward II took a vow to crusade, and clerics regularly preached the crusade in English churches while English chroniclers repeatedly included crusading events, taxes, and plans in their records.[94] Moreover, even though crusading efforts were not prospering when Auchinleck was compiled, English rulers and their people continued to be involved in various plans to regain the Holy Land.[95] Twenty-six embassies seeking assistance with crusading visited England between 1216 and 1307, crusades were preached in the 1290s, and the papacy imposed mandatory crusading taxes on the English Church in 1274, 1291, 1312 and 1333.[96] Edward I led a substantial force to the Middle East in the 1270s, renewed his vow to crusade in 1286, dispatched an advance force to the East in 1290, and planned a departure to the Holy Land with a large crusading force in 1293.[97] In 1306, Edward was still recognized throughout the West as a guiding light in the crusading movement and was the addressee of a treatise outlining plans to reclaim the Holy Land.[98] His son, Edward II, took the cross in 1313, and in 1313 and 1320 wrote "royal letters smooth[ing] the path for groups of Franciscans and Dominicans bound for the Holy Land on preaching missions to convert the infidel."⁹⁹ Even Edward III, who did not take the official crusading vow, repeatedly expressed publicly his willingness to crusade, and both he and his subjects were extensively involved in French plans for a crusade to the Holy Land between 1331 and 1336. Parliament even discussed the issue in 1332 and 1334.¹⁰⁰ In short, late medieval England prided itself on its role in pan-Christian crusading efforts and English people's participation in, and awareness of, such efforts were very much part of their sense of national identity. Saracens in *Seynt Mergrete* and *Seynt Katerine* explore this religious aspect of English identity. Through a convoluted evocation of historical Muslims, these texts offer an imaginative revision of late thirteenth-century crusading setbacks and enunciate a vision of Christian triumph somewhat similar to that espoused by writers advocating crusade in the early fourteenth century. The Saracens in these hagiographic tales thus help craft a vision of England as a nation deeply involved, and interested, in pan-Christian crusading efforts.

These two aspects of Christian Englishness—Christian education, and reflection on geo-political western Christian endeavors—are interwoven in the Auchinleck saints' lives discussed here. Other Auchinleck texts of lay piety demonstrate a similar linking of these two elements of English Christian identity, and reveal how each element seems to require invocation of the other. *On þe seven dedly sinnes* concludes its explicit effort to instruct English men, women and children in the basic articles of their faith in their own English language with an entreaty to God to

> Sende pees, þere is werre,
> And ȝiue cristenemen grace,
> In to þe holi lond to pace
> And sle Sarazins, þat beȝ so riue,
> And lete be cristenemen on liue. (288–92)

Thus, even texts that do not actually depict Saracens link vernacular explorations of Christian tenets to these eastern characters, and to the pan-Christian geo-political concerns of late medieval Europe.

SARACEN PERSECUTORS AND THE ELUCIDATION OF MODEL CHRISTIAN BEHAVIOR

One of the functions of representations of non-Christians in the medieval West was to clarify for Christians certain tenets of their faith. Cindy Vitto, discussing the figure of the virtuous pagan in Middle English texts, notes that this figure addresses not so much the issue of converting the non-Christian, but rather the long-standing theological debate "over the relative importance of grace and works in *Christian* salvation."[101] Similarly, Norman Daniel argues that the Christian theologian Raymon Lull, when he penned an imaginary debate between a Christian and a Muslim, "was interested, not in actual Muslim objections to the Christian dogma, but in those that he himself thought it might be reasonable for them to have."[102] Saracens in western texts about Christian theology are thus perhaps better read as loci of doctrinal clarification than as efforts at the mimetic representation of another religious group. By figuring forth what is supposedly opposed to Christianity, the Saracen in a saint's life defines Christian identity and ideological tenets, and gives voice to what might be a Christian audience's concerns about these ideals.

In *Seynt Katerine* and *Seynt Mergrete*, Saracens work especially well to clarify the role of the body, sensuality, and physical luxuries in a model Christian society. In particular, Saracens in these texts of virgin martyrdom articulate alternative ideas about the female body's sexual role in society, about people's proper relationship to physical luxuries, and about the types of bodies that should be worshipped by a community. Their ideas stand in opposition to those of the saint and God. As a result, Saracens illuminate, by contrast, ideal Christian tenets. Acting thus, the Saracens work effectively in a context of lay piety. Moreover, while clarifying Christian ideals, Saracens also voice earthly social concerns about aspects of those ideals, concerns that quite likely could have crossed the minds of lay readers and hearers. A lay audience, firmly implicated in socio-corporeal ties to other members of their community, might well have appreciated some of the points raised by Saracens about the social implications of the saint's model of community. The Saracens' Saracenness may ultimately suggest the essentially un-Christian nature of such socio-corporeal concerns, but their voicing of these concerns would certainly clarify for lay people what ought to be the good Christian's values.

In *Seynt Katerine* and *Seynt Mergrete*, one of the clearest points of difference between Saracens and saints is their respective ideas about a female body's sexuality. In accordance with stereotypical assertions of Saracen sensuality,[103] Saracens in these tales manifest an awareness of the female body as both physically attractive and a site for sexual intercourse. In *Seynt Katerine*, the Emperor Maxens is "forwonderd . . . / Of þat maidens fair vise" (105–6), and urges her to "Haue merci on þi feirhed!" (239) and recant her beliefs. In *Seynt Mergrete*, the sexual lens through which the Saracen persecutor views the saint is even more pronounced. When he first sees the saint tending her sheep, "Olibrious for hir fairnesse | ʒerne[s] hir to wiue" (48), and also decides that, even "ʒif sche be born of þral," "for hir michel feirhed, |, ...

Sche schal be mi leman | and haue gold to wal" (53–56). Such reactions, focussed on earthly beauty and indicative of sexual desire, stand in stark contrast to the attitudes articulated by Katerine and Mergrete. Katerine tells Maxens that Christ "is mi loue, he is mi spouse: / To swiche a leman take y me" (267–68), while Mergrete informs Olibrious's retainers "Ichaue ȝeuen mi maidenhed | to Jhesus Crist of heuen" (67). Both saints voice traditional Christian notions of virginity as a state of marriage to Christ, and of Christ as the virgin's bridegroom and lover.[104] In their model, there is no place for earthly sexuality; all such energies should be directed towards God, and he alone is the appropriate partner for a beautiful and exemplary Christian virgin. Their ideas quite distinctly contrast those of the Saracens. The Saracens, however, while they allow the saints to outline exemplary Christian virginity, also articulate an alternative, actively heterosexual vision of society and male-female relationships. The Saracen characters voice what might potentially be the less exemplary, sexually active, lay Christian's ideas about male and female bodies. Even though such attitudes, through their association with Saracen characters, are implied to be inferior and undesirable, their articulation allows these saints' lives to engage lay concerns more effectively.

Saracens also work in these two saints' lives to distinguish exemplary and non-exemplary ideas about people's relationship to the luxury goods of earthly society. Saracens clearly believe that corporeal delicacies are desirable, while the saints repeatedly voice the values of abstinence. For example, the Saracen Olibrious tries to entice Mergrete into his bed thus: "Trowe on me & be mi wiif: | wele þou schalt spede; / . . . . / Sikelatoun and purpel-pal | þat schal be þi wede, / Wiþ þe best metes in mi lond | wele y schal þe fede" (113–16). With these words, Olibrious offers Mergrete fine clothes, and delicious food—every bodily comfort she could desire. Similarly, Maxens volunteers to set Katerine up as a queen, with all the prestige and luxury that entails (241–42). Both saints, however, turn down these offers. Mergrete tells Olibrious "Þine wicke redes . . . | y do out of mi þouȝt" (117), while Katerine tells Maxens "Þou redest me to do gret sinne" (258). Katerine then immediately proceeds to clarify the doctrinal point for the audience: "What man wald ydampned be / For ani maner warldes winne?" (259–60). Olibrious and Maxens thus offer an opportunity for the saints to indicate to their audience the ever-present temptations of worldly sins such as Avarice and Gluttony that must be avoided by Christians. The Saracens, on the other hand, voice the attractiveness of fine clothes and delicious food, of luxuries and of wealth. Once again, the non-Christians articulate potential lay Christian distaste for the rejection of worldly luxuries asserted so forcefully by the saints.

Interestingly, the Saracens' very human (albeit unexemplary in Christian terms) attraction to luxuries and wealth may well have been shared by whoever commissioned or bought the Auchinleck manuscript. While no details of Auchinleck's original purchaser are known, most scholars agree that the manuscript must have been bought by someone who could afford some worldly luxuries. The sheer number of items in the book, as well as the inclusion of miniature illustrations, would have demanded a substantial outlay for materials and workmanship. Some scholars, such as Derek Pearsall and I. C. Cunningham, assert that the book is a product designed for mercantile consumption, while others, such as Thorlac Turville-Petre, argue that it was probably intended for a noble household, although perhaps not for the most senior or wealthy members of that household. [105] In either case, some excess wealth and interest in consumption of non-essential goods must underlie Auchinleck's compilation, a fact which would make Katerine's reminder about the emptiness of "warldes winne" particularly appropriate for the manuscript's original audience.

Saracens in *Seynt Mergrete* and *Seynt Katerine* also provide for their audience an alternative vision of the kind of bodies that deserve to be worshipped by communities. For them, bodies to be honored are bodies that enjoy all the trappings of worldly wealth. Olibrious states that if Mergrete accepts his offers, "Of alle þe wimen þat y wot | best hir schal be" (52). She will, in her possession of luxuries and of his favor, be foremost among women. Maxens develops this idea into a specifically religious form of worship. He tells Katerine that if she accepts his offers and recants,

"Hei3e & lowe [will] worþschipe þe
. . . .
3if þou wilt wirche after mi red:
A temple in þi worþschip make
Of marble ston, when þou art ded;
Among our godes þou schalt be sett
In siluer & in gold rede." (249–56)

Beauty, riches, and devotees are all connected in the model of worship offered by Saracens. A beautiful body, beautifully represented in the finest materials and ensconced in a luxurious temple, will form the center around which a religious community gathers. The saints, by contrast, offer the traditional Christian image of a suffering body around which, and by which, a community will be gathered and constructed. As the Emperor's wife is led off to execution, Katerine tells her to remember Christ "Þat sprad his bodi on þe tre, / As his swete wille was, / For to maken ous all fre" (550–52). Earlier, she bids converts "leue on Jhesu Crist, / Þat for mankin schadde his blod" (325–26). The body around which Christians unite is that of a bleeding, crucified man. Mergrete also mentions how Christ "wiþ his swete blod | . . . haþ ous alle bou3t" (275), and her hagiographer concludes with a prayer directed to "Jhesu, þat on þe rode was don | our soules forto borwe" (409). Similarly, the saints' own bodies, as they suffer, gather a community of potential converts around them. Katerine's scourged body, and the divine ministrations of God's angel, facilitate the conversion of Maxens's wife and of his knight Porfir when these two Saracens see "Ich wem & ich a wounde" of the saint being tended (314). Likewise, the spectacle of Mergrete's scourging gathers a crowd of potential Saracen converts who implore Mergrete "Haue merci on þi fair bodi | and þole þis paines no more!'" (148). Once again, the community gathering around a Christian gathers around a beaten and suffering body. All told, Saracens offer a vision of religious communities assembled around, and united by, beautiful, wealthily-adorned bodies, while the saints repeatedly remind Christians that the community to which they belong is centered on a suffering, bleeding, and dying body. If the Saracen religious communities in these tales represent the allure of worldly bodies, the Christian communities represent the abject underside and ultimate end of worldly bodies that wealthy Christians were ideally to keep in mind during their lives.[106]

All these contrasts between Christian and Saracen attitudes illuminate Christian ideals of female virginity and of general abstinence from worldly luxuries. The contrasts also clarify for a Christian audience the type of body Christians should worship—the naked suffering one rather than the finely clothed body of worldly success. Saracens in *Seynt Mergrete* and *Seynt Katerine* thus communicate to their audience certain Christian beliefs, and can be read as part of an effort at lay religious education of the "Inglisch." In this way, Saracens participate in Auchinleck's interpellation of a lay English Christian community as its audience. The historical pertinence of these saints' lives for Auchinleck's audience, however, extends beyond this. English people's participation in a pan-Christian geo-political and cultural identity was very much a part of their sense of Christian Englishness as well, and Saracens in *Seynt Mergrete* and *Seynt Katerine* also illuminate this aspect of English identity.

SARACENS AND MUSLIMS

If one distinctive aspect of the Saracens in *Seynt Katerine* and *Seynt Mergrete* is their role in promoting lay piety and defining an ideal Christian community, another is their relationship to history and to historical Muslims. As I have mentioned before, scholars of literary Saracens generally assert that these characters bear little or no resemblance to historical Muslims. In Auchinleck, however, certain representations of Saracens do evoke, in a convoluted way, aspects of late medieval Muslim civilization. The penultimate section of Chapter One discusses one such evocation. The Saracen persecutors in *Seynt Katerine* and *Seynt Mergrete* participate in another. In particular, while these Saracens' behaviors are stereotypical and inaccurate (as always, Saracens worship idols and are prone to fits of rage and intolerance), these figures are repeatedly linked to historical Muslims by their characterization, geographic locations, technological expertise, and wealth and power. In this way, familiar Saracen others metamorphose into rather less familiar evocations of historical Muslim Others, and these evocations facilitate the expression of fourteenth-century pan-Christian concerns about, and attitudes towards, the Middle East.

To understand how *Seynt Mergrete* and *Seynt Katerine* can be read in relation to Christian-Muslim interactions in the later Middle Ages, it is first necessary to indicate how the Saracen characters in these tales evoke historical Muslims. To begin with, the very presence of Saracen persecutors in *Seynt Mergrete* reflects a deliberate effort to characterize Saracens as earthly rather than fantastic creatures, and to write them into a lived, historical context. Traditionally, as mentioned earlier, this legend did not include explicitly Saracen persecutors, but did include a devil who appeared as a black-skinned man. It is very clear from the context of his appearance that this devil is part of a supernatural and superhuman battle between good and evil. He appears in Margaret's prison cell right after another devil, who appeared in the form of a dragon, swallowed her and burst apart. This is not a series of events that belongs on an earthly, quasi-historical plane; their supernatural character is very marked, and provoked expressions of skepticism from some hagiographers, while others omitted the unbelievable events altogether.[107] What fascinates me about the Auchinleck legend is its rewriting of this supernatural black-skinned demon as a fantastical creature with eyes on his toes, and the concomitant appearance of Saracen persecutors on the earthly plane. Four Auchinleck texts, *Þe King of Tars*, *Seynt Katerine*, *Guy of Warwick (Couplet Version)*, and *Guy of Warwick (stanzaic continuation)* explicitly identify Saracens as black-skinned people.[108] Thus, in Auchinleck, an association of Saracenness with black skin color is found at a number of points. These identifications help to show how the Saracen persecutors in *Seynt Mergrete* rewrite other tales of the saint that link black skin to the supernatural and the fantastic. In Auchinleck, a devil who is part of Margaret's hagiographic tradition and who resembles Saracens depicted elsewhere in the manuscript is rewritten so as to lose his skin color and appear more fantastical. At the same time, persecutors explicitly identified as Saracens, and thereby linked through manuscript context to black skin, torment Christ's saint during her earthly existence. What we see in Auchinleck, then, is a movement away from a depiction of black men as supernatural, hellish persecutors of Christians, and towards a depiction of black men as human, earthly persecutors of Christians. This is completely understandable in a post-Crusade western manuscript. As narratives of crusade had made clear in the centuries preceding Auchinleck's compilation, earthly, black-skinned enemies of Christians did exist.[109] Accordingly, the rewriting of the devil found in the Auchinleck *Seynt Mergrete* asserts that black-skinned opponents of Christianity are not fantastical imaginings on the level of dragons, but rather historical facts. As a result, *Seynt Mergrete* writes its events into a closer resemblance to lived situations in the later Middle Ages.

Geographic locations also link the Saracen persecutors in these hagiographic legends to historical Muslim-Christian conflict. The two saints in these Auchinleck tales are persecuted in Alexandria and Antioch, places that evoke crusading events and contexts. Katerine is persecuted by Maxens, the Emperor of Greece (10) in "þe borwe of Alisander" (29). The Greek reference, which Bella Millett suggests is a unique Auchinleck addition to Katherine's legend,[110] evokes in a late medieval context the Byzantine Empire of eastern Christendom. It might appear surprising to link Byzantine Greeks with Muslim persecutors and a Muslim city, but western crusaders repeatedly expressed dissatisfaction with the Greek empire and the assistance it offered them, and occasionally lumped the Byzantines together with Muslims as enemies to be fought and overcome. Indeed, western crusaders conquered and claimed parts of the Byzantine Empire as kingdoms for themselves, as happened in 1098 on the First Crusade when Bohemond of Taranto claimed Antioch for himself after it had been seized from the Muslims, and refused to return the city to its former Byzantine overlords despite an agreement to do so.[111] Similarly, the conquest of Constantinople in 1204 on the Fourth Crusade enacted in battle a western perception of the eastern Christians as enemies. The characterization of Saracens in *Seynt Katerine* thus evokes a Byzantine Christian Otherness as much as a Muslim one, and creates in this tale a generalized sense of Middle Eastern power and menace.

Setting Katerine's martyrdom in Alexandria further links her and her Saracen persecutors to crusading hotspots. The Auchinleck manuscript itself establishes Alexandria as a crusading center. *Guy of Warwick (stanzaic continuation)* recounts a battle between Christians and Saracens around "Alisaundre" (52. 4), and states that Christian captives from the battle are led to prison in "Alisaunder" (54. 4). Such literary references reflect Alexandria's lived history of Muslim-Christian conflict. The city, under Muslim control, was besieged by Christians in 1167, while campaigners on Saint Louis's crusade in 1249, which was aimed at Egypt and briefly conquered Damietta, seriously discussed "the possibility of moving . . . along the coast to take Alexandria."[112] Alexandria's name was thus linked with crusading actions against Muslims long before the time of Auchinleck's compilation. Indeed, a few decades after this compilation the city again figured large in crusading tales when, in 1365, Peter of Cyprus captured the city and looted it for six days before being forced to withdraw.[113] As Christopher Tyerman notes, this crusading endeavor involved a number of English nobles, and was duly reported in England.[114] The geographic positioning of *Seynt Katerine* thus situates the eponymous saint and her Saracen persecutors in a historical landscape rich with crusading associations, and develops the links between Saracen characters and historical Muslims.

The same is true of *Seynt Mergrete*. Born to natives of "Antiage" (6), St Mergrete is persecuted by the Mahoun-worshipping Olibrious, "lord . . . / Of Antiage" (41–42). The crusaders' capture of Antioch in 1098 after a seven-month siege was well known in the West not only through various chronicles but also through the circulation of the crusading cycle, the *Chanson d'Antioche*, which detailed many of the adventures of the First Crusaders and of the eventual Lord of Antioch, Bohemond.[115] Indeed, a copy of this tale was loaned to Henry III of England's queen, Eleanor, in May 1250, and scenes from it were "depicted in the queen's own Antioch Chamber at Westminster, at Clarendon, and in the Camera Rosamundae at Winchester Castle."[116] Records of the First Crusade also indicate that a Christian naval fleet composed in part of English ships and sailors "played an important role in maintaining the lifeline of food and supplies between Byzantine Cyprus and the crusaders [besieging Antioch] on the Syrian mainland."[117] According to Tyerman, English awareness of Antioch would also have been fostered by events such as Pain Peverel's endowment of Barnwell Priory with precious relics acquired by him while "on the Antioch campaign with Robert Curthose."[118] Antioch also served as a gathering point for forces linked to Louis VII of France's crusade in 1148, and was the site of what Jonathan Riley-Smith calls Eleanor of Aquitaine's "atrocious" behavior, for which her marriage to Louis VII of France was annulled a few years later.[119] Thus, although Antioch fell to the Muslims in 1268,[120] it had a long history of publicity in the West, and was clearly a crusading locale known in England. In Auchinleck's stanzaic version of *Guy of Warwick*, for example, Guy the pilgrim approaches "Antiage" (45. 2), only to be met outside the city by a Christian crusader captured by

Saracens. A tale of St Margaret's persecution by Saracens of Antioch in the 1330s would thus have evoked both the fact of contemporary Muslim control of the area, and the area's past engagement in Muslim-Christian conflicts.

Another point of connection between historical Muslims and these saints' lives Saracens is found in *Seynt Katerine*. Unlike many chronologically earlier versions of the legend, the Auchinleck text explicitly identifies as Saracen the man who designs a contraption of wheels to dismember Katerine:

> Þer com a Sarraȝin gon:
> Cursates, seyt þe boke, he hiȝt.
> "King," he seyd, "icham þi man.
> ȝete y can a turnament make:
> Swiche no herdestow neuer nan;
> Bi þan it be wrouȝt & sche it se,
> Anoþer þouȝt sche schal þenke on.
> Four wheles schal y make,
> Þe to schal turn oȝain to,
> Ful þicke þai schal be driuen
> Wiþ wiþerhokes mo & mo.
> Among þe four sche schal be don,
> Hir bodi forto wirche wo:
> To smale peces sche schal be rent,
> On erþe schal sche neuer go." (450–64)

While the contraption of the Katherine wheel is common to legends of the saint (indeed, a wheel is one of Katherine's iconographic attributes),[121] the association of this complex feat of engineering with a Saracen designer is not. The Saracen designer, however, evokes notions of Muslim technological superiority in the later Middle Ages. According to Steven Runciman, the medieval western Christian who traveled to Muslim lands was "uneasily aware that in most respects Moslem civilization was higher than his own."[122] Crusade chronicles repeatedly document western amazement at the architectural and technological advancement of Middle Eastern civilizations in the later Middle Ages, be they Muslim or Byzantine.[123] Similarly, there is no denying that medieval Muslims possessed much superior scientific knowledge, as can be seen in the fact that many medieval western writings on medicine were translations of Arabic texts.[124] The association of Cursates, the diabolical engineer, with Saracenness thus would seem to evoke medieval associations of technological expertise with historical easterners, both Muslim and Greek. Once again, Saracens in the Auchinleck saints' lives appear more closely related than usual to the historical Middle East.

The final link between Saracens and historical Muslims found in these texts is a rather traditional one, and is also true of other Saracens in Auchinleck. In *Seynt Mergrete* and *Seynt Katerine*, the Saracen persecutors repeatedly demonstrate their access to wealth and power. As mentioned above, Olibrious can offer Mergrete fine clothes and good food, while Maxens can offer Katerine a temple of marble and idols made of gold and silver. Both men also possess power. Olibrious is the lord of Antioch and Azie, while Maxens is the emperor of Greece who can summon scholars from all over his realm to debate religion with Katerine (145–52). The two Saracens also have the authority to effect the saints' physical suffering and earthly death. Like Saracens elsewhere in Auchinleck, these characters communicate to readers a sense of the wealth and power of the historical Muslim world. Crusaders repeatedly remarked the luxurious furnishings and clothing found in the East, while many of Europe's luxury goods such as fine materials and spices came from Muslim or eastern realms.[125] Similarly, Christian crusaders often learned firsthand the political and military might of Muslim rulers, particularly in the centuries following the First Crusade when Christian victories became scarce, and Muslim rulers such as Saladin reconquered Christian holdings in Outremer.[126] Powerful Saracens like the persecutors in these saints' lives, like Josiane's father in *Sir Beves*, like King Garsie in *Otuel a Kni3t*, like King Triamour in *Guy of Warwick (stanzaic continuation)*, like King Arguus in *Reinbrun*, and like the Soudan of Damascus in *Þe King of Tars* thus all represent in some form the menacing might of Muslim rulers in the later Middle Ages.

The characterization of Mergrete's persecutors, the two legends' associations with crusading locales, the technological expertise of the Saracen Cursates in *Seynt Katerine*, and the depiction of Saracens in positions of wealth and power all serve to link the Saracens in these saints' lives to historical Muslims (and, occasionally, to Byzantine Greeks). The hagiographic texts' evocation of historical locale and context, however, should not be read as part of an effort to represent accurately medieval Muslims. Saracens in these texts still worship multiple graven images in complete contravention of Muslim practices and prohibitions of images. They also participate in an active persecution of their Christian subjects, something by no means the norm in medieval Muslim polities which were, if anything, more tolerant of religious diversity than their western Christian counterparts.[127] However, even as these literary Saracens demonstrate the disjuncture between them and historical Muslims that has been identified by scholars, they also, through their aforementioned evocations of the East, communicate a sense of the power Muslim (and Byzantine) civilizations possessed, and of the menace and insecurity western Christian civilizations occasionally felt when confronted by the East. Medieval western hagiographers could envisage a realm in which Christians were persecuted by fictional Saracens precisely because historical Muslims possessed the might to defeat, conquer, oppress, and persecute Christians if they so desired. One can thus perceive in the Saracen persecutors of *Seynt Katerine* and *Seynt Mergrete* a trace of the historical actuality of medieval Muslims and, more clearly, a trace of the fear Middle Eastern powers provoked in late medieval Christians. Historical inaccuracy may be rife among Saracens, but in saints' lives at least, historical Muslim (and occasionally Byzantine) impressiveness can be dimly sensed in the figure of the Saracen persecutor. As a result, although the texts' actions bear little resemblance to actual events in the Middle East, they are moved from an atemporal, highly idealized and exemplary realm to a historical human plane of uneasy East-West coexistence and conflict. The Saracens in these saints' legends write the Christian religious ideals manifested into the lived geo-political context of Auchinleck's fourteenth-century readers and hearers. The evocation of a quasi-historical context enables these hagiographic legends to function as venues in which western attitudes to the East can be expressed, and in which recent western military humiliations at Muslim and Byzantine hands can be imaginatively redressed.

REJECTION AND IMAGINATIVE REDRESS

In the early fourteenth century, European crusading endeavors were not prospering. In 1261, western control of Constantinople, established in 1204 as a result of the Fourth Crusade, ended when Byzantine forces conquered the city and forcibly reclaimed it from their Christian cousins.[128] In 1291, Acre, the last foothold of western Christians in the Holy Land, fell to a huge force of Muslims from Egypt.[129] Physically, the western medieval Christian presence in the Holy Land ended with this defeat, but westerners were not to know this, and, as Jonathan Riley-Smith explains, "The fall of Acre . . . inspired the writing of a spate of crusade treatises, which continued to appear at intervals throughout the fourteenth century."[130] The fourteenth century was thus a period in the West when various writers repeatedly reminded European Christians of their defeats in the East, and of the need to mount a new effort to retake the Holy Land from "heathen" control. England was not isolated from this movement. Instead, the crusading prowess Edward I demonstrated in the 1270s, his dispatch of forces to the Holy Land in the 1290s, his diplomatic and financial preparations to crusade again, and his many military victories at home marked him as an ideal recipient of treatises about renewing the crusade.[131] One such treatise dedicated to Edward was that written around 1306 by Pierre Dubois, a Frenchman. In his *De recuperatione terre sancte*, Dubois laid out a plan for the conquest and conversion of the Holy Land as well as for the reconquest of Constantinople and its reclamation from "Paleologus, usurper of the empire of Constantinople."[132] The extensive detail of Dubois's plan reveals the amount of thought expended on plans to retake the Holy Land, while the treatise's focus on attacking Muslims *and* Byzantines makes both Muslims and eastern Christians enemies of the West. When situated in this historical context of which the English were very much aware, the actions of Saints Katerine and Mergrete take on a new aspect. Their behavior constitutes both a rejection of eastern culture as medieval westerners perceived it, and a literary assertion of Christian superiority that was far from historical reality, but that must have been rather comforting given recent Christian setbacks at Muslim and Byzantine hands, and given repeated calls to engage the Muslims anew and expel them from the Holy Land.

In the historical context of East-West interaction evoked by the Saracens in *Seynt Mergrete* and *Seynt Katerine*, the saints' repulsion of their persecutors' advances becomes more than a display of exemplary Christian virginity, self-abnegation and refusal of "warldes winne." It also enacts a rejection of what westerners identified as Muslim practices and products, and an assertion of western Christian superiority. For example, when read in historical context, the saints' rejection of their Saracen persecutors' sexual advances becomes a Christian refusal of the sensuality and sexual indulgence westerners stereotypically associated with medieval Muslims.[133] Given Christian ideals, this rejection of Saracen sensuality also functions as an assertion of Christian moral superiority to Muslims. Likewise, the two saints' refusal to be bribed by promises of wealth, fine food, and luxurious clothes can be read as a western Christian refusal of the wealth, spices, and fine materials of the East. Most European spices were imported by way of the Middle East, and fine silks and other materials also traveled this route. Jonathan Riley-Smith details the ways in which Outremer was very much an economic import-export hub for westerners, and indicates how mercantile concerns related to this fact shaped European policies both in the Middle East and at home.[134] Similarly, E. Jane Burns has traced the western association of fine materials with the East and with wealth,[135] while a recurring theme in Dubois's *De recuperatione terre sancte* is the need to reclaim the Holy Land in order both to curtail the exorbitant prices western merchants charge for goods obtained from Muslims, and to ensure an adequate supply of luxury items for the West. According to Dubois, "valuable commodities, abundant in those regions but rare and highly prized among us, would be transported to us Occidentals in adequate amounts at a reasonable price, once the world were made Catholic."[136] In the saints' lives studied here, however, the two Christian virgins reject as meaningless and worthless all the riches produced by the East, and thus diminish the value of the goods the East provided to the medieval West. The saints' deeds assert Christian superiority and disavow Christian Europe's reliance on Muslim traders and commodities.

Other aspects of these saints' lives, too, can be read as a western rejection of the Middle East and any cultural connections to it. The conflation of Greek and Saracen in the figure of St Katerine's persecutor Maxens, for example, refuses any notion of cross-cultural Christian unity. To identify Maxens as both "In Grece . . . an emp*erour*" (10) and a "Sarraʒin . . . ful strong" (21) makes eastern Christians and Muslims one and the same enemy of western Christians. A similar sense of common enmity can be discerned in the depiction of the "Gregeys" of "Costentyn-noble" in Auchinleck's *Guy of Warwick*. Although Guy aids the Emperor of Constantinople in his battles against Saracens, Guy finds himself repeatedly the target of treacherous acts by the Emperor's steward. Guy finally tells the Emperor that "[although] Ich haue þe serued wiþ gret honour; / ʒolden þou hast me iuel mi while" (4404–5), and adds that

> "Seþþe þou no miʒt nouʒt waranti me,
> Whar-to schuld y serui þe,
> On oncouþe man in thi lond,
> When þou no dost him bot schond?
> Harm me is, & michel misdo;
> Þer-fore ichil fram þe go." (4415–20)

Guy's experiences reflect western crusaders' distrust of eastern Christians, and a western sense that everyone of the East is a foe of some sort. Similarly, Dubois's treatise and his above-cited description of the Byzantine Emperor show that fourteenth-century westerners considered Muslims and Byzantine Christians alike to be enemies of Christ and wrongful possessors of Christian lands in the Middle East. Such conflation of different peoples and religions reflects western Europeans' failure to appreciate the historical and cultural distinctiveness of their eastern Christian cousins, and a concomitant desire to classify their religious fellows as foes.[137] The characterization of Katerine's persecutor as both Greek and Saracen thus constitutes a medieval western rejection of Christian connections linking East and West, and indicates a preference for viewing the Middle East as an undifferentiated space of enmity towards "true" Christians.

The above examples demonstrate how Saracen characters in *Seynt Mergrete* and *Seynt Katerine* participate in a pageant of western rejection of various aspects of the Middle East. Such fictional rejections imaginatively rewrite recent western military defeats at the hands of Greek and Muslim forces, and the westerners' subsequent expulsion from the Middle East. In these saints' lives, western dissociation from peoples of the Middle East becomes a willed, saintly rejection of all the enticements the Middle East can offer. As Mergrete and Katerine choose death over Saracen worship practices and life in a Saracen-controlled polity, they demonstrate for their audiences the virtue of Christian disengagement from peoples and places linked to the Middle East, and represent such disengagement as the product of virtuous Christian choice. This model of disengagement as choice clearly stands in contrast to the forcible historical ejection of westerners from the Middle East effected by Muslim and Greek armies in the late thirteenth century. The saints' lives thus recast the political severance of East and West historically caused by military defeat as a dissociation and rejection of the East willed by virtuous Christians. This revision places Christians in a position of power as the instigators of western disengagement in the Middle East, and thereby asserts Christian superiority.

The superiority of Christian virtue is also affirmed in other ways in *Seynt Mergrete* and *Seynt Katerine*. The two saints' ability to emerge unharmed from the torments imposed on them by their Saracen persecutors suggests the ultimate inefficacy of Saracens and their acts against model Christians. When Mergrete emerges from a vat of boiling water unscathed, and when the device of wheels designed to torture Katerine bursts asunder, the powerlessness of the Saracen persecutors in relation to these Christian heroes is clearly communicated. The saints' invulnerability suggests Christian imperviousness to Saracen and, by implication, Muslim and Byzantine power. The miraculous avoidance of torture at these points also represents Christian misfortunes at Saracen hands, when they do occur, as events willed by God rather than consequences of non-Christian power. Likewise, the assumption of the two saints into heaven and God's various signs of favor at the end of the saints' lives demonstrate the Christian God's power and affirm that the saints have been killed by Saracens only because God willed it. Such images, in the historical context of fourteenth-century western exile from the Holy Land, comfortingly assert the value of Christianity, as well as the power of a Christian God who will not allow his people to remain oppressed indefinitely, and who possesses the power to make everything right for the chosen ones who follow his precepts. *Seynt Mergrete* and *Seynt Katerine* thus emphasize the applicability of

Christian virtue to military success in the East, and suggest that Christian virtue will reap its own reward. This notion of sinlessness as a component of Christian recovery of the Holy Land was quite common among writers expounding plans for renewed crusade. Dubois, for example, repeatedly insists that corrupt and worldly clergy must give up their luxury goods if the Holy Land is to be reclaimed, and that warring western nobles must make peace among themselves if his plan is to succeed. Redressing western humiliations at Muslim hands is thus represented as requiring virtuous Christian action, and the balance of power between westerner and Middle Easterner is re-aligned so as to endow the western Christian with the power to decide his or her own destiny.

Recent western defeats in the Middle East are imaginatively redressed in more concrete ways as well in the saints' lives in Auchinleck. The acts of saints in these tales constitute a wholesale infiltration and destruction of non-Christian society by Christians. Such infiltration and destruction represent a Christian victory over Saracens and the historical Muslim civilization they evoke in *Seynt Mergrete* and *Seynt Katerine*. Interestingly, the notion of Christian victory by way of feminine infiltration was not unrelated to historical plans for recovery of the Holy Land. Dubois's treatise explicitly outlines ways in which attractive Christian women are to be raised who, through their marriages to Muslim leaders and interactions with Muslim women, will convert Muslims to Christianity.[138] This model posits the deconstruction of non-Christian society and the formation of a Christian community through the disruptive acts of good Christian women living within a non-Christian society. In addition, these women are to achieve the destruction of Muslim society by challenging Muslim ideas of marriage and the traditional bonds linking men and women in Muslim marriage.[139] Although Dubois's treatise certainly did not influence the general outlines of the tales studied here, which existed long before he wrote his piece, his ideas are intriguingly paralleled in *Seynt Mergrete* and *Seynt Katerine* and their narration of how female saints reconfigure, and thereby raze, the bonds that structure Saracen society. Evidently, ideas expounded in saints' lives could be extremely pertinent to medieval western ideas about renewing crusade and recapturing the Holy Land.

To be persecuted and martyred, a saint must needs introduce a new, unacceptable, and Christian mode of behavior into an already-established, non-Christian community. Accordingly, the saint is always presented as challenging and undermining a community's traditional structures. In *Seynt Mergrete* and *Seynt Katerine*, the Saracen characters indicate that the destructive potential of these saints revolves around their reconfigurations of the social and physical connections linking people in the Saracen polity. As in Dubois's model, one of the traditional socio-corporeal relationships repeatedly challenged, rejected or severed by the saints in *Seynt Mergrete* and *Seynt Katerine* is that between Saracen husband and wife. As mentioned above, Mergrete and Katerine behave in traditional saintly fashion by rejecting marriage and coupling in this life in favor of marriage to Christ. Physical sexuality is abandoned, and bonds of loyalty tie the saints to a heavenly bridegroom rather than an earthly one, thereby destroying the ties that bind traditional Saracen society together. The saints' disruption of traditional socio-corporeal bonds, however, consists not only of their own refusal of marriage, but also, in Katerine's case, of her encouragement to Saracen women to do the same. Katerine explicitly advises Maxens's Empress to abandon her earthly husband for God:

> "Certes, dame, y rede þe wel:
> Forsake Maxens & al his miȝt
> For þat ich kinges loue
> Þat made þe day & eke þe niȝt." (337–40)

When the Empress actually follows Katerine's advice later, her rejection of Maxens is introduced narratively by the line: "To hi*m* seyd his wiif, þe quen" (507). The reference to the empress's status as "wiif" emphasizes precisely the rupture of physical, familial bonds that is taking place according to Katerine's instructions. Maxens's response both enacts the severance of sexual and physical closeness that the Empress's decision entails, and indicates the concern with which he views this change in his relationship with his wife. Maxens tells her,

> "Bot þou forsake Jh*es*u Crist,
> Þis schal be þi iugement:
> First þine pappes of þi brest
> Wiþ iren hokes schal be rent;
> Biheueded schaltow þan be,
> Þi bodi on þe feld ysent,
> Wiþ houndes & wiþ foules to-drawe.
> And þis schal be mi comandment." (530–36)

The physical brutality of Maxens's judgement demonstrates clearly the severance of the sexual closeness that binds husband and wife together physically. His references to "forsak[ing] Jhesu Crist" as well as his assertion that "þis schal be mi comandment" simultaneously cast this severance as the direct result of his wife's decision to re-align her loyalties according to a Christian model, and to replace her physical links to Maxens with spiritual ones to Christ. The harshness of the judgement also communicates the seriousness with which Maxens views this Christian re-alignment of earthly, physical bonds in his community. Maxens's judgement makes clear to all the destructive effects of Christian challenges to his Saracen community's ideas about how people are connected. Not only are such challenges disruptive in themselves, but they also provoke socially disruptive, harsh punishments, as indeed they must, since they effectively break and rewrite the foundational bonds structuring a society and joining its members.

The saints, however, do not merely challenge the familial connections underpinning Saracen society; they also destroy and rewrite the bonds linking together large sections of the society in the political sphere, and thereby win a political victory for Christianity as well as a socio-cultural one. Maxens articulates a purportedly Saracen notion of the physical sconnections binding him and his soldiers together when, upon discovering that someone has disobeyed him and buried his wife, he demands, "who haþ þis don / Of min men þat y fede & cloþe!" (573–74). His words reveal a sense that looking after a person's physical needs should ensure that person's loyalty to his or her provider. Maxens essentially articulates a basic tenet of retainership: one fights for and obeys the person who pays one and looks after one's physical needs. Bonds of physical comfort and provision thus unite people.[140] Christ's saints, however, actively undermine the community created by such bonds. Katerine, for example, tells Porfir, Maxens's knight, of the joys of heaven, saying

> "Þer nis non in þat riche
> Þat honger haþ, cold no þrest;
> Þer is liif wiþouten ende,
> Þer is stede of ro & rest." (353–56)

The community to which she belongs, and to which she advocates belonging, is one untouched by the need for food, water, or clothing. Maxens's attention to those issues is therefore irrelevant in Katerine's spiritual, heavenly community, and the body's needs are a moot point. Her model of Christian community completely rewrites the bodily dependence and need upon which Maxens's community of male retainers is based.

When Porfir converts and thereby rejects the bonds that tie him to Maxens, he breaks the traditional, corporeal links yoking retainers and ruler together in the text's Saracen society. The sense of social destruction associated with this act is clearly articulated in Maxens's repeated lamentations. Maxens first says "Now haþ Porfir me forsake, / Þat was wardain of al mi liif" (597–98), but then continues:

> . . . "now ichaue forelorn
> Þe best kniȝt of al mi þede!
> He was min help & mi rede,
> Ouer-al at al mi nede.
> Þe wiche schal it abigge de(re)
> Þurch whom he haþ don þis dede!" (603–8)

The repetition of Maxens's woe indicates the extent of the loss he feels. Indeed, Maxens bewails this destruction of masculine, political bonds more vociferously than he does the destruction of the bonds linking him and his wife. Moreover, he explicitly attributes Porfir's rejection of retainership to Katerine and her efforts to Christianize Maxens's community. Maxens's attitude to her hardens from this point onwards. Not only does he vow to make her pay for what she has accomplished, but when she comes before him, he looks on her "Ful sternliche" (633), and says

> "Miche wo þou hast ous wrouȝt,
> Þou wiche ful of felonie,
> Þou hast me don mi folk forlese.
> Þat þou schalt ful dere abie!" (635–38)

In this speech he explicitly charges Katerine with having caused the destruction of his relationships with his people and with having wrought "ous" woe. Her efforts to rewrite the ties binding Maxens and his people have proven effective, and with such Christian rewriting she has destroyed the Saracen community. The social dangers of altering the physical, bodily modes through which people relate to each other are made clear, the Saracen community is destroyed, and Christianity emerges triumphant. In *Seynt Katerine*, then, we see enacted the rupture of a community evocative in convoluted ways of historical Muslim polities in the Middle East. In Auchinleck's tale of this saint's life, historical, western reverses at Muslim and Byzantine hands are narratively redressed and avenged by the destruction of a fictional Saracen society. Moreover, this destruction is effected by a feminine infiltration of Saracen society and through a female Christian's efforts to sever and rewrite the inter-personal bonds structuring that society. Ideas strangely similar to Dubois's model can thus be seen at work and, as he envisaged, non-Christian society is bested by Christianity.

CODA: CHRISTIANITY AND THE NEED FOR
PERSECUTION ON DEMAND

Christian martyrdom and the concomitant besting of a non-Christian society require persecution. Indeed, problems ensue when it appears in a saint's
passion that martyrdom, the ultimate end of persecution, may not be
achieved. For example, in *Seynt Mergrete* Mergrete's direct links to Christ
prove so impressive that her executioner, Malcous, converts and refuses to
behead her, saying "Þat nold y do, . . . | for al þis warld to winne; / Þi louerd
haþ wiþ þe speke | in wham þou leuest inne" (383–84). Margaret finally
orders him to behead her, and tells him that if he does not, he will not enter
heaven (385–93). Her identity and her place in God's model community
require her persecution, and she is ultimately responsible for ensuring that
her physical suffering follows the trajectory required for membership in the
heavenly host. To that end, she must undermine her efficacy of conversion
by ordering a recent convert to behave as though he has not converted. She
cannot fit in to the heavenly community she desires if everyone around her
starts behaving like a Christian. Mergrete's need for an un-Christian act of
murder to establish her identity as Christian martyr thus reveals a truism of
group identity: a community requires the existence of outsiders to define
itself. Christianity in particular, as a community of worship gathered around
suffering, dying bodies, requires an outsider to inscribe that suffering and
torment since Christians, ideally, are not supposed to do so. Without an outsider to enact the existence of an alternative belief, the truth and superiority
of Christian death cannot be demonstrated. In other words, the presence of
outsiders who are willing to kill to defend their ideas of religion is essential if
suffering bodies are to be made available for worship and veneration, and if
Christian ideals are to be presented as life and death issues. Fictional Saracens fulfill this need admirably. Their power, sensuality and vehemence
ensure their opposition to Christian saints, their cooperation in the creation
of a community of martyrs, and their clarification, through contrast, of
Christian ideologies.

Fictional Saracens are necessary for another reason, however: real-life
Muslims could not be depended upon to act sufficiently intolerantly
towards Christians. While Saracens in saints' lives may evoke aspects of historical Muslims, they differ greatly in this one respect. Fictional Saracens,
whatever their historical resonances, can always be relied upon to kill Christians, illuminate Christian ideals, and build a community of martyrs; historical Muslims cannot. The stories of Ramón Lull and of Father Livin, a
fourteenth-century monk, clearly demonstrate this fact.[141] Inflamed by ideas

of the glory of martyrdom and the enmity of Muslims to Christianity, both men moved to Muslim-controlled parts of Africa and started to preach conversion there. Both were disappointed by their failures to attract converts and to provoke the Muslim authorities to persecution of them. Instead, they were tolerated, and ignored. Both worked to become more controversial, but did not succeed in provoking Muslim ire until they, respectively, vituperated Islam in the market place and defiled the mosque on a holy day. Resigned, the Muslim rulers finally ordered their executions. These anecdotes illustrate clearly the disjuncture between western representations of active Saracen persecution of Christians and the historically more common medieval Muslim tolerance. They show that fictional Saracen persecutors were necessary in the West because they alone could be relied upon to behave just as Christians expected and desired.

While actual outsiders cannot be relied upon to behave in the ways necessary for a society's self-definition, they can be represented as behaving in the desired ways. This representation (or misrepresentation) of Others ensures the textual definition and demarcation of a group's identity. Nevertheless, fictional others with historical resonances, like the Saracens in these saints' lives, are the *most* useful characters to explore group identity because they communicate all the intensity of lived experiences of Otherness, while their fictionality ensures that they function optimally to define a group. Thus Saracens are necessary for medieval Christians because, since they are fictions, they will always persecute on demand, even as they may simultaneously evoke resonances of actual historical alterity.

Fictional Saracens work extremely well to define Christian identity in western texts, as the persecutors in Auchinleck's *Seynt Mergrete* and *Seynt Katerine* show. These characters complement other Auchinleck Saracens' explorations of Englishness by indicating that Englishness is a religious identity as well as a political, cultural, linguistic, and historical one. To be "Inglisch" in this manuscript is evidently to desire vernacular instruction in basic tenets of the Christian faith, and the Saracens of *Seynt Mergrete* and *Seynt Katerine* ably offer such instruction to a lay English audience. To be English in Auchinleck is also to be aware of crusading setbacks and triumphs, and of English participation in a pan-Christian geo-political and cultural identity. Saracens in these two saints' lives promote such awareness by sliding disconcertingly from being the familiar domestic others of medieval literature to being slightly menacing evocations of historical Middle Eastern Otherness. The Saracens' characterization, geographic affiliations, technological expertise, and power all communicate a sense of the historical existence of Muslims and Byzantine Greeks, and of Christian interactions with these societies in the Middle East. Saracens thus introduce contemporary historical resonances of western political expulsion from the Holy Land into the usually ahistorical genre of the saint's life. As a result, the actions of the saints in these saints' lives imaginatively revise late thirteenth-century crusading setbacks, and envision an overwhelming Christian triumph that would have gladdened the hearts of English proponents of crusade in the early fourteenth century.

Chapter Five

Saracens, Englishness, and Productive Violence in *Of Arthour and Of Merlin*[1]

INTRODUCTION

While the other chapters of this book examine Saracens in texts that, with the exception of *Sir Beves* and *Guy of Warwick,* are not explicitly related to England, this final chapter studies the representation of Saracens in a text intimately linked to England and its history. *Of Arthour and of Merlin* combines historical and romance material, and depicts in extensive detail King Arthur's rise to power. Although noted for its originary "Englishing" of French Arthurian tradition, Auchinleck's *Of Arthour and of Merlin* has not attracted much critical interest.[2] This may perhaps be explained by the poem's predilection for detailed and gory descriptions of martial encounters.[3] Indeed, accounts of the tale in Wells's and Severs's *Manuals of the Writings in Middle English* excoriate it for the many accounts of battles that "are too numerous, too prolonged, and too like each other,"[4] or simply "monotonous to the modern reader."[5] To focus on the number of battles, however, is to foreclose consideration of the implications of these battles, and to ignore the poem's somewhat unusual depiction of these battles as Saracen-Christian conflicts. The presence of Saracens represents a rather innovative insertion into an Arthurian tradition deeply involved in complicated questions of ethnic and political identity. This chapter examines the textual precedents for the appearance of Saracens in *Of Arthour and of Merlin* and then studies the various ways in which the Saracens here engage issues of English identity. Generally, the Saracens in this text expose the many ways in which "Inglisch" identity is a product of violence. Saracens in *Of Arthour and of Merlin* craft a vision of England as a great crusading nation, and indicate the geo-political benefits that accrue from crusade. They also explore the historically formative role of invasions and conquest in England, and reveal the hybrid nature of the "Inglisch" identity Auchinleck trumpets so proudly. Finally, Saracens in this text facilitate awareness of the ways in which war can define, stabilize and revitalize the English polity and its structures. Saracens in *Of Arthour and of Merlin* thus offer a variety of insights into the role of conflict and violence in the formation of "Inglisch" identity.

THE TEXTUAL ORIGINS OF *OF ARTHOUR AND OF MERLIN* AND ITS SARACENS

The nature of the Saracen presence in *Of Arthour and of Merlin* is perhaps best appreciated when the text is situated in the context of its literary history. The Auchinleck *Of Arthour and of Merlin* represents the earliest extant Middle English reworking of material from the French Arthurian tradition that developed out of the twelfth-century poems of Chrétien de Troyes.[6] *Of Arthour and of Merlin* translates a portion of the Old French vulgate prose cycle of Arthurian romances, a collection of texts also known as the Lancelot-Grail Cycle, the Vulgate Cycle, and the Pseudo-Map cycle.[7] This cycle consists of the *Estoire del saint graal,* the *Estoire de Merlin,* the *Lancelot, La Queste del saint graal,* and *La Mort Artu.*[8] *Of Arthour and of Merlin* is based upon material found in the *Estoire de Merlin.* This French text also possesses multiple names, and is known variously as the *Merlin ordinaire,* the French Prose *Merlin,* and *Merlin* as well as the *Estoire de Merlin.*[9] Ultimately, the prose tradition is believed to be based on a poetic work by Robert de Boron, known as *Merlin,* of which only a 502-line fragment remains.[10] Prose re-workings and significant additions constitute the extremely lengthy *Estoire de Merlin,* of which forty-six complete versions and nine fragments exist in manuscript form.[11]

The Auchinleck *Of Arthour and of Merlin* represents the earliest redaction of the *Estoire de Merlin* in English, and marks a return to poetic verse. The poem is 9938 lines long, and begins by depicting the turmoil created in England by King Costaunce's death, his heirs' failure to defend the realm against Saracen invaders, the usurpation of the throne by Fortiger, and Fortiger's alliance with the Saracens.[12] The poem then proceeds to recount the supernatural birth and infancy of Merlin, the return of Costaunce's rightful heir (Uter) to the throne, the begetting and childhood of Arthur, Arthur's accession to the throne, and Arthur's battles against unruly kings who refuse to acknowledge his overlordship. The final six thousand lines concentrate on Arthur's battles in a foreign kingdom against Saracens and on the many battles fought in England between invading Saracens and the rising generation of Round Table knights. The Auchinleck poem ends at this point, whereas the French *Estoire* proceeds to relate Arthur's return to England, the decisive expulsion of the Saracens, and the adventures of Arthur and his knights overseas.

While Auchinleck is the earliest extant version of *Of Arthour and of Merlin*, other manuscripts of the English poem do exist, although they recount much less of the action than Auchinleck does. These later versions are: London, Lincoln's Inn Library, Hale 150, which dates from c. 1450; Oxford, Bodleian Library, Douce 236, which has been dated to the last quarter of the fifteenth century by the *Middle English Dictionary*, and to the beginning of the fifteenth century by Kölbing and Moore, Meech, and Whitehall;[13] and London, British Library, Additional 27879 (also known as the Percy Folio Manuscript), which dates from the seventeenth century. A sixteenth-century transcription of sixty-two lines by John Stow also exists (London, British Library, Harley 6223), as does an early printed edition by Wynkyn de Worde (*Marlyn,* unique copy at Pierpont Morgan Library).[14] These later versions of the poem concentrate on Merlin's birth and events preceding Arthur's accession rather than on the troubled early days of Arthur's reign recounted in detail in the lengthy Auchinleck poem. Instead of narrating Arthur's rise to power and his many extended battles against Saracens, the later non-Auchinleck manuscripts terminate their narratives close to the 2000-line mark with the defeat and death of Fortiger (Lincoln's Inn), or with the accession of Uter (Percy and Douce).

Two other Middle English redactions of the *Estoire de Merlin* exist. The first is known as the English Prose *Merlin,* and is contained in the fifteenth-century manuscript Cambridge, University Library, Ff. 3. 11.[15] A fragment of a related manuscript is found in Oxford, Bodleian Library, Rawlinson Miscellany olim 1262, later 1370,[16] which has been dated to the fifteenth century.[17] The second English redaction of the *Estoire* is a verse translation of the French text by Henry Lovelich, a member of the London Company of Skinners. His work is found solely in Cambridge, Corpus Christi College, 80, and may date from as early as 1425,[18] although more usually it is dated c. 1450.[19] These fifteenth-century texts, which run to 697 pages and 27,582 lines respectively, translate more of the vulgate *Estoire* than *Of Arthour and of Merlin* does. They also differ from the Auchinleck text in that, like the French source, both "stress Merlin's role as the prophet of the Holy Grail,"[20] and open with the demonic conception of Merlin. The Auchinleck poem, by contrast, omits or truncates developments of the tale relating to the grail quest,[21] and opens with more chronicle-like attention to kings and their reigns, recounting the end of Costaunce's reign and the usurpation of the throne by Fortiger before introducing the story of Merlin's begetting.[22]

The web of textual relationships informing *Of Arthour and of Merlin* is both extensive and complicated, as is the case with most medieval Arthurian material. These relationships are important, however, in that they allow me to situate and explain the presence of Saracens in *Of Arthour and of Merlin*. The characters who invade "Engleterre" in the Old French *Estoire de Merlin* are usually called "Sesnes" or "Saines," terms designating Saxons. It is impossible to say whether this is always the case because the plethora of manuscripts of this tale, and their variety, have precluded the publication of a definitive critical edition. Two of the forty-six full manuscript versions have been edited and published: London, British Library, Additional 10292 (folios 76–101), which dates to 1316 and was published by Oskar Sommer as the base manuscript of his 1908 edition of the *Estoire de Merlin*,[23] and Paris, Bibliothèque nationale, 747, which dates to the thirteenth century and was the base manuscript for Micha's edition of the *Estoire de Merlin*. In my reading of these texts, of the variants they list, and of the recent English translation of the *Estoire de Merlin*,[24] I have not come across any reference to the invaders as "Sarrazins," the Old French term used to designate Saracens. The invaders are always Saxons or Irish. Moreover Macrae-Gibson, who consulted a variety of manuscripts of the Old French *Estoire* for his edition of *Of Arthour and of Merlin*, nowhere indicates any references in these French texts that would explain the appearance of Saracens as the invading peoples in the Auchinleck poem. Macrae-Gibson does, however, believe that a now-lost manuscript of the French *Estoire* may have been *Of Arthour and of Merlin*'s source, since the poem does not directly correlate to any of the extant manuscripts of the *Estoire de Merlin* that most closely resemble it. That now-lost manuscript may indeed have referred to the invaders troubling England as Saracens. The appearance of Saracens in *Of Arthour and of Merlin* might also reflect the influence of an antecedent, now-lost English version of the poem. Auchinleck and the other manuscripts of *Of Arthour and of Merlin*, however, appear to be the first extant versions of the *Estoire de Merlin* to identify the invaders of England as Saracen. All manuscript versions of the English poem characterize the foreign invaders troubling England after Costaunce's death as "Sarraȝin."[25] Auchinleck is the only manuscript of this group whose narrative extends past the time of Arthur's crowning, but it continues, after Arthur's accession, to call the invaders from abroad "Saracens." Indeed, the Auchinleck text resolutely refers to these invaders as "Sarraȝin," "paien," or "heþen." While it mentions that these pagans come from Saxony, Denmark or Ireland, it never uses the term "Saxon" to refer to them, even as a variant. Unlike the later, fifteenth-century English Prose *Merlin*, which uses the term "Sarazin" as a less frequent variant of "Saines" or Saxons,[26] the Auchinleck *Of Arthour and of Merlin* uses "Sarraȝin" as its only marker of pagan specificity.[27] The early fourteenth-century poem, then, represents what appears to be a rare tradition among *Estoire de Merlin* texts, although this may very well not be a unique tradition given the possible existence of now-lost or other-wise inaccessible (because unpublished) versions of the *Estoire de Merlin.*

While I have not found textual antecedents for Saracen invaders in extant and accessible versions of the *Estoire de Merlin,* the question of whether other Arthurian material may have influenced the appearance of Saracens in *Of Arthour and of Merlin* should be considered. One very likely source of influence is the vulgate prose cycle itself. In texts of this cycle other than the *Estoire de Merlin,* Saracens do occasionally appear as inhabi-tants of Britain, or as Saxons. [28] In Sommer's edition of the vulgate cycle, Saracens ("Sarrasin," "Sarra3ins") appear in *Lestoire del saint graal,* the tale of Joseph of Arimathea.[29] Here, Saracens populate both the Middle East, whence Joseph's voyages originate, and Britain ("grant bartaigne") where Joseph is to begin additional missionary work at God's behest. "Sara3ins" also appear in two places in the *Livre d'Artus,* which Sommer prints as a supplement to his edition of the vulgate prose cycle. *Livre d'Artus* is not a version or continuation of the vulgate *Estoire de Merlin,* but is a "redaction[ ] of an account of the reigns of Uter pandragon and Artus made at [a] dif-ferent date[ ] for the purpose of linking Robert de Boron's *Merlin* to the *Lancelot* part of the vulgate cycle."[30] The Saracens who appear only twice in this lengthy text are described once as Saxons, and once as allies of the Sax-ons whom Arthur fights. Unlike in *Of Arthour and of Merlin,* however, these Saracens appear only after Arthur's kingship has been long established, at a point in the text several episodes past the point at which Auchinleck ceases its tale of Arthur. All told, although Saracens do appear in these two Old French vulgate cycle texts, they figure only briefly in the action and are found in different contexts than they are in *Of Arthour and of Merlin.* They do, however, resemble the Saracens of Auchinleck in their presence in "grant bartaigne," and in their Saxonness. Some transposition of this Old French tradition may therefore have influenced the appearance of Saracens in *Of Arthour and of Merlin.*

English Arthurian tradition may also have influenced the *Of Arthour and of Merlin* redactor. In this tradition, no Saracen invaders of Britain appear in the Arthurian sections of La3amon, or in Robert Mannyng's *Chronicle.* In Mannyng's chronicle, however, there are Saracen-Saxon invaders of Scotland and of the "Norþe cuntre" in periods of British his-tory preceding Arthur's reign.[31] Saracens are also listed as allies of the Roman Emperor confronted by Arthur on the Continent long after he has firmly established himself as king in England and Britain. Interestingly, Mannyng also uses the term "Sare3in" very occasionally to describe pagan Anglo-Saxons such as Penda, "kyng of Lyndeseie," as well as to designate, in later periods, Muslim opponents of Christian crusaders in the Middle East.[32] At times, then, Mannyng uses the term "Sareȝin" so as to invoke the same connotations found in Auchinleck's use of it in *Of Arthour and of Merlin*. He does not, however, use the term in reference to the invaders of England during Arthur's reign. Robert of Gloucester, by contrast, does use "Saracen" to describe European pagan invaders of England in Arthur's time in the A-version of his chronicle.[33] According to the *Middle English Dictionary*, Robert of Gloucester's *Chronicle* (A-version) and *Of Arthour and of Merlin* are among the first English texts to link pagan Scandinavian invaders of England during Arthur's reign to the term "Saracen."[34] The Saracens in *Of Arthour and of Merlin* thus represent a somewhat uncommon, if not unprecedented, tradition in Arthurian material in English.[35]

Having laid out the complexity of the textual situation, and having indicated the possible antecedents underlying the Saracen invaders in *Of Arthour and of Merlin*, I am perfectly willing to accept that their appearance in this text may be neither originary nor unique, although it does seem to be uncommon. What fascinates me, however, is not the diachronic, literary history underlying the Saracen presence in *Of Arthour and of Merlin* (although this is important and interesting), but rather the ways in which this history shapes and complicates the Saracens of *Of Arthour and of Merlin*.

The textual tradition underlying *Of Arthour and of Merlin* identifies the invaders harrying Arthur's realm as Saxons and Irish, and although the term "Saxon" has been replaced by "paien," "heþen" or "Saracen" in Auchinleck, the foreign invaders in *Of Arthour and of Merlin* continue to originate from Saxony, Denmark, and Ireland, just as historical invaders of Britain did in the early Middle Ages.[36] King Angys, for example, "gadre[s] him folk wel felle / Of Danmark and of Sessoyne" (110–11). Many battles later, Arthur's nephew Wawayn vows, in Arthur's absence, to defend the kingdom against invading "painemes" who have arrived under the command of four "heþen kinges" from "Yrlond" (4728–29, 4752). Despite their European origins and historical links to the English people, however, the invaders are described repeatedly as Saracens. The Danish King Angys's kin, for example, are identified thus: "Of Danmark Sarraȝins / Þat were of Angys lins" (2067–68). In the battle between Wawayn's forces and the Irish, the narrator states of Wawayn's comrade Galathin that

> What Sarraȝin so he mett
> Wel soriliche he hem grett
> Þat wom euer þat he hitt
> Þe heued to þe chinne he slitt. (4809–12)

Effortlessly, the Saxons, Danes, and Irish become Saracen. Moreover, as in other Auchinleck texts, these Saracens are linked to the Middle East. Not only are they called "Saracens," a term that in Middle English signifies Turk, Arab, or Muslim as early as 1300 (see *MED* meaning (a)), but they also worship gods linked to the Middle East in the minds of western medieval Christians. For example, during the battle between Wawain's forces and the pagans from "Yrlond," the Irish Saracens make vows to "Mahoun" (5066), as do Saracens fighting Arthur (5775) and King Clarion of Northumberland (7497). These European-linked Saracens thus share other Saracens' adherence to Muslim worship of Muhammad as depicted by medieval Christians.[37] In addition, terms reflecting European contact with the Middle East and with Arabic military and governmental titles turn up when various leaders of the invaders are called "amiral" and "soudan" (7751; 7725, 7767, 7776). The Saracens of *Of Arthour and of Merlin* thus embody a hybrid mixture of European and eastern characteristics. The text conflates historical and textual Germanic pagans who invaded England with contemporary thirteenth- and fourteenth-century Middle Eastern Muslims.

These hybrid East-West Saracens introduce a new type of Saracen into the Auchinleck manuscript. Saracens in *Þe King of Tars, Seynt Katerine, Seynt Mergrete, Guy of Warwick (couplet version), Reinbrun gij sone of warwike, King Richard,* and *Sir Beves of Hamtoun* (the text that immediately precedes *Of Arthour and of Merlin*) are pagans of Middle Eastern or African geographic origin, and sometimes of different skin color. The color-changing sultan in *Þe King of Tars* rules Damascus, while the two saints are persecuted by black-skinned Saracens in Alexandria and Antioch. Guy fights a black-skinned Saracen near Antioch, while his son serves a Saracen king of Africa. Richard attacks Saracens in Acre, while Saracen kings rule Damascus and (somewhat inaccurately) Armenia in *Sir Beves. Of Arthour and of Merlin,* by contrast, presents hybrid northern European-Middle Eastern Saracens, and writes these Saracens into a narrative of English history. In some ways, these European-linked Saracens resemble those found in *Otuel a Kniʒt* who come from "Lumbardie" (17) and are found in Spain.[38] Those Saracens also combine European geographical specificity with vows by Mahoun and references to Middle Eastern governmental terms. They do not, however, represent a conflation of Middle Easternness with a Europeanness that is explicitly part of English history. The Saracens in *Of Arthour and of Merlin,* however, are linked to northern spheres, and participate in English history. The only other Auchinleck text even to hint at such Saracens is *Guy of Warwick (stanzaic continuation).* There Guy fights a giant "Out of Aufrike" (235. 8) who swears by the Saracen god "Apolin" (266.7) and yet serves the Christian king of Denmark who makes oaths on holy relics (253.1–12). This giant, named Colbrond, is never explicitly identified as a Saracen, but his monstrous size, his oaths, and his African origins imply that he may well be one.[39] The fact that he fights for Danish invaders of England links him, like the Saracens in *Of Arthour and of Merlin,* to English history. Thus *Guy (stanzaic continuation)* sketches out in one incident a connection between Saracens and Danes that *Of Arthour and of Merlin* expands and develops more fully in its narrative of ongoing invasions of England by hybrid East-West Saracens.

ARTHURIAN SARACENS AND THE REPRESENTATION OF ENGLISH IDENTITY

It seems logical that my last chapter about Saracens and the making of "Inglisch" identity in the Auchinleck manuscript should examine *Of Arthour and of Merlin.* This poem introduces Saracens into an insular Arthurian tradition already extensively interwoven with complicated assertions of Englishness and group identity. Arthur, historically, is a Briton king, and tales about him usually represent him as such. "Briton" and "English" are not co-extensive terms, and do not signify the same cultural and ethnic groups or identities. "Briton" refers to the Christianized Celtic people of Britain who inhabited that island when the Romans invaded it and who, according to Bede and others, were displaced when pagan Saxons, Frisians, Jutes, and Angles invaded the land during the European population movements of the fifth and sixth centuries. This displacement is believed to have pushed the Britons westward into Wales and Cornwall, as well as into Brittany. Arthur, inasmuch as he has been identified historically, has generally been identified as a Briton or Welshman not just by today's scholars, but also by the language and provenance of the texts in which he first appears.[40] The term "English," on the other hand, refers to the inhabitants of southern Britain descended from the Germanic invaders of the fifth and sixth centuries, some Britons and Celts, the Scandinavian invaders of the ninth and tenth centuries, and the French-speaking Norman invaders of 1066.[41] Despite this disjuncture between terms, tales of the Briton King Arthur frequently appear in medieval narratives of England and English identity such as William of Malmesbury's *De gestis regum Anglorum.*[42]

Because Arthur traverses the borders between Englishness and Britonness, he cannot help but raise questions of group identity and identification in the larger insular context. Indeed, this aspect of Arthur may explain his popularity: he offers different points of identification for the various groups implicated in both insular and English identities. J.S.P. Tatlock, Lee Patterson, and others have pointed out ways in which Arthur could be made to serve the ideological purposes of the Anglo-Normans.[43] For example, since tales of Arthur often cast the Saxons as enemies of Britain, the tales could be used to validate the Norman conquest of the Anglo-Saxon descendents of these people in 1066.[44] Roger Loomis has demonstrated how Edward I advanced his political ends through deployments of Arthur which emphasized the mythical king's ethnic multivalency.[45] For example, Edward I visited Glastonbury and there participated in a re-interment of Arthur's supposed bones in 1278.[46] This act effectively demonstrated the fact of the Briton king's death, and the concomitant falsity of prophecies foretelling Arthur's return from Avalon to lead the Welsh in time of need.[47] Welsh leaders had invoked such prophecies to rally support for uprisings against kings of England from Henry II's reign onwards,[48] and they were still doing so in Edward I's time.[49] In 1301, on the other hand, Edward I sought to advance other geo-political ends by deploying Arthur in a way that asserted that king's Englishness: he cited Arthur as a precedent for English overlordship of Scotland in a letter to Pope Boniface VIII.[50] In Edward I's use of him, then, Arthur oscillated between being Briton and being English. In *History on the Edge,* Michelle Warren has demonstrated the multitude of ways in which Arthur's origins and relations to various British identities are deployed in insular narratives about him. She shows how medieval authors of different ethnic and regional origins adapted the story of Arthur and of his relations to the various inhabitants of Britain to fit agendas both of colonization and of resistance. Her study makes clear the many ways in which Arthur's tale could be told, and the fluidity of identification of the ethnic groups involved in the tale depending on readers' and writers' own affiliations and interests.

Given this tradition, it is not surprising that a tale about Arthur in Auchinleck should from its outset both invoke Englishness and gesture towards the complexity of such an invocation in an Arthurian context. At the text's very opening, the reader is explicitly told that this tale is about "Inglond." Not only does the prologue offer a survey of the status of the English language in England, but the narrator informs the reader in the first three lines of the tale proper that "Now ich ȝou telle þis romaunce: / A king hiȝt while sir Costaunce / Þat regned in Inglond" (31–33). *Of Arthour and of Merlin* thus introduces its redaction of its French source with clear indications that it has re-cast this continental source to fit into an English Arthurian tradition. While the French *Estoire* and the later fifteenth-century English translations of this tale begin with Merlin's demonic conception, the Auchinleck poem opens with two specifically English-focussed contextualizations of the tale, one linguistic and the other geographic and political.[51] With these alterations to its French source, *Of Arthour and of Merlin* shifts the focus from the life of Merlin to England and the larger narrative of England's past. The poem's opening insists that this text is about England and its kings. Shortly thereafter, *Of Arthour and of Merlin* directly addresses the question of how this tale of Arthour, a Briton king, relates to an English audience. This poem describes the inhabitants of "Inglond," as "Þe Bretouns þat beþ Inglisse nov" (119). Moreover, in case there should be any confusion about the conflation of Britons and English, the poem states right before this "Ac Inglond was yhoten þo / Michel Breteyne wiþouten no" (117–18). In this way, the Auchinleck poem disposes of any possible cavils that it is not a story about England and the inhabitants of that realm. It demands that its "Inglisch" audience recognize that this is a tale of their kings and their origins, and it elides from consideration the complex and conflicted historical relationships between Briton and English inhabitants of Britain. Place of habitation defines identity, and re-naming replaces conquest as the explanation for the historical and linguistic development of the region.[52]

The presence of Saracens in a text that explicitly represents itself as a narrative about England's past has many implications. First, finding Saracens who are directly linked to Saxon and Danish invasions of England in a tale about King Arthur shows these characters' ability to elide geographic and temporal borders and to play an explicit role in narratives about English culture and history. *Saracens and the Making of English Identity* as a whole argues that Saracen characters in Auchinleck explore issues of group identity central to notions of Englishness in the early fourteenth century. *Of Arthour and of Merlin* offers decisive evidence that, far from being mimetic representations of Muslims tied exclusively to Arabic geography or ethnicity, Saracens are instead fluid and shifting ciphers of otherness that can be deployed in a variety of settings. They represent not a specific historical alterity, but rather the fact of cultural, political, and religious otherness. Accordingly, these figures can conflate within themselves various historical othernesses, both Middle Eastern and European, that speak to western European situations in the Middle Ages. Most importantly for this project, finding Saracens who incarnate historical invaders and settlers of England in a tale about Arthur demonstrates the ability of Saracens to participate intimately in explorations of "Inglisch" identity. Because of its content and setting, this poem writes Saracens directly into a relationship with England, English history, English kingship, and English identity. *Of Arthour and of Merlin* thus demonstrates that as the Saracens of Auchinleck explore the complexities of relations between ethnic and cultural groups, their explorations not only are relevant to Auchinleck's English context, but could have been perceived as such by readers of the manuscript in the fourteenth century. In other words, readers of the manuscript who had come upon the Saracens in Auchinleck's tale of Arthur and "Inglond" could have been guided by this text to read Saracen characters as connected in some way to Englishness. *Of Arthour and of Merlin* indicates definitively, and explicitly, the pertinence of Saracens and the issues they raise to the questions of English identity raised in Auchinleck as a whole.

SARACENS AND ENGLAND'S CRUSADING HERITAGE

As indicated in Chapter Four, awareness of crusade and of English participation in crusades was very much part of England's sense of itself as a Christian nation. *Of Arthour and of Merlin* reinforces this idea by depicting England as a realm with a long history of crusade. As the opponents of King Arthur and his knights anachronistically become Saracens, the legendary English/Briton king and his companions become crusaders. Indeed, the poet celebrates their martial accomplishments in terms that evoke crusade. Arthur slays "misbileueand paiem[s]" (5982) while

> . . . Wawain
> And his feren wiþ gret main
> Euerich of hem gan to bere
> Þurth a Sarraȝin wiþ his spere
> Afterwards swerdes þai drowe
> And sexten þousinde to grounde slowe
> Mani mouþe þe gres bot
> And griseliche ȝened God it wot
> Paiens floted in her blod—
> Ever is Cristes miȝt gode. (7101–10)

Such actions cast Arthur and his knights as vehicles of "Cristes miȝt" in a bloody battle against unbelievers, and link the characters to historical crusade heroes such as Richard I and his forces, described thus in the *Itinerarium Peregrinorum et Gesta Regis Ricardi:*

> King Richard pursued the Turks with singular ferocity, fell upon them and scattered them across the ground. No one escaped when his sword made contact with them; wherever he went his brandished sword cleared a wide path on all sides. Continuing his advance with untiring sword strokes, he cut down that unspeakable race . . . Constantly slaying and hammering away with their swords, the Christians wore down the terrified Turks . . . The rout of the enemy was so complete that for two

miles there was nothing to see except people running away, although they had previously been so persistent, swollen with pride and very fierce. Yet through God's aid their arrogance was so destroyed that they never ceased fleeing.[53]

Like Richard and his forces, Arthur and his knights, too, "slay[ ] and hammer[ ] away" at God's enemies, and in so doing represent God's power. They are clearly model crusaders, a fact which enhances their heroic status. Such enhancement of the Round Table's renown might seem unnecessary, but in the later Middle Ages crusade was considered the noblest endeavor of knighthood, and battling Saracens in the Holy Land was deemed the noblest form of crusade.[54] *Of Arthour and of Merlin* ensures that even though Arthur and his knights may not fight in the Holy Land, they do fight Saracens and garner all the prestige such battle bestows on Christians. The poem also ensures that Arthur, the hero of the insular Matter of Britain, does not suffer in comparison with Charlemagne, the hero of the Matter of France who repeatedly leads his forces against Saracen opponents and who appears in two Auchinleck texts. By re-casting Arthur's Saxon opponents as Saracens, *Of Arthour and of Merlin* allots to England's foundational king the same crusading glory as France's foundational king, and thereby quashes any suggestion that English crusading achievements might be inferior to French ones.

Indeed, the Auchinleck manuscript as a whole works to portray England as a nation with a long history of crusading prowess. Both *Sir Beves of Hamtoun* and *Guy of Warwick* depict specifically English knights fighting and defeating Saracens. In addition, *Guy of Warwick* puts words in Saracen characters' mouths that represent English warriors as particularly effective crusaders. When Guy is travelling incognito as a pilgrim in the Middle East, he identifies himself to one of his Saracen opponents only as an Englishman. The opponent (Amoraunt) replies "O, artow Inglis? . . . / Now wald mi lord Teruagaunt / Þat þou were Gij þe strong!" (*Stanzaic Continuation* 111. 1–3). Amoraunt then adds that he very much wishes to kill Guy because Guy has "destrud al our [Saracen] lawe" to the extant that "keuer schal we [Saracens] neuer more / þat he haþ don ous forlore" (*Stanzaic Continuation* 111.7–11). Evidently, English warriors like Guy pose a particular threat to Saracen practices and society. The manuscript's penultimate item, *King Richard*, also develops this idea of English crusading prowess. *King Richard* narrates Richard I's departure on crusade, his experience of French perfidy en route to the Holy Land, his battles against Saracens in the Holy Land, and his encounters with Saladin. Only six folios of the Auchinleck *King Richard* still exist today, but even they record Richard's departure, his troubles with the

French, and his opening maneuvers at the siege of Acre. In its original form, the romance would have offered many more descriptions of Richard and his men slaughtering Saracens. And in case any reader of Auchinleck might have skipped over the lengthy romance about Richard, the manuscript also devotes 150 lines of its *Liber Regum Anglie* (also known as the *Anonymous Riming Chronicle*) to an account of Richard's achievements on the Third Crusade. Originally, then, Auchinleck's *Of Arthour and of Merlin, Beves of Hamtoun, Guy of Warwick, Liber Regum Anglie,* and *King Richard* all recounted at length the crusading accomplishments of English rulers and retinues. When read in tandem, these texts would have sketched out a glorious history of English crusading achievement.

Such a history would likely have resonated positively with Auchinleck's fourteenth-century audience. As discussed in Chapter Four, English rulers and subjects repeatedly involved themselves in international crusading efforts, and took great pride in such involvement during this period. In addition to the kingly efforts described in Chapter Four, late medieval Englishmen also venerated crusading ancestors,[55] and even dated local charters "by reference to crusading activity and events in the East."[56] In short, English people's participation in crusading efforts was very much part of their identity. The Saracen presence in *Of Arthour and of Merlin* appeals to this sense of Englishness. Through the depiction of an explicitly English Arthur fighting Saracens instead of Saxons, *Of Arthour and of Merlin* affirms that England has long been a notable player on the international crusading stage, and reinforces popular notions of an English crusading heritage. A key alteration of the poem's French source produces a culturally resonant portrait of England for Auchinleck's fourteenth-century audience. Making Arthur's opponents Saracen also indicates with whom the audience is to identify. Whereas Saxon opponents might complicate the issue of identification by invoking a historical component of English identity, Saracen opponents ensure that the audience's loyalty will unquestioningly lie with the Christians depicted. All told, the Saracen presence in *Of Arthour and of Merlin* suggests a long history of English participation in Christian military endeavors, and emphasizes the Christianness of English identity.

SARACENS, HISTORY, AND THE HYBRID NATURE OF ENGLISH IDENTITY

While the depiction of Arthur's enemies as Saracens writes him and his knights into a narrative of crusade, it also writes Saracens into a narrative of English history. Arthur possessed a double status in the Middle Ages as both

romance hero and historical king, and readers of Auchinleck would have
found tales of him not just in *Of Arthour and of Merlin,* but also in the *Liber
Regum Anglie* on folios 304–17. This chronicle of English kings introduces
itself with the words "Here may men rede who so can / Hou Inglond first
bigan" (lines 1–2) and concludes with reference to the "ʒong king edward
[III]" (line 2357), listing Arthur among the historical rulers of England (lines
1057–1116). Thus, manuscript context as well as tradition reminds readers
of Arthur's historical status, and encourages them to consider what vision of
English history a tale of Arthur repelling Saracen invaders advances.

Considering this tale of Arthur as a narrative of England's past
demands recognition that, while the text's Saracens evoke England's crusading heritage, they also gloss over some of the specific conflicts that shaped
English identity. One such conflict is that among the English, Welsh and
Scots. In *Of Arthour and of Merlin,* Arthur is troubled early in his reign by
the refusal of various kings, including Angvisant of Scotland and Cradelman of North Wales, to acknowledge his sovereignty over them. Given
Arthur's explicit Englishness in this tale, his problems with these rulers
could not help but remind a fourteenth-century English audience of the
multiple confrontations between Edward I and the Welsh princes as well as
the ongoing war with Scotland. English kings repeatedly represented these
conflicts as the consequences of treasonous Welsh and Scottish refusals to
acknowledge England's rightful sovereignty over their realms.[57] By the end
of *Of Arthour and of Merlin,* though, the political and geographic divisions
among English, Welsh and Scots are overwritten and forgotten in the three
kings' vigorous martial opposition to invasion by Saracens. King Arthur, for
example, "After þis paiens fling / And mani of hem to deþ sting / Wiþ
scharp swerd of gode egge" (6423–25). The narrator later states that after
this battle, "Our men boþe gret and lite / Togider gaderd hem comonliche /
And comen hom nobleliche" (6446–48). The possessive "our" signals the
audience's responsibility to identify with these English forces. Such identifications, however, are not limited to the English when other insular peoples
are also fighting Saracens. For example, Cradelman of North Wales and his
men are accredited a few lines later with the slaughter of fifteen thousand
"heþen man" (6644), after which deed these Welsh forces are described as
"our kniʒtes and our barouns" (6703). The former enemy of King Arthur
thus becomes part of the English ruler's side in this battle. Angvisant of
Scotland and his forces, other erstwhile opponents of Arthur, are also in
their battles against Saracens described as "Our litel Cristen rout" (6838).
Thus, Saracens create a sense of unitary insular identity based on religion.
Because of their opponents' Saracenness, Arthur and the Scots and Welsh

kings become allies. In the twelfth century, identification with Christian crusading led William the Lion of Scotland to refuse to exploit to Scottish benefit the capture of Richard I on his way home from the Middle East, and even to contribute to Richard's ransom.[58] The same ability of crusade to overcome insular ethnic conflicts can be seen in *Of Arthour and of Merlin*'s depiction of the battles between Saracens and the Scots, Welsh and English inhabitants of Britain. The religious difference of the Saracens allows the text to downplay in its portrait of England's past the insular ethnic struggles that so troubled Britain in the early sections of the tale and, historically, in the thirteenth and fourteenth centuries.

The Saracens of *Of Arthour and of Merlin* also gloss over other historical complexities of English identity. The identification of invaders of England as Saracens shifts attention away from formative moments of England's past. The Saxon invasions of the fifth and sixth centuries laid part of the groundwork for the development of Anglo-Saxon language, literature and laws. All these institutions were still in existence when the Normans conquered England in 1066, and sufficiently established that they both survived the Conquest and ultimately melded with Norman institutions to help form the hybrid identity that was late medieval Englishness. This Saxon aspect of Englishness, which would complicate the text's easy equation of "Bretouns" with "Inglisse," is erased by the use of the appellation "Saracen" to describe pagan invaders from "Sessoyne." Such erasure undercuts the poem's efforts to present itself as a narrative of England's past, and facilitates the forgetting of significant components of English history and identity. Admittedly, the text does occasionally specify the Saxon origins of its Saracens, and this prevents the complete erasure of England's pagan invasions and settlement from the narrative. References to "Sessoyne," however, appear only twice in the 9938-line poem (lines 111, 6931), and are substantially outnumbered by the many references to Saracens. Moreover, although these rare geographic localizations might seem to remind readers of England's history, they actually facilitate a further forgetting of some aspects of this history. Because the Saracens in *Of Arthour and of Merlin* are identified as coming from Denmark and Ireland as well as Saxony, the poem effectively conflates the Saxon invasions of the fifth and sixth centuries with the Viking raids and settlements of the ninth and tenth centuries.[59] These later invasions also proved formative for Englishness,[60] but their chronological and historical specificity is elided from this poem by its decision to lump England's various pagan ancestors together under the rubric of "Saracens." The Saracens of *Of Arthour and of Merlin* thus shift attention away from particular pagan settlers of England's past, and downplay the role of specific conquests in shaping English identity. The

Normans are not mentioned at all, and the invasions that preceded that conquest are presented as naval incursions by late medieval infidels. The contemporary immediacy of religious crusade replaces historical specificity.

While the Saracens in *Of Arthour and of Merlin* reduce the historical specificity of the poem, these characters do make clear to readers the cultural consequences of historical invasions of England. One central incident involving the English and the Saracens foregrounds the cultural and physical hybridity of peoples that proceeds from conquest, and represents such intermixing as an undesirable but lived experience of English history. Early in the narrative, before Arthur is even conceived, Fortiger usurps the throne of England and finds himself menaced on all sides by English nobles outraged by his act. Fortiger invites the Saracen Angys,[61] whom he had formerly expelled from "Inglond"'s shores, to return to England with his Saracen followers and defend Fortiger against the men "þat wald him sle" (417). In exchange, Fortiger promises Angys "half his fe" (418). Angys returns with "Mani þousand" (421), and he and Fortiger battle the English nobles at Salesbiri. Fortiger and Angys win the victory (but only because they have a four to one advantage in numbers, the narrator tells us), and Fortiger draws and hangs the English opponents he catches, while

> Þe oþer he devoided alle
> Of lond and tour castel and halle
> And bi conseyl of Angys
> ȝaue it to Sarraȝins of pris. (471–74)

Fortiger thus kills or disinherits native nobles in favor of his foreign, pagan allies. The effects of conquest extend beyond death and dispossession, though. Sexual and cultural intermingling follow upon these actions, and such intermingling is portrayed not as a temporary situation, but as a long-term alteration to the cultural, political, and legal composition of England:

> Angys hadde verrament
> A douhter boþe fair and gent
> (Ac sche was heþen Sarraȝin)
> And Fortiger for loue fin
> Hir tok to fere and to wiue—
> And was curssed in al his liue
> For he lete Cristen wedde haþen
> And meynt our blod as flesche and maþen.
> Mani þousand was swiche in weddeloc
> As we finde writen in bok

Þer was wel neiȝe al þis lond
To þe Deuel gon an hond,
Festes he made gret and fele
And hadden al warldes wele
And held no better lawe
Þan þe hounde wiþ his felawe.
Þis last wel fel ȝere. (477–93)

Not only does Fortiger, the king, mingle blood with the Saracens, but many others do so as well, and this redefines "our blod," the lineage of the Christian Britons/English with whom the narrator identifies (484). We have here not a solitary instance of the sexual integration of foreigners into an English community (as in *Sir Beves*), but a pervasive intermingling of cultures in thousands of inter-faith marriages. The fears of such intermingling, so clearly demonstrated in *Sir Beves* and *Þe King of Tars,* are proven to be justified in *Of Arthour and of Merlin.* In this text, the large-scale economic and sexual integration of foreigners into English society sends the realm "To þe Deuel" and undermines the laws and order of the land (488, 491–92). The melding together of Saracen and Christian societies means the death or dispossession of Christians, the enfeoffing of Saracens, and the dissolution of native English genealogical purity and legal systems. Moreover, this economic, political, and cultural integration lasts "wel fel ȝere" (493). This passage, then, offers a portrait of the processes by which a native group's identity is altered by various and extended interactions with invaders and conquerors. Once Saracen invaders have settled in England, and taken up positions of economic, legal and political power and of sexual intimacy, they become a deep-rooted and inescapable presence within the native culture, and interact with it so as to produce a mixed culture in which two different groups are welded together indissolubly.

To envision English history in this way, as a narrative of invasion, conquest, and the intermingling of peoples over many years, is to envision English identity as neither unitary nor pure, but as a hybrid by-product of war and invasion. A brief consideration of Homi Bhabha's notion of hybridity both clarifies the nature of the English historical identity depicted in *Of Arthour and of Merlin* and illuminates the cause of the bloody violence narrated in the last 6000 lines of the poem. For Bhabha, hybridity is a state that challenges the idea that pure, unitary, and original cultural identities remain intact after a process of invasion and colonization. Hybridity is a performed and displayed awareness, on the part of the colonized, of the fact that they have absorbed some of the defining characteristics of their colonizers' culture,

and that neither they nor the colonizers retain a pure, unalloyed group identity and society. In other words, the term describes a state in which invaders
and invaded cannot be definitively differentiated, and in which "cultural differences are not simply *there* to be seen or appropriated."[62] No longer can the
colonizers draw boundaries between themselves and the colonized, and this
fact represents the power of hybridity. Hybridity displays the intermingling of
two cultures rather than the superimposition of one dominant culture upon
the other. Because hybridity "breaks down the symmetry and duality of
self/other, inside/outside," however, it menaces both groups' sense of
identity.[63] Both colonizers and colonized wish to disavow the interweaving
that has occurred and claim purity in their group's identity, but they cannot
erase the fact of their connection and intermingling. Hybridity demonstrates
that a clear line between colonized and colonizer can no longer be drawn.

The situation described in *Of Arthour and of Merlin* clearly does not
reproduce the Indian situation analyzed by Bhabha, but it does resemble it.
In the passage quoted above, *Of Arthour and of Merlin* depicts a cultural situation produced by conquest in which invaders and invaded can no longer be
differentiated, and in which intermingling lasts many years. The thousands
of inter-faith marriages and the long duration of the Saracen presence in
England mean that, after Fortiger's invitation to Angys, the identity of England's inhabitants is no longer unitary, but rather a hybrid mixture of Christian Englishness and foreign Saracenness. *Of Arthour and of Merlin* thus
advances a vision of "Inglisch" identity as a melding of invaders and invaded.
The same Saracens who elide historical specificity from the pagan invasions
offer a detailed portrait of the cultural processes through which those invasions formed Englishness. The depicted killing of English nobles, and the
economic, legal, political and sexual integration of Angys's Saracens into
English society, connote the very processes by which Angles, Saxons, Jutes,
Frisians, Danes, and Normans settled in England and became culturally
interwoven with the various inhabitants they found there. Thus, while *Of
Arthour and of Merlin* may not record the precise details of historical conquests of England, it clearly communicates to readers the hybridizing effects
of such conquests on "Inglisch" identity.

This is not to say, however, that such hybridity is perceived as desirable.
Bhabha suggests that intermingling and distaste for it can provoke futile
efforts to assert the purity of a group's identity and disavow the influence of
the other culture. This seems very much the case in *Of Arthour and of Merlin*.
The poem proffers an exceptionally negative vision of invasion and integration as cultural formation. The narrator depicts Saracen-English intermingling as unalloyed corruption and destruction. He likens it to maggot-ridden

meat (484), and suggests that it breeds the utter abandonment of human law (491–92). Accordingly, it is not surprising that the text next suggests that hybridization is reversible, that the invasive Saracen element of English identity can be excised. After an interlude narrating the birth of Merlin, *Of Arthour and of Merlin* describes how the hybrid English society created by Fortiger and the Saracens is destroyed by Costaunce's legal heirs. The heirs, Uter Pendragon and Aurilis Brosias, return home to fight Saracens, and eventually burn "Fortiger and wiif and child" (1891) to death. Uter and Aurilis then turn their attention to Angys and, after killing him, negotiate an agreement with his Saracens that they may return to the land whence they came (2036–44). The text thus implies that violence can easily reverse all the intermingling that occurred in Fortiger's reign and eradicate the Saracen presence from England, despite the thousands of inter-faith marriages. The desire to disavow and excise the foreign culture described in Bhabha's theory of hybridity illuminates this textual suggestion of reversibility. The idea, and hope, is that English identity can be re-purified, and disentangled from the Saracen "stren" (1667) of Fortiger and Angys. This eventuality, however, proves as impossible here as in Bhabha's India.

Repeatedly, *Of Arthour and of Merlin* suggests that a continued Saracen presence in England is the unavoidable consequence of Fortiger's interactions with Angys. Merlin proceeds, after Uter's coronation, to warn him and Aurilis that "Vp 3ou is comen a strong batayle / Of Sarra3ins of michel priss / Forto awreke þe douke Angys" (2080–82). Indeed, Saracens related to Angys and seeking to avenge him are still tormenting the inhabitants of England a generation later. After some years of respite, they turn up to trouble Uter's heir Arthur. Immediately after winning a victory over rebel kings, Arthur is informed by Merlin that

" . . . here is comand to þis lond
Gret hunger and here-gong
Sex hundred [þousand] Sarra3ins
Forto awreke þe douke Angis." (4083–86)

From this point until the end of the Auchinleck poem, Saracen invaders and pillagers are a constant presence in Arthur's realm, and the narrative focus of the tale. The Saracens who were so economically, politically, and sexually interwoven with the English early on in the poem simply cannot be excised from the text's record of English history and Arthur's kingship. Instead, their constant presence constitutes the tale of Arthur and his knights—they are the bodies upon which English knight after English knight proves his prowess, only to have to do so again a few hundred lines

later. Like a repressed and disavowed, but unavoidable, memory, the Saracens return constantly to haunt the land from which they have been
expelled. Their continuing presence testifies to the immanence and durability of invasion and conquest. Once combined, two cultural identities prove
extremely difficult to sever, however much people might desire to do so.

The Saracens in *Of Arthour and of Merlin,* thus depict the fact of
hybridity that lies at the origins of English history and identity. While the
text testifies to repeated English efforts to expel a Saracen presence from
England, it demonstrates the difficulty of effecting such an expulsion once
Saracens have been intimately interwoven into the cultural fabric of the
kingdom. Indeed, as the next section of this chapter will show, the Saracen
presence in this text proves formative in the definition, stabilization, and
revitalization of Arthur's English polity. Saracens in *Of Arthour and of Merlin*
thus demonstrate how hated invaders can come to play key roles in the realm
on which they prey. Their central presence in a tale of English history and
English kings promotes consideration of the various origins, and histories, of
English identity, and an awareness of the multiplicity of these origins and
histories.

In case there is any doubt that the Saracens of *Of Arthour and of Merlin*
relate to questions of origins, and that the moment of their integration into
English society is formative, it is interesting to note that the portion of narrative following the depiction of Saracen-Christian intermingling turns away
from the linear progression of English history to emphasize questions of origins and beginnings. Right after the reference to years of English-Saracen
intermingling, the narrative recounts the birth of Merlin. This tale, as in the
Estoire de Merlin, centers on questions of beginnings and parentage. Not
only is the origin of demons from the fall of the disobedient angels
recounted (639–74), but also the origin of redemption in Christ's birth, and
the demonic machinations that effect Merlin's conception. After Merlin
himself is born, he displays an uncanny ability to know and speak both his
own origins (1033–66), and those of people he meets (1063–144,
1316–77). Moreover, he does so repeatedly, thereby drawing attention to the
way in which origins are constructed and affirmed through repeated narration. Scholars have identified this type of concern with origins as characteristic of Old French literature. Howard Bloch discusses the phenomenon at
length in *Etymologies and Genealogies,* while E. Jane Burns has noted how the
French vulgate cycle that underlies *Of Arthour and of Merlin* constantly
returns its readers to "the sources and origins of characters and the narratives
they inhabit."[64] Merlin's engagement of this issue is particularly intriguing
because of its location in *Of Arthour and of Merlin.* Appearing right after a

portrait of cultural hybridization, the poem's mini- narrative of Merlin links the issue of origins to that of hybridity, thereby drawing attention to the ways in which cultures and identities, like Englishness, originate from hybridization.

Before concluding this discussion of hybridity in *Of Arthour and of Merlin,* the implications of finding Saracens at the origins of a hybridized English identity should be addressed. The term "Saracen" invokes at the heart of Englishness a powerful and much-feared fourteenth-century Other-ness—that of the Middle Eastern Muslim. While the Saracens enable a cer-tain generalization of the issues of identity and conquest being presented, they also introduce a pointed reminder of contemporary religious difference, and bring misbelief into a proximate and integral relationship with English history. The poem's portrait of the interweaving of English and Saracen cul-tures reminds readers of the paganism at the roots of English identity. The Germanic invaders of the fifth and sixth centuries, and the Viking invaders of the ninth and tenth centuries, were all pagan, and much of England's his-tory as recorded in early periods recounts the challenges and experiences of Christianizing these English ancestors.[65] Because the term "Saracen" evokes actual non-Christians encountered in the later Middle Ages, the term reminds readers of what it really means, in a Christian context, to be descended from non-believers, and allows fourteenth-century English read-ers to feel the religious strangeness that lies at their origins. Julia Kristeva points out in *Strangers to Ourselves* the role of internalized strangeness in the definition of one's identity. As she notes, what is radically external, what is different, must be expelled from one, or at least must be the object of efforts at expulsion, particularly when it is presented as lying at the heart of one's identity. When such efforts fail (as in *Of Arthour and of Merlin*), a sense of menace and uncanny strangeness ensues. Kristeva suggests that while this sensation is threatening, it also constitutes existence and subjectivity.[66] In her model, the internalization of threatening markers of alterity establishes a sense of identity. Saracens in *Of Arthour and of Merlin* effect this for English identity. The Saracens here, given their various associations both contempo-rary and historical, constitute the strangers within English identity, the prox-imate others who enable the construction of such an identity. They indicate the inconclusively rejected and intimate difference against which one defines oneself, and without which one lacks both aspects of oneself and the grounds for defining oneself. The Saracens demand consideration of the fact that multiple historical and religious origins underlie English identity, and that perhaps an identity like Englishness rests on what Kristeva calls the strange-ness within and what I would call the fact of hybridity at one's origins.

THE BLESSINGS OF THE BAD PENNY: SARACENS, PRODUCTIVE VIOLENCE, AND ENGLISH POLITICAL IDENTITY

Because Saracens in *Of Arthour and of Merlin* participate in a narrative noted as much for its many depictions of battle as for its concern with England's past, they demand consideration of the ways in which violence and "Inglisch" identity are intertwined. Saracens in this text clearly illustrate how the violence of crusade and conquest shaped fourteenth-century English identity, but they also explore the ways in which war can be politically productive in a domestic context. As mentioned above, Saracens in *Of Arthour and of Merlin* become, through their recurrent returns to England, a fact of life for the realm and its various rulers. They appear at the poem's beginning as the external menace that topples Moyne (Costaunce's heir) from the throne, they reappear as Fortiger's allies and a cultural graft onto English society, and thenceforth they are an inescapable preoccupation for Uter and his son Arthur. Having been intermingled with the English, the Saracens become an undesirable element of English identity that cannot be excised. They repeatedly sail in to kill Christians, challenge kings, pillage the land, and despoil the economic and social foundations of the English polity. These actions of war would seem to facilitate the polity's destruction. Moreover, such actions constitute the bulk of the text. The last 6000 lines of the 9938-line poem narrate in gory detail an apparently never-ending cycle of Saracen-Christian battle in England. The Saracens turn up, like a bad penny, and the violence of war follows in their wake. The fascinating aspect of such violence, however, is that it is found not in a tale of the end of King Arthur's reign (as in, for example, the alliterative *Morte Arthure*), but in a tale about Arthur's accession to kingship and rise to power. This is a poem about origins and beginnings, about the construction and creation of institutions and identities, not about the ends of reigns and the destruction of a society. Accordingly, the poem challenges its readers to make sense of what such violence, and what such a focus on violence, achieves in relation to Arthur's kingship and the English polity he rules. Upon consideration, it becomes apparent that the constant, violent Saracen actions in *Of Arthour and of Merlin* define, unify and revitalize the English polity and its structures. In particular, the battles provoked by Saracens enable the construction of Arthur's kingship and its legendary attributes, unite the various socio-political orders of Arthur's realm, re-subject to Arthur the unruly kings who challenge his right to kingship, and herald the revitalization of English political leadership.

A tale that depicts the destructive violence of war as a formative force in the establishment of King Arthur's rule and of a polity for him to rule over would have had many political resonances in England in the late thirteenth and early fourteenth centuries. First, because the king and polity depicted as shaped by war are Arthur and England, the text presents a vision of a legendary ruler and polity to which English kings were already attached by histories of England that listed Arthur as a prior king of the realm.[67] Indeed one chronicler, Pierre de Langtoft, even describes Edward I in Arthurian terms in his chronicle, thereby making explicit the connection between contemporary English kings and Arthur.[68] More significant, however, is the general relevance to early fourteenth-century England of a portrait of English polity and rulership that links these institutions explicitly and repeatedly with war. As Michael Prestwich points out in his introduction to *The Three Edwards,* the period spanned by these kings' reigns is "given a coherence by war."[69] Each of these kings found himself involved in wars either to extend and redefine his polity or to maintain his hold on power in England. Accordingly, Prestwich structures his entire book around the ways in which war shaped political, monarchical, and economic life in England from 1272–1377. He states:

> The importance of war in this period stretched far beyond . . . military history. The central constitutional development was the evolution of parliament, and it was the pressures of war that gave the institution much of its unique character. The need to obtain national consent for war taxation was of prime importance in the development of a system of representation, while the development of the parliamentary peerage was closely connected with the system used to summon magnates to fight. In economic terms, the burdens of recurrent taxation and the seizures of food supplied for the armies affected the prosperity of the countryside and were a matter for frequent complaint. Even the question of law and order was bound up with war. Criminals were given encouragement by the lavish grant of pardons in return for service on campaign, while the crown was on occasion compelled to reduce the severity of its policies as a concession in return for grants of taxation.[70]

As Prestwich makes clear, war and concomitant demands for men, money, and food were a central political force in the early fourteenth century, and affected multiple levels of English society. The violence of battle must also have been a fact of life for the many Englishmen who fought the Welsh, the Scots, and the French during this period. While the interplay between war and polity in *Of Arthour and of Merlin* in no way recreates the historical situation of the three Edwards' reigns, it does offer a pertinent portrait of how war affects the various members of a polity, and of how, even as it spreads chaos and menaces life and livelihood, war can construct kings, unify a polity, and restructure socio-political institutions.

Representing a polity shaped by war necessarily entails some consideration of war's gory disorder. When depicting the political benefits of war, the temptation might be to minimize the gruesomeness whence these benefits derive. *Of Arthour and of Merlin,* however, does not minimize the bloody chaos of war in any way.[71] Indeed, according to Macrae-Gibson, the English poet alters his French original so as to emphasize and amplify the violence contained in the source. The poet condenses passages linking battle scenes and passages of personal description found in the *Estoire de Merlin,* but translates closely and fully most of the original's battle descriptions, occasionally expanding the source when narrating "scenes of battle, cruelty, lamentation, and feasting."[72] Accordingly, to appreciate fully *Of Arthour and of Merlin*'s portrait of how a polity benefits from Saracen-Christian violence, one must recognize the horrors upon which these benefits, and Arthur's reign, are based in the text. Not to do so would both misrepresent the poem, which lovingly details all the chaos and carnage of war, and provide a false and simplistically positive vision of the origins from which Arthur's kingship emerges.

The horrific vision of war that the Saracens help to present is one of never-ending, indecisive battles, of bloody and gruesome physical encounters, and of pervasive social and economic destruction. The sense of never-ending and indecisive war is partly an effect of the sheer numbers of Saracens in this text. The redactor delights in offering detailed numbers and odds for the Christian-Saracen battles, and does so of his own initiative, often expanding less concrete or less numerically impressive references in the *Estoire de Merlin.*[73] In one battle, the narrator tells readers that "To þe brigge were comen wiþ gret pres / Of Sarraȝins xx þousinde / And wele mo also y finde" (8050–52). These twenty thousand Saracens are joined eleven lines later by a Saracen high king who simply appears "Wiþ so mani þousand Sarraȝins / Þat no man þerof couþe þe fins" (8065–66). While describing the battle that ensues, the narrator states that "Of Sarraȝin þer fouȝten ten and ten / Oȝain on of our men" (8075–76). Here, and elsewhere in the text, Saracens appear out of nowhere to join their fellows on various battlefields and outnumber their Christian opponents—they apparently constitute an unavoidable and massive presence in England. Consequently, no Christian victory (and almost all the text's twenty-four battles are Christian victories) marks a conclusive end to the conflict. For example, after Wawain and his forces have handily repelled twenty thousand Saracens and sent the invaders scurrying for reinforcements, they take shelter in Arundel, shut the gates, and ascend the walls only to "sei3e[ ] of heþen ful þe cuntreie" (8312), a vision which the narrator, true to form, elucidates as one hundred thousand fresh Saracens (8313–14). The long battle narrated by the poet means nothing—the Christians are now faced with even more Saracens to fight. The geographic extent of the encounters further develops the sense that the Saracen-Christian wars will never end. Not only does Arthur battle invading Saracens in Leodegan's (Guinevere's father's) kingdom of Carohaise, but the future knights of the Round Table valiantly oppose Saracens in England while Cradelman of North Wales, Angvisant of Scotland, and Lot of Orkney struggle with hordes of Saracen invaders in their realms. As a result, any individual victory seems both indecisive and incomplete, and war is presented as an ongoing and inevitable part of life in Arthurian Britain.

This, too, is the sense conveyed by the ending of the poem, which breaks off just after a battle between Arthur and the Saracens invading Leodegan's kingdom. The last incident depicted is the victorious return of Arthur and his allies to Leodegan's castle to rest, but there is no indication that this battle has been decisive—the Saracens have just fled, as they have many times before only to return later. Moreover, the last vision of England in the poem is of Wawain rescuing his own mother from Saracens who have abducted her and are abusing her. No decisive expulsion of Saracens has occurred there, either. Interestingly, this is not how the *Estoire* ends. That narrative continues on for much longer and depicts the final rout of the Saracens from all of Britain, Arthur's knighting of his Round Table warriors, and their martial endeavors as a unified group on the Continent. *Of Arthour and of Merlin,* by contrast, breaks off abruptly without a decisive resolution to the Saracen-Christian conflict besetting all of Britain. This ending would make sense if the manuscript had a lacuna here, an excised miniature or a missing folio. This, however, is not the case. Right after *Of Arthour and of Merlin* ends, a miniature that has been partially defaced appears,[74] and beneath it on the same page begins the next item *Þe wenche þat [lov]ed [a k]ing.* The Auchinleck scribe may not have chosen to end his poem thus—his exemplar may merely have broken off at this point—but he certainly makes no effort to conclude the tale more decisively by recounting a final rout of the Saracens, or by adding a couplet indicating the resolution of the conflict. Consequently, the poem ends on a note of irresolution. Readers of Auchinleck are presented with this inconclusive ending to *Of Arthour and of Merlin,* and left to make what they will of the ultimate indecisiveness of all the battles against the Saracens. Their perception, like ours, must have been of a rather permanent and unresolvable state of war and violence at the start of Arthur's reign over "Inglond."

The numerous indecisive battles recounted in *Of Arthour and of Merlin* contribute to a portrait of war as a state of bloody, inconclusive excess. Detailed references to gruesome carnage also develop this idea. Repeated cat-alogues of body parts, for example, communicate the gory plenty of war: "Oþer þe scholder oþer þe heued / Fro þe bodi was bireued / Oþer legge oþer fest" (4813–15). Another passage describes a similar scene of dismember-ment: "Heued of koruen smiten of arm / Bodi cleued into þe barm" (7951–52). Elsewhere, the narrator describes the aftermath of a battle between Christians and Saracens thus:

> Kni3tes and stedes þer laien aboute
> Þe heuedes of-smiten þe guttes out
> Heueden fet and armes þer
> Lay strewed eueriwher
> Vnder stede fet so þicke
> In crowes nest so doþe þe sticke,
> Sum storuen and sum gras gnowe
> Þe gode steden her guttes drowe
> Wiþ blodi sadels in þat pres. (9169–77)

Descriptions like this spread the carnage equally among Christians and Sara-cens, specifying neither in a portrait of gruesome excess. Twisted and torn wrecks of bodies litter the landscape, rivers run red with blood, and the sense of gory and all-pervasive war increases. The repeated depictions of such car-nage, like the numerous battles, suggest again the violent inconclusiveness of war. However many bodies are destroyed, more descriptions of destruction follow. Indeed, even severely wounded Saracens rise to fight again, as King Oriens does. After having been struck a powerful blow by Wawain, Oriens falls as if dead. Twenty lines later, however,

> Oriens his limes drou3
> And gan arise of his swou3
> . . .
> Vp he lepe wiþ chaufed blod
> So him no were nou3t bot god
> And asked anon ywis
> Newe armes and newe hors of priis
> And newe swerd and newe launce
> To nimen of his fon veniaunce. (7131–40)

Arthur's knights fell thousands of Saracens in an effort to rid England of its invaders, but such efforts prove futile. Still more Saracens arrive, or arise, to continue the violence. Arthur's kingdom becomes a site of never-ending carnage.

The destruction, moreover, is not just physical, nor is it confined to the military orders. A number of references depict the destruction of English economic prosperity and the persecution of all orders of society. Saracens pillage the goods of landholders, lay waste rural land, and burn men, women, and children. The economic breakdown effected by the Saracen invaders is made clear when Wawain and his brothers, coming to London[75] to seek knighthood at King Arthur's hands,

> . . . sei3en hem com swiþe ner
> Seuen hundred charged somer
> And seuen hundred cartes also
> And fiue hundred waines after go
> Ycharged alle wiþ ale and bred
> Wiþ fische and flesche and win red
> Robbed of men of þe cuntray. (4709–15)

Saracens are leading away all the produce of the land, and the English are left with nothing. Similar scenes occur in other parts of Britain (see lines 7559–65, 6965–75). In addition, as Wawain and his brothers come upon such economic destruction they also find evidence of Saracen slaughter of the non-fighting orders of society:

> [The four heathen kings] þe cuntre aboute Lounde
> Slowen and brent to þe grounde
> Men sei3e þe fer fer away
> Þennes ouer a iurnay,
> Man and wiif and children bo
> No hadde þai no pite to slo
> Þe folk schirsten so hei3e and loude
> Þat it schilled into þe cloude. (4733–40)

The references to family triads of men, women and children emphasize the social destruction wrought by the Saracens, and the way in which invasion preys on those from all walks of life and not just fighting men. In no way does the poem minimize the gruesomeness of war or elide war's pernicious socio-economic effects.

I have detailed at some length the nature of the violence depicted in *Of Arthour and of Merlin* in order to convey a sense of the pervasiveness of scenes of carnage and destruction in the last 6000 lines of this poem. Clearly, *Of Arthour and of Merlin* has no interest in minimizing the horrors of the

Saracen-Christian conflict that constitutes the narrative of Arthur's reign in this poem. The text paints a decidedly unflattering portrait of Arthur's early kingship as a period of brutal, gory, and continual violence, and of socio-economic destruction. Still, although the poem does not minimize the harshness of war and its effects on society, it steadfastly refuses to condemn these wars or wish them elsewhere. Instead, literary motifs introducing scenes of battle suggest the revitalizing effects of war, and gesture towards the fact that, in this poem, battles against Saracens benefit England. The origins of Arthur's kingship may be bloody, but they give birth to political glory.

The idea that the gory violence of the Saracen-Christian wars may not be all bad is communicated first by lyrical passages describing the joys and life force of nature that appear between depictions of gruesome, chaotic battle. Although a precedent for some of these passages can be found in the Old French *Estoire de Merlin,* the references in the source text are usually minimal, and do not wax lyrical the way the passages in *Of Arthour and of Merlin* do.[76] The English poem contains ten such passages, and most recount the re-greening of the countryside as spring comes,[77] the pleasures of summer, and the concomitant stirring of humanity in response to nature's beauty.[78] One such passage reads:

> Mirie is þentre of May
> Þe foules make miri play
> Maidens singgeþ and makeþ play
> Þe time is hot and long þe day
> Þe iolif niȝtingale singeþ
> In þe grene mede f[l]ou[r]es springeþ. (4675–80)

The sense of activity and mirth that underlies this passage is typical. Birds and maidens sing and play, flowers grow, and days are filled with heat and life rather than with carnage. What is fascinating is that such life-filled portraits usually link or introduce scenes of battle and carnage. For example, the passage quoted above appears immediately after Wawain and his brothers have decided to seek knighthood from Arthur, and is introduced by the lines "And ȝif þai no hadde togider ywent / Inglond hadde ben yschent" (4673–74). Right after the nature passage, Wawain and his brothers happen upon the havoc wrought by Saracens in the countryside outside London (lines 4709–40), and fight their first bloody battle against the invaders. Thus, the passage suggesting life, greenness, and mirth is sandwiched between a reference to the potential for England's destruction and a vision of carnage localized around London. Rebirth is situated in the midst of violence, and suggests a connection between violence and fecundity. A similar passage communicating the liveliness and beauty of summer appears after the narrator's assertion that he will "schewe werres and wo / In þis lond [England] þat weren þo—" (7615–16). Located between two descriptions of Saracens ravaging the Christian countryside, the passage reads:

> Mirie it is in somers tide
> Foules sing in forest wide
> Swaines gin on iustinge ride
> Maidens tiffen hem in pride. (7619–22)

Once again, a description of song and play, communicating a sense of animal and human activity, flowers in the space between scenes of destruction, death and pillaging. Thus, even as *Of Arthour and of Merlin* offers a portrait of carnage and incessant war, it occasionally links scenes of destruction to visions of burgeoning growth and life. This conveys the impression that the horrors of invasion and battle are interwoven with beauty and creation, thereby suggesting a productive element to the violence provoked by Saracens. The nature passages effectively frame and affirm the notion developed more explicitly by other events in the poem that the violence of war can be beneficial.

One of the main political benefits of the Saracen-Christian violence in *Of Arthour and of Merlin* is the construction of Arthur's kingship and its legendary attributes. As the title of the poem makes clear, this narrative of battle tells "Of Arthour," of how he succeeds to the throne, and of how he rules in the early years of his reign. As the full title demonstrates, however, this is not an independent process; this tale of Arthur is also a tale of Merlin. Merlin's role in the last 6000 lines of the poem is to instruct Arthur in the behaviors necessary to establish his legendary kingship. Merlin makes clear to readers, and to Arthur, the need for a king to display his power such that he overawes observers and thereby forces them to recognize his status as king. In other words, Merlin teaches Arthur the need to make a spectacle of kingship in order to reinforce one's position as king. The Saracens constitute the venue *par excellence* for such display. For example, when Arthur is battling Saracens in Leodegan's kingdom, Merlin deliberately provokes his protégé into appropriate manifestations of military might. At one point, when King Ban offers to do battle in Arthur's stead against a Saracen giant because Arthur is young and inexperienced, Merlin turns to Arthur and says "Wat abidestow coward king? / Þe paiem ȝif anon meteing!" (6343–44). Arthur, for shame, is

> . . . neiȝe wode
> In wratþe brent al his blod
> His hors he smiteþ and he forþ glod
> Oȝain king Saphiran he rode. (6345–48)

This battle, provoked by Merlin, results in Guinevere and all the watching ladies awarding Arthur "al þe priis" (6378). The renown of display thus redounds to Arthur's credit and helps to construct him as a noble leader in battle. Merlin also orchestrates Arthur's actions in other battles so that they may be noted as evidence of Arthur's nobility and leadership. For example, in the final battle recounted in the poem, Merlin charges Arthur that he has "iuel ʒolden þe kisseinge / Þat Gvenour him ʒaf at his arminge" (9241–42). As a result, Arthur redoubles his efforts against the Saracens and

> . . . tohewe[s] þat route
> Tofore biside and al about.
> Al wondred þat him seiʒe an
> And seyd he worþ a noble man. (9243–46)

Whereas earlier in the poem, at his coronation feast, Arthur's right to be king could be challenged by claims that he was not of noble birth, here his martial display demonstrates beyond a doubt the veracity of his noble origins and the validity of his claim to kingship.[79] Merlin also instructs Arthur in other appropriate kingly displays. When Leodegan awards to Arthur the Saracen booty he has captured in battle, Merlin advises the young king how to distribute this booty so as to communicate his worthiness to all observers: "Arthur nome it anon riʒtes / And parted it wel curtaisliche / Bi Merlins conseil sikerliche" (6458–60). Right after Arthur has done this, Leodegan summons him to take up lodging at court rather than in the humble inn where Arthur has heretofore stayed in Carohaise. Appropriate display means discernment of one's worthiness. Yet again, Saracens enable the public performance of Arthur's right to rule.

The association of monarchy with a need for spectacle and public display has long been accepted. As Foucault suggests in *Discipline and Punish,* much of what shapes power relations and society in a monarchy is the general knowledge of the monarch's special surplus of power in relation to his or her subjects.[80] The only way to maintain this sense of surplus power is to perform it, or have it performed for one by the actions of others.[81] Actions that draw attention to the specialness of the monarch, as here Arthur's martial efforts draw attention to his surplus of prowess, are thus vital to the maintenance of monarchical authority and to the continued existence of a political system of monarchical rule. Historically, late medieval monarchs certainly evinced a lively awareness of this, and carefully deployed spectacle to great political effect. Consider, for example, the symbolic implications of Edward I's decision to remove the supposed Crown of Arthur, as well as other regalia of Llywellyn ap Gruffyd's dynasty, from Wales to England.[82] As one contemporary chronicler put it, "et sic Wallensium gloria ad Anglicos, licet invite, est translata"[83] In this ritual act, Edward assumed and demonstrated his rights over Wales for all to see. His act displayed the validity of his claim to the overlordship of Wales. In *Of Arthour and of Merlin,* monarchical display serves a similar purpose: it makes manifest Arthur's right to rule and validates his kingship. Moreover, as the Saracens allow Arthur to display his monarchical identity, they allow him to solidify his claim to power and to affirm the nature of England's polity as a monarchy. Arthur's need for, and reliance on, display identify his polity as a monarchy. The Saracens of *Of Arthour and of Merlin* thus reveal the role of spectacle in the establishment both of a monarch and of his polity's identity.

The Saracens also serve as catalysts for socio-political associations that define Arthur's legendary court. When Merlin leads Arthur to Carohaise, he does so in order to effect the marriage of Arthur to Guinevere, and Saracens facilitate the achievement of this union so important to tales of Arthur's maturity. The Saracen invasion of Guinevere's father's kingdom offers Arthur a forum in which to exhibit his military prowess, and this exhibition convinces Leodegan to betroth his daughter to Arthur. As Arthur helps Leodegan to battle the invading Saracens, Arthur and his companions rescue Leodegan as that king is being led away into captivity by the Saracens (5862–94). This rescue and the massacre of Saracens that it entails clearly impress Leodegan:

> Michel wonder had Leodegan
> Þat swiche a litel poine of man
> So fele in so litel þrawe
> So manliche had yslawe,
> . . . .
> Þat he was deliuerd fram his fon
> He þonked Ihesu Crist anon. (5895–902)

Leodegan's favorable impression is reinforced by Arthur's performances in other battles against Saracens, and he subsequently decides to betroth Guinevere to Arthur and make Arthur heir to the kingdom of Carohaise (8609–25). Saracens thus play a key role in effecting a political alliance for Arthur and in arranging the marriage so central to Arthur's kingly identity and to Arthurian tradition.

Saracens also serve to establish the legendary company of Round Table knights. When Wawain and his brothers decide to seek knighthood from

Arthur and thereby end the discord between their uncle (Arthur) and their father (Lot of Orkney), they journey to London and come upon invading Saracens. Their battle against these Saracens leads to their acceptance by Arthur's constable Sir Do, and this marks the inception of Arthur's knightly company. Other young warriors subsequently come to seek Arthur and find themselves struggling mightily with Saracens only to have Wawain and his forces come to their aid. The two Ywains, Sagremor, Kay Destran, Kehedin, Dedinet the Savage, and the four Ywains of Arundel all find themselves in this position. The arrival of Wawain and his company always represents a much-needed reprieve for the Christians in a fierce battle, and ultimately unites the various newcomers in common service to Arthur. Fighting Saracens forges the chivalric and military fellowship that will define Arthur's court.

The bloody war against the Saracens also unites the various socio-political orders of Arthur's realm. When Wawain and his forces attack the Saracens harrying the countryside outside London, the inhabitants of that area gratefully join with them in this effort, and Wawain ends up leading a force of

> . . . . . four score kni3tes
> And fif hundred of squiers wi3t
> And tventi also þat schulden ben
> Kni3tes when þai mi3t her time sen
> And þ†re hundred of þe cuntray
> Boþe on fot and hors y say. (5135–40)

Wawain combines fighters from different paths of life in his army. He leads men who possess the wealth, status and training to fight on horses as well as men who fight on foot. In addition, Wawain's decision to send the recaptured booty to London gains him the support of the city aldermen and townspeople. When the constable summons the inhabitants of London to tell them what has happened, "Of þat cite þe alderman / Ich wiþ his ward cam," and 5000 of the 7000 subsequently sally forth to unite with Wawain's already-mixed forces in their fight against the Saracens (5095–96; 5097–130). Battling Saracens thus unites English nobles, rural workers, and townspeople. Bloody Saracen invasions strengthen the political and social fabric of Arthur's realm.

The advent of the Saracens also re-establishes English hegemony in Britain. When Arthur comes to power in this poem, a number of insular rulers, including those of Scotland, North Wales, Northumbria and Cornwall, challenge his overlordship. The arrival of Saracens, however, forces these kings to abandon plans to dethrone Arthur for plans to defend their realms. The Saracens redirect insular martial energies towards ends that do not threaten Arthur's kingship or the hegemony of the English polity. Just as battles against outsiders historically served to divert the military endeavors of magnates away from civil conflicts and into international ones, so in this poem battles against Saracens offer, from an English perspective, more politically beneficial directions for the military might of unruly subjects.[84] In addition, while the Saracen invasions end insular challenges to Arthur's kingship, they also promote the re-subjection of these kings to Arthur. As the depredations of the Saracens increase, the once rebellious kings lament their broken fealty to Arthur and their concomitant inability to call on him for military aid. King Yder of Cornwall, "acursse[s] oft þe time grim / Þat Arthour was wroþ wiþ him" (7717–18), while Lot of Orkney tears his hair and bewails the time "Þat he cunteked wiþ king Arthour" (8362). The ravages of the Saracens promote insular unity and the renewed overlordship of England within Britain.

Insular unity and English hegemony also benefit from the formation of Arthur's legendary band of knights. As these young men come to Arthur and fight Saracens for him in his absence, they end the political disunity of his larger realm. The reason for this is that most of these young knights are the sons of Arthur's erstwhile insular enemies, those rebellious subject kings described above. Wawain and his brothers, for example, are the sons of Lot of Orkney. Galathin, one of their companions, is the son of Nanters, another king who opposed Arthur. The two Ywains are sons of the King Uriens of Schorham who rejected Arthur's sovereignty earlier in the poem. These youths are also all nephews of Arthur (their mothers are various half-sisters of Arthur). Thus, their unity against the Saracens in Arthur's service not only reunites the island under Arthur, but also unites Arthur's extended family. Yet again, war against Saracens serves to reconstruct political bonds, here those between the king and powerful magnates related to him.

A sense of political renewal accompanies the strengthening of unity described above. Battles between Christians and Saracens facilitate the emergence of a new generation of leaders and the revitalization of the structures that define England politically. The battles record the rise to power of a new band of rulers and warriors explicitly characterized as youthful. For example, as Arthur battles Saracens in Leodegan's kingdom, the narrator repeatedly stresses his youth as well as his martial prowess. Arthur's company, with the exception of five loyal servitors of his father, is described as "Alle it were ȝong man" (5387). The women of Leodegan's court, watching the battle from the battlements, "ȝerne biheld king Arthour / And hadde wonder of his ȝingþe / Þat þer kidde swiche stre†ngþe" (6268–70). The future knights of Arthur's Round Table who fight Saracens so mightily in England are also described in terms that emphasize their youth. The narrator refers to Wawain and his brothers as "children" (4764, 4874, 4847, 4869, 5107, 5110), and while the term in this context means young and unproven rather than infant, it still connotes youthfulness and inexperience.[85] The two Ywains (Ywain and Ywain the Bastard), too, are identified as "children" (7795), and as "our 3ong man" (7868). Similarly, Dedinet the Savage, Ywain of the White Hand, Ywain of Lyonel, Ywain Desclavis le bel, and Ywain of Strangore are introduced as "3ong men of Arundel," and described as leading three hundred "3onglinges" (8263–65). The many references to youth, combined with the slaughter of Saracens effected by these men, represent these junior knights as a new generation of warriors coming to power. Every battle they fight against the Saracens manifests publicly their new status as military and political leaders, and suggests their ferocious ability to defend their polities and possessions. These young warriors represent the future greatness of England and of Arthur's reign. Not only do they offer, given their births and fellowship, the hope of a newly unified insular polity led by Arthur, but they also represent, through their victories, new military hope against the Saracens and the possibility of the eventual expulsion of these invaders.

The youngsters' performances against Saracens also reveal their forebears' decreased capacity for effective military and political leadership, and the concomitant assumption of power by the rising generation. For example, at one point when Arthur and his young knights are fighting Saracens in Leodegan's kingdom, they ride to the rescue of knights of Arthur's father's Round Table who have been unhorsed by Saracens (5933–47). Because these Round Table knights are not Arthur's fellows of future time (Wawain, Ywain and others), but knights of Uter's generation,[86] one sees in this episode the younger generation coming to the assistance and rescue of the older. The same sort of event occurs in another part of the poem when Wawain's father, King Lot, is bested by Saracen invaders. Lot decides to retreat and convey his wife and baby son (Mordred) to a distant safe fortress. Unfortunately, the fugitives do not escape the Saracens, and Lot's wife is captured. Lot is forced to choose between abandoning his wife and losing his life, and the end result is that Wawain comes upon his mother being whipped, beaten and dragged along by her hair by the Saracen giant Taurus (8427–58). Whereas Lot was unable to protect his queen, Wawain quickly disposes of the Saracens guarding her and kills Taurus. Once again, the up-and-coming generation comes to its forebears' assistance, and succeeds where they have failed. Repeatedly then, Saracens in *Of Arthour and of Merlin* precipitate a changing of the political guard, and the emergence of a new, younger generation of warriors and rulers.

Questions of the younger generation's accession to power characterize *chansons de geste* according to Sarah Kay and Peter Haidu.[87] This genre is also known for its attention to battles and conflict. Accordingly, it is perhaps unsurprising to find the two phenomena of war and succession linked in this tale.[88] However, I would like to consider in more detail the ways in which generational succession and the concomitant rejuvenation and reunification of a polity might be connected to, and dependent on, violence. In *Totem and Taboo,* Freud articulates a vision of social order as a structure premised upon violence and generational succession, that is to say the succession to power of a new generation, and their violent replacement of the older generation.[89] He discusses the actions of what he terms the primal horde, and argues that as the young men of this patriarchal horde grow envious of their father's access to women and control of the horde, they plot his death and eventually murder him. The guilt that arises from this act, though, is very powerful, as is the young men's fear that they, too, may become the victims of a violent murder plot. Consequently, they agree to follow the restrictions the primal father placed on their desires and practices even in the now-dead father's absence. Thus, while violence changes who sets the prohibitions that constitute social order, it does not change the prohibitions themselves. Violence does not redefine the social order; instead, it redefines who occupies the positions of power within that social order. The accession to power of Arthur and his company of youthful squires follows in some ways this model of power. Although the younger generation does not directly attack the older as in Freud's scenario, they achieve leadership roles within the polity by violent displays of martial prowess that are occasionally linked to their forebears. However, even as they rejuvenate the community of the realm, they ultimately only return it to the heyday of Arthur's father when their own fathers accepted Uter's overlordship and presented a united front of military and political might to the world. The practice of violence thus becomes the necessary act of accession, but does not in any way change the social order in which its practitioners operate. It is perhaps this ultimate inefficacy of violence—its ultimate inability to effect change—that explains why it seems to have such a revivifying role in *Of Arthour and of Merlin.* Violence here, as in Freud's model, serves as a pathway to power rather than a source of fundamental change. Violence becomes a method of renewing the social order rather than changing it, and is therefore much less menacing than it might appear.

This acceptance of violence as a fact of social and political life is very much in keeping with medieval ideas of knightly behavior. As Richard Kaeuper argues throughout *Chivalry and Violence,* medieval warriors' ideas of chivalry, of noble identity and behavior, were inextricably interwoven with an acceptance of violence as a way of life, and of profit as a worthy motive for violence. Many scholars of late medieval chivalry, in contrast, have characterized knightly violence and profit-taking through conflict as the dark underside of chivalry, an ugly truth which the rhetoric of idealized chivalry attempts to conceal and make more palatable.[90] As Kaeuper shows, however, medieval texts and knights themselves articulate no incompatibility between chivalric behavior on the one hand, and violence and plunder on the other.[91] Indeed, in *Of Arthour and of Merlin,* violence and the appropriate distribution of gifts characterize the noble King Arthur's reign, and effect his acceptance as king of England and overlord of Britain. To read late medieval knightly avowals of chivalry as concealments of "uglier" motivations such as bloodlust and booty thus seems rather contrary to medieval perceptions. Instead, medieval knights, at least as depicted in literature, seem very accepting of social models rooted in and upheld by violence and desires for personal benefit, models similar to that proffered by Freud in *Totem and Taboo.* Spring, as various medieval writers pointed out, was beautiful partly because it was the time to begin and renew wars, and to enjoy the violence and booty they entailed.[92] *Of Arthour and of Merlin* certainly links descriptions of spring and rebirth to conflict, and as a whole suggests that knightly violence and the plunder of war are integral parts of social and political structures.

In sum, rather than destroying the polity, Saracen-Christian violence revitalizes and reunifies the "Inglisch" realm. Just as, historically, the wars of Edward I, II, and III shaped the politics and governmental structures of their reigns and of England, so the incessant battles depicted here suggest a constructive role for war and violence in the establishment of a nation's political identity. One senses in *Of Arthour and of Merlin*'s violent portrait of the origins of Arthur's kingship that something new, and positive, and "Inglisch" (namely Arthur's legendary reign) grows out of the bloody socio-economic destruction and violence of Saracen invasion. Constructive effects of violent conflict can also be discerned in the general portrait of English history. Historically, the "Inglisch" identity so trumpeted in Auchinleck is precisely a hybrid conglomeration of Briton, Germanic, Scandinavian and French invasions, conquests, and interminglings. Accordingly, it is not surprising in a text so focussed on "Inglond" to find a portrait of a gruesome, brutal, and yet ultimately productive and fruitful experience of conflict and invasion.

CODA: VERNACULARITY, VIOLENCE, AND THE PROLOGUE

Given *Of Arthour and of Merlin*'s concern with origins and beginnings, it is appropriate, albeit literally preposterous, that I should conclude this chapter with a discussion of the poem's oft cited prologue. Scholars investigating the history of the English language or medieval notions of English identity frequently refer to this prologue in their studies.[93] The reasons for this are clear. After a brief invocation of Christ and the Virgin Mary, and a short discussion of schooling that offers "Freynsch and Latin eueraywhare" (18),[94] the poet launches into an enthusiastic assertion of English vernacular identity:

> Of Freynsch no Latin nil y tel more
> Ac on I[n]glisch ichil tel þerfore:
> Riȝt is þat I[n]glische vnderstond
> Þat was born in Inglond.
> Freynsche vse þis gentil man
> Ac euerich Inglische Inglische can,
> Mani noble ich haue yseiȝe
> Þat no Freynsche couþe seye,
> Biginne ichil for her loue
> Bi Ihesus leue þat sitt aboue
> On Inglische tel mi tale—
> God ous sende soule hale. (19–30)

With these words, unique to the Auchinleck version of the poem, the poet asserts the validity of using the English language for his tale, and identifies the ways in which this language serves as a marker of English identity in the early fourteenth century. He associates French and Latin with schools and training, and accordingly presents them as artificially acquired, not natively absorbed, means of communication in England.[95] Even the reference to the "gentil man" who uses French is qualified by a purported eyewitness report that many nobles do not know how to speak French. The English language becomes the natural and inclusive choice for the communication of a tale because "euerich Inglische Inglische can" (24). English language unites the inhabitants of England, and traverses socio-economic borders. It has become a definitive marker of people's geopolitical identities. The prologue thus identifies *Of Arthour and of Merlin* as a player in the culture wars between English and French in England. Whereas the French language has heretofore been valued, especially by nobles, the narrator asserts that its time as a language of insular culture has now passed, and that the language of insular culture henceforward must be "Inglische" because this is the only language that all inhabitants of the country understand. Accordingly, this prologue constitutes an enthusiastic interpellation of an early fourteenth-century "Inglisch" vernacular audience and identity.

The fact that the poet feels he has to assert so vehemently the validity of using the English language for his tale, however, reveals his awareness of England's history of invasion and conquest. As the references to French and Latin indicate, the poet's choice of the English language for his composition is neither straightforward nor obvious in the early fourteenth century. As Thorlac Turville-Petre has shown, this period witnesses a shift among writers in England from the use of Latin or French to the use of English for many scholarly and artistic texts.[96] The widespread use of French, of course, was a legacy of the Norman Conquest of England and the subsequent interweaving of Norman and English peoples. Even though the Norman Conquest occurred about 260 years before Auchinleck's compilation, the linguistic and artistic consequences of this invasion and of later influxes of French-speaking nobles into England under rulers such as Henry II and III still resonated in the early 1300s. Because of the lived effects of invasion, writers choosing to write in English at this time felt the need to assert forcefully the propriety of using the English language in their texts. *Of Arthour and of Merlin* is no exception, and introduces a text about invasions and efforts to expel foreign invaders from England's shores by announcing its composer's decision to break with a linguistic tradition created by the Norman Conquest. The poem's opening thus promotes readerly awareness of historically formative events in England, and establishes a backdrop of lived invasion for the poem's tale of Arthurian romance and English history. The prologue prepares the reader well for a vision of English identity and history as hybrid products of invasion and conquest.

Juxtaposing the proudly vernacular prologue with the bloody battles against Saracens depicted in *Of Arthour and of Merlin* also demands consideration of the historical connections between violence and the English language. Battles and invasions crafted the English language. The specific origins of the language (those that post-date its general Indo-European roots) date back to the Germanic pagan invasions of Britain in the fifth and sixth centuries. The melding of peoples effected by those invasions produced what became Old English,[97] the language that accounts today for a whole variety of English vocabulary, syntax, and grammar.[98] The later invasions by Scandinavian Vikings also contributed elements to the English language; the plural pronoun "they" derives from the languages of these invaders.[99] Similarly, the Norman Conquest of 1066 brought with it a huge variety of vocabulary.[100] Words such as "government," "empire," "justice" and "dinner" all represent borrowings of French words into English after the Conquest.[101] Thus, the very language the prologue trumpets, and the very vernacular identity it asserts, derive from bloody conflicts like those recounted in the poem. The prologue thus accords well with the larger poem's suggestions of the productivity of violence and conquest. The prologue and poem together offer a concrete reminder that the vernacular identity asserted so emphatically throughout the Auchinleck manuscript derives in part from invasions and battles, ugly and brutal as they may be, that change the societies in which people live and the language in which they communicate. Perhaps one may see in this the veracity of Walter Benjamin's claim that all records of culture are records of barbarism. *Of Arthour and of Merlin,* however, does not condemn barbarism; rather, in its prologue, its depiction of the hybrid origins of English identity, its portrait of Arthur's reign, and its multiple passages detailing the flowering of natural beauty within bloody carnage, it suggests that barbarism like that of the Saracen invasions is a necessary evil that can bear surprisingly attractive fruits.

Conclusion

As the prologue to *Of Arthour and of Merlin* shows, Saracen characters in Auchinleck complicate and enrich even very direct assertions of English vernacular identity. Without an awareness of the endemic violence provoked by *Of Arthour and of Merlin*'s Saracen invaders, the historical nature of the "Inglisch" identity trumpeted in the prologue and the full implications of the prologue's references to the Norman Conquest cannot be appreciated. Saracen characters in this text lay bare the violent, hybrid origins of the language and culture so proudly invoked in the prologue, and thereby constitute an important illumination of the "Inglisch" identity interpellated throughout Auchinleck. Functioning thus, these Arthurian Saracens epitomize the claim made throughout the pages of this book: Saracen characters in Auchinleck allow it to do more than merely assert an English vernacular identity; they enable the manuscript and its audience to explore the complexity of this identity and investigate the problems involved in defining and asserting it in the early fourteenth century.

All the Saracens in Auchinleck participate in important ways in this project. The noble Saracen knight, found in so many romances, promotes consideration of how a group defines and establishes its unique identity in a context of shared similarities. As a result, this figure illustrates the processes involved in England's efforts to differentiate itself from France and its French past in the early 1300s. Another common Saracen character is the Saracen princess who converts to Christianity for love of a Christian knight. This type of Saracen appears in Auchinleck's *Sir Beves,* and indicates the ways in which group and gender identities are linked, and how social, cultural, and familial identities are assumed, altered, and affirmed. In many ways, the Saracen princess resembles the foreign queen, a historical fixture in England in the early fourteenth century. As a result, *Sir Beves*'s Josiane reveals how these consorts crafted a place for themselves in English society, and shaped perceptions of English kings, their people, and England's place on the world stage. Although Josiane is tied to England through her marriage to Beves of Southampton, other Saracens in Auchinleck are never explicitly linked to England. This, however, does not prevent them from providing insight into some of the challenges facing the nation in the early fourteenth century. Saracens in Þe *King of Tars* and *Floris and Blauncheflur* exemplify this claim most clearly. As these romances of the East relate the interactions between Saracens and Christians in Damascus and Babylon, they explore the ways in which different peoples might be integrated, and show that such integration often promotes renewed and vehement assertions of two peoples' separateness. Similar vacillations between integration and differentiation can be discerned in English political rhetoric in the early fourteenth century as, for example, English kings encouraged enmity towards the Scots by emphasizing their cultural differences, and yet desired the incorporation of these same people into the English polity. While relations to other peoples certainly influenced assertions of "Inglisch" identity in the early fourteenth century, so too did relations to the divine. The Saracens in Auchinleck's saints' lives indicate that "Inglisch" identity in this manuscript is a religious identification as well as a political, linguistic, and historical one. Saracen persecutors illuminate central tenets of Christianity for a lay audience and thereby participate in the manuscript's efforts to promote lay piety in England. The Saracen persecutors also testify to English involvement in pan-Christian crusading endeavors, and to English interest in crusading setbacks at Muslim and Byzantine hands. While the Arthurian Saracens of Auchinleck further elaborate a vision of England as a crusading nation, they also reveal the hybridity of "Inglisch" identity and its relations to violence. As the Saracens of *Of Arthour and of Merlin* make clear, wars, invasions, and conquests formed Englishness both historically and politically, and contributed in no small part to the language which, in the fourteenth century, is coming increasingly to serve as a marker of this identity. Repeatedly, then, figures of religious otherness participate in Auchinleck's efforts to craft a vision of the English nation in the early 1300s.

As the Saracens of Auchinleck engage issues at stake in England, they show how medieval western depictions of Muslims could speak to the context of their production and circulation. Late medieval Saracens could connote foreigners close to home as well as Middle Easterners, and could address domestic concerns as well as western ideas of the East. The Saracens of Auchinleck exemplify this statement. At times they illuminate problems confronting England on the home front, while at other times they illustrate English perceptions of crusade and commitment to Christianity. At all times, however, these characters are relevant to the manuscript's audience. Thus,

although the Saracens in Auchinleck bear little or no resemblance to historical Muslims, they reveal a great deal about the "Inglisch" situation of their
production and circulation, and about the ways in which depictions of religious others intersect with articulations of a sense of national identity.

This is not to say that all Saracens necessarily function in this way.
Auchinleck has its own concerns and foci, and these construct a particular
network of manuscript associations within which Saracen characters res-
onate. It is difficult to say whether other English manuscripts from the late
thirteenth and early fourteenth centuries might have crafted a similar horizon of expectations for readers since not all manuscripts from this period
have survived, and, among those that have survived, Auchinleck enjoys a
somewhat anomalous status. As Derek Pearsall notes, Auchinleck "provides
the earliest extant text of all but a handful of its items," and contains primarily English texts of a "dominantly secular provenance."[1] It thereby stands in
marked contrast to "earlier and contemporary manuscript miscellanies, such
as Jesus College, Oxford, MS 29, British Library, Cotton Caligula A. ix,
Trinity College, Cambridge, MS 323, Bodleian Library Digby 2, Digby 86,
and British Library Harley 2253 . . . , which are dominated by clerkly and
educated interests, both religious and secular, and which accommodate Latin
and Anglo-Norman texts equally with English."[2] Other roughly contemporaneous manuscripts do exist, however, which share Auchinleck's emphasis
on vernacular texts, contain romances, and include Saracens. For example,
Oxford, Bodleian Library, Laud Miscellany 108 contains the *South English
Legendary, Havelok the Dane* and *King Horn.*[3] All material is in the vernacular, and the saints' lives and the romances share a decided interest in English
protagonists.[4] One also finds Saracens in this manuscript. *King Horn*
recounts the invasion of Horn's native kingdom by "Sarazyns lodlike and
blake" (line 1415), while the *Legendary* narrates the tale of St Christopher
who "was a saracen" (line 1) and depicts Thomas of Canterbury's father as a
crusader who eventually marries an "amirales" daughter when she converts to
Christianity. Laud 108 leans more heavily to religious texts than Auchinleck
does, and contains fewer Saracens. Its focus therefore differs from Auchinleck, despite the similarities they share, and Laud's Saracens should therefore
be studied in relation to its overarching concerns rather than Auchinleck's.

Another manuscript whose Saracens might have functioned similarly
to Auchinleck's is Cambridge, University Library, Gg 4.27 (2). Unfortunately, this manuscript exists today only as a single quire of fourteen leaves
dating to the first quarter of the fourteenth century.[5] Because of its fragmentary state, it is impossible to gain a full sense of Gg 4.27 (2)'s overarching
concerns and how its Saracen characters might have related to these. As it

exists now, however, this manuscript contains three Middle English texts that also appear in Auchinleck, *Floris and Blauncheflur, King Horn,* and the *Assumpcion de nostre dame.*[6] Two of the texts, *King Horn* and *Floris and Blauncheflur,* evoke Saracen locales and peoples.[7] However, Gg 4.27 (2) as it exists now does not seem to share Auchinleck's obsession with English identity. While all three extant texts are written in English, no text calls attention to its narration in English as opposed to any other language, and no text presents itself as an explicit commentary on English politics and history. Indeed, Gg 4.27 (2) as a whole contains no direct references to England or the English language. *King Horn,* to be sure, is categorized by scholars as a Matter of England romance, but the term "Inglond" never appears in the text and the romance's geographical evocation of England is notoriously unclear.[8] Generally, the Cambridge manuscript does not seem particularly invested in highlighting its texts' pertinence to England, and in this it differs significantly from Auchinleck. As a result, while the two manuscripts appear to share an interest in Saracens, Gg. 4. 27 (2)'s Saracens right now do not contribute to an exploration of "Inglisch" identity like that found in Auchinleck. Who knows, however, what horizon of expectations the complete manuscript might have offered originally?

I have included this sketch of the material landscape in which Auchinleck stands in order to indicate ways in which this manuscript and its Saracens may illuminate the functions of Saracens in other late medieval English manuscripts. Admittedly, Auchinleck is somewhat anomalous in its range of vernacular texts and in its explicit and repeated references to English language, history, geography and politics. Because of this, it is important not to generalize the ways in which its Saracens function to other English manuscripts of the period without a thorough consideration of those manuscripts' unique overarching interests. That said, however, there is no denying that Auchinleck and its Saracens demonstrate the value of placing texts about religious others in their manuscript contexts. Other manuscripts may not share the exact same interests as Auchinleck, nor its scope, but they, too, construct horizons of expectations that would have shaped their readers' interpretations of texts, and it is clear from this study of the Auchinleck manuscript that Saracens can interact with these horizons of expectations in rich and complex ways.

To conclude, the Saracens of medieval literature reveal much about western perceptions of racial and religious difference in the Middle Ages, but they also offer insight into more domestic concerns of the cultures that produced and consumed texts about them. When Saracens are situated within the material and historical contexts of their production and dissemination, their illumination of domestic concerns becomes more readily discernible. Within the context of the early fourteenth-century Auchinleck manuscript, Saracens serve to define the "Inglisch" identity asserted so stridently therein, and to explore the processes and problems involved in asserting such an identity in the 1330s. The Saracens of Auchinleck thus decisively demonstrate the various ways in which figures of religious alterity offer crucial insights into cultural and political debates in which their audiences are directly engaged. The manuscript therefore explains, at least in part, the popularity of Saracens in the late medieval West: these characters provided their audiences with the opportunity to examine purportedly exotic realms and people, but simultaneously ensured, through their inaccuracies and resemblances to Westerners, that such examination provided their audiences with ideas about, and clarifications of, the audiences' own concerns.

Notes

NOTES TO THE INTRODUCTION

1. Edward Said, *Orientalism* (New York: Vintage Books, 1979), 71.
2. Dorothee Metlitzki, *The Matter of Araby in Medieval England* (New Haven: Yale University Press, 1977), 209–10; Norman Daniel, *Heroes and Saracens: An Interpretation of the "chansons de geste"* (Edinburgh: University of Edinburgh Press, 1984), 3–4, 49–51, 72–73, 81, 133–54.
3. Recent scholars of Saracens have also drawn the same distinction. Jeffrey Jerome Cohen, for example, states that he uses the term *Saracen* "instead of *Muslim* in order to mark the category from the start as produced through the passionate investment of occidental fantasies and desires." Jeffrey Jerome Cohen, "On Saracen Enjoyment: Some Fantasies of Race in Late Medieval France and England," *Journal of Medieval and Early Modern Studies* 31, no. 1 (2001): 136, n. 3.

   To reflect a similar disparity between medieval western ideas about the Prophet Muhammad and actual Muslim ones, I use the Middle English term "Mahoun" to designate the object of Saracen worship depicted in my Auchinleck texts, and use the term "Muhammad" to refer to the Muslim Prophet. Norman Daniel offers a succinct argument in favor of this practice in *Heroes and Saracens*, 9–10.
4. Daniel, *Heroes and Saracens*, 8; William Wistar Comfort, "The Literary Role of Saracens in French Epic," *PMLA* 55 (1940): 629; *Oxford English Dictionary*, s.v. "Saracen."
5. Diane Speed, "The Saracens of *King Horn*," *Speculum* 65 (1990): 566. See also *OED*, s.v. "Saracen."
6. Diane Speed identifies this spelling as the product of French influence on Middle English. Speed, "Saracens of *King Horn*," 566. See also the list of forms given in the *Middle English Dictionary*, s.v. "Sarasin(e."
7. *MED*, s.v. "Sarasin(e," meanings (a) and (b) respectively.
8. Daniel, *Heroes and Saracens*, 8.
9. Speed, "Saracens of *King Horn*," 564–95. I am also inclined to question the *Middle English Dictionary* because one of the texts it cites as using the term

"Sarasin" to mean generic pagan (meaning (b)) is the thirteenth-century life of St Margaret of Antioch known as *Meidan Maregrete.* Given this saint's geographic associations with the East, it seems rather pedantic to insist that no connotation of Arab or Muslim could be associated with the word at this point. The *MED,* however, will not assert that the word can have eastern connotations until a Middle English text explicitly associates the word with geographic regions populated by Muslims in the Middle Ages. For an edition of *Meidan Maregrete,* see *Altenglische Legenden: Neue Folge,* ed. Carl Horstmann (Heilbronn: Heninger, 1881), 489–97.

10. Comfort, "The Literary Role of Saracens," 628–59; C. Meredith Jones, "The Conventional Saracens of the Songs of Geste," *Speculum* 17 (1942): 201–25.

11. Richard Southern, *Western Views of Islam in the Middle Ages* (Cambridge: Harvard University Press, 1962); Norman Daniel, *Islam and the West: The Making of an Image,* rev. ed. (Oxford: Oneworld Publications Ltd, 1993).

12. Metlitzki, *The Matter of Araby.*

13. Daniel, *Heroes and Saracens.*

14. Said, *Orientalism,* 1–110. The articles by Comfort and Jones are wholly devoted to the identification of stereotypes and conventions, while especially pertinent sections of the books by other scholars include Daniel, *Heroes and Saracens,* 35–38, 46–51, 62, 92, 116–22, 193, 263, 278–79, and Metlitzki, *Matter of Araby,* 160–250.

15. John Tolan, *Saracens: Islam in the Medieval European Imagination* (New York: Columbia University Press, 2002); Sharon Kinoshita, "The Politics of Courtly Love: *La Prise d'Orange* and the Conversion of the Saracen Queen," *Romanic Review* 86 (1995): 265–87; idem, "'Pagans are wrong and Christians are right': Alterity, Gender, and Nation in the *Chanson de Roland,*" *Journal of Medieval and Early Modern Studies* 31, no. 1 (2001): 79–112; Lynn Tarte Ramey, *Christian, Saracen and Genre in Medieval French Literature* (New York: Routledge, 2001).

16. Carol Falvo Heffernan, *The Orient in Chaucer and Medieval Romance* (Cambridge: D. S. Brewer, 2003); Geraldine Heng, *Empire of Magic: Medieval Romance and the Politics of Cultural Fantasy* (New York: Columbia University Press, 2003). Other significant work on Saracens is found in the essays included in the *Journal of Medieval and Early Modern Studies* 31, no. 1 (2001), a special issue devoted to the topic of "Race and Ethnicity in the Middle Ages." A number of studies of Chaucer's use of the East have also emerged recently, including Brenda Deen Schildgen, *Pagans, Tartars, Moslems, and Jews in Chaucer's Canterbury Tales* (Gainesville: University Press of Florida, 2001) and the collection of essays in Kathryn Lynch, ed. *Chaucer's Cultural Geography* (New York: Routledge, 2002).

17. John Tolan notes that, for Europeans, "the Muslim world [was] a civilization seen as a rival and a threat through the Middle Ages and beyond."

Saracens, xxiii. See Metlitzki, *Matter of Araby,* 16–56 for a discussion of the superiority of Muslim scientific and technological knowledge in the Middle Ages. Christian awareness of Muslim wealth and sophistication is discussed in Steven Runciman, *The First Crusade and the Foundation of the Kingdom of Jerusalem,* vol. 1 of *A History of the Crusades* (Cambridge: Cambridge University Press, 1951), 88; Jonathan Riley-Smith, *The Crusades: A Short History* (New Haven: Yale University Press, 1987), 188–89; and Christopher Tyerman, *England and the Crusades 1095–1588* (Chicago: University of Chicago Press, 1988), 293. See Southern, *Western Views,* 3, 42, and 105, and Metlitzki, *Matter of Araby,* 129, 248 for discussion of the military menace posed by Muslims to medieval western Christendom.

18. My thinking about depictions of otherness has been influenced by a number of theorists. Said's influence is clear from the body of the text, but I am also indebted to the writings of Bhabha on hybridity, stereotypes and mimicry, and to writings by Kristeva, Lacan, and Levinas. Homi Bhabha, *The Location of Culture* (London: Routledge, 1990); Julia Kristeva, *Strangers to Ourselves,* trans. Leon S. Roudiez (New York: Columbia University Press, 1991); Jacques Lacan, *The Seminar of Jacques Lacan: Book II—The Ego in Freud's Theory and in the Technique of Psychoanalysis, 1954–1955,* ed. Jacques-Alain Miller and trans. Sylvana Tomaselli (New York: W. W. Norton and Company, 1991); idem, "On a question preliminary to any possible treatment of psychosis," in *Ecrits: A Selection,* trans. Alan Sheridan (New York: W. W. Norton and Company, 1977); Emmanuel Levinas, "Time and the Other," in *The Levinas Reader,* ed. Sean Hand (Oxford: Blackwell, 1989), 37–58; idem, *Totality and Infinity,* trans. Alphonso Lingis (Pittsburgh: Duquesne University Press, 1969).

19. Dorothee Metlitzki's *The Matter of Araby* is one substantial exception to the rule, since her book examines representations of "Araby" in many genres and texts. She, too, however fails to consider manuscript context. John Tolan does discuss Old French representations of Saracens in vernacular *chansons de geste,* but he devotes most of his attention to Latinate and religious texts. The broad scope of his project in *Saracens* also precludes focus on one manuscript.

20. Andrew Taylor, "Authors, Scribes, Patrons, and Books," in *The Idea of the Vernacular: An Anthology Of Middle English Literary Theory, 1280–1520,* ed. Jocelyn Wogan-Browne, Nicholas Watson. Andrew Taylor, and Ruth Evans (University Park: Pennsylvania State University Press, 1999), 356.

21. This idea of a horizon of expectations was developed by Hans Robert Jauss, and is most readily accessible in the collection of essays in *Toward an Aesthetic of Reception,* trans. Timothy Bahti (Minneapolis: University of Minnesota Press, 1982).

22. Admittedly, a few lines of French appear in items 20 and 40, and the manuscript includes the Latin words it is translating in items 15 and 36 as well as

an occasional Latin phrase in items 8 and 10. However, the English language predominates even in these items, and all the manuscript items are conceived of, and presented, as works in English, a fact which is especially noteworthy given the manuscript's date of assembly.

23. Derek Pearsall and I. C. Cunningham, introduction to *The Auchinleck Manuscript: National Library of Scotland Advocates' MS 19. 2. 1 (facsimile)* (London: Scolar Press, 1977), vii.

24. Auchinleck currently exists in an incomplete state. The original scribal numbering of items in the manuscript indicates that the first item today's readers encounter is actually the sixth item of the original manuscript, and that items have been lost between current items 32 (*Otuel a Kni3t*) and 33 (*Kyng Alisaunder*), and between items 34 (*The Thrush and the Nightingale*) and 35 (*The Sayings of St Bernard*). Some of the remaining items such as *Kyng Alisaunder, King Richard* and *The Wench that [Lov]ed [A K]ing* exist in a fragmentary state. Other items lack either folios or groups of lines removed when earlier readers cut out most of the manuscript's illustrations. Of the forty-four items extant, however, most are sufficiently well preserved to be studied. For a full list of the manuscript's items, please see the Appendix.

25. Jean Harpham Burrows, "The Auchinleck Manuscript: Contexts, Texts and Audience" (Ph. D. diss., University of Washington, 1988), 1.

26. Laura Hibbard Loomis, "The Auchinleck Manuscript and a Possible London Bookshop of 1330–1340," in *Adventures in the Middle Ages: A Memorial Collection of Essays and Studies* (New York: Burt Franklin, 1962), 186.

27. For a full list of its contents, please see the Appendix.

28. For a full list of the editions and studies of Auchinleck texts by Horstmann, Kölbing and Zupitza, see Pearsall and Cunningham, introduction to *Auchinleck Manuscript (facsimile)*, xviii–xxiv.

29. Loomis, "Auchinleck Manuscript and a Possible London Bookshop," 150–87; idem, "Chaucer and the Auchinleck Manuscript: *Thopas* and *Guy of Warwick*," in *Adventures*, 131–49; idem, "Chaucer and the Breton Lays of the Auchinleck Manuscript," in *Adventures*, 111–30; idem, "The Auchinleck *Roland and Vernagu* and the Short *Chronicle*," *Modern Language Notes* 60 (1945): 94–97.

30. Judith Weiss, "The Auchinleck MS. and the Edwardes MSS," *Notes and Queries* 16 (1969): 444–46; Judith Mordkoff, "The Making of the Auchinleck Manuscript: The Scribes at Work" (Ph. D. diss., University of Connecticut, 1981); Timothy Shonk, "A Study of the Auchinleck Manuscript: Bookmen and Bookmaking in the Early Fourteenth Century," *Speculum* 60 (1985): 71–91; Frederick Porcheddu, "Editing the Auchinleck: Textual Criticism and the Reconstruction of a Medieval Manuscript (Auchinleck Manuscript)" (Ph. D. diss., Ohio State University, 1994); Ralph Hanna, "Reconsidering the Auchinleck Manuscript," in *New Directions in Later*

Medieval Manuscript Studies (Essays from the 1998 Harvard Conference), ed. Derek Pearsall (York: University of York Medieval Publications, 2000): 91–102.

31. Eve Salisbury has edited a version of "Bevis of Hampton," in *Four Romances of England: King Horn, Havelok the Dane, Bevis of Hampton, Athelston,* ed. Ronald B. Herzman, Graham Drake, and Eve Salisbury (Kalamazoo: Western Michigan University Medieval Institute Publications, 1999), 187–340; Susan Crane analyzes some of the manuscript's romances in *Insular Romance: Politics, Faith and Culture in Anglo-Norman and Middle English Literature* (Berkeley: University of California Press, 1986).

32. Loomis, "Auchinleck Manuscript and a Possible London Bookshop," 151.

33. These manuscripts are formally identified as, respectively, Oxford, Bodleian Library, Eng. poet. a. 1, and London, British Library, Harley 2253.

34. Seth Lerer, *Chaucer and His Readers: Imagining the Author in Late Medieval England* (Princeton: Princeton University Press, 1993); Derek Pearsall, ed., *Studies in the Vernon Manuscript* (Cambridge D. S. Brewer, 1990); Susanna Fein, ed., *Studies in the Harley Manuscript: The Scribes, Contents, and Social Contexts of British Library MS Harley 2253* (Kalamazoo: Western Michigan University Medieval Institute Publications, 2000).

35. Andrew Taylor, *Textual Situations: Three Medieval Manuscripts and Their Readers* (Philadelphia: University of Pennsylvania Press, 2002). One might also mention in this connection Elizabeth Scala's work, especially chapter 1 of *Absent Narratives, Manuscript Textuality, and Literary Structure in Late Medieval England* (New York: Palgrave Macmillan, 2002), 1–36.

36. Thorlac Turville-Petre, *England the Nation: Language, Literature, and National Identity, 1290–1340* (Oxford: Clarendon Press, 1996), 108–41; Burrows, "Auchinleck Manuscript: Contexts, Texts and Audience."

37. Titles listed are those used by Pearsall and Cunningham in their introduction to *Auchinleck Manuscript (facsimile),* xix-xxiv. Round brackets indicate titles provided by Pearsall and Cunningham for items in the manuscript that lack original titles because of manuscript lacunae. Square brackets indicate original titles reconstructed from extant letters in the manuscript. Titles without brackets are the original manuscript titles for items.

38. This text exists in an extremely fragmentary state in Auchinleck. Because of this, the word "Sarazin" does not appear in the extant lines, but the place names of "Grece," "Perce," and "Ynde" do. Since these names connote the East elsewhere in Auchinleck, and since other versions of the poem do include the term "Sarazin," I include *Kyng Alisaunder* in my list here. An edition of the Auchinleck text can be found in G. V. Smithers, ed., *Kyng Alisaunder,* 2 vols., Early English Text Society, o.s., 227, 327 (London: Oxford University Press, 1952), 1: 364–89. See 1: 368, 387 for the geographic references listed above. See, 2: 216 for a listing of where the term "Sarazin" is used in other more fully preserved versions of the text. The text

Notes to the Introduction

can run to about 8000 lines in its full state. Pearsall and Cunningham suggest that perhaps as many as five gatherings are missing from the manuscript at this point. See introduction, *Auchinleck Manuscript (facsimile)*, xxiii. The line count provided here is based on the digital facsimile. *The Auchinleck Manuscript (Digital Version 1.1.)*, ed. David Burnley and Alison Wiggins (National Library of Scotland: http://www.nls.uk/auchinleck/, July 5 2003), accessed August 13, 2004.

39. References to Saracens appear in two sections of this chronicle. At one point the King of France sends King Aþelston of England (king during Guy of Warwick's time) a spear "þat charlmain was won to bere / Oʒaines sarraʒines in bataile" (lines 1637–8; "sarraʒines" also appear in line 1645 in the same context). The other references to Saracens occur in the account of the reign of Richard I (lines 2037–187). There might have been references to Saracens in the account of the reign of Edward I (lines 2304–44), as the chronicle does mention his crusading vow, but nine lines have been lost at that point due to the excision of an illumination on the verso side of the folio. "Two Manuscripts of the Middle English *Anonymous Riming Chronicle*," ed. Marion Crane Carroll and Rosemond Tuve *PMLA* 46 (1931): 115–54.

40. This text also exists in an extremely fragmentary state in Auchinleck. Most versions of it run to about 7000 lines, and Pearsall and Cunningham suggest that at least three gatherings of the manuscript are missing at this point. See introduction, *Auchinleck Manuscript (facsimile)*, xxiv. Again, the line count provided is based on *The Auchinleck Manuscript (Digital Version 1.1.)*, ed. Burnley and Wiggins.

41. The term that most frequently appears in Auchinleck to describe the English community to which it appeals is "Inglisch" or "Englisse." I use the manuscript spelling "Inglisch" at various points in the text when I wish to signal the fluidity and contingency of English identity in the fourteenth century and thereby remind readers that Auchinleck's uses of the term "Inglisch" do not lie on as established, stable, and familiar ground as uses of the term "English" today. See Turville-Petre, *England the Nation*, v, 1–26 for a discussion of the variety of meanings associated with the term "Inglisch" in early fourteenth-century England

42. Burrows, "Auchinleck Manuscript: Contexts, Texts and Audience," 9–10, 37, 98–103, 119–23, 181–83, 190–91; Felicity Riddy, "Reading for England: Arthurian Literature and National Consciousness," *Bibliographical Bulletin of the International Arthurian Society* 43 (1991): 317–18; Albert C. Baugh and Thomas Cable, *A History of the English Language*, 4th ed. (Englewood Cliffs, NJ: Prentice-Hall, Inc., 1993), 142.

43. Emma Mason, "Legends of the Beauchamps' Ancestors: The Use of Baronial Propaganda in Medieval England," *Journal of Medieval History* 10 (1984): 25–40.

44. Turville-Petre, *England the Nation,* 122–30.
45. Benedict Anderson, *Imagined Communities: Reflections on the Origins and Spread of Nationalism,* rev. ed. (London: Verso, 1991), 1–36.
46. Ibid, 6.
47. Heng, *Empire of Magic,* 99.
48. John Gillingham, "Foundations of a Disunited Kingdom," in *Uniting the Kingdom?: The Making of British History,* ed. Alexander Grant and Keith J. Stringer (Routledge: London, 1995), 48–64; idem, "Henry of Huntingdon and the Twelfth-Century Revival of the English Nation," in *Concepts of National Identity in the Middle Ages,* ed. Simon Forde, Lesley Johnson, and Alan V. Murray, Leeds Texts and Monographs, n. s., 14 (Leeds: Leeds Studies in English, 1995), 75–101; Lesley Johnson, "Imagining Communities: Medieval and Modern," in *Concepts of National Identity,* ed. Forde, Johnson, and Murray, 1–20 (many other essays in this collection also argue in favor of medieval nations); Thorlac Turville-Petre, "The 'Nation' in English Writings of the Early Fourteenth Century," in *England in the Fourteenth Century: Proceedings of the 1991 Harlaxton Symposium,* ed. Nicholas Rogers (Stamford: Paul Watkins, 1993), 128–39 as well as *England the Nation;* Riddy, "Reading for England," 314–32; Diane Speed, "The Construction of the Nation in Middle English Romance," in *Readings in Medieval English Romance,* ed. Carol Meale (Cambridge: D. S. Brewer, 1994), 135–57; Heng, *Empire of Magic,* especially 63–113. Relevant, too, is the recent collection of essays, *Imagining a Medieval English Nation,* ed. Kathy Lavezzo (Minneapolis: University of Minnesota Press, 2004).
49. *MED,* s.v. "nacioun," meanings 1 (a) and 1 (b).
50. Louis Althusser, "Ideology and Ideological State Apparatuses," in *Lenin and Philosophy and Other Essays,* trans. Ben Brewster (New York: New Left Books, 1971), 121–73.
51. I am thinking here not only of eleventh-century Norman invaders, but also of the many influxes of Angevins and Poitevins over the course of the twelfth and thirteenth centuries as Henry II and III established their rule over the realm.
52. The questions of bilingualism, and of the stage by which Normans considered themselves "English" are discussed in George E. Woodbine, "The Language of English Law," *Speculum* 18 (1943): 395–436; R. M. Wilson, "English and French in England: 1100–1300," *History* 23 (1943): 37–60; William Rothwell, "The Role of French in Thirteenth-Century England," *Bulletin of the John Rylands Library* 58 (1976): 445–66; Ian Short, "On Bilingualism in Anglo-Norman England," *Romance Philology* 33 (1980): 467–79; idem, "Patrons and Polyglots: French Literature in Twelfth-Century England," *Anglo-Norman Studies* 14 (1991): 229–49; idem, "*Tam Angli quam Franci:* Self-Definition in Anglo-Norman England," *Anglo-Norman Studies* 18 (1995): 153–75; and Gillingham, "Henry of Huntingdon," 75–101.

53. R. A. Lodge discusses linguistic "hierarchies of prestige" and "High-" vs "Low-" status uses of languages in "Language Attitudes and Linguistic Norms in France and England in the Thirteenth Century," in *Thirteenth Century England IV: Proceedings of the Newcastle Upon Tyne Conference 1991,* ed. P. R. Coss and S. D. Lloyd (Woodbridge, Suffolk: Boydell, 1992), 73–84.

54. I use the term "Britain" to refer to the entirety of the island of Great Britain and to the various polities and peoples found there in the fourteenth century. When I wish to speak of distinct polities and peoples, I use the terms "England/English," "Scotland/Scots," and "Wales/Welsh."

55. Heng, *Empire of Magic,* 72.

56. Given the number and length of texts in Auchinleck involving Saracens, *Saracens and the Making of English Identity* cannot examine all texts with the same thoroughness and level of detail. Accordingly, I have chosen to concentrate more heavily on texts that are fairly complete, and invoke fragmentary texts like *Kyng Alisaunder* and *King Richard* as additional illustrations of points laid out more fully in relation to other texts.

NOTES TO CHAPTER ONE

1. I usually refer to these three tales as one unit narrating the life experiences of Guy (*Guy of Warwick*). When I wish to distinguish among the three texts or cite one in particular, I will use *Guy of Warwick (couplet version)* to describe the first, and *Guy of Warwick (stanzaic continuation),* and *Reinbrun gij sone of warwike* to describe the other two.

2. On this point, see Comfort, "Literary Role of Saracens," 631, 632, 648, 659; Jones, "Conventional Saracens," 207, 209–10, 214; Metlitzki, *Matter of Araby,* 177–87; Daniel, *Heroes and Saracens,* 30, 35–51, 78, 178–79, 193, 224, 278–79.

3. Jones, "Conventional Saracens," 203–4; Daniel, *Heroes and Saracens,* 38, 46–47, 116.

4. I use the term "class" to denote a general relationship to means of production. I use it in this context to indicate the ways in which ideas about wealth and appropriate rewards for knightly service unite knights on opposing sides of a conflict, and distinguish them as a body from peasants whose labor finances knighthood and the rewards system on which it operates. In other words, I use the term to indicate the ways in which knights from various regions resemble each other more closely than they do the peasants who till their lands.

5. May McKisack, *The Fourteenth Century: 1307–1399* (1959; reprint, Oxford: Oxford University Press, 1991), 163.

6. Ibid.

7. Ibid, 162–63.

8. Ibid, 118–19.
9. Ibid, 119.
10. See May McKisack's chapter "The Origins of the Hundred Years War" in *The Fourteenth Century,* 105–26 and Christopher Allmand, *The Hundred Years War: England and France at War c. 1300-c. 1450* (Cambridge: Cambridge University Press, 1989), 6–20 for helpful descriptions of this situation of increasing French-English tension.
11. All references to *King Richard* are to line numbers in the transcription provided in *The Auchinleck Manuscript (Digital Facsimile Version 1.1),* http://www.nls.uk/auchinleck/mss/richard.html, accessed September 3, 2004.
12. H. M. Smyser, "Charlemagne Legends," in *A Manual of the Writings in Middle English 1050–1500,* vol. 1, *Romances,* ed. J. Burke Severs (New Haven: The Connecticut Academy of Arts and Sciences, 1967), 88.
13. Ibid. In particular, the Old French *Estoire de Charlemagne* adds to the Latin *Pseudo-Turpin* a summary of the *Descriptio qualiter Karolus Magnus clavum et coronam Domini a Constantinopoli Aquis Grani detulerit,* characterized by Smyser as "an ecclesiastical version of the story which also lies behind the *Pèlerinage de Charlemagne.*"
14. Lines 8–9 of "Roland and Vernagu," in *The Taill of Rauf Coilyear With the Fragments of Roland and Vernagu and Otuel,* ed. Sidney Herrtage, Early English Text Society, e.s., 37 (London: N. Trübner & Company, 1882), 37–61. Henceforth all line numbers will be given in parentheses after the quotation within the main body of the chapter.
15. William of Malmesbury was writing in 1125, fifty-nine years after the event. Scholars (usually arguing about the origin of the *Chanson de Roland*) either accept William's claim as the trustworthy report of actual combatants' tales and of an oral *Roland* tradition, or they dismiss it as a construction of William's which some say testifies to the *Chanson*'s popularity after being written down around 1100. See Ferdinand Lot, "Etudes sur les légendes épiques françaises, V: la *Chanson de Roland.* A propos d'un livre récent," *Romania* 54 (1928): 357–80 in support of William's accuracy. See Pierre Le Gentil, *The Chanson de Roland,* trans. Francis F. Beer (Cambridge: Harvard University Press, 1969), 18, 30–31 for the opposing view. Robert Fawtier's discussion, although dated, lays out the bones of the problems clearly. See Robert Fawtier, *La Chanson de Roland: étude historique* (Paris: E. de Boccard, 1933), 76–81.

The actual words William uses are "Tunc cantilena Rollandi inchoata, ut martium viri exemplum pugnatoros accenderet, inclamatoque Dei auxilio, praelium consertum" [Then, with the song of Roland having been chanted so that the martial example of the man might inflame the fighters, and with the help of God having been invoked, the battle was joined]. William of Malmesbury, *De gestis regum Anglorum,* ed. William Stubbs, Rolls Series, no. 90, 2 vols. (London: Eyre & Spottiswoode, 1889), 2: 302. Translation

mine. Wace, too, writing his *Roman de Rou* around 1160, depicts the jon-
gleur Taillefer narrating the *Chanson de Roland* at the Battle of Hastings. See
Fawtier, *Chanson de Roland*, 77; and Joseph J. Duggan, "Medieval Epic as
Popular Historiography: Appropriation of Historical Knowledge in the Ver-
nacular Epic," in *La Littérature historiographique des origines à 1500*, ed.
Hans Ulrich Gumbrecht, Ursula Link-Heer, and Peter-Michael Spangen-
berg, vol. 11, tome 1 of *Grundriss der romanischen literaturen des mittelalters*
(Heidelberg: C. Winter, 1986), 287.

16. Ambroise, *L'Estoire de la guerre sainte, histoire en vers de la troisième croisade
    (1190–1192) par Ambroise*, ed. Gaston Paris (Paris: Imprimerie nationale,
    1897), lines 8479–518. For a translation, see *The Crusade of Richard Lion-
    Heart (Estoire de la guerre sainte)*, trans. Merton Hubert (New York: Colum-
    bia University Press, 1941), lines 8479–518.

17. Smyser, "Charlemagne Legends," 88.

18. This is the date assigned to the manuscript by F. Guessard and H.
    Michelant, preface to *Otinel: chanson de geste*, ed. F. Guessard and H.
    Michelant (Paris: F. Vieweg, 1859), ix.

19. This manuscript was formerly known as the Mende manuscript from the
    Archives de Lozère.

20. This manuscript was formerly known as Phillipps 8345. All dates and bibli-
    ographic information for Anglo-Norman texts and manuscripts, unless oth-
    erwise noted, are taken from Ruth J. Dean and Maureen Boulton,
    Anglo-Norman Literature: A Guide to Texts and Manuscripts (London: Anglo-
    Norman Texts Society, 1999).

21. André de Mandach, *Naissance et développement de la chanson de geste en
    Europe*, vol. 1, *La Geste de Charlemagne et de Roland* (Geneva: Droz, 1961),
    348–49.

22. The dates for these manuscripts are taken from Gisela Guddat-Figge, *Cata-
    logue of Manuscripts Containing Middle English Romances* (Munich: Wilhelm
    Fink Verlag, 1976). Another text from London, British Library, Additional
    31042, *The Sege of Melayne*, is usually included in the English Otuel group
    since some scholars believe it to be a prequel to *Otuel*. *The Sege of Melayne*
    narrates the deeds of the same Saracen villain, Garcy, who appears in the
    Otuel stories, and sets its action in the same locale (Lombardy) as the Otuel
    tales. There is, however, no reference to Otuel in this text. See Smyser,
    "Charlemagne Legends," 93–94 for a discussion of the text and the prob-
    lems involved in viewing it as a prequel to the Otuel stories. For editions of
    the fifteenth-century Middle English tales of Otuel, see *Firumbras and
    Otuel and Roland*, ed. Mary Isabelle O'Sullivan, Early English Text Society,
    o. s., 198 (London: Oxford University Press, 1935); and *The Sege off
    Melayne, The Romance of Duke Rowland and Sir Otuell of Spayne, and a frag-
    ment of The Song of Roland*, ed. Sidney J. Herrtage, Early English Text Soci-
    ety, e. s., 35 (1880; reprint Millwood, NY: Kraus Reprint, 1981).

23. R. N. Walpole, "Charlemagne and Roland: A Study of the Source of Two Middle English Metrical Romances, *Roland and Vernagu* and *Otuel and Roland*," *University of California Publications in Modern Philology* 21 (1944): 388.

24. It should be pointed out that a number of scholars have accepted the suggestion made by Gaston Paris in the nineteenth century that some Middle English Otuel texts, particularly *Roland and Vernagu* and the Fillingham *Otuel and Roland*, represent the fragmentary remains of a now-lost Middle English tail-rhyme romance called **Charlemagne and Roland* which translated into English the *Estoire de Charlemagne* and interpolated into it a translation of *Otuel*. No material evidence that such a text existed has been found, however, and the fact remains that Auchinleck is the earliest extant English Otuel narrative. Walpole, "Charlemagne and Roland," 392–95.

25. This manuscript was formerly known as the Firmin Didot manuscript and lacked lines 1–911 and 1082–189. It had been dated to the second half of the thirteenth century.

26. This version consists of two strips from a binding, containing parts of lines 1641–43 and 1672–96.

27. This date is taken from Charles Hardwick and H. R. Luard, *A Catalogue of the Manuscripts Preserved in the Library of the University of Cambridge*, vol. 2 (Cambridge: Cambridge University Press, 1857). Other manuscript dates, unless explicitly noted, are taken from Eugen Kölbing, introduction to *The Romance of Sir Beves of Hamtoun*, ed. Eugen Kölbing, Early English Text Society, e. s., 46, 48, 65 (1885–86, 1894; reprint, 3 vols. in 1, Millwood, NY: Kraus Reprint Company, 1978), vii-xliii.

28. This date is taken from Montague Rhodes James, *A Descriptive Catalogue of the Manuscripts in the Library of Gonville and Caius College* (Cambridge: Cambridge University Press, 1907).

29. According to Ker, different scholars have dated this manuscript to the reigns of Henry III-Edward I, Richard II, and Edward IV. N. R. Ker, *Medieval Manuscripts in British Libraries* (Oxford: Clarendon Press, 1983), 3: 362. Most *Beves* scholars seem to concur with the later datings, and identify Auchinleck as the earliest English version. See Kölbing, introduction to *Sir Beves*, viii; Charles W. Dunn, "Romances Derived from English Legends," in *A Manual of the Writings in Middle English 1050–1500*, vol. 1, *Romances*, ed. J. Burke Severs (New Haven: The Connecticut Academy of Arts and Sciences, 1967), 25.

30. It should be pointed out that *Sir Beves* enjoyed a wide circulation in Europe in the Middle Ages. According to Dunn, "Romances Derived from English Legends," 26, the "original Anglo-Norman romance of c. 1200" became a Continental French romance in the early thirteenth century, a Welsh text ca. 1250–75, a Middle English text in the early fourteenth century, a Norse prose tale in the fourteenth century, and an Irish prose text in the fifteenth

century. In addition, the Continental French version of the tale spawned a number of other language versions of *Sir Beves*. It metamorphosed into a French prose text in the fifteenth century, "into a Dutch prose version printed in 1502, and into a series of Italian versions." In addition, "a Yiddish poetic version, derived from Italian and frequently reprinted, was composed in 1501, and this eventually served as the source for a Rumanian translation (1881)" while a Russian version appeared in the early sixteenth century.

31. Eve Salisbury, introduction to "Bevis of Hampton," in *Four Romances of England,* 187–89.

32. Ibid, 187; Dunn, "Romances Derived from English Legends," 26.

33. The ten relatively complete versions are found in Cambridge, Corpus Christi College, 50; Cologny-Geneva, Bodmeriana Library, Manuscripts 67 and 168; London, British Library, Manuscripts Additional 38662, Harley 3775, and Royal 8 F. IX; London, College of Arms, Arundel XXVII, New Haven, Yale University, Beinecke Library 591; Paris, Bibliothèque nationale, fonds français 1669; and Wolfenbuttel, Herzog August Library, Aug. The six fragmentary versions are: Cambridge, University Library, Additional 2751, no. 16; Nottingham University Library, Oakham Parish Library, Bx 1756 S 4; Oxford, Bodleian Library, Rawlins d.913 (13679); Oxford, Corpus Christi College, 491; Ripon, Ripon Cathedral, XVII.F.33; York, Minster Library 16.I.7. Dean and Boulton, *Anglo-Norman Literature,* 90–91.

34. Alison Wiggins identifies these fragments as Aberystwyth, National Library of Wales, Binding Fragments 578 in her notes on *Guy* in the digital facsimile of the Auchinleck Manuscript. Gisela Guddat-Figge identifies these fragments as Aberystwyth, National Library of Wales, 572. Guddat-Figge, *Catalogue of Manuscripts,* 73.

35. Dunn, "Romances Derived from English Legends," 28, 217–18.

36. The Sloane fragment has been dated to the mid-late fourteenth century by Alison Wiggins, to 1375–1400 by Charles Dunn, and to the early fifteenth century by Gisela Guddat-Figge. Wiggins, *Auchinleck Manuscript (Digital Facsimile Version 1.1),* notes to *Guy of Warwick;* Dunn, "Romances Derived from English Legends," 218; Guddat-Figge, *Catalogue of Manuscripts Containing Middle English Romances,* 213.

37. Turville-Petre, *England the Nation,* 108–41.

38. Loomis, "The Auchinleck Manuscript and a Possible London Bookshop," 150–87.

39. For example, Norman Daniel discusses them in his study of French *chansons de geste, Heroes and Saracens*.

40. Susan Crane, *Insular Romance*.

41. *A Manual of the Writings in Middle English 1050–1500,* vol. 1, *Romances,* ed. J. Burke Severs (New Haven: The Connecticut Academy of Arts and Sciences, 1967).

42. Paul Strohm, "The Origin and Meaning of Middle English *Romaunce*," *Genre* 10 (1977): 1–28; idem, "*Storie, Spelle, Geste, Romaunce, Tragedie:* Generic Distinctions in the Middle English Troy Narratives," *Speculum* 46 (1971): 348–59.

43. *MED,* s. v. "gest(e." The *OED* records no use of "chanson de geste" in English before the nineteenth century. See *OED,* s. v. "chanson de geste."

44. Sarah Kay, *The Chansons de geste in the Age of Romance: Political Fictions* (Oxford: Clarendon Press, 1995), 2.

45. Ibid.

46. Kay, *Chansons de geste,* 4–12.

47. Margaret Adlum Gist, *Love and War in the Middle English Romances* (Philadelphia: University of Pennsylvania Press, 1947), 8; Dieter Mehl, *The Middle English Romances of the Thirteenth and Fourteenth Centuries* (London: Routledge & Kegan Paul, 1968), vii, 2–6, 28, 50; Crane, *Insular Romance,* 6–12, 135–74.

48. *Otinel: chanson de geste,* ed. F. Guessard and H. Michelant (Paris, F. Vieweg, 1859), 13–14, 16, 23–26.

49. *The Song of Roland, An Analytical Edition,* vol. 2, *II. Oxford Text and English Translation,* ed. and trans. Gerard J. Brault (University Park: Pennsylvania State University Press, 1978), lines 3221–3223. All quotations from this poem will henceforth be indicated by line numbers in parentheses within the text. The English translation reads thus: " . . . large-headed men . . . / On their spines, along the length of their backs, / They have bristles like pigs." All English quotations from the *Chanson de Roland* are from Brault's facing page edition.

50. *The Romance of Sir Beves of Hamtoun,* ed. Eugen Kölbing, Early English Text Society, e.s., 46, 48, 65 (1885–86, 1894; reprint, 3 vols. in 1, Millwood, NY: Kraus Reprint Company, 1978), line 2506. All quotations of *Sir Beves* are taken from this edition of the Auchinleck text, and henceforth line numbers will be given in parentheses after the quotation.

51. All quotations from *Guy of Warwick* are taken from *The Romance of Guy of Warwick: Edited from the Auchinleck MS. in the Advocates' Library, Edinburgh and from MS. 107 in Caius College, Cambridge,* ed. Julius Zupitza, Early English Text Society, e.s., 42, 49, 59 (1883, 1887, 1891; reprint, 3 vols. in 1, Oxford: Oxford University Press, 1966). References to *Guy of Warwick (couplet version)* are to line numbers in this edition, while references to *Guy of Warwick (stanzaic continuation)* and *Reinbrun gij sone of warwike* are to stanza and then line numbers within the stanza as Zupitza did not continuously number lines when editing these stanzaic texts.

52. "Otuel a Kni3t," in *The Taill of Rauf Coilyear With the Fragments of Roland and Vernagu and Otuel,* ed. Sidney Herrtage, Early English Text Society, e.s., 37 (London: N. Trübner & Company, 1882), 65–124, lines 899 and 903. All quotations of *Otuel* derive from this edition and will henceforth

be identified by line numbers in parentheses within the main body of the chapter.

53. Daniel, *Heroes and Saracens,* 103.

54. Richard Kaeuper, *Chivalry and Violence in Medieval Europe* (Oxford: Oxford University Press, 1999), 172.

55. Ambroise, *L'Estoire de la guerre sainte,* lines 5649–56.

56. This idea was commonplace among knights in the later Middle Ages. As John Barnie states, from the beginnings of crusading "amongst the knights themselves the pious desire to recover the Holy City was always inextricably involved with the pursuit of land and plunder." John Barnie, *War in Medieval English Society: Social Values in the Hundred Years War, 1337–1399* (Ithaca: Cornell University Press, 1974), 58. On this point about crusading knights' greed, see also Steven Runciman, *The First Crusade,* 113; idem, *The Kingdom of Acre and the Later Crusades,* vol. 3 of *A History of the Crusades* (Cambridge: Cambridge University Press, 1954), 351; Robert Bartlett, *The Making of Europe: Conquest, Colonization and Cultural Change 950–1350* (Princeton: Princeton University Press, 1993), 90–91. Service in warfare in the late thirteenth and fourteenth centuries was also a "profitable enterprise," involving opportunities to enrich oneself from wages, booty, ransoms, and fees for sub-contracting war-bands for military leaders. Lee Patterson, *Chaucer and the Subject of History* (Madison: University of Wisconsin Press, 1991), 172. On this point, see also Barnie, *War in Medieval English Society,* 33–38; Peter Coss, *The Knight in Medieval England, 1000–1400* (Conshohocken, PA: Combined Books, 1993), 104–8. Given this western context, it is not surprising to find historical Saracens represented as possessing the same interest. Ambroise, for example, reports that Saladin viewed the arrival of Christian reinforcements at the siege of Acre as an economic windfall, saying "'Now our booty is increased.'" Ambroise, *The Crusade of Richard Lion-Heart,* trans. Merton Hubert, line 2884. For the original French, see Ambroise, *L'Estoire de la guerre sainte,* line 2884.

57. This idea that violence and battle somehow communicate divine positions was part of the historical attitude of crusaders. For them, however, it was not God's status that was manifested in battle, but their own. Both regular troops and clerics on crusade interpreted success or failure on the battlefield as a comment on their relative sinfulness or lack thereof in God's eyes. When military encounters went well, God was pleased with the moral state of the Christians, while when things went poorly for Christians, it was accepted that God was punishing them for their misdeeds. Chroniclers thus explain the Fall of Acre in 1291, the vicissitudes of conflict at Antioch in 1098, and the Fall of Jerusalem in 1187. See, respectively, *Chronicon de Lanercost,* ed. Joseph Stevenson (Edinburgh: Bannatyne Club, 1839), 138–39; Matthew Paris, *Chronica majora,* ed. H. R. Luard, 7 vols., Rolls Series, no. 57 (London: Longman, 1872–83), 2: 83–84; and *Itinerarium*

peregrinorum et gesta regis Ricardi, auctore, ut videtur, Ricardo canonico Sanctae Trinitatis Londoniensis, vol. 1 of *Chronicles and Memorials of the Reign of Richard I,* ed. William Stubbs, Rolls Series, no. 38 (London: Longman, 1864–65), 5–6, 14–16. The same idea underlay clerical efforts to improve the moral tone of the Christian camp when Saracen fortunes were in the ascendant. To regain God's favor for the Christians, the clerics doled out stiff punishments and called for intense penitential rites. See Matthew Paris, *Chronica majora,* 2: 83–84.

58. The contrast between this situation and that found, for example, in Wolfram von Eschenbach's *Parzival* is striking. Unlike Guy, Parzival receives spiritual guidance from relatives and religious hermits, and is represented as requiring repeated mentoring before he can achieve his destiny.

59. This notion of religious self-sufficiency is not confined to the focal texts of this chapter; it was a commonplace of tales about knights and of knightly attitudes in the later Middle Ages, as Kaeuper points out repeatedly in the section of his book detailing relations between clerics and knights (Kaeuper, *Chivalry and Violence,* 41–88). The tales here, however, belong to a relatively small subset of texts which use Saracen figures and conversions to make this point.

60. This is how John Barnie summarizes the incident in *War in Medieval English Society,* 71. Froissart's original French account of the incident reads thus: "li connestables de France et li contes de Tankarville . . . se doubtèrent d'eulz meismes que il n'escheissent en ce parti et entre mains d'arciers, qui point ne les cognuissent. Ensi que il regardoient aval en grant doubte ces gens tuer, il perçurent un gentil chevalier englès, qui n'avoit c'un oel, que on clamoit monsigneur Thumas de Hollandes, et cinq ou six bons chevaliers avoecques lui: lequel monsigneur Thumas ravisèrent bien, car il s'estoient aultre fois veu et compagniet l'un l'autre à Grenade et en Prusse et en aultres voiages, ensi que chevalier se truevent. Si furent tout reconforté quant il le veirent; si l'appellèrent en passant, et li disent: "Monsigneur Thumas, . . . parles à nous!" Quant li chevaliers se oy nommer, il s'arresta tous quois et demanda: "Qui estes vous, signeur, qui me cognissiés?" Li dessus dit signeur se nommèrent et disent: "Nous sommes telz et telz. Venés parler à nous en ceste porte, et nous prendés à prisonniers." Quant li dis messires Thumas oy ceste parolle, si fu tous joians, tant pour ce que il les pooit sauver que pour ce qu'il avoit, en yaus prendre, une belle aventure de bons prisonniers, pour avoir cent mil moutons." Jean Froissart, *Chroniques de Jean Froissart,* ed. Siméon Luce, 15 vols. (Paris: Mme Ve Jules Renouard, 1872), 3 (1342–1346): 143–44.

61. Coss, *The Knight,* 4, 35–46, 112–15, 123–34; Crane, *Insular Romance,* 6–9, 20–23, 43–51, 176–78.

62. Geraldine Heng also mentions chivalric knighthood's ability to problematize articulations of national identity. She states, "it is in popular, not

courtly, romance that the impetus toward nation formation can be most readily read: chivalric productions being, above all, the ideological property of elites whose caste interests are typically overriding, and whose class culture touts chivalry as an international formation with loyalties that exceed the merely local or national." Although I agree that chivalric class culture can impede articulations of nation, Heng's claims about chivalric vs popular romance seem somewhat problematic. Her definition of popular romance as romances extant in multiple manuscripts and "traversed by utopian fictions of class unity and justice" seems to exclude the Matter of France romances discussed here, and I am not sure that it entirely suits the Matter of England texts discussed here which do exist in multiple manuscripts, but which do not offer substantial visions of the utopian world Heng describes. These four texts, however, clearly participate in articulations of a sense of English nationhood, whether through their use of the English language, their celebration of heroes from Warwick and Southampton, or their subtle consideration of the problems involved in making an assertion of English identity in the early fourteenth century. Heng, *Empire of Magic,* 72–73.

63. The English themselves perceived and experienced such problems in the later Middle Ages. Ambroise, for example, charges two crusaders with wrecking a Christian attack on Saracens by their eagerness to prove themselves most courageous in battle. Ambroise, *L'Estoire de la guerre sainte,* lines 6411–65. Similarly, John Barnie notes that in the Hundred Years War "[Sir Hugh] Calveley almost lost the battle of Auray for the English by refusing to take command of the rearguard on the grounds that it was dishonorable and an insult." *War in Medieval English Society,* 90.

64. Indeed, Lee Patterson points out the problems of a social group's investment in violence as a means of advancement and differentiation when he discusses the English nobility of the later fourteenth century. According to him, "between 1351 and 1400, about 25 percent of all the peers who died succumbed to violence in one form or another, a fact that was not unrelated to the failure of the direct male line in a quarter of the noble families every twenty-five years throughout the fourteenth and fifteenth centuries." Patterson, *Chaucer and the Subject of History,* 191.

65. My thinking on this point has been influenced by the ideas about non-differentiation, violence, and rivalry articulated by René Girard in *Violence and the Sacred,* trans. Patrick Gregory (Baltimore: Johns Hopkins University Press, 1977), 49–64, 145–58.

66. See McKisack, *The Fourteenth Century,* 4

67. Juliet Vale, *Edward III and Chivalry: Chivalric Society and its Context 1270–1350* (Woodbridge, Suffolk: Boydell Press, 1982), 65.

68. As Geoffrey Barrow notes, the Scots and English were basically at war from 1296 to 1328, and from 1333 to 1357. Geoffrey Barrow, "Frontier

and Settlement: Which Influenced Which? England and Scotland, 1100–1300," in *Medieval Frontier Societies,* ed. Robert Bartlett and Angus MacKay (Oxford: Clarendon Press, 1989), 21.

69. Juliet Vale, *Edward III and Chivalry,* 65.
70. Comfort, "Literary Role of Saracens," 207, 214; Daniel, *Heroes and Saracens,* 3–4, 46–51, 72–73, 81, 133–54, 165–78.
71. In Middle English, the term "wille" primarily refers to the appetitive and volitional faculty of the soul (*MED,* meaning 1). In some cases, this means that the term connotes unpremeditated or involuntary desire, particularly sexual desire (*MED,* meaning 2a). In the instances discussed here, however, "wille" connotes a desire or state linked to deliberate action, conscious decision or an act of agency, as in *MED* meanings 5 a and b, or 7a. See *MED,* s. v. "wil(le."
72. I should point out that this lie is not found in most other manuscripts of the Middle English *Sir Beves.* According to Kölbing's edition, most texts do not have Beves take this radical step of asserting his own death. See variants printed for lines 1305–12. The event is found in the Anglo-Norman *Boeve,* however: "'Paumer,' ceo dist Boefs, 'vus oi parler de nent, / Car le emfaunt est pendu dount jeo vus oi tochant." *Der anglonormannische Boeve de Haumtone,* ed. Albert Stimming, Bibliotheca Normannica, no. 7 (Halle: Max Niemeyer, 1899), lines 846–47.
73. Augustine, *Confessiones,* ed. and trans. Pierre de Labriole (Paris: Société d'édition "Les Belles lettres," 1956). For an English translation, see *Confessions,* trans. Henry Chadwick (Oxford: Oxford University Press, 1991).
74. This aspect of Augustine's theology is discussed in Lawrence G. Duggan, "'For Force is Not of God'? Compulsion and Conversion from Yahweh to Charlemagne," in *Varieties of Religious Conversion in the Middle Ages,* ed. James Muldoon (Gainsville: University Press of Florida, 1997), 50–58; and in Karl Morrison, *Understanding Conversion* (Charlottesville: University of Virginia Press, 1992), 24, 79, 152.
75. Morrison, *Understanding Conversion,* xii-xvi, xix, 4–14, 22–24.
76. See Chapter Three, "Monstrous Intermingling and Miraculous Conversion: Negotiating Cultural Borders in *Þe King of Tars,*" for a full discussion of ideas about cultural integration in Auchinleck.
77. *Chronicle of Lanercost 1272–1346,* trans. Herbert Maxwell (Edinburgh: Maclehose and Sons, 1913), 44–45. The Latin reads "minus sui solatii providus." *Chronicon de Lanercost,* ed. Stevenson, 118.
78. *The King of Tars: Edited from the Auchinleck MS Advocates 19. 2. 1,* ed. Judith Perryman (Heidelberg: Carl Winter Universitätsverlag, 1980), lines 799, 928–30. All quotations of *Þe King of Tars* are taken from this edition unless otherwise indicated. All references to the text of the poem are to line numbers in this edition, and will henceforth be indicated within parentheses in the text. For a full discussion of this incident, see Chapter Three.

79. *Chronicle of the Third Crusade: a Translation of the Itinerarium peregrinorum et gesta regis Ricardi,* trans. Helen Nicholson (Aldershot: Ashgate, 1997), 90, 247. The Latin descriptions read thus: "Inter oppugnantes erat quædam gens larvalis nimis vehemens et pertinax, natura deformis, sicut et aliis erat dissimilis animis, nigro colore, enormi statura, feritate immanes," and "gens larvalis, colore nigerrimo." See *Itinerarium peregrinorum,* 83, 262.

80. Barnie, *War in Medieval English Society,* 34. See pages 33–38 for a detailed survey of the role of booty and personal advancement in the early years of the Hundred Years War.

81. Few extant manuscripts contain Matter of France texts while many more contain stories of Arthur.

82. Walpole, "Charlemagne and Roland," 388.

83. In the Old French manuscript, Charlemagne simply prays that Roland be saved and Otuel converted, while Otuel describes his visit from the Holy Spirit as an influence on his heart. No variants from the Anglo-Norman version are listed for these lines by Guessard and Michelant, thus the idea of will seems particular to Auchinleck. *Otinel,* ed. Guessard and Michelant, 18, 21.

84. See Chapter Five for a full discussion of this prologue.

85. Daniel, *Heroes and Saracens,* 192.

86. Jews had been expelled from England in 1290, and heresy was not yet a problem facing the political authorities. Thus, a 1330s audience would have been much less familiar with conversion than with a change in political allegiance. This latter change in one's group identity was much more common given the political turbulence of early fourteenth-century England (see later discussion). For a discussion of why heresy was not a problem in England until Lollardy emerged, see Gordon Leff, *Heresy in the Later Middle Ages: The Relation of Heterodoxy to Dissent, c. 1250–c. 1450* (Manchester: Manchester University Press, 1967), 1: 33 n. 2.

87. Jonathan Elukin, "From Jew to Christian?: Conversion and Immutability in Medieval Europe," in *Varieties of Religious Conversion in the Middle Ages,* ed. James Muldoon (Gainsville: University Press of Florida, 1997), 171.

88. See lines 1780–811. All references to the Old French and Anglo-Norman *Otinel* are to the edition by Guessard and Michelant, and will henceforth be indicated by line numbers within the body of the text.

89. Benjamin Z. Kedar, "Multidirectional Conversion in the Frankish Levant," in *Varieties of Religious Conversion in the Middle Ages,* ed. James Muldoon (Gainsville: University Press of Florida, 1997), 194.

90. *Chronicle of Lanercost,* trans. Maxwell, 32, 81, 128–29, 308. The same points are made in the Latin *Chronicon de Lanercost,* ed. Stevenson, on pages 111–12, 140–41, 169, 292–93.

91. McKisack, *The Fourteenth Century,* 25–29.

92. Allmand, *The Hundred Years War,* 8.

93. Ibid, 7–10.
94. McKisack, *The Fourteenth Century,* 105–7.
95. Although *Þe King of Tars* is not one of the main texts discussed in this chapter, I have included a brief reference to it here because one part of the tale works well with *Otuel a Kniȝt* to illustrate the limitations of willed changes of identity.
96. As Louise Fradenburg notes, ideally the Christian knight was "to uphold the rightness and sameness of western Christendom against the threat of the Eastern other." Louise Fradenburg, *City, Marriage, Tournament: Arts of Rule in Late Medieval Scotland* (Madison: University of Wisconsin Press, 1991), 198. This function was a popular one, as evidenced by widespread English support, at all levels of society, for crusades to the Holy Land in the thirteenth and fourteenth centuries. See Christopher Tyerman, "The Holy Land and the Crusaders of the Thirteenth and Fourteenth Centuries," in *Crusade and Settlement,* ed. Peter Edbury (Cardiff: University College Press Cardiff, 1985), 108–109; Simon Lloyd, *English Society and the Crusade, 1216–1307* (Oxford: Clarendon Press, 1988), 246. When fighting the infidel, European knights were not assaulting other Christians and committing violence against the other estates. Indeed, Urban II is reported to have pointed this out explicitly when preaching the Crusade in 1095. According to a thirteenth-century English chronicle entry variously attributed to both Roger of Wendover and Matthew Paris, Urban said to his largely knightly audience, "'Let your zeal in this expedition atone for the rapine, theft, homicide, and fornication, the adulteries, and deeds of incendiarism by which you have provoked the Lord to anger." Roger of Wendover, *Roger of Wendover's Flowers of History Formerly Ascribed to Matthew Paris,* trans. J. A. Giles (1849; reprint, Llanerch, Wales: Felinfach, 1993–96), vol. 1, bk. 2, 377. The Latin reads "Rapinas, furta, homicidia, fornicationes, adulteria, incendia, quibus Deum ad iracundiam provocastis, in hac expeditione redimite." See Matthew Paris, *Chronica majora,* 2: 46.
97. For an interesting discussion of the depictions of giants and the cultural functions they served in the Middle Ages, see Jeffrey Jerome Cohen, *Of Giants: Sex, Monsters and the Middle Ages* (Minneapolis: University of Minnesota Press, 1999).
98. A fuller discussion of the issues raised in this section appears in "The Anxieties of Encounter and Exchange: Saracens and Christian Heroism in *Sir Beves of Hamtoun,*" *Florilegium* 21 (2004): 135–58. I am grateful to *Florilegium* for permission to reproduce parts of that discussion here.
99. Geraldine Heng, "Cannibalism, the First Crusade, and the Genesis of Medieval Romance," *Differences* 10 (1998): 107.
100. Steven Runciman, *The Kingdom of Jerusalem and the Frankish East 1100–1187,* vol. 2 of *A History of the Crusades* (Cambridge: Cambridge

University Press, 1952), 101; Sarah Lambert, "Heroines and Saracens," *Medieval World* 1 (1991): 3–4.

101. *Chronicle of the Third Crusade,* 23. The Latin original of this passage reads: "aggravata est manus Domini super populum Suum, si tamen recte dixerimus Suum, quem conversationis immunditia, vitæ turpitudo, vitiorum fœditas fecerat alienum. Jam enim eousque flagitiorum consuetudo proruperat, ut omnes, abjecto erubescentiæ velo, palam et passim ad turpia declinarent." See *Itinerarium Peregrinorum,* 5.

102. Roger of Wendover, *Roger of Wendover's Flowers of History,* vol. 2, bk. 2, 527. For the Latin, see Roger of Wendover, *Flores historiarum,* ed. H. R. Hewlett, 3 vols., Rolls Series, no. 84 (London: Eyre and Spottiswoode, 1886–89), 2: 373–74. It reads "Item in palatio suo Achonensi fecit convivari Saracenos, et fecit eis habere mulieres Christianas saltatrices ad ludendum coram eis, et ut dicebatur, commiscebantur eis. Item, fœdus quod iniit cum Soldano, nemo scivit qua conditione tractatum fuit inter eos, nisi ipse solus; veruntamen manifeste videbatur, quod magis approbaret, secundum quod perpendi poterat per gestus exteriores, legem Saracenorum, quam legem fidei nostræ quia in multis ritus ipsorum imitatus est."

103. Pierre Dubois, *The Recovery of the Holy Land,* trans. Walther I. Brandt (New York: Columbia University Press, 1956), 114. The original Latin of this passage reads: "Si enim habitatores illius terre male vivant . . . si homines quasi ex omnibus mondi partibus ibi congregati male vivere incipiant, et assuescant talem modum vivendi, consuetudini que est altera natura quoniam naturam alterat, non emendationi, deputando?" Pierre Dubois, *De Recuperatione terre sancte: traité de politique générale par Pierre Dubois,* ed. Ch-V. Langlois (Paris: Alphonse Picard, 1891), 46–47.

104. Dubois, *Recovery,* 124 (*De Recuperatione,* 57).

105. Lambert, "Heroines and Saracens," 3.

106. This Christmas Day incident and the battle that follows are unique to the Middle English versions of *Sir Beves* and do not turn up in the Anglo-Norman.

107. The *Gesta Francorum* records St George's appearance at Antioch, while Raymond of Aguilers' *Historia Francorum* narrates the saint's appearance on the march to Jerusalem and his insistence that his relics be carried to Jerusalem by the crusaders. St George is even said by some to have appeared on the walls of Jerusalem to inspire crusaders, a manifestation recorded in Jacobus de Voragine's life of St George in the *Legenda Aurea.* I would like to thank Jonathan Good for drawing my attention to these references. See *Gesta Francorum et aliorum Hierosolimitanorum / The Deeds of the Franks and the Other Pilgrims to Jerusalem,* ed. and trans. Rosalind Hill (London: Thomas Nelson, 1962), 69; Raymond of Aguilers, "Historia Francorum qui ceperunt Iherusalem," in *Recueil des historiens des croisades:*

historiens occidentaux, vol. 3 (Paris: Imprimerie impériale, 1866), 232–309, page 290; Jacobus de Voragine, *Legenda aurea: edizione critica,* ed. Giovanni Paolo Maggioni, 2 vols. (Florence: Sismel edizioni del Galluzzo, 1998).

108. Jonathan Good, *"Argent a Cross Gules:* The Origins and English Use of the Arms of St George," paper delivered at the 38th International Congress of Medieval Studies at Kalamazoo, Michigan, May 9 2003.

109. *Calendar of Patent Rolls, 1350–54* (London: HMSO, 1907), 127. I am again indebted to Jonathan Good for these references.

110. Judith Weiss, "The Major Interpolations in *Sir Beves of Hamtoun,*" *Medium Ævum* 48 (1979): 72, 72 n. 6.

111. This is Weiss's central argument in "Major Interpolations." See her article for a full examination of the issues and evidence.

NOTES TO CHAPTER TWO

1. I am here drawing upon Judith Butler's notion of the performative nature of gender. She argues that masculine and feminine behaviors are not inherently natural actions for people, but are instead culturally determined actions that individuals perform. Her theory thus allows a role to individual agency in the construction of culture and gender, and opens a pathway for cultural resistance. Judith Butler, *Gender Trouble* (New York: Routledge, 1990), 1–34.

2. Various literary sources have been identified as possibly underlying this figure's appearance in medieval literature. These potential sources include: "the classical figure of Medea, a story in Seneca's sixth *controversia,* tales in the *Arabian Nights,* an episode in the tenth-century Byzantine epic *Digenes Akrites,*" and episodes in works by the first-century Jewish historian, Josephus that were known to the Latin Middle Ages as the *De bello Judaico* and the *Antiquitates Judaicae.* Mark Balfour, "Moses and the Princess: Josephus' *Antiquitates Judaicae* and the *Chansons de Geste,*" *Medium Ævum* 64 (1995): 1.

3. Orderic Vitalis, *The Ecclesiastical History of Orderic Vitalis,* ed. and trans. Marjorie Chibnall, (Oxford: Clarendon Press, 1975), 5: 354–79; Matthew Paris, *Chronica majora,* 3: 90.

4. See *Vita et passio Sancti Thomae Cantuariensis archiepiscopi et martyris,* in *Patrologiae cursus completus series Latina,* ed. J. Migne, 221 vols. (Paris: Frères Garnieri, 1844-), 190: 346–49.

5. Interestingly, she does not always obtain the Christian husband of her choice. In Orderic's story of Bohemond, for example, the Saracen princess Melaz ends up marrying Bohemond's kinsman Roger of Salerno rather than Bohemond himself as she had originally requested. Orderic Vitalis, *Ecclesiastical History,* 5: 378–79.

6. See Jacqueline DeWeever, *Sheba's Daughters: Whitening and Demonizing the Saracen Woman in Medieval French Epic* (New York: Garland, 1998), xvii, xix, 55–88.

7. To my knowledge, none of the chronicle accounts listed above has been confirmed by independent sources.

8. DeWeever, *Sheba's Daughters*, xii, 3–29, 39–54.

9. *The Romance of Sir Beves of Hamtoun,* ed. Eugen Kölbing, lines 521–22. All quotations of *Sir Beves* are taken from this edition of the Auchinleck text, and henceforth line numbers will be given in the main body of the chapter in parentheses after the quotation.

10. May McKisack, *The Fourteenth Century,* 79–83.

11. For a description of the application of this epithet to Isabella, see Hilda Johnstone, "Isabella, the She-Wolf of France," *History* 21 (1936): 208–18.

12. McKisack, *The Fourteenth Century,* 81.

13. For a summary of theological and ecclesiastical positions on marriage as well as a careful nuancing of how such ideas were reformulated and implemented by confessors at the local level, see Jacqueline Murray, "Thinking About Gender: The Diversity of Medieval Perspectives," in *Power of the Weak: Studies on Medieval Women,* ed. Jennifer Carpenter and Sally-Beth MacLean (Urbana: University of Illinois Press, 1995): 1–26.

14. See Lois Huneycutt, "Intercession and the High-Medieval Queen: The Esther Topos," in *Power of the Weak,* ed. Carpenter and MacLean, 126–46; John Carmi Parsons, "The Queen's Intercession in Thirteenth-Century England," in ibid, 147–77; Peggy McCracken, *The Romance of Adultery: Queenship and Sexual Transgression in Old French Literature* (Philadelphia: University of Pennsylvania Press, 1998).

15. Fradenburg, *City, Marriage, Tournament,* 74.

16. Ibid, 252.

17. When Beves wins King Yuor's Saracen kingdom of Mombraunt, Josiane finds herself enthroned as that country's queen.

18. Indeed, one wonders whether any male Saracen could raise the question of how gender plays into constructions of group and personal identities because he, like most medieval male characters, functions as the norm. When the norm is implicitly masculine, it is necessary for female characters to demonstrate and raise problems that may not be encountered in masculine experiences of traversing group borders and defining identities.

19. For a discussion of the influence of Esther's story on Henry I's Anglo-Saxon queen Matilda and her self-construction as a mediatrix, see Huneycutt, "Intercession and the High-Medieval Queen." For a discussion of Marian imagery and the intercessory roles of thirteenth-century English queens, see Parsons, "The Queen's Intercession in Thirteenth-Century England." Parsons also suggests that in the later Middle Ages in England, the Esther topos

was more frequently associated with noblewomen and the Marian model with queens (159).

20. On this point see also Paul Strohm, "Queens as Intercessors," in *Hochon's Arrow: The Social Imagination of Fourteenth-Century Texts* (Princeton: Princeton University Press, 1992), 95–119.

21. Jean Froissart, *Chroniques de Jean Froissart*, 4 (1346–1356): 61–62. While the incident described took place and was recorded after Auchinleck is believed to have been completed, this account serves to indicate general motifs of English queenly intercession in circulation in the fourteenth century.

22. Strohm, "Queens as Intercessors," 99.

23. Translated in Strohm, "Queens as Intercessors," 100. The French account reads "Ha! gentilz sires, puis que je apassai le mer par deça en grant peril, si com vous savés, je ne vous ay riens rouvet ne don demandet. Or vous pri jou humlement et requier en propre don que, pour le fil sainte Marie et pour l'amour de mi, vous voelliés avoir de ces six hommes merci." Froissart, *Chroniques*, 4 (1346–1356): 62.

24. Strohm, "Queens as Intercessors," 101.

25. Fradenburg points out that the power of the liminal lies in its very status of usually being excluded from power. Fradenburg, *City, Marriage, Tournament*, 74.

26. Interestingly, the story of Esther, too, indicates that the interceding Esther importuned her husband while on her knees. Esther 8: 3, Vulgate Bible.

27. It should be noted that at the time of this incident, Philippa's pregnancy was not nearly as evident as Froissart implies. Parsons writes, in personal correspondence cited by Strohm, that "Philippa's pregnancy is exaggerated for effect, if not invented outright: 'Calais surrendered on 5 August 1347. If Philippa bore William in May 1348, she may well not even have known she was pregnant at the time. She cannot possibly have been pregnant when she crossed the channel.'" Strohm, "Queens as Intercessors," 102 n. 6. It should also be pointed out that motifs of pregnant queens interceding with their husbands are not limited to historical narratives, but turn up as well in romances like *Athelston*. There, however, the dynamic of the situation changes rapidly when the king defies generic expectations and, instead of yielding to his wife, kicks her in the stomach and murders his heir. "Athelston," in *Four Romances of England*, 356–57.

28. It should be noted that, historically, queenly intercession was not always as efficacious as Philippa's proved at Calais. For example, Richard II's queen, Anne of Bohemia, knelt to intercede for Simon Burley's life to the Duke of Gloucester at the Merciless Parliament in 1388, but to no avail. McKisack, *The Fourteenth Century*, 458.

29. The performative aspects of Josiane's speech and actions have also been noted and discussed by Myra Seaman in "Engendering Genre in Middle

English Romance: Performing the Feminine in *Sir Beves of Hamtoun*," *Studies in Philology* 98 (2001): 49–75. Seaman's discussion, however, concentrates on how Josiane's behaviors problematize "traditional generalizations about romance gender dynamics" rather than on how Josiane's behaviors enable her negotiation of two different cultural groups. Seaman, "Engendering Genre," 52.

30. While the term "God" would seem theologically to apply to both the Christian and Muslim God since they are the same deity, it must be pointed out that in Middle English romances, Saracens do not ever call their deity "God" to my knowledge. Instead, they swear by "Mahoun" or "Tervagaunt" or "Apolin." Such a depiction of Saracen practices concurs with medieval Christians' frequent refusals (or inabilities?) to perceive that they and Muslims worshipped the same God. Admittedly, some ecclesiastical scholars did consider Islam a heretical sect of Christianity, but there was by no means unanimous acceptance of this theory, nor does it appear from the romances that this theory was ever fully developed in fictional depictions of Saracens.

31. Interestingly, when Beves later rejects Josiane's love, she curses him with reference to Mahoun (see lines 1118–24), apparently reverting to Saracenness when Christian utterances seem to be of no avail in achieving her particular desires.

32. See Weiss "Major Interpolations," 71–76; Eve Salisbury, introduction to "Bevis of Hampton," in *Four Romances of England,* 187–99. See my discussion of the manuscript tradition of *Sir Beves* in Chapter One for the full titles, dates, and locations of the Anglo-Norman and Middle English manuscripts of the tale.

33. *Der anglonormannische Boeve de Haumtone.* Stimming used Paris, Bibliothèque nationale, nouvelles acquisitions françaises 4532 for lines 1–1268, and Leuven, University Library, G.170 (destroyed in World War II) for lines 913–3850.

34. All references to non-Auchinleck versions of *Sir Beves* are to variants listed in Kölbing's edition. In this section, I reference Manchester, Chetham Library, 8009 (also known as Mun. A. 6. 31; Version M in Kölbing); Cambridge, Gonville and Caius College, 175 (Version E in Kölbing); and Cambridge, University Library, Ff. 2. 38 (Version C in Kölbing). His readings have been checked against Jennifer Fellows's parallel-text edition of *Sir Beves* in "*Sir Beves of Hamtoun:* Study and Edition" (Ph. D. diss., Cambridge University, 1979), but I have retained Kölbing's versions for convenience of access.

35. The same emphasis on performance as a way of changing one's group identity can be seen in the actions of Beves. After Beves affirms his Christian identity by destroying the idols of Saracen worshippers, he introduces himself as Ermin's messenger to Brademond with a speech in which he swears by Mahoun, Tervagaunt, and Apolin (1379–80). Beves himself thus highlights the rhetorical performance of religious identity.

36. Seaman also discusses Josiane's rhetorical deployment of gender stereotypes. She states that Josiane "consciously appropriates the stereotypically feminine role in order to manipulate others in the romance." Seaman, "Engendering Genre," 64. Seaman's larger discussion of Josiane's use of gender stereotypes can be found on pp. 64–68. It should be noted that my discussion of Josiane was written as part of a dissertation completed and defended before I came upon Seaman's article.

37. In some ways, these ends appear altruistic as in Philippa's plea for six men's lives. It should not be forgotten, however, that queenly intercession was also a way for the queen to claim power by demonstrating her access to the king and possession of his favor. This was particularly important for a foreign queen. Brought to a new country, bereft of the status and customs of her home, the new queen was essentially forced to demonstrate her access, through her husband's regard and esteem, to a certain power and position in order to establish herself among her new people and earn some respect. This could be done in many ways; for example, by bearing the king's heir and thus demonstrating physically her sexual closeness to, and influence on, the king. John Carmi Parsons explains that intercession, too, could effect the same result. He states: "Evidence points to an increase in such [intercessionary] activity as widowhood neared or childbearing ended, implying that queens exploited the role with public relations in mind, or to manifest the strength of their marriages after they ceased to give the most obvious proof of intimacy with their husbands [i.e. pregnancy]." Parsons, "The Queen's Intercession," 151.

38. Josiane again invokes ideals of womanhood in lines 3658–82, when she implores her Saracen captor to permit her to " do [her] nedes in priuite" since "kende hit is, wimman te be / Schamfaste and ful of corteisie" (3661–63). She thus wins for herself an opportunity to employ herbs to disfigure herself and make herself unattractive to the Saracen king for whose pleasure she has been abducted.

39. Bhabha describes such an event in India in the nineteenth century in "Signs Taken for Wonders," and shows how in this case Christian religious rhetoric, often deployed to colonial ends (not only in the age of Empire but also in the Middle Ages, I might add), was deployed by Indians in a manner that frustrated their colonial oppressors and thus constituted a subtle act of resistance and refusal. Bhabha, "Signs Taken for Wonders: Questions of Ambivalence and Authority Under a Tree Outside Delhi, May 1817," in *The Location of Culture*, 102–22.

40. Consider the work of Anne McClintock, and her discussion of constructions of British womanhood and "Britannia" in the nineteenth century, or some of the essays in *Nationalisms and Sexualities* about the ways in which women and ideas about them are deployed in inter-group conflicts. Anne McClintock, *Imperial Leather: Race, Gender, and Sexuality in the Colonial*

Conquest (New York: Routledge, 1995); *Nationalisms and Sexualities,* ed. Andrew Parker, Mary Russo, Doris Sommer, and Patricia Yaeger (New York: Routledge, 1992).

41. Consider, for example, the extremely restrictive Taliban model of the Muslim woman and her role in society. See Valentine M. Moghadan, "Revolution, Islam and Women: Sexual Politics in Iran and Afghanistan," in *Nationalisms and Sexualities,* 424–50. I should point out, too, as many people have noted, that this model of behavior is by no means a generic Muslim model. Most Muslim regimes do not circumscribe women's activities and learning as narrowly as the Taliban did.

42. *Der anglonormannische Boeve de Haumton,* line 1712.

43. It is interesting that in constructions of knightly identity, the lady's role is often that of spectator of the knightly body. In some ways this is a reversal of contemporary notions of gender and specularity in which the woman's body is the object of the gaze. Consequently, one must interrogate contemporary notions of the gazer's superior position in relation to the object, since I do not think the lady watching the knight is in a particularly powerful position in medieval romances and hierarchies. Her role calls into question the applicability to cultures of display of this notion of object of the gaze.

44. For the characterization of Saracen princesses, see F. M. Warren, "The Enamoured Moslem Princess in Orderic Vital and the French Epic," *PMLA* 29 (1914): 341–58; Comfort, "Literary Role of Saracens," 628–59; Charles A. Knudson, " Le thème de la princesse sarrasine dans *La Prise d'Orange,*" *Romance Philology* 22 (1969): 449–62; and Micheline de Combarieu, "Un personnage épique: la jeune musulmane," in *Mélanges de langue et littérature françaises du moyen âge offerts à Pierre Jonin, Senefiance* 7 (1979): 183–96.

45. Sarah Lambert, "Heroines and Saracens," 9.

46. I should point out that this is represented more clearly by female Saracen convert figures than by male ones who, as shown in Chapter One, resemble their Christian counterparts closely, and manifest similar values, modes of deportment, and notions of battle. It is left to the feminized, gendered figure to explore and expose the challenges of gender norms when changing group identities, which is unsurprising given the tendency in the Middle Ages to view the male as the norm and neutral base for thinking about the individual.

47. I also cannot believe that the Auchinleck compilers would willingly omit any reference to their beloved and ubiquitous "Inglond."

48. Norman Daniel discusses this phenomenon in a number of Old French texts in *Heroes and Saracens,* 57.

49. The Egerton, Naples and Gonville and Caius College manuscripts all include this reference to "Mahoun" by Beves, while the Chetham and Cambridge University Library manuscripts do not.

50. Robert C. Stacey, "The Conversion of Jews to Christianity in Thirteenth-Century England," *Speculum* 67 (1992): 277.

51. Ibid.
52. Ibid, 278.
53. Ibid, 280.
54. James Brundage, *Law, Sex, and Christian Society in Medieval Europe* (Chicago: University of Chicago Press, 1987), 196, 207, 238.
55. The Latin Council Decree reads "In nonnullis provinciis a christianis Judaeos seu Saracenos habitus distinguit diversitas; sed in quibusdam sic quaedam inolevit confusio, ut nulla differentia discernantur. Unde contingit interdum, quod per errorem christiani Judaeorum seu Saracenorum, et Judaei seu Saraceni christianorum mulieribus commisceantur. Ne igitur tam damnatae commixtionis excessus per velamentum erroris hujusmodi, excusationis ulterius possint habere diffugium; statuimus, ut tales utriusque sexus in omni christianorum provincia, et in omni tempore, qualitate habitus publice ab aliis populis distinguantur, cum etiam per Mosen hoc ipsum legatur eis injunctum." H.J. Schroeder translates this as "In some provinces a difference of dress distinguishes the Jews and Saracens from the Christians, but in others confusion has developed to such a degree that no difference is discernible. Whence it happens sometimes through error that Christians mingle with the women of Jews and Saracens, and, on the other hand, Jews and Saracens mingle with those of the Christians. Therefore, that such ruinous commingling through error of this kind may not serve as a refuge for further excuse for excesses, we decree that such people of both sexes (that is, Jews and Saracens) in every Christian province and at all times be distinguished in public from other people by a difference of dress, since this was also enjoined on them by Moses." See *Disciplinary Decrees of the General Councils (Text, Translation, and Commentary)*, ed. and trans. H. J. Schroeder (London: B. Herder Book Company, 1937), 290, 584.
56. Steven Kruger, "Conversion and Medieval Sexual, Religious, and Racial Categories," in *Constructing Medieval Sexuality*, ed. Karma Lochrie, Peggy McCracken, and James A. Schultz (Minneapolis: University of Minnesota Press, 1997), 169, 167.
57. Elukin, "From Jew to Christian?," 183.
58. Kruger, "Conversion and Medieval Sexual, Religious, and Racial Categories," 169.
59. Ibid, 169–70. In this passage, Kruger quotes from Salo Wittmeyer Baron, *A Social and Religious History of the Jews*, 2nd ed, 18 vols. (New York: Columbia University Press, 1952–83), 11: 79
60. This marriage was not to Josiane's liking and was arranged by her father during Beves's seven-year imprisonment in Brademond's dungeon. As a mark of her love for Beves, Josiane used a magic ring during this time to preserve her virginal body from Yuor's sexual advances as a husband. In this way, she maintained the virginity requisite for marriage to Beves later in the text. Her act here recalls that of Chrétien de Troyes's heroine Fenice, in

Cliges, who also preserved her virginity in marriage through a magic trick. Interestingly, this part of the French romance is set in the East, and Chrétien explicitly ends his tale with a joking comment that Fenice's deceptive behavior is the reason why present-day Muslim women are confined to a harem. In some ways, then, Josiane's deceptiveness and ability to perform her way into identities may be read as a literary trait of Saracen women in the Middle Ages. When it comes down to sexual integration, however, Josiane's ability to pass herself off as whatever she pleases is challenged.

61. I am indebted to Jennifer Fellows for cognizance of Auchinleck's uniqueness at this point as it is something she first pointed out to me in conversation. The manuscript's uniqueness is clearly seen upon consultation of Fellows's parallel-text edition. Auchinleck's uniqueness at this point is also discussed in Linda Marie Zaerr, "Medieval and Modern Deletions of Repellent Passages," in *Improvisation in the Arts of the Middle Ages and Renaissance,* ed. Timothy J. McGee (Kalamazoo: Western Michigan University Medieval Institute Publications, 2003): 222–46.

62. Jennifer R. Goodman, *Chivalry and Exploration 1298–1630* (Woodbridge, Suffolk: Boydell Press, 1998).

63. For a number of entries expressing anxiety and bitterness about Henry's efforts to accommodate his "uterine brothers," see Matthew Paris's record of the year 1247 in his *Chronica majora,* 4: 590–655, especially 627–29, 650.

64. Isabella wanted this Despenser banished from court because he had actively been working to secure an annulment for Edward II and had also been instrumental in the sequestration of Isabella's estates, a diminution of her financial and political power that Isabella vehemently opposed. *Chronicon de Lanercost,* ed. Stevenson, 254; McKisack, *The Fourteenth Century,* 81.

65. *Chronicon de Lanercost,* ed. Stevenson, 254; McKisack, *The Fourteenth Century,* 82.

66. McKisack, *The Fourteenth Century,* 83–98.

67. Fradenburg, *City, Marriage, Tournament,* 172–224.

68. McCracken, *Romance of Adultery,* 2, 23, 31, 49, 57, 60, 117–18.

69. Ibid, 49, 60, 52.

70. Andrew Parker, Mary Russo, Doris Sommer, and Patricia Yaeger, introduction to *Nationalisms and Sexualities,* 6.

71. Joachim Bumke, *The Concept of Knighthood in the Middle Ages,* trans. W. T. H. and Erika Jackson (New York: AMS Press, Incorporated, 1982), 29.

72. Peter Coss, *The Knight in Medieval England,* 62.

73. Simon Lloyd, *English Society and the Crusade,* 204–7.

74. Ibid.

75. Vale, *Edward III and Chivalry,* 2, 16–22.

76. *Chronicle of Bury St Edmunds 1212–1301,* ed. and trans. Antonia Gransden (London: Nelson, 1964), 63–64, 172; Lloyd, *English Society and the Crusade,* 29–35.

77. Pierre Dubois proposed a plan for the renewed conquest and settlement of the Holy Land around 1306 and addressed it to Edward I. Pierre Dubois, *De recuperatione terre sancte,* 1.
78. Vale, *Edward III and Chivalry,* 3, 35–46, 56–93.
79. While Beves's mother may here incarnate the medieval stereotype of female lascivity, there is no textual evidence that she is consciously performing this identity.
80. Barnaby C. Keeney, "Military Service and the Development of Nationalism in England, 1272–1327," *Speculum* 22 (1947): 544. Keeney is here summarizing and translating writs published in F. Palgrave, *Parliamentary Writs and Writs of Military Summons* (London: Record Commission, 1827–34), vol. 2, pp. 96–97, 107, 280–81, 476 (nos. 12, 13, 17, 63, and 70).
81. *The Chronicle of Lanercost,* trans. Maxwell, 122. The Latin reads: "Nam unanimiter et qui prælationis officio et qui prædicationis functi sunt, consiliis et exhortationibus tam publice quam occulte, aures et animos principum et plebium corruperunt, ut adversum regem ac gentem, qui eos salubriter salvaverat, hostiliter animarentur; asserentes erronee abundantioris esse justitiæ ipsos quam Sarracenos impetere." *Chronicon de Lanercost,* ed. Stevenson, 165–66.

NOTES TO CHAPTER THREE

1. Portions of this chapter first appeared in "Marking Religion on the Body: Saracens, Categorization, and *The King of Tars," Journal of English and Germanic Philology* 104 (2005): 219–38. I am grateful to *JEGP* and the University of Illinois Press for permission to republish those portions here.
2. The one exception to this statement is Thorlac Turville-Petre, who does mention *Þe King of Tars* in his discussion of Auchinleck. Turville-Petre, *England the Nation,* 127–28.
3. Roger of Wendover, *Roger of Wendover's Flowers of History,* vol. 2, bk. 2, 336–37. The Latin reads "Venit ergo ad hoc omne genus hominum perversorum in Angliam cum mulieribus ac parvulis, ut, expulsis indigenis a regno et penitus exterminatis, ipsi jure perpetuo terram possiderent." See Roger of Wendover, *Flores historiarum,* 2:148.
4. Matthew Paris, *Chronicles of Matthew Paris: Monastic Life in the Thirteenth Century,* ed. and trans. Richard Vaughan (New York: St Martin's Press, 1984), 81–128. The Latin entry is found in Matthew Paris, *Chronica majora,* 4: 590–655.
5. Matthew Paris, *Chronicles,* 87, 110. The Latin passages read: "Quod multis Angliæ naturalibus et indigenis, qui se spretos censuerunt, molestum videbatur et absurdum," and "et sic in magna parte devoluta est Anglicana nobilitas ad advenas et ignotos." See Matthew Paris, *Chronica majora,* 4: 598, 629.

6. Matthew Paris, *Chronicles,* 124. The Latin reads "quia usque ad odium advenarum elatio cum obprobriis Anglorum constantiam provocavit." See Matthew Paris, *Chronica majora,* 4: 649.

7. *Chronicle of Bury St Edmunds,* 27. The Latin reads "Romanorum eciam bona ubicumque inuenta, . . . diripiebant et ecclesias eorum uel conferebant uel cui uolebant tradebant, et similiter de alienigenis faciebant." See facing page Latin in *Chronicle of Bury St Edmunds.*

8. *The Chronicle of Lanercost,* trans. Maxwell, 194. The Latin reads: "Ipse enim, credens se in comitatu pro suo perpetuo confirmatum, cum esset alienigena et de sola gratia regis tantum honorem adeptus, jam in tantam superbiam est erectus quod omnes nobiles comites terræ contempsit." *Chronicon de Lanercost,* ed. Stevenson, 216. The issue of sexuality and difference may also be at stake in this characterization of Gaveston given ideas about the possible homosexual relationship between Edward and Gaveston, and contemporary chroniclers' discomfort with the evident close relationship between the two men. The Lanercost chronicler merely states that English nobles disliked Edward's familiarity with Gaveston and his public references to Gaveston as his brother (ibid, 210).

9. *The Anonimalle Chronicle 1307 to 1334 From Brotherton Collection MS 29,* ed. and trans. Wendy R. Childs and John Taylor, Yorkshire Archæological Society Record Series, vol. 147 (Leeds: University of Leeds Printing Service for the Yorkshire Archæological Society, 1991), 137. This edition is based on Leeds, Leeds University Brotherton Library, Brotherton Collection 29. The French states "En cel temps a Everwyk les Hanautz oscirent nutaundre moltz des Engleis," and narrates the Stanhope Park debacle thus: "et quei par envie qe les (les: *repeated*) grauntz avoient devers les Henautz, et que par fausine et compassement dascuns grantz de la terre, les Escoz eschaperent hors del dit park." *Anonimalle Chronicle,* 136.

10. Rees Davies, "Frontier Arrangements in Fragmented Societies: Ireland and Wales," in *Medieval Frontier Societies,* ed. Robert Bartlett and Angus MacKay (Oxford: Clarendon Press, 1989), 77, 89.

11. Geoffrey Barrow, "Frontier and Settlement," 21.

12. *The Chronicle of Lanercost,* trans. Maxwell, 128–129. The original Latin reads: "gentem ipsam . . . falsam et ingratam beneficiis a rege Edwardo perceptis" and "ipsi . . . absurdissime dixerint sacramentum suum regi Edwardo ex mera necessitate factum, ac proinde ex necessitate infringendum." *Chronicon de Lanercost,* ed. Stevenson, 169.

13. Keeney, "Military Service," 544–45.

14. Ibid, 534–49.

15. "Two Manuscripts of the Middle English *Anonymous Riming Chronicle,*" lines 477–78, 675–6, 783–812, 837–58, 967–82, 995–1002, 1582–94, 1736–49, 2304–25.

16. I am using "Soudan" as the proper name for the Saracen king since he is not given any designation other than his title. For this reason, I do not always put the Middle English word into quotation marks.

17. *The King of Tars,* ed. Judith Perryman, line 580. All quotations of *Þe King of Tars* are taken from this edition unless otherwise indicated. All references to the text of the poem are to line numbers in this edition, and will henceforth be indicated within parentheses in the text.

18. Lillian Herlands Hornstein, "A Study of Historical and Folklore Sources of *The King of Tars*" (Ph. D. diss., New York University, 1940); idem, "A Folklore Theme in the *King of Tars,*" *Philological Quarterly* 20 (1941): 82–87; idem, "The Historical Background of *The King of Tars,*" *Speculum* 16 (1941): 404–14; idem, "New Analogues to the 'King of Tars,'" *Modern Language Review* 36 (1941): 433–42; Robert J. Geist, "On the Genesis of *The King of Tars,*" *Journal of English and Germanic Philology* 42 (1943): 260–68; Judith Perryman, introduction to *The King of Tars,* 42–50.

19. The Tartars are more commonly called Mongols or Tatars now. I use the medieval term "Tartars" and the more modern term "Mongols" interchangeably.

20. Perryman, introduction to *The King of Tars,* 44.

21. Ibid.

22. *Chronicle of Bury St Edmunds,* 154–55. The Latin reads "Noua gaudia noua felicitas nuper nobis de orientis partibus illuxerunt. Sane Cassan rex magnus Tartarorum Cham, id est inperator [sic], constituit regem Hermenie principem et ducem exercitus sui. Vnde ultimo die mensis Decembris inter duas magnas ciuitates Gamel' et Damascum primum contra soldanum Babilonie bellum commisit. Ibidem Saraceni uicti fuerunt et mortui. Soldanus igitur in ciuitatem Gamel' fugit. Quem Tartarorum dominus cum toto exercitu insecutus obsedit et cepit dictam ciuitatem. Soldanus igitur fugit Damascum ubi primo ex utraque parte multa milia Saracenorum ceciderunt; sed tandem omnes soldani copie fuse fuerunt. Soldanus autem cum quinque tantum sociis fugam iniit per solitudinem Babilonie usque Algar. Soldanus misit post hec imperatori Cassando xxx. equos oneratos auro, mandans ei quod uellet tenere de eo omnes terras suas. Cassan uero aurum retinuit nichil prorsus respondens nunciis, asserens se proprium et non alterius thesaurum recepisse. Eya sic euacuatis inimicis Christianorum et extinctis magnus Cham restituit Christianis omnes terras quas antiquitus possidebant." See facing page Latin in *Chronicle of Bury St Edmunds.*

23. Perryman, introduction to *The King of Tars,* 45.

24. Ibid.

25. Geist, "Genesis of *The King of Tars,*" 261. For the *Annales Polonorum* entry, see *Annales Polonorum,* ed. Richard Röpell and William Arndt, in MGH, Scriptores [in folio] 19 (Hanover: Hahn, 1866), 640. The entry reads "Rex eciam Thartarorum ibidem venit et obedienciam Romane ecclesie promisit

et fidem confessus est, a quo et coronam suscepit. In territorio Cracoviensi natus est puer cum dentibus, qui statim ut natus est cepit loqui; sed cum esset baptizatus, mox et dentes amisit et loquelam. Vixit autem tribus annis et mortuus est."

26. Geist, "Genesis of *The King of Tars*," 261.

27. Perryman, introduction to *The King of Tars*, 45; Röpell and Arndt, introduction to *Annales Polonorum*, 609.

28. Röpell and Arndt, introduction to *Annales Polonorum*, 609.

29. Perryman, introduction to *The King of Tars*, 42.

30. As Lillian Herlands Hornstein notes, the tale also appears in later chronicles, including Thomas Walsingham's *Historia Anglicana*, ed. Henry T. Riley, Rolls Series, no. 28 (London: Longman, 1863), 1: 77, 113. The Walsingham *Historia* dates from 1377–1422 in its time of compilation according to Hornstein, "Historical Background," 404, n. 2, and its entries are "clearly derived from the other Anglo-Latin texts" according to Hornstein in "New Analogues," 435. Other post-Auchinleck chronicles containing analogous narratives include a Germano-Latin "Chronicon" written by Jean de Vietring around 1343 and found in *Fontes rerum Germanicarum*, ed. J. F. Böhmer, Vol. 1 (Stuttgart: J. G. Cotta, 1843), 314 as well as various recensions of this manuscript; two Franco-Latin chronicles of c. 1350, one by Gilles Le Muisit, *Chronique et annales*, ed. H. Lemaître (Paris: La Société de l'histoire de France, 1806), 114–15, and the other the "Chronicon Muevini," in *Recueil des chroniques de Flandre*, ed. J. J. de Smet, Collection chroniques belges inédites, vol. 2 (Brussels: M. Hayez, 1841), 470; and, finally, a German chronicle of 1386–1400, *Österreichische Chronik von den 95 Herrschaften*, ed. J. Seemüller, MGH, Scriptores [in folio] 6 (Hanover: Hahn, 1909), 138–39.

31. *Flores historiarum*, ed. H. R. Luard, Rolls Series, no. 95, vol. 3 (London: Eyre and Spottiswoode, 1890), 107, 300.

32. Giovanni Villani, *Istorie Fiorentine*, ed. P. Massai, Vol. 4, bk. 8 (Milan: Società tipografica de' classici italiani, 1802–3), 49–53.

33. Rishanger, *Chronica et annales*, ed. H. T. Riley, Rolls Series, no. 28 (London: Longman, 1865), 2: 189–90.

34. *Acta Aragonensia: Quellen zur deutschen, italienischen, französischen, spanischen, zur Kirchen- und Kultur-geschichte aus der diplomatischen Korresponden Jaymes II (1291–1327)*, ed. H. Finke (Berlin: W. Rothschild, 1908), 2:746.

35. *Annales Sancti Rudberti Salisburgenses*, ed. G. H. Pertz, MGH, Scriptores [in folio] 9 (Hanover: Hahn, 1851), 806.

36. Ottokar, *Österreichische Reimchronik*, ed. J. Seemüller, MGH, Deutsche Chroniken 5 (Hanover: Hahn, 1890–93), 253–56.

37. Perryman, introduction, 46.

38. Hornstein, "New Analogues," 434. It should be noted, however, that the black-to-white trope did exist elsewhere long before it was linked, in

Auchinleck, to this chronicle narrative. Frank Snowden analyzes the trope in relation to early Christian interpretations and the Classical tradition in *Blacks in Antiquity: Ethiopians in the Greco-Roman Experience* (Cambridge: Harvard University Press, Belknap Press, 1970), 196–215, and Thomas Hahn notes the appearances of this trope in the twelfth-century "History of the Rood Tree," in *History of the Holy Rood Tree: A Twelfth Century Version of the Cross-Legend,* ed. Arthur S. Napier, Early English Text Society, o. s. 103 (London: Kegan Paul, Trench, Trübner & Company Limited, 1894), 2–17, and in the c. 1325 *Cursor Mundi,* ed. Richard Morris, Early English Text Society, o. s. 59 (London: Kegan Paul, Trench, Trübner & Company Limited, 1874–93), 2: lines 8072–124. See Thomas Hahn, "The Difference the Middle Ages Makes: Color and Race before the Modern World," *Journal of Medieval and Early Modern Studies* 31, no. 1 (2001): 12–15, 33, n. 45.

39. Perryman, introduction, 42–44 offers a helpful summary of the various narratives.

40. See *Chronicon de Lanercost,* ed. Stevenson, 104. A translation of the entry can be found in *The Chronicle of Lanercost,* trans. Maxwell, 21–22.

41. Alan Harding, *England in the Thirteenth Century* (Cambridge: Cambridge University Press, 1993), 310–12.

42. *Chronicle of Lanercost,* trans. Maxwell, 22–23. The Latin reads: "tam gratiose erga regem et suos se habuit quod mores in melius mutavit, idioma Gallicum et Anglicum eum docuit, et de indumentis et esculentis honestius instituit." *Chronicon de Lanercost,* ed. Stevenson, 105.

43. Perryman, introduction, 35 asserts that "There is no direct source of the Middle English *K[ing of] T[ars]*."

44. Perryman, introduction, 11.

45. Ibid, 15. Perryman later also postulates that the Auchinleck *King of Tars* might have been translated from a now-lost French romance or chronicle entry (39), but bases this postulation on the assumption that the manuscript was the product of a London bookshop. This theory was put forward by Laura Hibbard Loomis in "The Auchinleck Manuscript and a Possible London Bookshop," 150–87. Loomis's bookshop theory, however, has been challenged by the more recent work of Judith Weiss, "The Auchinleck MS. And the Edwardes MSS," 444–46; A. I Doyle and M. B. Parkes, "The Production of Copies of the *Canterbury Tales* and the *Confessio Amantis* in the Early Fifteenth Century," in *Medieval Scribes, Manuscripts and Libraries: Essays Presented to N. R. Ker,* ed. M. B. Parkes and Andrew G. Watson (London: Scolar Press, 1978), 163–210; Judith Mordkoff, "The Making of the Auchinleck Manuscript;" Timothy Shonk, "A Study of the Auchinleck Manuscript," 71–91; and Frederick Porcheddu, "Editing the Auchinleck." Accordingly, Perryman's postulation may be premised upon an erroneous notion of the manuscript's assembly.

46. One might think, for example, of the lines about pig-like Saracens in *The Song of Roland,* quoted in Chapter One.
47. Perryman, introduction, 59.
48. See Metlitzki, *Matter of Araby,* 189–92 for a discussion of this literary stereotype.
49. Perryman, introduction, 59.
50. Brundage, *Law, Sex, and Christian Society,* 196.
51. David Nirenberg, *Communities of Violence: Persecution of Minorities in the Middle Ages* (Princeton: Princeton University Press, 1998), 136–40.
52. As Sharon Kinoshita points out, the literary trope of "amor de lonh" is often found in French troubadour lyrics, a number of which celebrate "the hero's overwhelming passion for a woman he has never seen." Sharon Kinoshita, "The Politics of Courtly Love," 269, n. 7. The article as a whole offers a fascinating discussion of "amor de lonh," its use by French poets, and its role in *La Prise d'Orange.*
53. Jaufré Rudel, "Lanquan li jorn son lonc en may," in Alfred Jeanroy, ed., *Les Chansons de Jaufré Rudel,* Classiques français du moyen age, no. 15 (Paris: Honoré Champion, 1924), 12–15.
54. Jaufré Rudel certainly fits into this category as his poem represents him, a western man, desiring a woman in Saracen lands. Similarly, the French hero Guillaume's love for the Saracen queen Orable is a central part of *La Prise d'Orange.* See *La Prise d'Orange: chanson de geste de la fin du XIIe siècle,* ed. Claude Regnier, 7th ed. (Paris: Klincksieck, 1986). For a translation, see *William, Count of Orange: Four Old French Epics,* trans. Glanville Price, Lynette Muir, and David Hoggan (London: Dent, 1975).
55. Chaucer's *Man of Law's Tale* also describes a Saracen man becoming enamoured of a Christian woman, although there the Saracen offers to convert to Christianity whereas in *Þe King of Tars* the Sultan insists that his wife convert to the Saracen faith. The Auchinleck *King of Tars,* of course, pre-dates the *Man of Law's Tale* and is often numbered among the sources and analogues of Chaucer's later text.
56. See Metlitzki, *Matter of Araby,* 209–10, and Daniel, *Heroes and Saracens,* 133–78 regarding the utter inaccuracy of this representation of Muslim worship practices. See Michael Camille, *The Gothic Idol: Ideology and Image-Making in Medieval Art* (Cambridge: Cambridge University Press, 1989), for an interesting discussion of medieval Christians' concerns about idolatry and its relation to their own worship practices.
57. Perryman's emendation here does not supply the word "heþen" where it is missing. The Auchinleck text clearly reads "heþþen," and Perryman's desire to normalize spellings leads her to emend the word. *The Auchinleck Manuscript (facsimile),* folio 9r.
58. *Chronicle of the Third Crusade,* 156. The Latin reads "Porro modus habitudinis formam trahit ex animo præsidentis; talis nimirum erit forma

prædicati, qualem permiserit natura subjecti." See *Itinerarium peregrino-rum*, 155–56.

59. Susan Crane, *The Performance of Self: Ritual, Clothing, and Identity During the Hundred Years War* (Philadelphia: University of Pennsylvania Press, 2002), 102–3. The passage from *Silence* is taken from Heldris of Cornwall, *Silence*, ed. and trans. Sarah Roche-Mahdi (East Lansing, Michigan: Colleagues Press, 1992), lines 6672–74.

60. It is interesting to note, too, the role of idols in this undercutting of difference. Throughout *The Gothic Idol*, Michael Camille argues that the fondness of Christians for representing Saracens and Jews as idol-worshippers stemmed from Christian concerns about the veneration of saintly and religious images and symbols in relation to the commandment not to idolatrize. Interestingly, the miniature located at the start of the Auchinleck *King of Tars* underlines the similarities between Christians and idol-worshippers by contrasting one figure's idol worship with two figures' veneration of the Crucifix. The illustration thus calls into question the postulated differences between the two religions. *The Auchinleck Manuscript (facsimile)*, folio 7r.

61. The Vulgate Bible passage reads: "quam ob rem relinquet homo patrem suum et matrem et adherebit uxori suae et erunt duo in carne una" (Gn 2:24). The Douay-Rheims version translates the passage as "Wherefore a man shall leave father and mother, and shall cleave to his wife: and they shall be two in one flesh."

62. Brundage, *Law, Sex, and Christian Society*, 382.

63. Nirenberg, *Communities of Violence*, 155. Jacquart and Thomasset explain this notion of mingling blood when they point out that in the Middle Ages male sperm was considered "man's purest blood," and was understood to mix with women's blood in reproduction. Danielle Jacquart and Claude Thomasset, *Sexuality and Medicine in the Middle Ages*, trans. Matthew Adamson (Princeton: Princeton University Press, 1988), 60.

64. See Chapter Two for a detailed enumeration of these prohibitions. In the eleventh and early twelfth centuries, before the prohibition in Gratian's *Decretum* circulated widely, Muslim-Christian marriages did occasionally occur, usually in Spain or in the kingdom of Outremer (see Brundage, *Law Sex, and Christian Society*, 194). Even then, however, such unions were frowned upon by Church authorities in the West. For example, Steven Runciman notes that in 1114 "the Patriarch Arnulf was severely scolded by Pope Paschal for having performed a marriage ceremony between a Christian and a Moslem lady." Steven Runciman, *The Kingdom of Jerusalem and the Frankish East*, 101.

65. Daniel, *Heroes and Saracens*, 74; Comfort, "Literary Role of Saracens," 657–58. Besides Þe *King of Tars* I know of only one other medieval romance that squarely depicts Saracen-Christian sex: Wolfram von Eschenbach's

Parzival. In *Parzival,* however, the Saracen queen Belacane and the Christian knight Gahmuret know each other's religious affiliations at the time of
intercourse.

66. Wolfram von Eschenbach, *Parzival,* trans. A. T. Hatto (New York: Penguin,
     1980), 40. For an illuminating discussion of this figure, see S. Van D'Elden,
     "Black and White: Contact with the Mediterranean World in Medieval
     German Narrative," in *The Medieval Mediterranean: Cross-Cultural Con-
     tacts,* ed. M. Chiat and K. Reyerson (St. Cloud, MN: Medieval Studies at
     Minnesota, 1988), 112–18.

67. Nirenberg, *Communities of Violence,* 21.

68. *Chronicle of Lanercost,* trans. Maxwell, 22. The Latin reads: "ursi non viri
     præferens pignus, utpote frustum informe carnis, non filium." *Chronicon de
     Lanercost,* ed. Stevenson, 104.

69. Hornstein, "Folklore Theme," 84.

70. Ibid.

71. Both Gahmuret and Feirefiz abandon Saracen lovers for Christian ones in
     Parzival.

72. The Auchinleck manuscript labels the offspring "flesche" seven times
     (lines 580, 607, 622, 639, 662, 752, and 772). Between birth and bap-
     tism, only two exceptions to calling the offspring "flesche" are found in
     Auchinleck. First, its parents call it a "child" when it is born (592, 604).
     Their use of the term "child" highlights the tragedy of the un-child-like
     nature of their offspring. Second, the text itself labels the "flesche" a
     "child" when the Sultan promises to convert if the "flesche" should
     become a "child" (704), but the text then reverts to referring to the off-
     spring as "flesche." Here, then, Christianity is directly linked to the
     potential child within the lump. By contrast, the Vernon and Simeon
     manuscripts, after describing the "flesche" that appears at birth, always
     call the inter-faith offspring ""the child" or "hit" or "wrecche" where
     Auchinleck uses the term "flesche." For "child," see Perryman's variants
     for lines 622, 662, 772. For "hit" see Perryman's variants for lines 607,
     639. For "wrecche," see Perryman's variants for line 752. The Vernon
     manuscript has been edited by F. Krause in "Kleine Publicationen aus der
     Auchinleck-Hs: IX. The king of Tars," *Englische Studien* 11 (1888), 1–62.
     In this article, the Vernon variants can be read in a facing-page format
     beside the Auchinleck text. The relevant lines in Krause's numbering are
     lines 550, 562, 580, 601, 620, and 662.

73. Joan Cadden, *Meanings of Sex Difference in the Middle Ages: Medicine, Sci-
     ence, and Culture* (Cambridge: Cambridge University Press, 1993), 121.

74. Jacquart and Thomasset, *Sexuality and Medicine,* 139, 141.

75. Ibid, 85.

76. Gerald of Wales, *Journey Through Wales and the Description of Wales,* trans.
     Lewis Thorpe (New York: Penguin, 1978), 191.

77. David Williams, *Deformed Discourse: The Function of the Monster in Mediaeval Thought and Literature* (Montreal: McGill-Queen's University Press, 1996), 175.
78. Ibid, 83, 59.
79. See Julia Kristeva, "Semiotics of Biblical Abomination," and " . . . *Qui tollis peccata mundi,*" in *Powers of Horror: An Essay on Abjection,* trans. Leon S. Roudiez (New York: Columbia University Press, 1982), 90–132.
80. Williams, *Deformed Discourse,* 4–6.
81. This relates to the notion of the splitting of the subject as it enters language and learns that it must conform to a social construction outside itself even if that construction is completely foreign, or harmful to it. This learning to conform means that the subject must split itself, divide its true desires and drives from the appearance it maintains in society to be loved by others.
82. Kristeva, *Powers of Horror,* 11, 9.
83. Ibid, 8.
84. Ibid, 18.
85. Ibid, 4.
86. Consider the use of rhetorics of otherness against various opponents of papal power in the later Middle Ages as discussed by Norman Housley in "Crusades Against Christians: Their Origins and Early Development," in *Crusade and Settlement,* ed. Peter Edbury (Cardiff: University College Cardiff Press, 1985), 17–36. For a similar point, see Gordon Leff, *Heresy in the Later Middle Ages,* 1: 22–24. Consider also late medieval rhetoric about heretics as discussed by Gordon Leff in 1: 34–47; Bernard Hamilton in *The Medieval Inquisition* (New York: Holmes and Meier Publishers, Incorporated, 1981), 29–34; and R. I. Moore in *The Formation of a Persecuting Society: Power and Deviance in Western Europe, 950–1250* (New York: Blackwell, 1987), 11–27.
87. Lisa Lampert, *Gender and Jewish Difference from Paul to Shakespeare* (Philadelphia: University of Pennsylvania Press, 2004), 78.
88. Caroline Walker Bynum, *The Resurrection of the Body in Western Christianity 200–1336* (New York: Columbia University Press, 1995), 10, 256–71. As Bynum makes clear, the idea that soul gave form to body was one shared by "thinkers such as Albert the Great, Thomas Aquinas, and Giles of Rome" (256). This idea was not universally accepted, as Bynum shows in her discussion of the condemnations and revisions of the idea in the late thirteenth century (271–77). These condemnations, however, seem to have died out or been rescinded by the early fourteenth century (277–78).

    Generally, the formative power of the soul was believed to be exercised on bodily matter in the womb. Bynum refers to "the ensouling of the fetus in the womb" in her discussion of late thirteenth- and early fourteenth-century ideas about the soul-body relationship (263). Normally, then, a child would receive its soul and form in the womb. The "flesche," however, was neither Christian nor Saracen in the womb (being a mix), and thus may not have been able to receive a soul until it was baptized and one identity firmly asserted.

89. Acts 9: 1–30 Vulgate Bible, translated in Douay-Rheims Bible.
90. Augustine, *Confessiones,* 8.12.28–30. For an English translation, see *Confessions,* trans. Henry Chadwick.
91. Morrison, *Understanding Conversion,* xv–xxii, 11, 22, 46–49, 57, 93–94, 114–24, 156–57.
92. Augustine, *Confessiones,* 10.31.44–43.70.
93. Acts 9: 26–28 Vulgate Bible.
94. This aspect of conversion clearly informs the conversions of Otuel and Josiane discussed earlier in this book.
95. Some scholars read the fact that the Princess is pursued by black hounds in her dream (lines 421–56) as clear indication of the Soudan's blackness. No explicit reference to the Soudan is made in the description of the dream hounds, however, and these hounds are symbolic dream figurations rather than a clear statement about the lived world of the text and the Soudan's biological skin color.
96. Bernard of Clairvaux, *On the Song of Songs,* trans. Kilian Walsh (Kalamazoo, MI: Cistercian Publications, 1976), 2: 89. The sermon number is 28, Section 2. Bruce Holsinger suggests some modifications to Walsh's translation (the italicized words), and I have accepted these. See Bruce Holsinger, "The Color of Salvation: Desire, Death, and the Second Crusade in Bernard of Clairvaux's *Sermon on the Song of Songs,*" in *The Tongue of the Fathers: Gender and Ideology in Twelfth-Century Latin,* ed. David Townsend and Andrew Taylor (Philadelphia: University of Pennsylvania Press, 1998), 168. The Latin reads: "Agnosco denigratae formam naturae; agnosco tunicas illas pelliceas, protoplastorum peccantium habitum. Denique semetipsum denigravit formam servi accipiens in similitudinem hominum factus et habitu inventus ut homo." See Bernard of Clairvaux, *Sermones super cantica canticorum,* vol. 1 of *S. Bernardi opera,* ed. J. Leclercq, H. M. Rochais, and C. H. Talbot (Rome: Editiones Cistercienses, 1957), 193.
97. Holsinger, "The Color of Salvation," 168.
98. *Chronicle of Lanercost,* trans. Maxwell, 44. The Latin states that the scholar was found "muta loquela, quasi in extremis agentem; sed, quod valde mirandum est, toto corpore ita tetra effigie obtectum ut Æthiopem squalidum potius crederes quam Christianum." *Chronicon de Lanercost,* ed. Stevenson, 118.
99. *Chronicle of Lanercost,* trans. Maxwell, 45. The Latin reads "paulatim a specie fuliginea ad propriam formam restitutus est." *Chronicon De Lanercost,* ed. Stevenson, 119.
100. Henry Louis Gates Jr., "Introduction: Writing 'Race' and the Difference It Makes," in *"Race," Writing, and Difference,* ed. Henry Louis Gates, Jr. (Chicago: University of Chicago Press, 1986), 5.

101. Medieval ideas about race and ethnicity are complex, and have recently been explored in a special issue of the *Journal of Medieval and Early Modern Studies* 31, no. 1 (2001). As various articles in this collection demonstrate, some scholars believe that the term "race" should not be applied to the Middle Ages at all, while others believe that the term and its modern connotations of biological and physiological appearance are relevant to the Middle Ages and that not using the term constitutes an elision of history. Still other scholars indicate that in the Middle Ages terms designating racialized identities were used to differentiate peoples whom we today consider ethnically but not racially different. See for these respective opinions, William Chester Jordan, "Why 'Race'?" *Journal of Medieval and Early Modern Studies* 31, no. 1 (2001): 165–74; Jeffrey Jerome Cohen, "On Saracen Enjoyment," ibid, 113–46; Robert Bartlett, "Medieval and Modern Concepts of Race and Ethnicity," ibid, 39–56. As race has become a more popular topic of medievalists' studies, various discussions referencing *Þe King of Tars* have appeared. Most of these mention only the Soudan's conversion. See Kruger, "Conversion," 164–65; Thomas Hahn, "The Difference the Middle Ages Makes," 15; and Cohen "On Saracen Enjoyment," 121. Geraldine Heng discusses both the lump and the Soudan in *Empire of Magic,* 227–37.

102. Her bloodlust might also arise from a desire to obliterate from her memory her own close brush with succumbing to Saracenness.

103. Heffernan, *The Orient in Chaucer and Medieval Romance,* 84.

104. Kathleen Coyne Kelly, "The Bartering of Blauncheflur in the Middle English *Floris and Blauncheflur,*" *Studies in Philology* 91 (1994): 101–10; Heffernan, *The Orient in Chaucer and Medieval Romance,* 83–107. Kelly refers to her "darker reading" on page 102 of her article.

105. E. Jane Burns, *Courtly Love Undressed: Reading Through Clothes in Medieval French Culture* (Philadelphia: University of Pennsylvania Press, 2002), 213.

106. Indeed, even scholars who find the tale troubling do so because of its content, not because the intermingling of cultural inheritances is itself jarring or unharmonious.

107. All references to *Floris and Blauncheflur* are to line numbers in F. C. De Vries's edition of the four Middle English versions. Unless specified otherwise, lines are quoted from the Auchinleck version. *Floris and Blauncheflur: A Middle English Romance Edited with Introduction, Notes, and Glossary,* ed. F. C. De Vries (Groningen: Druk, 1966).

NOTES TO CHAPTER FOUR

1. Hippolyte Delehaye, *Legends of the Saints: An Introduction to Hagiography,* trans. V.M. Crawford (Notre Dame: University of Notre Dame 1961), 24–25.

2. Patrick J. Geary, *Living With the Dead in the Middle Ages* (Ithaca: Cornell University Press, 1994), 20.

3. See Geary, *Living With the Dead*, 21–22 for a well-reasoned refutation of Thomas Heffernan's assertion that saints' biographies were intended as models for imitation (Heffernan, *Sacred Biography: Saints and Their Biographers in the Middle Ages* (New York: Oxford University Press, 1988), 5). Geary points out that in many Merovingian and Carolingian hagiographic documents, saints' lives are not "to be emulated but rather to be admired. They glorify God; they do not provide models for mortals" (22). Geary also notes that "in glorifying God, they [saints' lives] also glorify the individual saint, the place he or she lived or was buried, the community where God chose to be glorified through his saints" (22). Thus, saints' lives function and acquire meaning in very particular local contexts as well as in larger Christian ones.

4. The term "saints' lives" usually refers to hagiographic texts that record all events in a saint's life from birth to death. The term "passion" usually refers to hagiographic texts that focus on the sufferings and martyrdom of saints. *Seynt Mergrete* and *Seynt Katerine* both focus on the sufferings and martyr-dom of their eponymous saints, but they also begin their narration at the saint's birth, and identify themselves as, respectively, "vie" (line 4) and "liif" (line 6). For this reason, I will call them "saints' lives" rather than "passions."

5. Christopher Tyerman, *England and the Crusades*; Simon Lloyd, *English Society and the Crusade*.

6. Information about Saint Katherine and narratives of her life is drawn from Saara Nevanlinna and Irma Taavitsainen, introduction to *Saint Katherine of Alexandria: The Late Middle English Prose Legend in Southwell Minster MS 7*, ed. Saara Nevanlinna and Irma Taavitsainen (Cambridge: D. S. Brewer, 1993), and from Jocelyn Wogan-Browne and Glyn Burgess, introduction to *Virgin Lives and Holy Deaths: Two Exemplary Biographies for Anglo-Norman Women*, trans. Jocelyn Wogan-Browne and Glyn S. Burgess (London: Everyman, 1996).

7. Nevanlinna and Taavitsainen, introduction to *Saint Katherine*, 4; Wogan-Browne and Burgess, introduction to *Virgin Lives*, xix.

8. Nevanlinna and Taavitsainen, introduction to *Saint Katherine*, 5.

9. This is the traditional understanding of events. Wogan-Browne and Burgess point out, however, that "there is no record of Catherine's shrine before European pilgrims and crusaders sought it out in the Third Crusade (began 1189), [thus] the cult [of St Katherine] may well have been transmitted from Rouen to Sinai rather than the other way round." Wogan-Browne and Burgess, introduction to *Virgin Lives*, xxi.

10. Nevanlinna and Taavitsainen, introduction to *Saint Katherine*, 5.

11. Ibid.

12. Wogan-Browne and Burgess, introduction to *Virgin Lives*, xxi.

13. Ibid.
14. Nevanlinna and Taavitsainen, introduction to *Saint Katherine*, 5.
15. Wogan-Browne and Burgess, introduction to *Virgin Lives*, xxi–xxii.
16. Ibid, xxii.
17. See S. R. T. O. D'Ardenne and E. J. Dobson, introduction to *Seinte Katerine: Re-edited from MS Bodley 34 and the other Manuscripts*, ed. S.R.T.O. D'Ardenne and E.J. Dobson, Early English Text Society, s.s., 7 (Oxford: Oxford University Press, 1981), xii–xx for a discussion of the various Latin tales of St Katherine.
18. For example, versions of the Mombritius-type life of St Margaret apparently served as sources for the Old English versions of her life. See Mary Clayton and Hugh Magennis, introduction to *The Old English Lives of St Margaret*, ed. Mary Clayton and Hugh Magennis (Cambridge: Cambridge University Press, 1994), 17.
19. William Granger Ryan, introduction to *The Golden Legend: Readings on the Saints*, by Jacobus de Voragine, trans. William Granger Ryan (Princeton: Princeton University Press, 1993), 1: xii–xiv. The most recent critical edition of the Latin *Legenda aurea* is Jacobus de Voragine, *Legenda aurea: edizione critica*.
20. Ryan, introduction to *The Golden Legend*, xiii.
21. Nevanlinna and Taavitsainen, introduction to *Saint Katherine*, 7.
22. Wogan-Browne and Burgess, introduction to *Virgin Lives*, xxii.
23. Ibid.
24. Nevanlinna and Taavitsainen, introduction to *Saint Katherine*, 6.
25. Ibid; see also Wogan-Browne and Burgess, introduction to *Virgin Lives*, xxii.
26. The availability of these manuscripts is shown by the use of both the Vulgate and the *Legenda aurea* versions of St Katherine's legend as sources for English versions of the tale. The Vulgate is believed to have served as the main source of the life of St Katherine found in the early thirteenth-century Katherine Group, while both the Vulgate and the *Legenda aurea* have been identified as sources of the Auchinleck *Seynt Katerine*. The *Legenda* has also been identified as one source of the thirteenth-century *South English Legendary*. The earliest dated manuscript of the *Legenda* in England (Cambridge, University Library, Ff. V. 31) is from 1299. See Nevanlinna and Taavitsainen, introduction to *Saint Katherine*, 7–8 on these points.
27. Wogan-Browne and Burgess, introduction to *Virgin Lives*, xxiii.
28. Nevanlinna and Taavitsainen, introduction to *Saint Katherine*, 6. This is the text translated by Wogan-Browne and Burgess in *Virgin Lives*.
29. The earliest manuscript of this poem (Paris, Bibliothèque nationale, nouvelles acquisitions françaises, 4503) dates to 1200 (Wogan-Browne and Burgess, introduction to *Virgin Lives*, xxiv). The Anglo-Norman text has been edited by William Macbain as *The Life of St. Catherine by Clemence of*

Barking, ed. William Macbain (Oxford: Anglo-Norman Text Society, 1964), and has been translated into English in *Virgin Lives*.

30. See Anne Savage and Nicholas Watson, introduction to "St Katherine," in *Anchoritic Spirituality: Ancrene Wisse and Associated Works*, trans. Anne Savage and Nicholas Watson (New York: Paulist Press, 1991), 260.

31. Katherine Lewis, *The Cult of St Katherine of Alexandria in Late Medieval England*, (Woodbridge, Suffolk: Boydell Press, 2000).

32. A full listing of these, up to and including the story's appearance in Caxton's 1483 version of the *Golden Legend*, is offered by Charlotte D'Evelyn in "Saints' Legends" in *A Manual of the Writings in Middle English 1050–1500*, ed. J. Burke Severs, vol. 2 (Hamden: Connecticut Academy of Arts and Sciences, 1970), 410–41, 556–635. I draw heavily on her piece for the general overview of Middle English legends of St Katherine provided in this paragraph.

33. The Katherine Group consists of *Seinte Katerine, Seinte Marherete, Seinte Iuliene*, the *Epistel of Meidenhad* (also known as *Hali Meidenhad*), and *Sawles Warde*. This is the collection found in Oxford, Bodleian Library, Bodley 34. London, British Library, Royal 17 A. xxvii contains the three saints' lives as well as *Sawles Warde*, while London, British Library, Cotton Titus D. xviii contains *Seinte Katerine, Hali Meidenhad*, and *Sawles Warde*. This collection of texts has attracted much scholarly interest for both its language and its evidence of female spirituality and anchoritism in England in the thirteenth century. For an overview of the scholarship on these texts and their implications for Middle English literature, see Bella Millett, *Annotated Bibliographies of Old and Middle English Literature: II. Ancrene Wisse, the Katherine Group, and the Wooing Group* (Cambridge: D. S. Brewer, 1996).

34. Charlotte D'Evelyn, "Saints' Legends," 413.

35. Ibid, 600.

36. Ibid, 600–602.

37. Ibid, 600–601.

38. Bella Millett, "The Audience of the Saints' Lives of the Katherine Group," *Reading Medieval Studies* 16 (1990): 132.

39. Information about St Margaret and the dissemination of her legend in Greek, Latin, and English is drawn from *Seinte Marherete þe Meiden ant Martyr*, ed. and intro. Frances M. Mack, Early English Text Society, o. s., 193 (London: Oxford University Press, 1934), as well as from Clayton and Magennis, introduction to *Old English Lives of St Margaret*.

40. Clayton and Magennis, introduction to *Old English Lives of St Margaret*, 3.

41. Ibid.

42. *Seinte Marherete*, ed. Mack, ix; Clayton and Magennis, introduction to *Old English Lives of St Margaret*, 3.

43. *Seinte Marherete*, ed. Mack, ix.

44. Ibid.

45. Clayton and Magennis, introduction to *Old English Lives of St Margaret*, 5–6.
46. Ibid, 7.
47. *Seinte Marherete*, ed. Mack, ix–x.
48. Clayton and Magennis, introduction to *Old English Lives of St Margaret*, 7–24. In more detail, these versions are, respectively, BHL 5303 found in a variety of manuscripts from the ninth century onward as well as in Mombritius's print *Sanctuarium*; a newly-identified version found in a variety of continental manuscripts dating from the eighth through the eleventh centuries; BHL 5304; BHL 5305; BHL 5306, found in London, British Library, Cotton Caligula A. viii and in Hereford, Cathedral Library, P.2.V; and BHL 5308. See pages 7–24 for a full discussion and analysis.
49. *Seinte Marherete*, ed. Mack, xxxiii.
50. See Clayton and Magennis, introduction to *Old English Lives of St Margaret*, 41 for an indication of the variety of Latin manuscripts containing Margaret's legend in England up to the Norman Conquest. See the above discussion of the availability of *Legenda aurea* manuscripts in England for an indication of how accessible her story would have been in the later Middle Ages.
51. Clayton and Magennis, introduction to *Old English Lives of St Margaret*, 72–77.
52. Ibid, 80–82. Clayton and Magennis note that "The presence of relics of Margaret in England is not surprising, given that her relics had been translated from the East to San Pietro della Valle near Lake Bobena in Italy in 908 and that Bobena was on the route which English pilgrimages commonly took to Rome" (82).
53. Clayton and Magennis, introduction to *Old English Lives of St Margaret*, 80. See also Bella Millett and Jocelyn Wogan-Browne, introduction to their edition of the Katherine Group *Seinte Marherete* in *Medieval English Prose for Women: Selections from the Katherine Group and the Ancrene Wisse*, ed. Bella Millett and Jocelyn Wogan-Browne (Oxford: Clarendon Press, 1990), xxii.
54. *Seinte Marherete*, ed. Mack, xi.
55. For details of the Anglo-Norman lives of St Margaret, see the relevant section in *Hagiographies: histoire internationale de la littérature hagiographique latine et vernaculaire en occident des origines à 1550*, ed. Guy Philippart, vol. 1 (Turnhout: Brepols, 1994). For editions of two of the Anglo-Norman lives, see Frederic Spencer, "The Legend of St Margaret," *Modern Language Notes* 5 (1890): 71–5, 107–111.
56. See *The Old English Lives of St Margaret* for an extensive scholarly analysis of the Old English lives of St Margaret, and for an edition of the Cotton and Corpus Christi College texts.
57. My overview of the various Middle English versions of *St Margaret* draws upon Charlotte D'Evelyn's bibliography in "Saints' Legends," 606–8.

58. D'Evelyn, "Saint's Legends," 413.
59. Ibid, 607. Consult D'Evelyn for a full listing of the fifteenth-century recensions.
60. *Seinte Marherete*, ed. Mack, xxxiii.
61. D'Evelyn, "Saint's Legends," 607.
62. Ibid.
63. Ibid.
64. Nevanlinna and Taavitsainen, introduction to *Saint Katherine*, 8. The critical edition of the *Legenda aurea* is that by Maggioni, while a critically edited version of the Vulgate St Katherine, based on a collation of eighteen manuscripts, is found in *Seinte Katerine: Re-edited from MS Bodley 34 and the other Manuscripts*, ed. S. R. T. O. D'Ardenne and E. J. Dobson, Early English Text Society, s.s., 7 (Oxford: Oxford University Press, 1981).
65. See D'Evelyn, "Saints' Legends," 607 and E. Krahl, *Untersuchungen über vier Versionen der mittelenglische Margaretenlegende* (Berlin, 1889), 18, 24, 53.
66. The phrase "antecedent texts" here refers to English texts chronologically prior to Auchinleck and to the Latin texts identified as general sources of Auchinleck. "Antecedent texts" do not here include any Greek texts or any Latin texts not identified as sources of *Seynt Katerine* and *Seynt Mergrete*.
67. It is interesting to note the unconcern with which the English poet attaches a Greek Emperor to Saracen beliefs. This in many ways reflects the confusion many crusaders felt when faced with eastern Christians. Although the easterners were supposed allies, the western Christians never seemed quite able to accept them as fellow Christians, a fact that may have facilitated the Fourth Crusade's metamorphosis into a conquest by western Christians of the eastern Christian center of Constantinople. See later discussion in chapter.
68. All references to this text are to *Seynt Katerine* as edited in *Altenglische Legenden: Neue Folge*, ed. C. Horstmann (Heilbronn: Henninger, 1881), pages 242–59. Line numbers will henceforth be indicated in parentheses in the text as references.
69. Given the large number of manuscripts of these Latin legends, and the editing problems this entails, any assertion I make about the contents of these Latin texts is necessarily made with the proviso "according to the critical edition I consulted, and the manuscripts upon which that edition was based." The edition of Jacobus de Voragine's *Legenda aurea* I consulted is that by Giovanni Maggioni, and the edition of the Vulgate St Katherine I consulted is that offered in *Seinte Katerine*, ed. D'Ardenne and Dobson.
70. See *Seinte Katerine*, ed. D'Ardenne and Dobson, 106. All subsequent references are to page numbers in this edition and will be indicated in parentheses within the text.

71. See the Old French etymology presented in the *MED*, s. v. "maumet," which clearly links the term to [w]estern terms for Muhammad. See also Michael Camille, *The Gothic Idol.*

72. References to the *South English Legendary* version of Katherine's legend are to line numbers in *The South English Legendary: Edited from Corpus Christi College Cambridge MS. 145 and British Museum MS. Harley 2277 With Variants from Bodley MS. Ashmole 43 and British Museum MS. Cotton Julius D. IX,* ed. Charlotte D'Evelyn and Anna J. Mill, Early English Text Society, o.s., 235, 236, 244 (London: Oxford University Press, 1967), II: 533–43. The text of "Seinte Katerine" is taken from London, British Museum, Harley 2277, which has been dated to c. 1300.

73. These manuscript versions have both been edited by Horstmann, and are found in *Altenglische Legenden,* pages 242–59 and 260–64.

74. See *Altenglische Legenden,* pages 165–173 for an edition of a Katherine text from the fifteenth-century *Northern Homily Collection.*

75. See *Saint Katherine of Alexandria: The Late Middle English Prose Legend in Southwell Minster MS 7,* ed. Saara Nevanlinna and Irma Taavitsainen (Cambridge: D. S. Brewer, 1993) for an edition of this text.

76. All references to the Auchinleck *Seynt Mergrete* are to line numbers in the edition in *Altenglische Legenden,* pages 225–35. These line numbers will henceforth be indicated in parentheses in the text. It should be noted that one of the problems with Horstmann's edition is his decision to reproduce as one line every two short lines of the Auchinleck text. He links the two lines with a caesura indicated thus: |, and numbers these composite lines as one line. Although I feel this editing of Auchinleck distorts the manuscript text, I have followed his edition for convenience as it is the most recent print edition of the Auchinleck text. Because of this choice, my line numbers refer, as his do, to his composite lines.

77. All references to the Mombritius text are to page numbers in the version edited by Mary Clayton and Hugh Magennis from Paris, Bibliothèque nationale, fonds latins 5574 and found in *The Old English Lives of St Margaret.* This tenth-century manuscript was written in Anglo-Saxon England.

78. *The Old English Lives of St Margaret,* 206. Clayton and Magennis translate thus: "she saw another devil sitting there in the form of a black man, with his hands fastened to his knees" (207).

79. *Seynt Mergrete* is item 4 in Auchinleck as it exists today. Item 2 is *Þe King of Tars,* which contains a black Soudan, and Item 5 is *Seynt Katerine,* whose Saracens are explicitly identified as black, as noted above. Black Saracens also appear much later in the manuscript in *Guy of Warwick (Couplet Version)* where Guy is said to have gained plenty of treasure from fighting "Sarrazins blake" (4460) and in *Guy of Warwick (stanzaic continuation)* where Guy battles the Saracen Amoraunt, who is "As blac . . . as brodes brend" (62.10)

80. *The Old English Lives of St Margaret*, 124. This version is that found in the late eleventh-century legend in London, British Library, Cotton Tiberius A. iii.

81. Ibid, 162. This version is the early twelfth-century legend in Cambridge, Corpus Christi College 303.

82. Ibid, 112. This version is that found in the late eleventh-century legend in London, British Library, Cotton Tiberius A. iii.

83. Ibid, 152. This version is the early twelfth-century legend in Cambridge, Corpus Christi College 303.

84. All references to the Katherine Group *Seinte Marherete* are to page numbers in the edition of her life in *Medieval English Prose for Women*, ed. Millett and Wogan-Browne.

85. The translation at this point reads "much blacker than any black man" (61). *Seinte Marherete*, ed. Millett and Wogan-Browne. Note how this version, like Auchinleck, distinguishes between human and supernatural blackness.

86. All references to the Margaret legend in the *South English Legendary* are to line numbers in *The South English Legendary*, I: pages 291–302. This text is edited from an early fourteenth-century manuscript of the *Legendary*: Cambridge, Corpus Christi College 145.

87. All references to *Meidan Maregrete* are to line numbers in the edition in *Altenglische Legenden*, pages 489–97.

88. See D'Evelyn, "Saints Legends," 607.

89. References are to line numbers in the edition in *Altenglische Legenden*, pages 236–41. This manuscript was formerly known as Ashmole 61.

90. See *Altenglische Legenden*, 446–453 for an edition of Lydgate's text.

91. See the Appendix for a complete list of items in Auchinleck.

92. All references are to line numbers in *Þe pater noster undo on englissch*, ed. E. Kölbing, *Englische Studien* 9 (1886): 47–9.

93. All references are to line numbers in *On þe seven dedly sinnes*, ed. E. Kölbing, *Englische Studien* 9 (1886): 43–6.

94. Tyerman, *England and the Crusades*, 84–85, 160–67; Lloyd, *English Society*, 10, 35–36, 57–67, 98, 100, 245, 246

95. In 1261, western control of Constantinople ended and in 1291, Acre, the last foothold of western Christians in the Holy Land, fell to a huge force of Muslims from Egypt. See Jonathan Riley-Smith, *The Crusades*, 185, 204–7.

96. Lloyd, *English Society*, 29; Tyerman, *England and the Crusades*, 229, 235.

97. The 1293 passagium eventually came to naught because of developments in Scottish-English relations. See Tyerman, *England and the Crusades*, 230–40 for a discussion of Edward I's involvement with crusading.

98. In *De recuperatione terre sancte* Pierre Dubois, a Frenchman, laid out a plan for the conquest, conversion, and acculturation of the Holy Land and dedicated it to the ruler he identified as best suited to leading this effort: Edward I of England.

99. Tyerman, *England and the Crusades*, 242–45.
100. Ibid, 246–49.
101. Cindy Vitto, "The Virtuous Pagan in Middle English Literature," *Transactions of the American Philosophical Society* 79.5 (1989): 89, my italics.
102. Daniel, *Islam and the West*, 20
103. Ibid, 124, 168–70; Metlitzki, *Matter of Araby*, 206–7.
104. See Millett, "Audience," 128. For a sampling of scholarship on the subject of virginity as marriage to Christ, see John Bugge, *Virginitas: An Essay in the History of a Medieval Ideal* (The Hague: Nijhoff, 1975); Caroline Walker Bynum, *Jesus as Mother: Studies in the Spirituality of the High Middle Ages* (Berkeley: University of California Press, 1982); *Hali Meiðhad*, ed. Bella Millett (London: Oxford University Press, 1982), and Frances Beer, *Women and Mystical Experience in the Middle Ages* (Cambridge: D. S. Brewer, 1992).
105. For the costs involved in producing a manuscript, see Michael Camille, "Labouring for the Lord: The Ploughman and the Social Order in the Luttrell Psalter," *Art History* 10 (1987): 423–54. For Pearsall's and Turville-Petre's ideas about Auchinleck's audience, see, respectively, Pearsall and Cunningham, introduction to *The Auchinleck Manuscript (facsimile)*, viii, and Turville-Petre, *England the Nation*, 113–14, 134–38.
106. The theological point made here by the saints' lives would certainly link well with the Auchinleck *Desputisoun bitven þe bodi & þe soul*.
107. See Jacobus de Voragine, *Legenda aurea* and the *South English Legendary*, for versions of the legend wherein the narrator expresses skepticism about the dragon-like demon's appearance and swallowing of Margaret. See *The Old English Lives of St Margaret* for descriptions of versions like the Casinensis version that omit this incident altogether, or state that the dragon-demon burst as it rushed at Margaret rather than after swallowing her.
108. For a discussion of blackness in *Þe King of Tars*, a text found earlier in the manuscript than the two saints' lives, see Chapter Three. The reference to blackness in *Seynt Katerine* (the item that immediately follows *Seynt Mergrete*) consists, as mentioned earlier, of the statement that Katerine is persecuted by "sarra3ins so blake" (426), while Guy fights black Saracens in the Middle East (see *Couplet Version* line 4460 and *Stanzaic Continuation* stanza 62, line 10).
109. See, for example, the references to black skin color in *Chronicle of the Third Crusade*, 90, 247.
110. Millett, "Audience," 145.
111. See Runciman, *The First Crusade and the Foundation of the Kingdom of Jerusalem*, 152–275 for a description of Bohemond's antipathy to the Byzantines and his claiming of Antioch. The same events are described in Riley-Smith, *The Crusades*, 27–33, 40–43.
112. See Riley-Smith, *The Crusades*, 84, 160.

113. Ibid, 228.
114. Tyerman, *England and the Crusades*, 290–93.
115. Bohemond of Antioch also enjoyed considerable press due to Orderic Vitalis's rather fantastic story about Bohemond's capture by Muslims and the Muslim captor's daughter's infatuation with him and subsequent conversion to Christianity. Orderic Vitalis, *Ecclesiastical History*, 5: 354–79.
116. Tyerman, *England and the Crusades*, 117.
117. Ibid, 19.
118. Ibid, 23.
119. See Riley-Smith, *The Crusades*, 101–2.
120. Tyerman, *England and the Crusades*, 86.
121. Nevanlinna and Taavitsainen, introduction to *Saint Katherine*, 17; Wogan-Browne and Burgess, introduction to *Virgin Lives*, xx–xxi.
122. Runciman, *The First Crusade and the Foundation of the Kingdom of Jerusalem*, 88. See Metlitzki, *Matter of Araby*, 16–56 for a discussion of the superiority of Muslim scientific and technological knowledge in the Middle Ages.
123. See Robert of Clari, *The Conquest of Constantinople*, trans. Edgar Holmes McNeal (1936; reprint, Toronto: University of Toronto Press, 1996), 101–13; *Chronicle of the Third Crusade*, 88, 91, 109–10, 114–16, 196–97, 206, 210.
124. The much-quoted authority Avicenna was actually an Arab, Ibn Sina, whose writings had been translated into Latin.
125. See Riley-Smith, *The Crusades*, 188–89; Tyerman, *England and the Crusades*, 293; and Burns, *Courtly Love Undressed*, 1–16, 179–229.
126. Saladin reconquered Jerusalem in 1187, while in 1291 Acre fell and the western Christian control of formerly Muslim lands ended.
127. Daniel, *Islam and the West*, 143–46.
128. Riley-Smith, *The Crusades*, 185.
129. Ibid, 205–7.
130. Ibid, 209. See also Antony Leopold, *How to Recover the Holy Land: The Crusade Proposals of the Late Thirteenth and Fourteenth Centuries*. Aldershot: Ashgate, 2000.
131. Tyerman, *England and the Crusades*, 235–36.
132. Pierre Dubois, *Recovery*, 157. The Latin reads "Peryalogum detentorem imperii Constantinopolis." See Pierre Dubois, *De recuperatione*, 90.
133. See Pierre Dubois, *De recuperatione*, 2, 57 (*Recovery*, 70, 124); Daniel, *Islam and the West*, 124, 168–70; Metlitzki, *Matter of Araby*, 206–7, 217.
134. Riley-Smith, *The Crusades*, 188–89.
135. Burns, *Courtly Love Undressed*, 1–16, 179–229.
136. Pierre Dubois, *Recovery*, 120. The Latin reads: "Per hujusmodi, . . . contingeret nobis occidentalibus communicari res preciosas, in partibus illis habundantes, nobis deficientes et apud nos carissimas, satis pro modico

nobis communicari, mondo catholicorum ordinato." *De recuperatione*, 53. See also *De recuperatione* 14, 53–57, 89 (*recovery*, 82, 120–24, 157).

137. Steven Runciman, *The Kingdom of Jerusalem and the Frankish East 1100–1187*, 101.
138. Pierre Dubois, *De recuperatione*, 57 (*Recovery*, 124).
139. Ibid.
140. Evidently, this model of society was part of life in the medieval West as well. In this saint's life, however, such attitudes are cast as an explicitly Saracen attention to bodily comfort and to worldly issues. Accordingly, Katerine's destruction of this type of society can be read as a decidedly anti-Saracen act.
141. See Daniel, *Islam and the West*, 141–46 for these stories.

NOTES TO CHAPTER FIVE

1. Portions of this chapter first appeared in "Violence, Saracens, and English Identity in *Of Arthour and of Merlin*," *Arthuriana* 14, no. 2 (2004): 17–36. I am grateful to *Arthuriana* for permission to reprint them here.
2. Elizabeth Sklar discusses the Englishing of the poem in "*Arthour and Merlin*: The Englishing of Arthur," *Michigan Academician* 8 (1975–76): 49–57. I know of only one other article that discusses the full romance at length: Nicole Clifton, "*Of Arthour and of Merlin* as Medieval Children's Literature," *Arthuriana* 13, no. 2 (2003): 9–22. There is also a Ph.D. dissertation by Karen Haslanger Vaneman, "Interpreting the Middle English Romance: The Audience in *Of Arthour and of Merlin*" (Ph. D. diss., Wayne State University, 1986). Most references to the poem consist of passing citations of it in discussions of English identity, as found, for example, in Riddy, "Reading for England," 317–18 and Turville-Petre, *England the Nation*, 21, 125–27.
3. O. D. Macrae-Gibson, introduction to *Of Arthour and of Merlin*, ed. O. D. Macrae-Gibson, vol. 2, Early English Text Society, o. s., 268 (London: Oxford University Press, 1973), 9–14, 18–19.
4. John Edwin Wells, *A Manual of the Writings in Middle English 1050–1400*, rev. ed. (New Haven: Connecticut Academy of Arts and Sciences, 1926), 44.
5. Helaine Newstead, "Arthurian Legends," in *A Manual of the Writings in Middle English 1050–1500*, ed. J. Burke Severs, vol. 1 (New Haven: Connecticut Academy of Arts and Sciences, 1967), 48.
6. Sklar, "Englishing," 50.
7. Norris J. Lacy, preface to *Introduction; The History of the Holy Grail; The Story of Merlin*, vol. 1 of *Lancelot-Grail: The Old French Arthurian Vulgate and Post-Vulgate in Translation* (New York: Garland, 1993), ix.
8. Ibid. For a full discussion of the complicated evolution and transmission of this cycle, see E. Jane Burns, "Introduction," in *Introduction; The History of the Holy Grail; The Story of Merlin*, xv-xxxiii.

9. Macrae-Gibson, introduction to *Of Arthour and of Merlin,* 2.

10. Ibid, 3. This fragment is found in Paris, Bibliothèque nationale, 20047 (s. xiii ex). For more information about this fragment, see *Merlin: roman du XIIIe siècle,* ed. Alexandre Micha (Geneva: Librairie Droz, 1979), xiii.

11. See *Merlin: roman du XIIIe siècle,* xiv-xix for a complete list of manuscripts, including dates.

12. Fortiger is the name this text assigns to the figure known more commonly in English history as Vortigern.

13. *Arthour and Merlin nach der Auchinleck-Hs. Nebst zwei Beilagen,* ed. Eugen Kölbing (Leipzig: Altenglische Bibliothek, 1890), xviii; S. Moore, S. B. Meech, and H. Whitehall, *Middle English Dialect Characteristics and Dialect Boundaries: Preliminary Report,* Language and Literature, vol. xiii (Ann Arbor: University of Michigan Publications, 1935), 55.

14. There is also a transcript of the Auchinleck version by Walter Scott (Oxford, Bodleian Library, Douce 124). All information on the non-Auchinleck manuscripts of the poem is taken from Macrae-Gibson, introduction to *Of Arthour and of Merlin,* 40–44.

15. Newstead, "Arthurian Legends," 49; Jocelyn Price, "Prose *Merlin* (2)," in *New Arthurian Encyclopedia,* ed. Norris Lacy (New York: Garland, 1991), 373.

16. Price, "Prose *Merlin* (2)," 373.

17. *Merlin [English Prose],* ed. H. B. Wheatley, Early English Text Society, o. s., 10, 21, 36, 112 (Hertford: Stephen Austin, 1869–98), 3: ccxlix.

18. Newstead, "Arthurian Legends," 49.

19. Valerie M. Lagorio, "Henry Lovelich," in *New Arthurian Encyclopedia,* ed. Norris Lacy (New York: Garland, 1991), 283; Henry Lovelich the skinner, *Merlin,* ed. E. A. Kock, Early English Text Society, o. s., 185, e.s., 93, 112 (London: Humphrey Milford, 1904–32), 1: frontspiece.

20. Lagorio, "Henry Lovelich," 283.

21. Sklar, "Englishing," 55.

22. The later and shorter manuscript versions of the English poem share this chronicle-like opening and revision of the Old French source with Auchinleck. Sklar and Macrae-Gibson suggest that the chronicle-like opening mimics, and may have been influenced by, the structure of formative insular Arthurian texts such as Geoffrey of Monmouth's *Historia regum Britanniae* and Laȝamon's *Brut.* See Sklar, "Englishing," 56; Macrae-Gibson, introduction to *Of Arthour and of Merlin,* 23. Some other traces of this earlier insular tradition's influence can be found in the Auchinleck poem's excision of material about Mordred's incestuous parentage which is found in the French *Estoire.* As Macrae-Gibson points out, "The Mordred of Wace and Laȝamon is clearly legitimate; they expand Geoffrey of Monmouth's simple statement that he was Arthur's *nepos.*" Macrae-Gibson, introduction to *Of Arthour and of Merlin,* 8–9. Macrae-Gibson discusses the areas in which

insular texts and Wace, rather than the vulgate *Estoire,* may have influenced the composition of *Of Arthour and of Merlin* on pages 20–32 of the introduction to his edition.

23. *Lestoire de Merlin,* vol. 2 of *The Vulgate Version of the Arthurian Romances,* ed. H. Oskar Sommer (Washington: The Carnegie Institute of Washington, 1908–13).

24. "The Story of Merlin," trans. Rupert T. Pickens in *Introduction; The History of the Holy Grail; The Story of Merlin.*

25. See, for example, Auchinleck, line 1822 (page 135); Lincoln's Inn, line 1939 (page 134); and Percy, line 2068 (page 150). All references to *Of Arthour and of Merlin* are to the Auchinleck version contained in *Of Arthour and of Merlin,* ed. O. D. Macrae-Gibson, vol. 1, Early English Text Society, o. s., 268 (London: Oxford University Press, 1973). All references to this text will henceforth be indicated by reference to line numbers in Macrae-Gibson's edition, and these numbers will be listed in parentheses in the body of the text. Macrae-Gibson's edition also presents the other manuscript versions of *Of Arthour and of Merlin* on facing pages to the Auchinleck version. Citations of these other manuscript versions have been listed so as to identify the manuscript version, line numbers, and, if necessary for clarity, page numbers of lines quoted.

26. For references to "Sarzin" invaders, see *Merlin [English Prose],* ed. H. B. Wheatley, 49, 50, 54, 55, 94, 172, 174, 194, 209, 210, 307, 325, 327, 330, 333, 335, 336, 342, 351, 664. To see the comparatively more frequent use of the term "Saine" or "Saxon," see Wheatley's glossary.

27. I should point out that "Saracen" is an appellation that could mean unlocalized pagan in Middle English as early as 1250 according to the *Middle English Dictionary,* s. v. "Sarasin(e," meaning (b). There are, however, some problems with this definition given the choice of text as exemplar by the *MED* (see my note in the "Introduction"). The term is more commonly associated with Middle Eastern pagans (note the *MED* decision to list this association as part of meaning (a) for the term), and does reflect contact with the Arab world. See Norman Daniel, *Heroes and Saracens,* 8. Thus, the term "Sarasin(e" itself does connote some specificity even if that specificity remains unelaborated in certain Middle English texts.

28. As noted in the Introduction, I use the term "Britain" to refer to the entirety of the island that includes England, Scotland, Wales and Cornwall. If I wish to refer to the kingdom of the historical Britons, I use the term "Britannia." See the essays in *Uniting the Kingdom?* for very good discussions of "British" vs. "English" identities and histories, and of the imperialist slippage that in the eighteenth and nineteenth centuries led to the reduction of the term "British" to purely English histories, identities and kings. *Uniting the Kingdom?: The Making of British History,* ed. Alexander Grant and Keith J. Stringer (Routledge: London and New York, 1995).

29. *Lestoire del saint graal,* vol. 1 of *The Vulgate Version of the Arthurian Romances,* ed. H. Oskar Sommer (Washington: The Carnegie Institution of Washington, 1908–13).

30. H. Oskar Sommer, note opening *Le Livre d'Artus,* vol. 7 of *The Vulgate Version of the Arthurian Romances,* ed. H. Oskar Sommer (Washington: The Carnegie Institution of Washington, 1908–13).

31. Robert Mannyng of Brunne, *The Chronicle,* ed. Idelle Sullens (Binghamton: Center for Medieval and Early Renaissance Studies, State University of New York at Binghamton, 1996), Part 1: lines 6484–534.

32. Ibid, 1: 15271, 15290; 2: 3416–55.

33. Robert of Gloucester, *The Metrical Chronicle of Robert of Gloucester,* ed. William Aldis Wright, Rolls Series, no. 86, 2 vols. (London: Eyre and Spottiswoode, 1887), 1: lines 4522, 4692.

34. The *MED* does list *King Horn* (dated to c. 1300) as the earliest example of the use of the term "Saracen" to describe pagan invaders of England, especially Danes or Saxons. As Diane Speed has shown, however, no explicit lines in this text link the Saracens Horn fights with Denmark or Saxony, and there may be equally good reasons to read these Saracens as examples of Middle Eastern Saracens. In addition, *King Horn* is not an Arthurian text, thus *Of Arthour and of Merlin* is among the first Arthurian texts in English to describe Saxon invaders as Saracens. Speed, "The Saracens of *King Horn,*" 564–95.

35. It is impossible to discern what may have been the general case in England as an extensive amount of Anglo-Norman Arthurian material remains unpublished. There may very well be references to Saracen invaders of Arthur's realm in some versions of the extremely popular Anglo-Norman *Brut,* which is found in over one hundred manuscripts but has yet to be edited, although Julia Marvin is presently working on such an edition. Some manuscripts of Wace's *Roman de Brut* do occasionally identify the invaders invited into Britain by Mordred at the end of Arthur's reign as Saracens, but other manuscripts do not. For versions where the term "Saracen" is applied to these invaders, see Wace, *Le Roman de Brut par Wace publié d'après les manuscrits des bibliothèques de Paris,* ed. Le Roux de Lincy (Rouen: Edouard Frère, 1836), 2: 228. A recent edition of Wace based on London, British Library, Additional 45103, and Durham, Cathedral Library, C. iv. 27 (I), does not identify the same invaders as Saracens. See *Wace's Roman de Brut, A History of the British Text and Translation,* ed. and trans. Judith Weiss (Exeter: University of Exeter Press, 1999), 332.

36. The Saxons invaded Britain, along with other Germanic pagan tribes in the fifth and sixth centuries A.D. Irish raids on Britain also happened in the early Middle Ages (consider the story of St. Patrick's origins). The Vikings, some of whom sailed in from Denmark and some of whom had allies in, and links to, Ireland, raided Britain in the ninth and tenth centuries, and

established a significant presence there (consider the co-existence of the Danelaw region with the Anglo-Saxon kingdom of Wessex).

37. The chronological impossibility of this, since Arthur's purported historical reign pre-dated the foundation of Islam, is of course not mentioned.

38. The Saracens in *Otuel* evoke a historical Muslim presence in Europe in ways that Danish Saracens do not. From 711 onwards, Muslims constituted a significant cultural presence in Spain. One offshoot of this presence and the crusades it provoked was a literary tradition that Charlemagne fought Saracens in Spain. This tradition underlies a number of Matter of France texts, including *Otuel* and *Roland and Vernagu.*

39. Colbrond's African origins suggest he might be Saracen because, as we find out in *Reinbrun,* Arguus, the King of "Aufrik," is a Saracen who swears by Mahoun, has Saracens in his army, and hangs and draws all who believe in "godes lawe" (30.1–12).

40. According to Helaine Newstead, the earliest reference to Arthur is an oblique one in a Welsh elegy known as *The Gododdin* and dated to roughly 600 A.D. After that, one finds more detailed references to Arthur in the *Historia Brittonum* written in Latin c. 830 (pseudo-Nennius), which lists Arthur's victories against the Saxons and refers to local legends attached to his name in Wales. Around 995, the *Annales Cambriae* recount in Latin Arthur's victory at Badon and the battle of Camlann where Arthur and Mordred fell. A tenth-century Welsh poem, the *Spoils of Annwn,* narrates Arthur's disastrous expedition to the Celtic Otherworld of Annwn, and the Welsh prose romance *Culhwch and Olwen* (c. 1100) also tells of this tale as well as of Arthur's experiences as the leader of a group of personages with supernatural powers. In the first decade of the twelfth century, stone-carvers at Modena Cathedral depicted the abduction of Guinevere and identified the characters involved with carved names that represent transitional forms between the original Welsh words and those of the later French romances. Scholars believe that these carvings were probably based on a tale told by a French-speaking Breton. Around 1136, Geoffrey of Monmouth wrote in Latin prose his *Historia regum Britanniae,* the chronicle that was to become the base for most subsequent historical and romance narratives of Arthur. See Newstead, "Arthurian Legends," 38–39.

41. Given the mixed origins of English identity in various invasions and settlements of the early Middle Ages, I refer to it as a hybrid identity. For a definition of the terms "hybrid" and "hybridity" as I use them, see later portion of this chapter.

42. William of Malmesbury, *De gestis regum Anglorum,* ed. and trans. R. A. B. Mynors, completed by R. M. Thomson and M. Winterbottom, 2 vols. (Oxford: Clarendon Press, 1998–99).

43. The foundational text on this issue is J. S. P. Tatlock, *The Legendary History of Britain: Geoffrey of Monmouth's 'Historia regum Britanniae' and its Early*

Vernacular Versions (Berkeley: University of California Press, 1950). Other scholars have also discussed the matter of Arthur's ideological usefulness for Anglo-Normans. See Gordon H. Gerould, "King Arthur and Politics," *Speculum* 2 (1927): 33–51; Lee Patterson, *Negotiating the Past* (Madison: University of Wisconsin Press, 1987), 204–10; James Noble, "Patronage, Politics, and the Figure of Arthur in Geoffrey of Monmouth, Wace, and Laȝamon," *Arthurian Yearbook* 2 (1992): 159–78; Martin B. Schichtman and Laurie Finke, "Profiting from the Past: History as Symbolic Capital in the *Historia regum Britanniae*," *Arthurian Literature* 12 (1993): 1–35; Michelle Warren, *History on the Edge: Excalibur and the Borders of Britain, 1100–1300* (Minneapolis: University of Minnesota Press, 2000).

44. Tatlock, *Legendary History*, 308; Noble, "Patronage," 161–62; Schichtman and Finke, "Profiting from the Past," 15.

45. Roger Sherman Loomis, "Edward I, Arthurian Enthusiast," *Speculum* 28 (1953): 114–27.

46. Michael Prestwich, *Edward I*, rev. ed. (New Haven: Yale University Press, 1997), 120.

47. Mary Giffin, "Cadwalader, Arthur, and Brutus in the Wigmore Manuscript," *Speculum* 16 (1941): 109, 114; Michelle Warren, *History on the Edge*, 76.

48. W. A. Nitze, "The Exhumation of King Arthur at Glastonbury," *Speculum* 9 (1935): 355–61; Giffin, "Cadwalader," 109, 114, 119; J. S. P. Tatlock "Geoffrey and King Arthur in 'Normannicus Draco,'" *Modern Philology* 31 (1933): 1–18, 115–25.

49. Maurice Powicke, *King Henry III and the Lord Edward* (Oxford: Clarendon Press, 1947), 2: 724; Loomis, "Edward I, Arthurian Enthusiast," 114, 116; Harding, *England in the Thirteenth Century*, 181.

50. Prestwich, *Edward I*, 121, 492; Loomis, "Edward I, Arthurian Enthusiast," 121–22. Copies of the letter containing this citation were sent out to many contemporary chroniclers and dutifully included by them in their records. Prestwich, *Edward I*, 492.

51. See Sklar, "Englishing," 52–54 for a discussion of various ways in which this poem rewrites and re-casts the geographic focus of the French original from France to England.

52. For a discussion of similar elisions in the Arthurian material of Laȝamon and Robert of Gloucester, see Warren, *History on the Edge*, 89–112.

53. *Chronicle of the Third Crusade*, ed. and trans. Helen J. Nicholson, 254–55. The Latin reads: "Ibi rex Ricardus, singularis, ferus, Turcos insectatur, invadit, passim prosternit; cujus gladium non fuit qui ab eo tactus effugeret. Ipse enim, quacunque se ageret, viam undique late patentem vibrans gladium effecit. Qui cum infatigabiliter progrediendo continuatis gladii percussionibus nefandam gentem, velut quis falce messem metendo, contereret, cæteri morientium exemplo turbati, viam cedebant ampliorem . . . Con-

stanter cædendo gladiis malleant Christiani, expavescentes contabescunt Turci . . . Eximie quidem repellebatur illa gens inimica, ita quod infra duo milliaria non videretur nisi gens tantum fugitiva, quæ prius exstiterat tam pertinax, et fastu tumida, et ferocissima: sed auxiliante Deo, sic periit eorum arrogantia, qui nec etiam cessaverunt fugere." *Itinerarium Peregrinorum,* 270–72.

54. Tyerman, *England and the Crusades,* 4, 91, 165; Lloyd, *English Society and the Crusade,* 97–98. For a discussion of various clerical efforts to direct knightly violence towards crusading ends, see Kaeuper, *Chivalry and Violence,* 75. See also the purported words of Urban II in his eleventh-century sermon preaching the crusade. According to Fulcher of Chartres, Urban II said "Now will those who once were robbers become *Christi milites;* those who fought brothers and relatives will justly fight barbarians; those who once were mercenaries for a few farthings will obtain eternal reward." Similarly, Baldric of Dol reports Urban saying "If you wish to save your souls, either abandon the profession of arms or go boldly forth as *Christi milites* and hasten to the defence of the Eastern church." Carl Erdmann, *The Origin of the Idea of Crusade,* trans. Marshall W. Baldwin and Walter Goffart (Princeton: Princeton University Press, 1977), 339–40. Fulcher's Latin text reads, "Nunc fiant Christi milites, qui dudum exstiterunt raptores. Nunc jure contra barbaros pugnent, qui olim adversus fratres et consanguineos dimicabant. Nunc æterna præmia nanciscantur, qui dudum pro solidis paucis mercenarii fuerunt." Fulcher of Chartres, "Historia Iherosolymitana," in vol. 3 of *Recueil des historiens des croisades: historiens occidentaux* (Paris: Imprimerie impériale, 1866), 324. Baldric's Latin text reads, "Porro si vultis animabus vestris consuli, aut istiusmodi militiæ cingulum quantocius deponite, aut Christi milites audacter procedite, et ad defendendam Orientalem Ecclesiam velocius concurrite." Baldric of Dol, "Historia Jerosolimitana," in vol. 4 of *Recueil des historiens des croisades: historiens occidentaux* (Paris: Imprimerie impériale, 1879), 14.

55. For a description of the ways in which Henry III and Edward II sought to venerate in art the crusading deeds of Robert Curthose of Normandy, Richard I, and Edward I, see Lloyd, *English Society and the Crusade,* 198–200. See page 200 for a discussion of the aristocratic understanding of "combat with the infidel as an admirable means of winning prestige and honor for their line as well as themselves."

56. Ibid, 246.

57. Harding, *England in the Thirteenth Century,* 309–13.

58. John Gillingham, "Foundations of a Disunited Kingdom," 63.

59. Although the Germanic invasions of the fifth and sixth centuries also involved Danes, Danes are more usually associated with the later Viking invasions and the subsequent establishment of the Danelaw and of Danish kings such as Sweyn and Cnut in England.

60. Consider, for example, the establishment of the Danelaw in northeastern England and the linguistic influence of these Scandinavian invader-settlers on fundamental elements of the English language such as the adoption of "they" as the plural nominative pronoun in the later Middle Ages.

61. This is the text's name for the historical figure more commonly known as Hengist.

62. Bhabha, *Location of Culture,* 114.

63. Ibid, 116.

64. R. Howard Bloch, *Etymologies and Genealogies: A Literary Anthropology of the French Middle Ages* (Chicago: Chicago University Press, 1983); Burns, "Introduction," xxvii.

65. Consider Bede's *Ecclesiastical History,* for example, or the various narratives of St. Augustine of Canterbury in chronicles of English history like the Auchinleck *Liber regum Anglie.* Bede, *Bede's Ecclesiastical History of the English People,* ed. Bertram Colgrave and R. A. B. Mynors (1969; reprint, Oxford: Clarendon Press, 1991); "Two Manuscripts of the Middle English *Anonymous Riming Chronicle,*" ed. Carroll and Tuve, 115–54.

66. See Kristeva, *Strangers to Ourselves,* 169–92.

67. William of Malmesbury, *De gestis regum Anglorum;* Geoffrey of Monmouth, *Historia regum Britanniae of Geoffrey of Monmouth,* ed. A. Griscom (London: Longmans and Green, 1929).

68. Prestwich, *Edward I,* 122; Pierre de Langtoft, *Chronicle of Pierre de Langtoft in French Verse,* ed. Thomas Wright, Rolls Series, no. 47, 2 vols. (London: Longmans and Green, 1868), 2: 266, 326.

69. Michael Prestwich, *The Three Edwards: War and State in England 1272–1377* (London: Methuen, 1980), 2.

70. Ibid.

71. The poem's refusal to minimize such bloody chaos is often excoriated by scholars (see Wells, Newstead, Macrae-Gibson) but, as Macrae-Gibson points out, such a bloody and violent focus was evidently not so unappealing to medieval readers. See Wells, *A Manual,* 44; Newstead, "Arthurian Legends," 48; Macrae-Gibson, introduction to *Of Arthour and of Merlin,* 9.

72. Macrae-Gibson, introduction to *Of Arthour and of Merlin,* 18.

73. Ibid, 13.

74. *The Auchinleck Manuscript (facsimile),* folio 256v

75. See Sklar, "Englishing," 53–54, for a discussion of how the repeated references to London, and its appellation as "London," mark a distinct change from the Old French sources of this poem, and constitute further evidence of a determined effort to focus this poem explicitly on England.

76. Macrae-Gibson, introduction to *Of Arthour and of Merlin,* 68–71.

77. I refrain from identifying all these passages as "reverdi" because this term connotes spring explicitly, and some of the passages situate themselves in summer or, in the case mentioned below, fall. Nine of the ten, though,

could certainly be described as "reverdi" for their presentation of a vision of burgeoning life and growth.

78. The one exception is the passage at lines 4199–204:

In time of winter alange it is
Þe foules lesen her blis
Þe leues fallen of þe tre
Rein alangeþ þe cuntre
Maidens leseþ here hewe,
Ac euer hye louieþ þat be trewe.

Interestingly, this passage concludes the battle between Arthur and his untrue subject kings, and precedes the arrival of the Saracens whose presence gives rise to the continual battles of the remainder of the poem. The passage thus appears at the nadir of disunity in "Inglond," and that may explain the sense of decrepitude communicated in this portrait of fall.

79. It is partially the possibility that Arthur may not be of noble birth that leads the unruly kings to rebel against him at his coronation feast. Display like this puts to rest any queries of such a nature and affirms Arthur's right to be king.

80. Michel Foucault, *Discipline and Punish: The Birth of the Prison,* trans. Alan Sheridan (1977; reprint, New York: Vintage Books, 1995).

81. In other words, people's actions must suggest the surplus, the excess of the monarch. Foucault indicates this in *Discipline and Punish* when he traces out the ways in which the violent torture and dismemberment of traitors in public worked to manifest the excess violence and the excess power of the monarch. Scanlon addresses the same issue in his discussion of a king's need to have others speak for him so as to preserve the notion of the king as an entity beyond the realm of human language and speech, that is to say an entity possessed of so much power that he occupies another type of realm beyond the human. Larry Scanlon, "The King's Two Voices: Narrative and Power in Hoccleve's *Regement of Princes,*" in *Literary Practice and Social Change in Britain, 1380–1530,* ed. Lee Patterson (Berkeley: University of California Press, 1990), 221–26, 229–40.

82. Prestwich, *Edward I,* 202–4.

83. "And thus the glory of the Welsh was translated to the English, albeit unwillingly [on the Welsh part]." See "Annales monasterii de Waverleia, A.D. 1–1291," in *Annales monastici,* ed. H. R. Luard, Rolls Series, no. 36, 5 vols. (London: Longman, 1864–69), 2: 401. Translation mine.

84. Historically, one might consider the reigns of Edward I and III as periods when English magnates' military energies were redirected into international endeavors to aggrandize England, and away from the civil discord and political challenges to kingly power that marked the less outward-looking reigns of these kings' fathers (Henry III and Edward II, respectively).

85. *MED,* s. v. "child," meanings 5 and 6.

86. *Of Arthour and of Merlin* presents the Round Table as a creation of Merlin's during Uter Pendragon's reign.

87. Sarah Kay, *The Chansons de geste*; Peter Haidu, *The Subject of Violence: The Song of Roland and the Birth of the State* (Bloomington: Indiana University Press, 1993).

88. To readers who object that this poem represents an Arthurian romance, I would direct attention to my discussion of romance versus *chanson de geste* in Chapter One.

89. Sigmund Freud, *Totem and Taboo*, trans. James Strachey (New York: Norton, 1950).

90. For a summary of various scholars' thoughts on chivalry, violence, and profit as well as an articulation of his vision of this relationship, see Lee Patterson, *Chaucer and the Subject of History*, 170–79.

91. Kaeuper, *Chivalry and Violence*, 8–9, 22–29, 35, 79, 84, 132, 164, 176–85, 194–98, 205–6.

92. Ibid, 161–62.

93. See Baugh and Cable, *History of the English Language*, 142; Turville-Petre, *England the Nation*, 108–41; and Burrows, "The Auchinleck Manuscript: Contexts, Texts and Audience."

94. This comment refers to the fact that children in England at this time were generally schooled in French and Latin rather than English. It was not until after the Plague (1348–50) that English became a language of instruction in grammar schools, but there is evidence from c. 1250 on of a decreased native familiarity with French. Around this time a number of manuals for learning French circulated and, later in the century, monasteries and universities had to legislate students' use of French or Latin rather than English in daily conversations. Baugh and Cable, *History of the English Language*, 136, 146.

95. For discussions of the relationship between the English and French languages in England after the Norman Conquest, see the articles listed in the Introduction.

96. Turville-Petre, *England the Nation*, 8–22, 39–40, 71–76.

97. It should be noted that not only is Old English probably a product of the mixing of Frisians, Jutes, Angles, and Saxons within Britain, but that it also incorporates, in place names, elements of the ancient Briton language. Baugh and Cable, *History of the English Language*, 88.

98. See Baugh and Cable, *History of the English Language* for a study of the various Old English influences in Present Day English. One need only think, for example, of the verb forms "I run," I "ran" (i.e. of vocalic alteration as an indication of tense) to perceive the formative role of the Anglo-Saxon invasions and settlements on today's English language.

99. Baugh and Cable, *History of the English Language*, 90–103.

100. Ibid, 163–70.

101. Ibid, 165–66.

NOTES TO THE CONCLUSION

1. Pearsall and Cunningham, introduction to *The Auchinleck Manuscript (facsimile)*, viii.
2. Ibid.
3. It also includes some later fifteenth-century additions, but these do not concern us here as they are not contemporaneous with Auchinleck's compilation. According to Rosamund Allen, there is some debate about whether two or three different hands can be discerned in the *Legendary* in Laud 108, but most scholars agree in dating these hands to the late thirteenth or early fourteenth centuries. The romances are written in a different, but roughly contemporaneous hand, and occupy their own booklet. See Rosamund Allen, introduction to *King Horn: An Edition Based on Cambridge University Library MS Gg. 4.27 (2)*, ed. Rosamund Allen (New York: Garland, 1984), 8–9. There is some debate about when the romances and the *Legendary* were combined, and there is a possibility that they were bound together in the fifteenth century (Ibid, 12). This late conjoining would mean that the generic mixture of saints' lives and romances that heightens Laud's similarities to Auchinleck occurred long after Auchinleck's compilation. Some evidence supports the later binding date, while other evidence suggests that the romances and saints' lives were bound together earlier (Ibid, 10–11, 102–3). Because there is a solid possibility that the romances and saints' lives were bound together around the time of their writing, I mention Laud 108 here as a book that not only shares vernacularity and Saracens with Auchinleck, but also romances.
4. The two romances belong to the Matter of England, while the *Legendary* includes many English saints, among them Dunstan, Oswold, Alban, Wolston, and Thomas Beckett. See the entries for these saints in *The Early South-English Legendary of Lives of Saints: I. MS Laud, 108, in the Bodleian Library*, ed. Carl Horstmann, Early English Text Society, o.s., 87 (1887; reprint, Millwood, NY: Kraus Reprint Company, 1973).
5. This information is taken from M.B. Parkes and Richard Beadle's appendix to *The Poetical Works of Geoffrey Chaucer: A Facsimile of Cambridge University Library MS Gg. 4. 27*, ed. M.B. Parkes and Richard Beadle (Cambridge: D.S. Brewer, 1979–80) 3: 68. Rosamund Allen concurs with this dating. See her introduction to *King Horn*, 3 and 101, n. 5.
6. It should be noted that the two manuscripts' versions of the Horn story and of the Assumption differ significantly. The version of *King Horn* contained in Auchinleck is usually referred to by its unique title *Horn childe & maiden rimnild*. It differs from other stories of Horn and Rimenild, among other things, in that the invaders of Horn's homeland are not explicitly identified

as Saracens. The Auchinleck *Assumpcion* resembles that of Cambridge University Library Gg 4.27 (2) in that it narrates the assumption of the Virgin Mary, but the two versions of the tale are listed as separate entities by Pearsall and Cunningham in their introduction to *The Auchinleck Manuscript (facsimile),* xxi, and by D'Evelyn, "Saints' Legends," 451, 643.

7. The Cambridge *Floris and Blauncheflur* sets its events in "Babilloine" (line 129), while *King Horn* depicts explicitly Saracen characters (see lines 40, 613, 640, 1351 and 1409) who seem to represent Muslim invaders; they are described as "blake" (line 1351) and evince a clear interest in rewriting the religious faith of Horn's homeland of Suddenne (lines 61–68). All references to the Cambridge *Floris and Blauncheflur* are to line numbers in De Vries's parallel-text edition of the romance. All references to *King Horn* are to line numbers in *King Horn: An Edition Based on Cambridge University Library MS Gg. 4.27 (2),* ed. Rosamund Allen (New York: Garland, 1984). For the characterization of the Saracens of *King Horn* as representations of Muslims, see Diane Speed, "Saracens of *King Horn,*" 564–95.

8. As Rosamund Allen notes, Horn's land of origin, Suddenne, has been identified variously by scholars as part of south Devon, Denmark, Surrey, south Scotland and the Isle of Man. References to Westnesse and Estnesse merely compound the topographical confusion, especially when combined with compass directions such as "west" and "est." Indeed, the resemblance of place-names such as Suddenne and Westnesse to generic compass points works against their immediate recognition and identification as parts of England. See *King Horn,* ed. Rosamund Allen, 267, n. 147; 318, n. 966.

    King Horn's lack of clarity in this regard is perhaps most visible when compared with the topography of the Auchinleck *Horn Childe and Maiden Rimnild.* This text begins by describing Horn's father as one "of kinges tvo / . . . / Þat weld al Ingelond" (lines 7–9) and refers six more times to "Inglond." The Auchinleck text also includes many specific references to places north of the Humber, all of which serve to craft a full and detailed portrait of an English locale. Details of *Horn Childe* also lend themselves more readily to evocations of English history. *King Horn* nowhere prompts its latest editor to discuss the possibility of precise historical analogues to events in the text while *Horn Childe* (especially the section on Horn's father, Haþeolf) leads its latest editor to devote thirteen pages to a discussion of historical events in England that may well have influenced *Horn Childe.* All references to *Horn Childe and Maiden Rimnild* are to line numbers in *Horn Childe and Maiden Rimnild edited from the Auchinleck MS, National Library of Scotland, Advocates' MS 19.2.1,* ed. Maldwyn Mills (Heidelberg: Carl Winter, 1988). See Maldwyn Mills, introduction to *Horn Childe,* 40–41, 58–68, 73–76.

Appendix

ITEMS CONTAINED IN THE AUCHINLECK MANUSCRIPT

Titles are those used in the introduction to the facsimile of the manuscript by Derek Pearsall and I. C. Cunningham. Items' manuscript titles are provided where extant; postulated readings are signaled by square brackets. If the manuscript title has not survived, a text's conventional title is provided in round brackets. A number of items begin and/or end imperfect, but only exceptional fragmentation has been noted here. Please consult the listing of contents by Pearsall and Cunningham, pp. xix-xxiv, for detailed information about lacunae, foliation, gatherings, editions, etc.

1. (The Legend of Pope Gregory)
2. Þe King of Tars,
3. (The Life of Adam and Eve)
4. Seynt Mergrete
5. Seynt Katerine
6. (St Patrick's Purgatory and the Knight, Sir Owen; *also* Owayne Miles)
7. Þe desputisoun bitven þe bodi & þe soule
8. (The Harrowing of Hell)
9. (The Clerk Who Would See the Virgin; *also* A Miracle of the Virgin)
10. (Speculum Gy de Warewyke; *also* Epistola Alcuini)
11. (Amis and Amiloun)
12. (Life of St Mary Magdalene)
13. [Anna our] leuedis moder
14. [On þe seven dedly] sinnes
15. Þe pater noster vndo on englissch
16. (The Assumption of the Blessed Virgin)
17. (Sir Degare)
18. (The Seven Sages of Rome)
19. (Floris and Blauncheflur)

20. (The Sayings of the Four Philosophers)
21. (List of names of Norman barons, *i.e.* The Battle Abbey Roll)
22. (Guy of Warwick)
23. (Guy of Warwick, *stanzaic continuation*)
24. Reinbrun gij sone of warwike
25. Sir beves of hamtoun
26. Of arthour & of merlin
27. Þe wenche þat [lou]ed [a k]ing
28. [A penni]worþ [of wi]tte
29. Hou our leuedi saute was ferst founde
30. Lay le freine
31. (Roland and Vernagu)
32. Otuel a kniȝt
33. (Kyng Alisaunder), fragmentary (number of gatherings missing)
34. (The Thrush and the Nightingale)
35. (The Sayings of St Bernard; *also* The Three Foes of Mankind)
36. Dauid þe king
37. (Sir Tristem)
38. (Sir Orfeo)
39. (The Four Foes of Mankind)
40. Liber Regum Anglie (*also* The Anonymous Short English Metrical Chronicle)
41. Horn childe & maiden rimnild
42. (Alphabetical Praise of Women)
43. King Richard, fragmentary (number of gatherings missing)
44. Þe Simonie (*also* Poem on the Evil Times of Edward II)

Bibliography

Anonymous medieval texts are listed under their titles, not under their editors' names. Collections of secondary essays are also listed by title and not by editor's name.

MEDIEVAL TEXTS

Acta Aragonensia: Quellen zur deutschen, italienischen, französischen, spanischen, zur Kirchen- und Kultur-geschichte aus der diplomatischen Korresponden Jaymes II (1291–1327). Edited by H. Finke. Berlin: W. Rothschild, 1908.

Altenglische Legenden: Neue Folge. Edited by Carl Horstmann. Heilbronn: Heninger, 1881.

Ambroise. *L'Estoire de la guerre sainte, histoire en vers de la troisième croisade (1190–1192) par Ambroise*. Edited by Gaston Paris. Paris: Imprimerie nationale, 1897.

———. *The Crusade of Richard Lion-Heart (Estoire de la guerre sainte)*. Translated by Merton Hubert with notes by John LaMonte. New York: Columbia University Press, 1941.

Der anglonormannische Boeve de Haumtone. Edited by Albert Stimming. Bibliotheca Normannica, no. 7. Halle: Max Niemeyer, 1899.

"Annales monasterii de Waverleia, A.D. 1–1291." In *Annales monastici*, edited by H. R. Luard. 5 vols. Rolls Series, no. 36. London: Longman, 1864–69.

Annales Polonorum. Edited by Richard Röpell and William Arndt. MGH, Scriptores [in folio] 19. Hanover: Hahn, 1866.

Annales Sancti Rudberti Salisburgenses. Edited by G. H. Pertz. MGH, Scriptores [in folio] 9. Hanover: Hahn, 1851.

The Anonimalle Chronicle 1307 to 1334 From Brotherton Collection MS 29. Edited and translated by Wendy R. Childs and John Taylor. Yorkshire Archæological Society Record Series, vol. 147. Leeds: University of Leeds Printing Service for the Yorkshire Archæological Society, 1991.

Arthour and Merlin nach der Auchinleck-Hs. Nebst zwei Beilagen. Edited by Eugen
  Kölbing. Leipzig: Altenglische Bibliothek, 1890.
"Athelston." In *Four Romances of England: King Horn, Havelok the Dane, Bevis of
  Hampton, Athelston,* edited by Ronald B. Herzman, Graham Drake, and Eve
  Salisbury, 341–84. Kalamazoo: Western Michigan University Medieval Insti-
  tute Publications, 1999.
*The Auchinleck Manuscript: National Library of Scotland Advocates' MS 19. 2. 1 (fac-
  simile).* Introduced by Derek Pearsall and I. C. Cunningham. London: Scolar
  Press, 1977.
The Auchinleck Manuscript (Digital Version 1.1.). Edited by David Burnley and Ali-
  son Wiggins. National Library of Scotland: http://www.nls.uk/auchinleck/,
  July 5 2003. Accessed August-September, 2004.
Augustine. *Confessiones.* Edited and translated by Pierre de Labriole. Paris: Société
  d'édition "Les Belles lettres," 1956.
———. *Confessions.* Translated by Henry Chadwick. Oxford: Oxford University Press,
  1991.
Baldric of Dol. "Historia Jerosolimitana." In *Recueil des historiens des croisades: histo-
  riens occidentaux.* Vol. 4. Paris: Imprimerie impériale, 1879.
Bede. *Bede's Ecclesiastical History of the English People.* Edited by Bertram Colgrave
  and R. A. B. Mynors. 1969. Reprint, Oxford: Clarendon Press, 1991.
Bernard of Clairvaux. *On the Song of Songs.* Vol. 2. Translated by Kilian Walsh. Kala-
  mazoo, MI: Cistercian Publications, 1976.
———. *Sermones super cantica canticorum.* Vol. 1 of *S. Bernardi opera.* Edited by J.
  Leclercq, H. M. Rochais, and C. H. Talbot. Rome: Editiones Cistercienses,
  1957.
"Bevis of Hampton." In *Four Romances of England: King Horn, Havelok the Dane,
  Bevis of Hampton, Athelston,* edited by Ronald B. Herzman, Graham Drake,
  and Eve Salisbury, 187–340. Kalamazoo: Western Michigan University
  Medieval Institute Publications, 1999.
Calendar of Patent Rolls, 1350–54. London: HMSO, 1907.
Chronicle of Bury St Edmunds 1212–1301. Edited and translated by Antonia Grans-
  den. London: Nelson, 1964.
The Chronicle of Lanercost 1272–1346. Translated by Herbert Maxwell. Glasgow:
  James Maclehose and sons, 1913.
*Chronicle of the Third Crusade: a Translation of the Itinerarium peregrinorum et gesta
  regis Ricardi.* Translated by Helen Nicholson. Aldershot: Ashgate, 1997.
Chronicon de Lanercost. Edited by Joseph Stevenson. Edinburgh: Bannatyne Club,
  1839.
Clemence of Barking. *The Life of St. Catherine by Clemence of Barking.* Edited by
  William Macbain. Oxford: Anglo-Norman Text Society, 1964.
Disciplinary Decrees of the General Councils (Text, Translation, and Commentary).
  Edited and translated by H.J. Schroeder. London: B. Herder Book Company,
  1937.

The Early South-English Legendary of Lives of Saints: I. MS Laud, 108, in the Bodleian Library. Edited by Carl Horstmann, Early English Text Society, o.s., 87. 1887. Reprint, Millwood, NY: Kraus Reprints Company, 1973.

Lestoire de Merlin. Vol. 2 of *The Vulgate Version of the Arthurian Romances.* Edited by H. Oskar Sommer. Washington: The Carnegie Institute of Washington, 1908–13.

Lestoire del saint graal. Vol. 1 of *The Vulgate Version of the Arthurian Romances.* Edited by H. Oskar Sommer. Washington: The Carnegie Institution of Washington, 1908–13.

Firumbras and Otuel and Roland. Edited by Mary Isabelle O'Sullivan. Early English Text Society, o.s.,198. London: Oxford University Press, 1935.

Flores historiarum. Edited by H. R. Luard. 3 vols. Rolls Series, no. 95. London: Eyre and Spottiswoode, 1890.

Floris and Blauncheflur: A Middle English Romance. Edited by F. C. De Vries. Groningen: Druk, 1966.

Fontes rerum Germanicarum. Edited by J. F. Böhmer. Vol. 1. Stuttgart: J. G. Cotta, 1843.

Fulcher of Chartres. "Historia Iherosolymitana." In *Recueil des historiens des croisades: historiens occidentaux.* Vol. 3. Paris: Imprimerie impériale, 1866.

Geoffrey of Monmouth. *Historia regum Britanniae of Geoffrey of Monmouth.* Edited by A. Griscom. London: Longmans and Green, 1929.

Gerald of Wales. *Journey Through Wales and the Description of Wales.* Translated by Lewis Thorpe. New York: Penguin, 1978.

Gesta Francorum et aliorum Hierosolimitanorum / The Deeds of the Franks and the Other Pilgrims to Jerusalem. Edited and translated by Rosalind Hill. London: Thomas Nelson, 1962.

Gilles Le Muisit. *Chronique et annales.* Edited by H. Lemaître. Paris: La Société de l'histoire de France, 1806.

Giovanni Villani. *Istorie Fiorentine.* Edited by P. Massai. Vol. 4, bk. 8. Milan: Societá tipografica de' classici italiani, 1802–3.

Hali Meiðhad. Edited by Bella Millett. London: Oxford University Press, 1982.

Henry Lovelich the skinner. *Merlin.* Edited by E. A. Kock. Early English Text Society, o.s., 185, e.s. 93, 112. London: Humphrey Milford, 1904–32.

Horn Childe and Maiden Rimnild edited from the Auchinleck MS, National Library of Scotland, Advocates' MS 19.2.1. Edited by Maldwyn Mills. Heidelberg: Carl Winter, 1988.

Itinerarium peregrinorum et gesta regis Ricardi, auctore, ut videtur, Ricardo canonico Sanctae Trinitatis Londoniensis. Vol. 1 of *Chronicles and Memorials of the Reign of Richard I.* Edited by William Stubbs. Rolls Series, no. 38. London: Longman, 1864–65.

Jacobus de Voragine. *Legenda aurea: edizione critica.* Edited by Giovanni Paolo Maggioni. 2 vols. Florence: Sismel edizioni del Galluzzo, 1998.

——. *The Golden Legend: Readings on the Saints.* Translated by William Granger Ryan. Princeton: Princeton University Press, 1993.

Jaufré Rudel. "Lanquan li jorn son lonc en may." In *Les Chansons de Jaufré Rudel*, edited by Alfred Jeanroy. Classiques français du moyen age, no. 15. Paris: Honoré Champion, 1924.

Jean Froissart. *Chroniques de Jean Froissart*. Edited by Siméon Luce. Paris: Mme Ve Jules Renouard, 1873.

King Horn: An Edition Based on Cambridge University Library MS Gg. 4.27 (2). Edited by Rosamund Allen. New York: Garland, 1984.

The King of Tars: Edited from the Auchinleck MS Advocates 19. 2. 1. Edited by Judith Perryman. Heidelberg: Carl Winter Universitätsverlag, 1980.

"King Richard." In *The Auchinleck Manuscript (Digital Version 1.1.)*. Edited by David Burnley and Alison Wiggins. National Library of Scotland: http:/www.nls.uk/auchinleck/mss/richard.html, July 5 2003. Accessed September 3, 2004.

"Kleine Publicationen aus der Auchinleck-Hs: IX. The king of Tars." Edited by F. Krause. *Englische Studien* 11 (1888): 1–62.

Kyng Alisaunder. Edited by G. V. Smithers. 2 vols. Early English Text Society, o.s., 227, 327. London: Oxford University Press, 1952.

Liber Regum Anglie. See "Two Manuscripts of the Middle English *Anonymous Riming Chronicle*."

Le Livre d'Artus. Vol. 7 of *The Vulgate Version of the Arthurian Romances*. Edited by H. Oskar Sommer. Washington: The Carnegie Institution of Washington, 1908–13.

Matthew Paris. *Chronica majora*. Edited by H. R. Luard. 7 vols. Rolls Series, no. 57. London: Longman, 1872–83.

———. *Chronicles of Matthew Paris: Monastic Life in the Thirteenth Century*. Edited and translated by Richard Vaughan. New York: St Martin's Press, 1984.

Meidan Maregrete. In *Altenglische Legenden: Neue Folge*, edited by Carl Horstmann, 489–97. Heilbronn: Heninger, 1881.

Merlin [English Prose]. Edited by H. B. Wheatley. Early English Text Society, o.s., 10, 21, 36, 112. Hertford: Stephen Austin, 1869–98.

Merlin: roman du XIIIe siècle. Edited by Alexandre Micha. Geneva: Librairie Droz, 1979.

Of Arthour and of Merlin. Edited by O. D. Macrae-Gibson. 2 vols. Early English Text Society, o.s., 268, 279. London: Oxford University Press, 1973.

The Old English Lives of St Margaret. Edited by Mary Clayton and Hugh Magennis. Cambridge: Cambridge University Press, 1994.

On þe seven dedly sinnes. Edited by Eugen Kölbing. In *Englische Studien* 9 (1886): 43–6.

Orderic Vitalis. *The Ecclesiastical History of Orderic Vitalis*. Edited and translated by Marjorie Chibnall. 6 vols. Oxford: Clarendon Press, 1969–80.

Österreichische Chronik von den 95 Herrschaften. Edited by J. Seemüller. MGH, Scriptores [in folio] 6. Hanover: Hahn, 1909.

Otinel: chanson de geste. Edited by F. Guessard and H. Michelant. Paris, F. Vieweg, 1859.

Ottokar. *Österreichische Reimchronik*. Edited by J. Seemüller. MGH, Deutsche Chroniken 5. Hanover: Hahn, 1890–93.

"Otuel a Kniʒt." In *The Taill of Rauf Coilyear With the Fragments of Roland and Vernagu and Otuel,* edited by Sidney Herrtage, 65–124. Early English Text Society, e.s., 37. London: N. Trübner & Company, 1882.

Þe pater noster undo on englissche. Edited by Eugen Kölbing. In *Englische Studien* 9 (1886): 47–9.

Pierre de Langtoft. *Chronicle of Pierre de Langtoft in French Verse.* Edited by Thomas Wright. 2 vols. Rolls Series, no. 47. London: Longmans and Green, 1868.

Pierre Dubois. *De recuperatione terre sancte: traité de politique générale par Pierre Dubois.* Edited by Ch.-V. Langlois. Paris: Alphonse Picard, 1891.

———. *The Recovery of the Holy Land.* Translated by Walther I. Brandt. New York: Columbia University Press, 1956.

The Poetical Works of Geoffrey Chaucer: A Facsimile of Cambridge University Library MS Gg. 4. 27. Edited and Introduced by M.B. Parkes and Richard Beadle. 3 vols. Cambridge: D.S. Brewer, 1979–80.

La Prise d'Orange: chanson de geste de la fin du XIIe siècle. Edited by Claude Régnier. 7th ed. Paris: Klincksieck, 1986.

Raymond of Aguilers. "Historia Francorum qui ceperunt Iherusalem." In *Recueil des historiens des croisades: historiens occidentaux.* Vol. 3. Paris: Imprimerie impériale, 1866.

Recueil des chroniques de Flandre. Edited by J. J. de Smet. Collection chroniques belges inédites, vol. 2. Brussels: M. Hayez, 1841.

Rishanger. *Chronica et annales.* Edited by H. T. Riley. 2 vols. Rolls Series, no. 28. London: Longman, 1865.

Robert of Clari. *The Conquest of Constantinople.* Translated by Edgar Holmes McNeal. 1936. Reprint, Toronto: University of Toronto Press, 1996.

Robert of Gloucester. *The Metrical Chronicle of Robert of Gloucester.* Edited by William Aldis Wright. 2 vols. Rolls Series, no. 86. London: Eyre and Spottiswoode, 1887.

Robert Mannyng of Brunne. *The Chronicle.* Edited by Idelle Sullens. Binghamton: Center for Medieval and Early Renaissance Studies, State University of New York at Binghamton, 1996.

Roger of Wendover. *Flores historiarum.* Edited by H. R. Hewlett. 3 vols. Rolls Series, no. 84. London: Eyre and Spottiswoode, 1886–89.

———. *Roger of Wendover's Flowers of History Formerly Ascribed to Matthew Paris.* Translated by J. A. Giles. 2 vols. 1849. Reprint, Llanerch, Wales: Felinfach, 1993–96.

"Roland and Vernagu." In *The Taill of Rauf Coilyear With the Fragments of Roland and Vernagu and Otuel,* edited by Sidney Herrtage, 37–61. Early English Text Society, e.s., 37. London: N. Trübner & Company, 1882.

The Romance of Guy of Warwick: Edited from the Auchinleck MS. in the Advocates' Library, Edinburgh and from MS. 107 in Caius College, Cambridge. Edited by Julius Zupitza. Early English Text Society, e.s., 42, 49, 59. 1883, 1887, 1891. Reprint, Millwood, NY: Kraus Reprints Company, 1966.

The Romance of Sir Beves of Hamtoun. Edited by Eugen Kölbing. Early English Text Society, e.s., 46, 48, 65. 1885–86, 1894. Reprint, Millwood, NY: Kraus Reprints Company, 1978.

"Saint Katherine." In *Anchoritic Spirituality: Ancrene Wisse and Associated Works.* Translated by Anne Savage and Nicholas Watson, 259–87. New York: Paulist Press, 1991.

Saint Katherine of Alexandria: The Late Middle English Prose Legend in Southwell Minster MS 7. Edited by Saara Nevanlinna and Irma Taavitsainen. Cambridge: D. S. Brewer, 1993.

The Sege off Melayne, The Romance of Duke Rowland and Sir Otuell of Spayne, and a fragment of The Song of Roland. Edited by Sidney J. Herrtage. Early English Text Society, e.s., 35. 1880. Reprint, Millwood, NY: Kraus Reprint, 1981.

Seinte Katerine: Re-edited from MS Bodley 34 and the other Manuscripts. Edited by S. R. T. O. D'Ardenne and E. J. Dobson. Early English Text Society, s.s., 7. Oxford: Oxford University Press, 1981.

"Seinte Marherete." In *Medieval English Prose for Women: Selections from the Katherine Group and the Ancrene Wisse,* edited by Bella Millett and Jocelyn Wogan-Browne. Oxford: Clarendon Press, 1990.

Seinte Marherete þe Meiden ant Martyr. Edited by Frances M. Mack. Early English Text Society, o.s., 193. London: Oxford University Press, 1934.

"Seynt Katerine." In *Altenglische Legenden: Neue Folge,* edited by Carl Horstmann, 242–59. Heilbronn: Heninger, 1881.

"Seynt Mergrete." In *Altenglische Legenden: Neue Folge,* edited by Carl Horstmann, 225–35. Heilbronn: Heninger, 1881.

The Song of Roland, An Analytical Edition. Vol. 2, *II. Oxford Text and English Translation.* Edited and translated by Gerard J. Brault. University Park, Pennsylvania: Pennsylvania State University Press, 1978.

The South English Legendary: Edited from Corpus Christi College Cambridge MS. 145 and British Museum MS. Harley 2277 With Variants from Bodley MS. Ashmole 43 and British Museum MS. Cotton Julius D. IX. Edited by Charlotte D'Evelyn and Anna J. Mill. Early English Text Society, o.s., 235, 236, 244. London: Oxford University Press, 1967.

"The Story of Merlin." Translated by Rupert T. Pickens. In *Introduction; The History of the Holy Grail; The Story of Merlin.* Vol. 1 of *Lancelot-Grail: The Old French Arthurian Vulgate and Post-Vulgate in Translation.* New York: Garland, 1993.

Thomas Walsingham. *Historia Anglicana.* Edited by Henry T. Riley. 2 vols. Rolls Series, no. 28. London: Longman, 1863.

"Two Manuscripts of the Middle English *Anonymous Riming Chronicle.*" Edited by Marion Crane Carroll and Rosemond Tuve. In *PMLA* 46 (1931): 115–54.

Virgin Lives and Holy Deaths: Two Exemplary Biographies for Anglo-Norman Women. Translated by Jocelyn Wogan-Browne and Glyn S. Burgess. London: Everyman, 1996.

Vita et passio Sancti Thomae Cantuariensis archiepiscopi et martyris. In *Patrologiae cursus completus series Latina,* edited by J. Migne. 221 vols. Paris: Frères Garnieri, 1844-. 190: 346–49.

Wace. *Le Roman de Brut par Wace publié d'après les manuscrits des bibliothèques de Paris.* Edited by Le Roux de Lincy. Rouen: Edouard Frère, 1836.

——. *Wace's Roman de Brut, A History of the British Text and Translation.* Edited and translated by Judith Weiss. Exeter: University of Exeter Press, 1999.

William, Count of Orange: Four Old French Epics. Edited by Glanville Price. Translated by Glanville Price, Lynette Muir, and David Hoggan. London: Dent, 1975.

William of Malmesbury. *De gestis regum Anglorum.* Edited by William Stubbs. 2 vols. Rolls Series, no. 90. London: Eyre and Spottiswoode, 1889.

——. *De gestis regum Anglorum.* Edited and translated by R. A. B. Mynors. Completed by R. M. Thomson and M. Winterbottom. 2 vols. Oxford: Clarendon Press, 1998–99.

Wolfram von Eschenbach. *Parzival.* Translated by A. T. Hatto. New York: Penguin, 1980.

SECONDARY TEXTS

Allmand, Christopher *The Hundred Years War: England and France at War c. 1300-c. 1450.* Cambridge: Cambridge University Press, 1989.

Althusser, Louis. "Ideology and Ideological State Apparatuses." In *Lenin and Philosophy and Other Essays,* translated by Ben Brewster, 121–73. New York: New Left Books, 1971.

Anderson, Benedict. *Imagined Communities: Reflections on the Origins and Spread of Nationalism.* Rev. ed. London: Verso, 1991.

Balfour, Mark. "Moses and the Princess: Josephus' *Antiquitates Judaicae* and the *Chansons de Geste.*" *Medium Ævum* 64 (1995): 1–16.

Barnie, John. *War in Medieval English Society: Social Values in the Hundred Years War, 1337–1399.* Ithaca: Cornell University Press, 1974.

Barrow, Geoffrey. "Frontier and Settlement: Which Influenced Which? England and Scotland, 1100–1300." In *Medieval Frontier Societies,* edited by Robert Bartlett and Angus MacKay, 3–22. Oxford: Clarendon Press, 1989.

Bartlett, Robert. *The Making of Europe: Conquest, Colonization and Cultural Change 950–1350.* Princeton: Princeton University Press, 1993.

——. "Medieval and Modern Concepts of Race and Ethnicity." *Journal of Medieval and Early Modern Studies* 31, no. 1 (2001): 39–56.

Baugh, Albert C., and Thomas Cable. *A History of the English Language.* 4th ed. Englewood Cliffs, NJ: Prentice-Hall, Inc., 1993.

Beer, Frances. *Women and Mystical Experience in the Middle Ages.* Cambridge: D. S. Brewer, 1992.

Bhabha, Homi. *The Location of Culture.* London: Routledge, 1994.

Bloch, R. Howard. *Etymologies and Genealogies: A Literary Anthropology of the French Middle Ages.* Chicago: Chicago University Press, 1983.

Brundage, James. *Law, Sex, and Christian Society in Medieval Europe.* Chicago: University of Chicago Press, 1987.

Bugge, John. *Virginitas: An Essay in the History of a Medieval Ideal.* The Hague: Nijhoff, 1975.

Bumke, Joachim. *The Concept of Knighthood in the Middle Ages.* Translated by W. T. H. Jackson and Erika Jackson. New York: AMS Press, Incorporated, 1982.

Burns, E. Jane. *Courtly Love Undressed: Reading Through Clothes in Medieval French Culture.* Philadelphia: University of Pennsylvania Press, 2002.

——. "Introduction." In *Introduction; The History of the Holy Grail; The Story of Merlin.* Vol. 1 of *Lancelot-Grail: The Old French Arthurian Vulgate and Post-Vulgate in Translation,* xv-xxxiii. New York: Garland, 1993).

Burrows, Jean Harpham. "The Auchinleck Manuscript: Contexts, Texts and Audience." Ph. D. diss., University of Washington, 1988.

Butler, Judith. *Gender Trouble.* New York: Routledge, 1990.

Bynum, Caroline Walker. *Jesus as Mother: Studies in the Spirituality of the High Middle Ages.* Berkeley: University of California Press, 1982.

——. *The Resurrection of the Body in Western Christianity 200–1336.* New York: Columbia University Press, 1995.

Cadden, Joan. *Meanings of Sex Difference in the Middle Ages: Medicine, Science, and Culture.* Cambridge: Cambridge University Press, 1993.

Calkin, Siobhain Bly. "The Anxieties of Encounter and Exchange: Saracens and Christian Heroism in *Sir Beves of Hamtoun,*" *Florilegium* 21 (2004): 135–58

——. "Marking Religion on the Body: Saracens, Categorization, and *The King of Tars,*" *Journal of English and Germanic Philology* 104 (2005): 219–38.

——. "Violence, Saracens, and English Identity in *Of Arthour and of Merlin,*" *Arthuriana* 14, no. 2 (2004): 17–36.

Cambridge History of the English Language. Vol. 2, *1066–1476.* Edited by Norman Blake. Cambridge: Cambridge University Press, 1992.

Camille, Michael. "Labouring for the Lord: The Ploughman and the Social Order in the Luttrell Psalter." *Art History* 10 (1987): 423–54.

——. *The Gothic Idol: Ideology and Image-Making in Medieval Art.* Cambridge: Cambridge University Press, 1989.

Chaucer's Cultural Geography. Edited by Kathryn Lynch. New York: Routledge, 2002.

Clifton, Nicole. "*Of Arthour and of Merlin* as Medieval Children's Literature." *Arthuriana* 13, no. 2 (2003): 9–22.

Cohen, Jeffrey Jerome. *Of Giants: Sex, Monsters and the Middle Ages.* Minneapolis: University of Minnesota Press, 1999.

——. "On Saracen Enjoyment: Some Fantasies of Race in Late Medieval France and England." *Journal of Medieval and Early Modern Studies* 31, no. 1 (2001): 113–46.

Comfort, William Wistar. "The Literary Role of Saracens in French Epic." *PMLA* 55 (1940): 628–59.

Concepts of National Identity in the Middle Ages. Edited by Simon Forde, Lesley Johnson, and Alan V. Murray. Leeds Texts and Monographs, n. s., 14. Leeds: Leeds Studies in English, 1995.

Coss, Peter. *The Knight in Medieval England 1000–1400.* Conshohocken, PA: Combined Books, 1993.

Crane, Susan. *Insular Romance: Politics, Faith and Culture in Anglo-Norman and Middle English Literature.* Berkeley: University of California Press, 1986.

———. *The Performance of Self: Ritual, Clothing, and Identity During the Hundred Years War.* Philadelphia: University of Pennsylvania Press, 2002.

Daniel, Norman. *Heroes and Saracens: An Interpretation of the "chansons de geste."* Edinburgh: University of Edinburgh Press, 1984.

———. *Islam and the West: The Making of an Image.* Rev. ed. Oxford: Oneworld Publications Ltd, 1993.

Davies, Rees. "Frontier Arrangements in Fragmented Societies: Ireland and Wales." In *Medieval Frontier Societies,* edited by Robert Bartlett and Angus MacKay, 77–100. Oxford: Clarendon Press, 1989.

de Combarieu, Micheline. "Un personnage épique: la jeune musulmane." In *Mélanges de langue et littérature françaises du moyen âge offerts à Pierre Jonin. Senefiance* 7 (1979): 183–96.

D'Evelyn, Charlotte. "Saints' Legends." In *A Manual of the Writings in Middle English 1050–1500.* Vol. 2, edited by J. Burke Severs. (Hamden: Connecticut Academy of Arts and Sciences, 1970).

de Mandach, André. *Naissance et développement de la chanson de geste en Europe.* Vol. 1, *La Geste de Charlemagne et de Roland.* Geneva: Droz, 1961.

DeWeever, Jacqueline. *Sheba's Daughters: Whitening and Demonizing the Saracen Woman in Medieval French Epic.* New York: Garland, 1998.

Dean, Ruth J., and Maureen Boulton. *Anglo-Norman Literature: A Guide to Texts and Manuscripts.* London: Anglo-Norman Texts Society, 1999.

Delehaye, Hippolyte. *Legends of the Saints: An Introduction to Hagiography.* Translated by V.M. Crawford. Notre Dame: University of Notre Dame 1961.

Doyle, A. I., and M. B. Parkes. "The Production of Copies of the *Canterbury Tales* and the *Confessio Amantis* in the Early Fifteenth Century." In *Medieval Scribes, Manuscripts and Libraries: Essays Presented to N. R. Ker,* edited by M. B. Parkes and Andrew G. Watson, 163–210. London: Scolar Press, 1978.

Duggan, Joseph J. "Medieval Epic as Popular Historiography: Appropriation of Historical Knowledge in the Vernacular Epic." In *La Littérature historiographique des origines à 1500,* edited by Hans Ulrich Gumbrecht, Ursula Link-Heer, and Peter-Michael Spangenberg, 285–311. Vol. 11, tome 1 of *Grundriss der romanischen literaturen des mittelalters.* Heidelberg: C. Winter, 1986.

Duggan, Lawrence G. "'For Force is Not of God'? Compulsion and Conversion from Yahweh to Charlemagne." In *Varieties of Religious Conversion in the*

Middle Ages, edited by James Muldoon, 50–58. Gainsville: University Press of Florida, 1997.

Dunn, Charles W. "Romances Derived from English Legends." In *A Manual of the Writings in Middle English 1050–1500.* Vol. 1, *Romances,* edited by J. Burke Severs, 17–37. New Haven: The Connecticut Academy of Arts and Sciences, 1967.

Elukin, Jonathan. "From Jew to Christian?: Conversion and Immutability in Medieval Europe." In *Varieties of Religious Conversion in the Middle Ages,* edited by James Muldoon, 170–88. Gainsville: University Press of Florida, 1997.

Erdmann, Carl. *The Origin of the Idea of Crusade.* Translated by Marshall W. Baldwin and Walter Goffart. Princeton: Princeton University Press, 1977.

Fawtier, Robert. *La Chanson de Roland: étude historique.* Paris: E. de Boccard, 1933.

Fellows, Jennifer. "*Sir Beves of Hamtoun:* Study and Edition." Ph. D. diss., Cambridge University, 1979.

Foucault, Michel. *Discipline and Punish: The Birth of the Prison.* Translated by Alan Sheridan. 1977. Reprint, New York: Vintage Books, 1995.

Fradenburg, Louise (Aranye). *City, Marriage, Tournament: Arts of Rule in Late Medieval Scotland.* Madison: University of Wisconsin Press, 1991.

Freud, Sigmund. *Totem and Taboo.* Translated by James Strachey. New York: Norton, 1950.

Gates Jr., Henry Louis. "Introduction: Writing 'Race' and the Difference It Makes." In *"Race," Writing, and Difference,* edited by Henry Louis Gates, Jr., 1–20. Chicago: University of Chicago Press, 1986.

Geary, Patrick J. *Living With the Dead in the Middle Ages.* Ithaca: Cornell University Press, 1994.

Geist, Robert J. "On the Genesis of The King of Tars." *Journal of English and Germanic Philology* 42 (1943): 260–68.

Gerould, Gordon Hall. "King Arthur and Politics." *Speculum* 2 (1927): 33–52.

Giffin, Mary. "Cadwalader, Arthur, and Brutus in the Wigmore Manuscript." *Speculum* 16 (1941): 109–21.

Gillingham, John. "Foundations of a Disunited Kingdom." In *Uniting the Kingdom?: The Making of British History,* edited by Alexander Grant and Keith J. Stringer, 48–64. Routledge: London and New York, 1995.

———. "Henry of Huntingdon and the Twelfth-Century Revival of the English Nation." In *Concepts of National Identity in the Middle Ages,* edited by Simon Forde, Lesley Johnson, and Alan V. Murray, 75–101. Leeds Texts and Monographs, n. s., 14. Leeds: Leeds Studies in English, 1995.

Girard, René. *Violence and the Sacred.* Translated by Patrick Gregory. Baltimore: Johns Hopkins University Press, 1977.

Gist, Margaret Adlum. *Love and War in the Middle English Romances.* Philadelphia: University of Pennsylvania Press, 1947.

Good, Jonathan. "*Argent a Cross Gules:* The Origins and English Use of the Arms of St George." Paper presented at the 38th International Congress of Medieval Studies at Kalamazoo, Michigan, May 9 2003.

Goodman, Jennifer R. *Chivalry and Exploration 1298–1630.* Woodbridge, Suffolk: Boydell Press, 1998.

Guddat-Figge, Gisela. *Catalogue of Manuscripts Containing Middle English Romances.* Munich: Wilhelm Fink Verlag, 1976.

Hagiographies: histoire internationale de la littérature hagiographique latine et vernaculaire en occident des origines à 1550. Vol. 1, edited by Guy Philippart. Turnhout: Brepols, 1994.

Hahn, Thomas. "The Difference the Middle Ages Makes: Color and Race before the Modern World." *Journal of Medieval and Early Modern Studies* 31, no. 1 (2001): 1–37.

Haidu, Peter. *The Subject of Violence: The Song of Roland and the Birth of the State.* Bloomington: Indiana University Press, 1993.

Hamilton, Bernard. *The Medieval Inquisition.* New York: Holmes and Meier Publishers, Incorporated, 1981.

Hanna, Ralph. "Reconsidering the Auchinleck Manuscript." In *New Directions in Later Medieval Manuscript Studies (Essays from the 1998 Harvard Conference),* edited by Derek Pearsall, 91–102. York: University of York Medieval Publications, 2000.

Harding, Alan. *England in the Thirteenth Century.* Cambridge: Cambridge University Press, 1993.

Hardwick, Charles, and H. R. Luard. *A Catalogue of the Manuscripts Preserved in the Library of the University of Cambridge.* Vol. 2. Cambridge: Cambridge University Press, 1857.

Heffernan, Carol Falvo. *The Orient in Chaucer and Medieval Romance.* Cambridge: D. S. Brewer, 2003.

Heffernan, Thomas. *Sacred Biography: Saints and Their Biographers in the Middle Ages.* New York: Oxford University Press, 1988.

Heng, Geraldine. "Cannibalism, the First Crusade, and the Genesis of Medieval Romance." *Differences* 10 (1998): 98–174.

———. *Empire of Magic: Medieval Romance and the Politics of Cultural Fantasy.* New York: Columbia University Press, 2003.

Holsinger, Bruce. "The Color of Salvation: Desire, Death, and the Second Crusade in Bernard of Clairvaux's Sermon on the Song of Songs." In *The Tongue of the Fathers: Gender and Ideology in Twelfth-Century Latin,* edited by David Townsend and Andrew Taylor, 156–86. Philadelphia: University of Pennsylvania Press, 1998.

Hornstein, Lillian Herlands. "A Study of Historical and Folklore Sources of *The King of Tars.*" Ph. D. diss., New York University, 1940.

———. "A Folklore Theme in the *King of Tars.*" *Philological Quarterly* 20 (1941): 82–87.

———. "The Historical Background of *The King of Tars.*" *Speculum* 16 (1941): 404–14.

———. "New Analogues to the 'King of Tars,'" *Modern Language Review* 36 (1941): 433–42.

Housley, Norman. "Crusades Against Christians: Their Origins and Early Development." In *Crusade and Settlement,* edited by Peter Edbury, 17–36. Cardiff:
University College Cardiff Press, 1985.

Huneycutt, Lois. "Intercession and the High-Medieval Queen: The Esther Topos."
In *Power of the Weak: Studies on Medieval Women,* edited by Jennifer Carpenter
and Sally-Beth MacLean, 126–46. Urbana: University of Illinois Press, 1995.

Imagining a Medieval English Nation. Edited by Kathy Lavezzo. Minneapolis: University of Minnesota Press, 2004.

Jacquart, Danielle, and Claude Thomasset. *Sexuality and Medicine in the Middle Ages.*
Translated by Matthew Adamson. Princeton: Princeton University Press, 1988.

James, Montague Rhodes. *A Descriptive Catalogue of the Manuscripts in the Library of
Gonville and Caius College.* Cambridge: Cambridge University Press, 1907.

Jauss, Hans Robert. *Toward an Aesthetic of Reception.* Translated by Timothy Bahti.
Minneapolis: University of Minnesota Press, 1982.

Johnson, Lesley. "Imagining Communities: Medieval and Modern." In *Concepts of
National Identity in the Middle Ages,* edited by Simon Forde, Lesley Johnson,
and Alan V. Murray, 1–20. Leeds Texts and Monographs, n. s., 14. Leeds:
Leeds Studies in English, 1995.

Johnstone, Hilda. "Isabella, the She-Wolf of France." *History* 21 (1936): 208–18.

Jones, C. Meredith. "The Conventional Saracens of the Songs of Geste." *Speculum*
17 (1942): 201–25.

Jordan, William Chester. "Why 'Race'?" *Journal of Medieval and Early Modern Studies* 31, no. 1 (2001): 165–74.

Kaeuper, Richard. *Chivalry and Violence in Medieval Europe.* Oxford: Oxford University Press, 1999.

Kay, Sarah. *The Chansons de geste in the Age of Romance: Political Fictions.* Oxford:
Clarendon Press, 1995.

Kedar, Benjamin Z. "Multidirectional Conversion in the Frankish Levant." In *Varieties of Religious Conversion in the Middle Ages,* edited by James Muldoon.
Gainsville: University Press of Florida, 1997.

Keeney, Barnaby C. "Military Service and the Development of Nationalism in England, 1272–1327." *Speculum* 22 (1947): 534–49.

Kelly, Kathleen Coyne. "The Bartering of Blaunchflur in the Middle English *Floris
and Blauncheflur.*" *Studies in Philology* 91 (1994): 101–10.

Ker, N. R. *Medieval Manuscripts in British Libraries.* Vol. 3. Oxford: Clarendon
Press, 1983.

Kinoshita, Sharon. "The Politics of Courtly Love: *La Prise d'Orange* and the Conversion of the Saracen Queen." *Romanic Review* 86 (1995): 265–87.

———. "'Pagans are wrong and Christians are right': Alterity, Gender, and Nation in
the Chanson de Roland." *Journal of Medieval and Early Modern Studies* 31, no.
1 (2001): 79–112

Knudson, Charles A. " Le thème de la princesse sarrasine dans *La Prise d'Orange.*"
Romance Philology 22 (1969): 449–62.

Krahl, E. *Untersuchungen über vier Versionen der mittelenglische Margaretenlegende.* Berlin, 1889.

Kristeva, Julia. *Powers of Horror: An Essay on Abjection.* Translated by Leon S. Roudiez. New York: Columbia University Press, 1982.

———. *Strangers to Ourselves.* Translated by Leon S. Roudiez. New York: Columbia University Press, 1991.

Kruger, Steven. "Conversion and Medieval Sexual, Religious, and Racial Categories." In *Constructing Medieval Sexuality,* edited by Karma Lochrie, Peggy McCracken, and James A. Schultz, 158–79. Minneapolis: University of Minnesota Press, 1997.

Lacan, Jacques. "On a question preliminary to any possible treatment of psychosis." In *Ecrits: A Selection,* translated by Alan Sheridan, 179–225. New York: W. W. Norton and Company, 1977

———. *The Seminar of Jacques Lacan: Book II—The Ego in Freud's Theory and in the Technique of Psychoanalysis, 1954–1955.* Edited by Jacques-Alain Miller and translated by Sylvana Tomaselli. New York: W. W. Norton and Company, 1991.

Lacy, Norris. Preface to *Introduction; The History of the Holy Grail; The Story of Merlin.* Vol. 1 of *Lancelot-Grail: The Old French Arthurian Vulgate and Post-Vulgate in Translation.* New York: Garland, 1993.

Lagorio, Valerie M. "Henry Lovelich." In *New Arthurian Encyclopedia,* edited by Norris Lacy, 283–84. New York: Garland, 1991.

Lambert, Sarah. "Heroines and Saracens." *Medieval World* 1 (1991): 3–9.

Lampert, Lisa. *Gender and Jewish Difference from Paul to Shakespeare.* Philadelphia: University of Pennsylvania Press, 2004.

Leff, Gordon. *Heresy in the Later Middle Ages: The Relation of Heterodoxy to Dissent, c. 1250-c. 1450.* Manchester: Manchester University Press, 1967.

Le Gentil, Pierre. *The Chanson de Roland.* Translated by Francis F. Beer. Cambridge: Harvard University Press, 1969.

Leopold, Antony. *How to Recover the Holy Land: The Crusade Proposals of the Late Thirteenth and Fourteenth Centuries.* Aldershot: Ashgate, 2000.

Lerer, Seth. *Chaucer and His Readers: Imagining the Author in Late Medieval England.* Princeton: Princeton University Press, 1993.

Levinas, Emmanuel. "Time and the Other." In *The Levinas Reader,* edited by Sean Hand, 37–58. Oxford: Blackwell, 1989.

———. *Totality and Infinity.* Translated by Alphonso Lingis. Pittsburgh: Duquesne University Press, 1969.

Lewis, Katherine. *The Cult of St Katherine of Alexandria in Late Medieval England.* Woodbridge, Suffolk: Boydell Press, 2000.

Lloyd, Simon. *English Society and the Crusade, 1216–1307.* Oxford: Clarendon Press, 1988.

Lodge, R. A. "Language Attitudes and Linguistic Norms in France and England in the Thirteenth Century." In *Thirteenth Century England IV: Proceedings of the*

Newcastle Upon Tyne Conference 1991, edited by P. R. Coss and S. D. Lloyd, 73–84.Woodbridge, Suffolk: Boydell, 1992.

Loomis, Laura Hibbard. "Chaucer and the Auchinleck Manuscript: *Thopas* and *Guy of Warwick.*" In *Adventures in the Middle Ages: A Memorial Collection of Essays and Studies,* 131–49. New York: Burt Franklin, 1962. First published in *Essays and Studies in Honor of Carleton Brown,* 111–28. New York: New York University Press, 1940.

———. "Chaucer and the Breton Lays of the Auchinleck Manuscript." In *Adventures in the Middle Ages: A Memorial Collection of Essays and Studies,* 111–30. New York: Burt Franklin, 1962. First published in *Studies in Philology* 38 (1941): 14–33.

———. "The Auchinleck Manuscript and a Possible London Bookshop of 1330–1340." In *Adventures in the Middle Ages: A Memorial Collection of Essays and Studies,* 150–87. New York: Burt Franklin, 1962. First published in *PMLA* 57 (1942): 595–627.

———. "The Auchinleck *Roland and Vernagu* and the Short *Chronicle.*" *Modern Language Notes* 60 (1945): 94–97.

Loomis, Roger Sherman. "Edward I, Arthurian Enthusiast." *Speculum* 28 (1953): 114–27.

Lot, Ferdinand. "Etudes sur les légendes épiques françaises, V: *la Chanson de Roland.* A propos d'un livre récent." *Romania* 54 (1928): 357–80.

A Manual of the Writings in Middle English 1050–1500. Vol. 1, *Romances,* edited by J. Burke Severs. New Haven: The Connecticut Academy of Arts and Sciences, 1967.

Mason, Emma. "Legends of the Beauchamps' Ancestors: The Use of Baronial Propaganda in Medieval England." *Journal of Medieval History* 10 (1984): 25–40.

McClintock, Anne. *Imperial Leather: Race, Gender, and Sexuality in the Colonial Conquest.* New York: Routledge, 1995.

McCracken, Peggy. *The Romance of Adultery: Queenship and Sexual Transgression in Old French Literature.* Philadelphia: University of Pennsylvania Press, 1998.

McKisack, May. *The Fourteenth Century: 1307–1399.* 1959. Reprint, Oxford: Oxford University Press, 1991.

Mehl, Dieter. *The Middle English Romances of the Thirteenth and Fourteenth Centuries.* London: Routledge & Kegan Paul, 1968.

Metlitzki, Dorothee. *The Matter of Araby in Medieval England.* New Haven: Yale University Press, 1977.

Millett, Bella. "The Audience of the Saints' Lives of the Katherine Group." *Reading Medieval Studies* 16 (1990): 127–56.

———. *Annotated Bibliographies of Old and Middle English Literature: II. Ancrene Wisse, the Katherine Group, and the Wooing Group.* Cambridge: D. S. Brewer, 1996.

Moghadan, Valentine M. "Revolution, Islam and Women: Sexual Politics in Iran and Afghanistan." In *Nationalisms and Sexualities,* edited by Andrew Parker, Mary Russo, Doris Sommer, and Patricia Yaeger. New York: Routledge, 1992.

Moore, R. I. *The Formation of a Persecuting Society: Power and Deviance in Western Europe, 950–1250.* New York: Blackwell, 1987.

Moore, S., S. B. Meech, and H. Whitehall. *Middle English Dialect Characteristics and Dialect Boundaries: Preliminary Report.* Language and Literature, vol. 13. Ann Arbor: University of Michigan Publications, 1935.

Mordkoff, Judith. "The Making of the Auchinleck Manuscript: The Scribes at Work." Ph. D. diss., University of Connecticut, 1981.

Morrison, Karl F. *Understanding Conversion.* Charlottesville: University of Virginia Press, 1992.

Murray, Jacqueline. "Thinking About Gender: The Diversity of Medieval Perspectives." In *Power of the Weak: Studies on Medieval Women,* edited by Jennifer Carpenter and Sally-Beth MacLean, 147–77. Urbana: University of Illinois Press, 1995.

Nationalisms and Sexualities. Edited and introduced by Andrew Parker, Mary Russo, Doris Sommer, and Patricia Yaeger. New York: Routledge, 1992.

Newstead, Helaine. "Arthurian Legends." In *A Manual of the Writings in Middle English 1050–1500.* Vol. 1, *Romances,* edited by J. Burke Severs, 38–77. New Haven: Connecticut Academy of Arts and Sciences, 1967.

Nirenberg, David. *Communities of Violence: Persecution of Minorities in the Middle Ages.* Princeton: Princeton University Press, 1998.

Nitze, W. A. "The Exhumation of King Arthur at Glastonbury." *Speculum* 9 (1935): 355–61.

Noble, James. "Patronage, Politics, and the Figure of Arthur in Geoffrey of Monmouth, Wace, and Laȝamon." *Arthurian Yearbook* 2 (1992): 159–78.

Palgrave, F. *Parliamentary Writs and Writs of Military Summons.* Vol. 2 London: Record Commission, 1827–34.

Parsons, John Carmi. "The Queen's Intercession in Thirteenth-Century England." In *Power of the Weak: Studies on Medieval Women,* edited by Jennifer Carpenter and Sally-Beth MacLean, 147–77. Urbana: University of Illinois Press, 1995.

Patterson, Lee. *Negotiating the Past.* Madison: University of Wisconsin Press, 1987.

———. *Chaucer and the Subject of History.* Madison: University of Wisconsin Press, 1991.

Porcheddu, Frederick. "Editing the Auchinleck: Textual Criticism and the Reconstruction of a Medieval Manuscript (Auchinleck Manuscript)." Ph. D. diss., Ohio State University, 1994.

Powicke, Maurice. *King Henry III and the Lord Edward.* Oxford: Clarendon Press, 1947.

Prestwich, Michael. *The Three Edwards: War and State in England 1272–1377.* London: Methuen, 1980.

———. *Edward I.* Rev. ed. New Haven: Yale University Press, 1997.

Price, Jocelyn. "Prose *Merlin* (2)." In *New Arthurian Encyclopedia,* edited by Norris Lacy, 373–74. New York: Garland, 1991.

Ramey, Lynn Tarte. *Christian, Saracen and Genre in Medieval French Literature.* New York: Routledge, 2001.

Riddy, Felicity. "Reading for England: Arthurian Literature and National Consciousness." *Bibliographical Bulletin of the International Arthurian Society* 43
(1991): 314–32.

Riley-Smith, Jonathan. *The Crusades: A Short History.* New Haven: Yale University
Press, 1987.

Rothwell, William. "The Role of French in Thirteenth-Century England." *Bulletin
of the John Rylands Library* 58 (1976): 445–66.

Runciman, Steven. *The First Crusade and the Foundation of the Kingdom of Jerusalem.*
Vol. 1 of *A History of the Crusades.* Cambridge: Cambridge University Press,
1951.

———. *The Kingdom of Jerusalem and the Frankish East 1100–1187.* Vol. 2 of *A History of the Crusades.* Cambridge: Cambridge University Press, 1952.

———. *The Kingdom of Acre and the Later Crusades.* Vol. 3 of *A History of the Crusades.*
Cambridge: Cambridge University Press, 1954.

Said, Edward. *Orientalism.* New York: Vintage Books, 1979.

Scala, Elizabeth. *Absent Narratives, Manuscript Textuality, and Literary Structure in
Late Medieval England.* New York: Palgrave Macmillan, 2002.

Scanlon, Larry. "The King's Two Voices: Narrative and Power in Hoccleve's *Regement
of Princes.*" In *Literary Practice and Social Change in Britain, 1380–1530,* edited
by Lee Patterson, 216–47. Berkeley: University of California Press, 1990.

Schichtman, Martin B., and Laurie Finke. "Profiting from the Past: History as Symbolic
Capital in the *Historia regum Britanniae.*" *Arthurian Literature* 12 (1993): 1–35.

Schildgen, Brenda Deen. *Pagans, Tartars, Moslems, and Jews in Chaucer's Canterbury
Tales.* Gainesville: University Press of Florida, 2001.

Seaman, Myra. "Engendering Genre in Middle English Romance: Performing the
Feminine in *Sir Beves of Hamtoun.*" *Studies in Philology* 98 (2001): 49–75.

Shonk, Timothy. "A Study of the Auchinleck Manuscript: Bookmen and Bookmaking in the Early Fourteenth Century," *Speculum* 60 (1985): 71–91.

Short, Ian. "On Bilingualism in Anglo-Norman England." *Romance Philology* 33
(1980): 467–79.

———. "Patrons and Polyglots: French Literature in Twelfth-Century England,"
Anglo-Norman Studies 14 (1991): 229–49.

———. "*Tam Angli quam Franci:* Self-Definition in Anglo-Norman England." *Anglo-
Norman Studies* 18 (1995): 153–75.

Sklar, Elizabeth. "*Arthour and Merlin:* The Englishing of Arthur." *Michigan Academician* 8 (1975–76): 49–57.

Smyser, H. M. "Charlemagne Legends." In *A Manual of the Writings in Middle English 1050–1500.* Vol. 1, *Romances,* edited by. J. Burke Severs, 80–91. New
Haven: The Connecticut Academy of Arts and Sciences, 1967.

Snowden, Frank. *Blacks in Antiquity: Ethiopians in the Greco-Roman Experience.*
Cambridge: Harvard University Press, Belknap Press, 1970.

Southern, Richard. *Western Views of Islam in the Middle Ages.* Cambridge: Harvard
University Press, 1962.

Speed, Diane. "The Saracens of King Horn." *Speculum* 65 (1990): 564–95.

———. "The Construction of the Nation in Middle English Romance." In *Readings in Medieval English Romance,* edited by Carol Meale, 135–57. Cambridge: D. S. Brewer, 1994.

Spencer, Frederic. "The Legend of St Margaret." *Modern Language Notes* 5 (1890): 71–5, 107–111.

Stacey, Robert C. "The Conversion of Jews to Christianity in Thirteenth-Century England." *Speculum* 67 (1992): 263–83.

Strohm, Paul. "*Storie, Spelle, Geste, Romaunce, Tragedie*: Generic Distinctions in the Middle English Troy Narratives." *Speculum* 46 (1971): 348–59

———. "The Origin and Meaning of Middle English Romaunce." *Genre* 10 (1977): 1–28.

———. "Queens as Intercessors." In *Hochon's Arrow: The Social Imagination of Fourteenth-Century Texts,* 95–120. Princeton: Princeton University Press, 1992.

Studies in the Harley Manuscript: The Scribes, Contents, and Social Contexts of British Library MS Harley 2253. Edited by Susanna Fein. Kalamazoo: Western Michigan University Medieval Institute Publications, 2000.

Studies in the Vernon Manuscript. Edited by Derek Pearsall. Cambridge: D. S. Brewer, 1990.

Tatlock, J. S. P. "Geoffrey and King Arthur in 'Normannicus Draco.'" *Modern Philology* 31 (1933): 1–18, 115–25.

———. *The Legendary History of Britain: Geoffrey of Monmouth's 'Historia regum Britanniae' and its Early Vernacular Versions.* Berkeley: University of California Press, 1950.

Taylor, Andrew. "Authors, Scribes, Patrons, and Books." In *The Idea of the Vernacular: An Anthology Of Middle English Literary Theory, 1280–1520,* edited by Jocelyn Wogan-Browne, Nicholas Watson. Andrew Taylor, and Ruth Evans, 353–65. University Park: Pennsylvania State University Press, 1999.

———. *Textual Situations: Three Medieval Manuscripts and Their Readers.* Philadelphia: University of Pennsylvania Press, 2002.

Tolan, John V. *Saracens: Islam in the Medieval European Imagination.* New York: Columbia University Press, 2002.

Turville-Petre, Thorlac. "The 'Nation' in English Writings of the Early Fourteenth Century." In *England in the Fourteenth Century: Proceedings of the 1991 Harlaxton Symposium,* edited by Nicholas Rogers, 128–39. Stamford: Paul Watkins, 1993.

———. *England the Nation: Language, Literature, and National Identity, 1290–1340.* Oxford: Clarendon Press, 1996.

Tyerman, Christopher. "The Holy Land and the Crusaders of the Thirteenth and Fourteenth Centuries." In *Crusade and Settlement,* edited by Peter Edbury, 105–12. Cardiff: University College Press Cardiff, 1985.

———. *England and the Crusades 1095–1588.* Chicago: University of Chicago Press, 1988.

Uniting the Kingdom?: The Making of British History. Edited by Alexander Grant and Keith J. Stringer. Routledge: New York, 1995.

Vale, Juliet. *Edward III and Chivalry: Chivalric Society and its Context 1270–1350.* Woodbridge, Suffolk: Boydell Press, 1982.

Van D'Elden, S. "Black and White: Contact with the Mediterranean World in Medieval German Narrative." In *The Medieval Mediterranean: Cross-Cultural Contacts,* edited by M. Chiat and K. Reyerson, 112–18. St. Cloud, MN: Medieval Studies at Minnesota, 1988.

Vaneman, Karen Haslanger. "Interpreting the Middle English Romance: The Audience in *Of Arthour and of Merlin.*" Ph. D. diss., Wayne State University, 1986.

Vitto, Cindy. "The Virtuous Pagan in Middle English Literature." *Transactions of the American Philosophical Society* 79.5 (1989): 1–100.

Walpole, R. N. "Charlemagne and Roland: A Study of the Source of Two Middle English Metrical Romances, *Roland and Vernagu* and *Otuel and Roland.*" *University of California Publications in Modern Philology* 21 (1944): 385–451.

Warren, F. M. "The Enamoured Moslem Princess in Orderic Vital and the French Epic." *PMLA* 29 (1914): 341–58.

Warren, Michelle. *History on the Edge: Excalibur and the Borders of Britain, 1100–1300.* Minneapolis: University of Minnesota Press, 2000.

Weiss, Judith. "The Auchinleck MS. and the Edwardes MSS." *Notes and Queries* 16 (1969): 444–46.

———. "The Major Interpolations in *Sir Beves of Hamtoun.*" *Medium Ævum* 48 (1979): 71–76.

Wells, John Edwin. *A Manual of the Writings in Middle English 1050–1400.* Rev. ed. New Haven: Connecticut Academy of Arts and Sciences, 1926.

Williams, David. *Deformed Discourse: The Function of the Monster in Mediaeval Thought and Literature.* Montreal: McGill-Queen's University Press, 1996.

Wilson, R. M. "English and French in England: 1100–1300." *History* 23 (1943): 37–60.

Woodbine, George E. "The Language of English Law." *Speculum* 18 (1943): 395–436.

Zaerr, Linda Marie. "Medieval and Modern Deletions of Repellent Passages." In *Improvisation in the Arts of the Middle Ages and Renaissance,* edited by Timothy J. McGee, 222–46. Kalamazoo: Western Michigan University Medieval Institute Publications, 2003.

Index